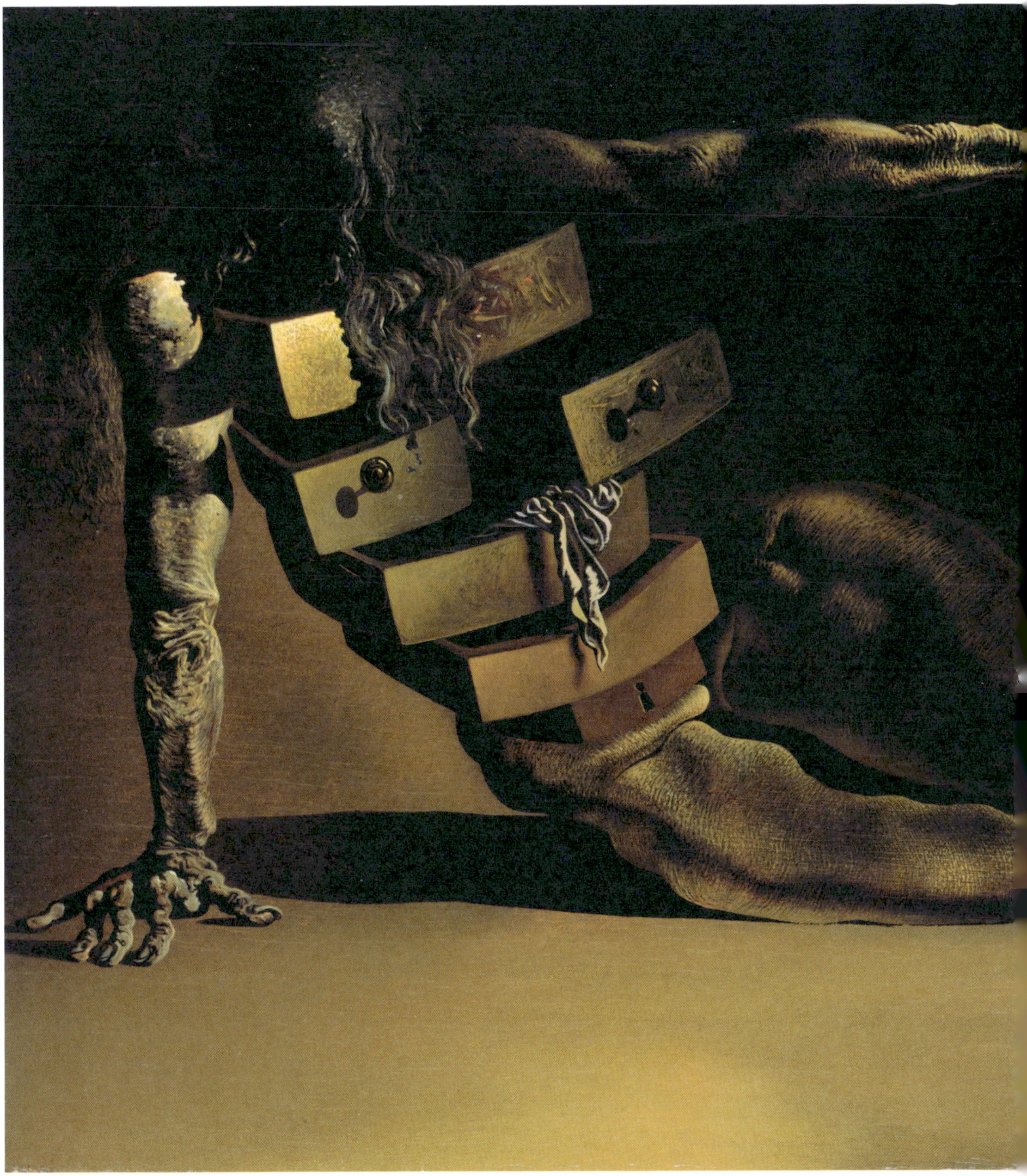

fi
SALVADOR DALÍ, *Le c*
(The Anthropomo
Kunstsammlung Nordrh
Cat.

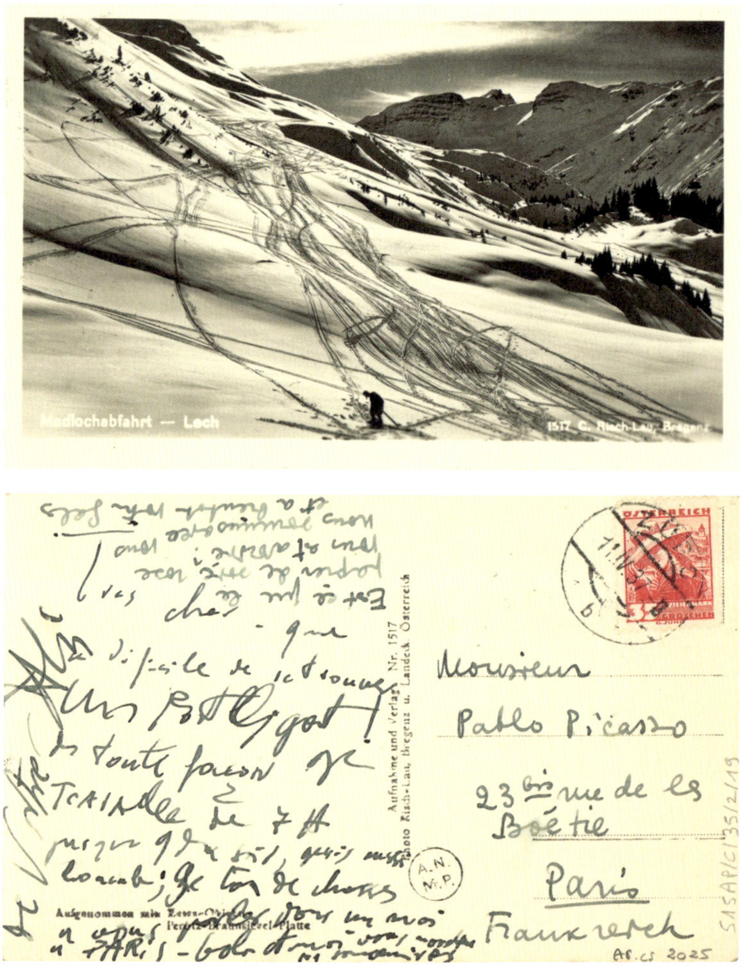

fig. 4
SALVADOR DALÍ, postcard to Pablo Picasso
sent from Lech am Arlberg, April 11, 1937
Musée national Picasso, Paris

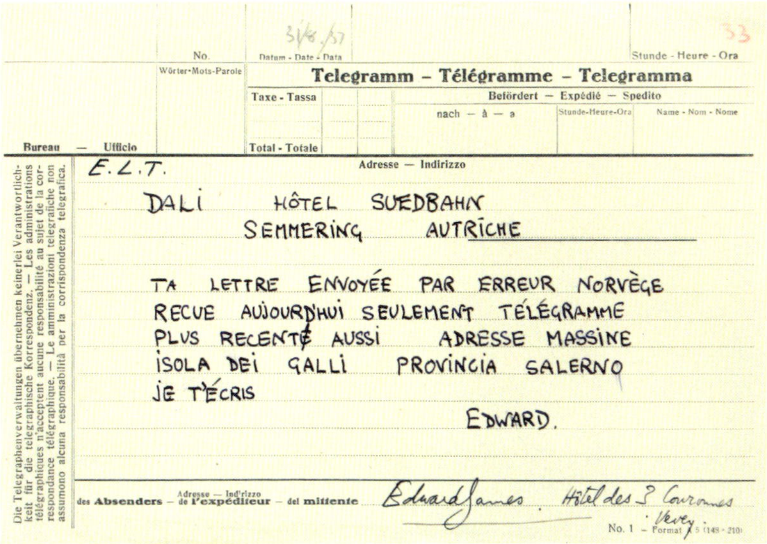

33

No. | Datum - Date - Data 31/8/37 | Stunde - Heure - Ora
Wörter-Mots-Parole

Telegramm – Télégramme – Telegramma

Taxe - Tassa | Befördert – Expédié – Spedito
nach – à – a | Stunde-Heure-Ora | Name - Nom - Nome

Bureau – Ufficio | Total - Totale

Die Telegraphenverwaltungen übernehmen keinerlei Verantwortlichkeit für die telegraphische Korrespondenz. – Les administrations télégraphiques n'acceptent aucune responsabilité au sujet de la correspondance télégraphique. – Le amministrazioni telegrafiche non assumono alcuna responsabilità per la corrispondenza telegrafica.

E.L.T.

Adresse – Indirizzo

DALI HÔTEL SUEDBAHN
SEMMERING AUTRICHE

TA LETTRE ENVOYÉE PAR ERREUR NORVÈGE
RECUE AUJOURDHUI SEULEMENT TÉLÉGRAMME
PLUS RECENTE AUSSI ADRESSE MASSINE
ISOLA DEI GALLI PROVINCIA SALERNO
JE T'ÉCRIS
EDWARD.

Adresse des Absenders – Adresse de l'expéditeur – Indirizzo del mittente: Edward James. Hôtel des 3 Couronnes Vevey.

No. 1 – Format A 5 (148 × 210)

fig. 2
EDWARD JAMES, telegram to Salvador Dalí
at Südbahnhotel in Semmering, August 31, 1937
West Dean College of Arts and Conservation

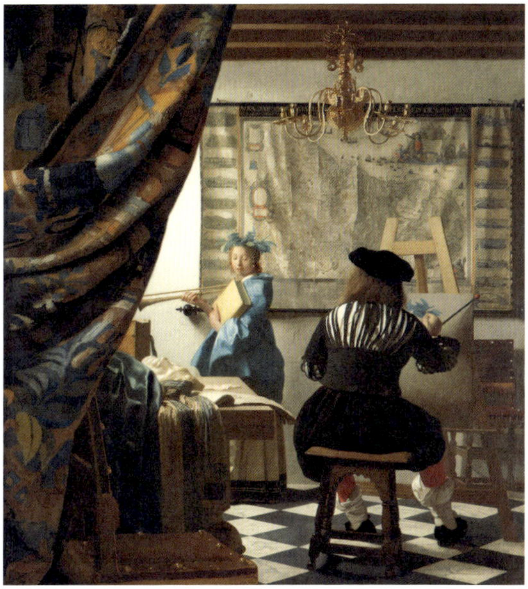

fig. 3
JOHANNES VERMEER VAN DELFT
The Art of Painting, about 1666/68, Kunsthistorisches
Museum Vienna (formerly Czernin Collection)
On each of his voyages to Vienna
Dalí visited Vermeer's *The Art of Painting*
in the Czernin Collection (→ p. 10).

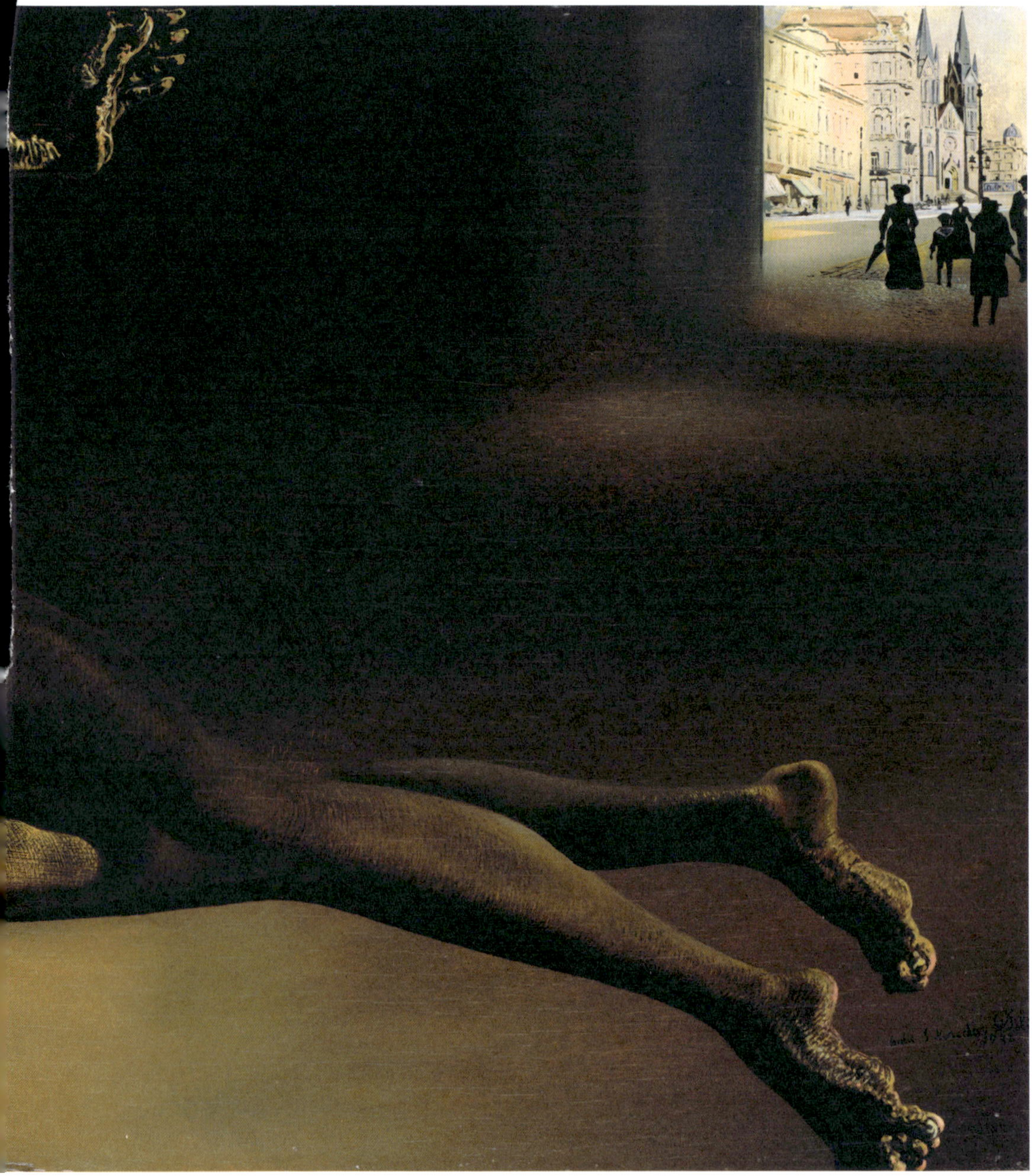

. 5
binet anthropomorphique
phic Cabinet), 1936
n-Westfalen, Düsseldorf
. P 444

DALÍ – FREUD

AN OBSESSION

VERLAG DER BUCHHANDLUNG
WALTHER UND FRANZ KÖNIG

PROLOGUE

FOREWORD

Stella Rollig

Salvador Dalí and Sigmund Freud: the art of one is inconceivable without the theories of the other. They seem inexorably linked. Dalí, the young, eccentric Catalan artist, even today the most colorful figure among the Surrealists, and Freud, the Viennese doctor, founder of psychoanalysis, commentator on culture and religion. When they met for the first and only time in July 1938 in London, where Freud was living in exile, they were separated not only by language barriers and an age difference of forty-eight years, but also by very different attitudes to art. What united them, however, was their profound interest in the human psyche and its hidden depths. Dalí had had access to translations of Freud's writings since the 1920s and had studied them intensely. Prompted by this, from 1926 onward, he began to investigate the poetics of Surrealism and developed a new pictorial language that uniquely characterizes his work to this day. He worshipped Freud and was driven by his desire to meet him. After several unsuccessful attempts to meet Freud in Vienna, a meeting was finally arranged in London in summer 1938, thanks to the stubborn insistence of Stefan Zweig and

Edward James. The artist later remembered the following detail about the meeting: "While I was crossing the old professor's yard I saw a bicycle leaning against the wall, and on the saddle, attached by a string, was a red rubber hot-water bottle, which looked full of water, and on the back of the hot-water bottle walked a snail! The presence of that assortment seemed strange and inexplicable in the yard of Freud's home. Contrary to my hopes we spoke little but we devoured each other with our eyes."[1]

Dalí's personality and the painting *Metamorphosis of Narcissus* (→fig. 17), which he had brought with him, also made an abiding impression on Freud and led him to reassess his ideas about Surrealism, as he wrote the following day to Stefan Zweig: "I really have reason to thank you for the introduction which brought me yesterday's visitors. For until then I was inclined to look upon surrealists, who have apparently chosen me for their patron saint, as absolute (let us say 95 per cent, like alcohol) cranks. The young Spaniard, however, with his candid fanatical eyes and his undeniable technical mastery, has made me reconsider my opinion. It would in fact be very interesting to investigate analytically how a picture like this came to be painted."[2] They were unable to further intensify their relationship before Freud died in September 1939.

On the basis of some hundred or so paintings, drawings, surrealist objects, photographs, films, books, magazines, letters, and other documents, this exhibition explores the fascination that Freud exerted on the artist and examines the meeting of the two from various perspectives. Taking this unusual meeting as its starting point, the exhibition looks at other influential encounters in the artist's life, for example with the poet Federico García Lorca and the filmmaker Luis Buñuel in the Residencia de Estudiantes in Madrid. These two in particular, together with the histologist and Nobel Prize winner Santiago Ramón y Cajal and his drawings of nerve tissue, ultimately became the catalysts for Dalí's Surrealist works. A further focus of the exhibition is the artist's family background, which he regularly explored in his paintings.

Thanks to the generous support of international institutions and private collections, the Belvedere has been able to place selected works by Dalí and his artistic career in a psychoanalytical context.

My particular thanks go to the Fundació Gala-Salvador Dalí in Figueres, the Museo Nacional Centro de Arte Reina Sofía Madrid, the Dalí Museum in Saint Petersburg (Florida), West Dean College of Arts and Conservation, the Museu de Montserrat in Barcelona, the Museo de Arte Contemporáneo and the Museo Nacional Thyssen-Bornemisza in Madrid, the Musée des Beaux-Arts de Brest, the Peggy Guggenheim Collection Venice, the Wadsworth Atheneum Museum of Art in Hartford (Connecticut), the Meadows Museum, Southern Methodist University Dallas, the Eli and Edythe Broad Art Museum at Michigan State University, the Hamburger Kunsthalle, the Ulla and Heiner Pietzsch Collection in Berlin, the Esther Grether Family Collection, the Centro Federico García Lorca in Granada, the Fundación Federico García Lorca, the Instituto Cajal, CSIC Madrid, the Fundación Mapfre, the Gregorio Prieto Foundation, the Freud Museum London, the Sigmund Freud Privatstiftung in Vienna, the Museo Patio Herreriano in Valladolid, and the Galerie Natalie Seroussi for making major works from their collections available for the exhibition.

Furthermore, I would especially like to thank Jaime Brihuega Sierra, curator of the exhibition, who was ably assisted by Stephanie Auer from the Belvedere. The project was several years in the making and I am most grateful to Johannes Ramharter and his team at PONTE: Organisation für kulturelles Management, who have assisted us from the outset. I am also very grateful to Eva Lorenzo for her support with the project coordination.

My special thanks go to Stephanie Auer, Juan Manuel Bonet, Jaime Brihuega Sierra, Ulrike Kadi, Robert Lubar Messeri, Agustín Sánchez Vidal, and Ingrid Schaffner for their leading contributions to this publication, whose design was in the experienced hands of Willi Schmid. Further thanks are due to Eva Lahnsteiner for her tireless work in producing this catalogue, Rebecca Law, Nick Somers, and Jessica West for the English translations, Betti Moser for her meticulous copy-editing, and my assistant Johanna Hofer for her competent support.

I am also particularly grateful to the Belvedere's Exhibition Management and Tatjana Gawron for their smooth collaboration, Monica Strinu for the exhibition graphics, and Margula Architects for its professional design. My thanks also go to Joan Dolç for the short film produced especially for the exhibition.

Finally, I would like to thank the Art Education and Communications & Marketing departments and all members of the Belvedere staff involved in preparing this exhibition.

1 Salvador Dalí, *The Secret Life of Salvador Dalí*, translated by Haakon M. Chevalier (New York, 1993), p. 24.
2 Sigmund Freud, *The Letters of Sigmund Freud*, selected and edited by Ernst L. Freud, translated by Tania & James Stern, (New York, 1975), pp. 448–49.

DALÍ – FREUD: A REVELATION

Stephanie Auer

Vienna, April 25, 1937: Salvador Dalí arrives at Hotel Krantz-Ambassador (→fig. 1).[1] He has only one aim: to meet Sigmund Freud, whose findings about the unconscious were a crucial discovery for him. The artist hopes that Freud will confirm his "paranoiac-critical method," which he sees as his most important contribution to Surrealism.

Once again, however, this hope, which had already brought Dalí to Vienna several times before,[2] was not to be fulfilled. In his autobiographical notes he recalls:[3]

> "On each of these voyages I did exactly the same thing: in the morning I went to see the Vermeer in the Czernin Collection, and in the afternoon I did *not* go to visit Freud because I invariably learned that he was out of town for reasons of health. [...] I remember with a gentle melancholy spending those afternoons walking haphazardly along the streets of Austria's ancient capital. [...] I held long and exhaustive imaginary conversations with Freud; he even came home with me once and stayed all night clinging to the curtains of my room in the Hotel Sacher."[4]

Dalí's recollections of his visits to Vienna form the starting point for an exhibition about the artist, highlighting his complex family relationships and following his development from discovering Freud's writings to finally meeting the founder of psychoanalysis in London, where Freud was then living in exile, in 1938. It takes us to the Residencia de Estudiantes in Madrid in the 1920s, where Dalí found a hub of open discussion and interdisciplinary exchange between avant-garde artists and academics. It was in this fertile atmosphere that he first came across Freud's work, which was published in Spanish translation from 1922 onwards. Reading *The Interpretation of Dreams* was one of the most important discoveries in the young artist's life and seized him with a "real vice of self-interpretation."[5] Freud's writings gave him access to his hidden fears, desires, and obsessions, whose origins he traced back to his complex family relationships, and it enabled him to give expression to them in pictorial form. While, in the early 1920s, Dalí still seems like a seeker, with works that show his intensive study of European avant-garde movements, his paintings toward the end of the 1920s—including major works such as *The Lugubrious Game* (→p. 91)—already begin to hint at his deepening connection with Freud's writings and the Surrealist movement. The painting's motifs attest to "dream, images, and hypnagogic visions [...] of an obscure and sensational world discovered by Freud,"[6] as he explained in a lecture at the Museum of Modern Art in New York in 1935. In their combination of Freudian concepts with motifs from Dalí's personal cosmos, his Surrealist images of that time are unmistakably rooted in the artist's "neurotic struggles."[7] These creations could not be "translated into colloquial language" and could "only be interpreted by psychoanalysts," as Dalí stated in an interview with the *Neues Wiener Journal,* while at the same time expressing the hope: "Sigmund Freud led the way. He will understand us."[8] Dalí's expectations were not to be fulfilled until the meeting in London, because Freud's attitude to Surrealist theories until then had mainly been one of skepticism and incomprehension. In a letter to André Breton, Freud admitted that, in spite of Breton's interest in and enthusiasm for his research, he could not clearly understand "what Surrealism is and what it is after." "It could be," he said, "that I am not in any way made to understand it; I am at such a distant position from art."[9]

Unlike Breton, who had already succeeded in meeting Freud in 1921, Dalí's repeated attempts to meet his revered idol in Vienna never bore fruit. He nevertheless commemorated Vienna as the birthplace of psychoanalysis in his 1936 painting *City of Drawers (The Anthropomorphic Cabinet)* (→fig. 5). The work not only expresses Dalí's admiration for Freud—with the open drawers in the upper body of the reclining woman representing the innermost recesses of her unconscious mind—it also recalls Vienna's cityscape, as the houses in the brightly lit street scene in the background may be interpreted as a *capriccio* of buildings from Vienna's 9th district, where Freud lived, including St. Canisius Church on Lustkandlgasse.[10]

Dalí's only documented visit to Vienna took place during an extended trip to Austria, undertaken by the artist and his wife Gala in 1937, together with the poet and patron Edward James, traveling from Seefeld in Tyrol via Zürs am Arlberg (→fig. 4) to Semmering (→fig. 2). The overwhelming impression of the Austrian Alps is reflected in the painting *Metamorphosis of Narcissus* (1937, →fig. 17). This picture is not only closely connected to Dalí's visit to Austria, but was also the work the artist took with him to his meeting with Freud in order to demonstrate his paranoiac-critical method. Neither the visit by Dalí and Gala to the Austrian Alps nor the later meeting with Freud would have been possible without James's help. It was thanks to him that Stefan Zweig, who was also in exile in London, approached Freud with Dalí's long-held wish to meet him. Zweig used all of his powers of persuasion to convince Freud, extolling Dalí as a "fanatical admirer" who, "despite all his little follies," was "perhaps the only genius of modern painting." (→p. 153). His efforts did not go unrewarded, and on July 19, 1938, Dalí finally met Freud, accompanied by Zweig and James. The correspondence and autobiographical recollections of all four protagonists speak of unfulfilled hopes and of a completely unexpected change of heart, and shed light from a number of different perspectives on the meeting at 39 Elsworthy Road, where Freud was living at the time.

Dalí's ambitious aim of obtaining Freud's psychoanalytic approval for his paranoiac-critical method remained unsatisfied. "Two geniuses had met without making sparks,"[11] Dalí disenchantedly summed up the events, which he processed at length in his memoirs. For Freud, by contrast, the meeting with Dalí prompted him to rethink his attitude to Surrealism. Until then he had regarded the Surrealists as "absolute (let us say 95 percent, like alcohol) cranks,"[12] but he admitted the following day that "the young Spaniard with his candid fanatical eyes and his undeniable technical mastery has made me reconsider my opinion," saying that "it would be very interesting to investigate analytically how a picture like this came to be painted."[13] In spite of his initial disappointment at the encounter with his hero, Dalí—after learning of the content of this letter and Freud's change of view—became convinced that their meeting had marked a turning point in Freud's appreciation of art. "[...] if we had met earlier, or several times," concluded Dalí, "some of his views on art might have been modified. My paranoia-critical method would have opened new vistas to him."[14]

1 "In Wien eingetroffen [...] im Hotel Krantz-Ambassador: [...] Maler Salvador Dali, Paris," *Neues Wiener Journal*, April 25, 1937, p. 19.

2 In his autobiography Dalí claims to have made three trips to Vienna. To date, only the visit in April 1937 has been documented; see Salvador Dalí, *The Secret Life of Salvador Dalí*, translated by Haakon M. Chevalier (New York, 1942), p. 23.

3 Ibid.

4 It could not be confirmed that Dalí stayed at Hotel Sacher.

5 Dali, *Secret Life*, (see note 2), p. 183.

6 Quoted from *La vie publique de Salvador Dalí*, exh. cat., Georges Pompidou, Paris (Paris, 1980), p. 43.

7 Peter Gorsen, *Salvador Dalí, der "kritische Paranoiker"* (Frankfurt am Main, 1983), p. 7.

8 "Harlekinade der Kunst: Sinn und Unsinn einer verballhornten Kunst—Gespräch mit Salvador Dalí, dem Führer der Surrealisten," in *Neues Wiener Journal*, August 14, 1937, p. 8.

9 Sigmund Freud to André Breton, December 26, 1932, translation quoted from Frederick B. Davis, "Three Letters from Sigmund Freud to André Breton," J Am Psychoanal Assoc (1973), https://articulosparapensar.files.wordpress.com/2013/10/three-letters-from-sigmund-freud-to-andrc3a9-breton.pdf (accessed on October 28, 2021).

10 Linus Klumpner, "Brennende Giraffen, die Greuel des Gebirges und kein Treffen mit Sigmund Freud—Salvador Dalí und Österreich," master's dissertation, University of Salzburg, 2013, pp. 73–74.

11 *The Unspeakable Confessions of Salvador Dalí as told to André Parinaud*, translated by Harold J. Salemsom (London, 1977), p. 121.

12 Sigmund Freud, *The Letters of Sigmund Freud*, selected and edited by Ernst L. Freud, translated by Tania and James Stern, (New York, 1993), pp. 448–49.

13 Ibid.

14 *The Unspeakable Confessions* (see note 11), p. 121.

SIGMUND FREUD
1856 – 1939,
Austrian doctor,
neuropathologist,
depth psychologist,
cultural theorist
and critic of religion,
founder of psycho-
analysis

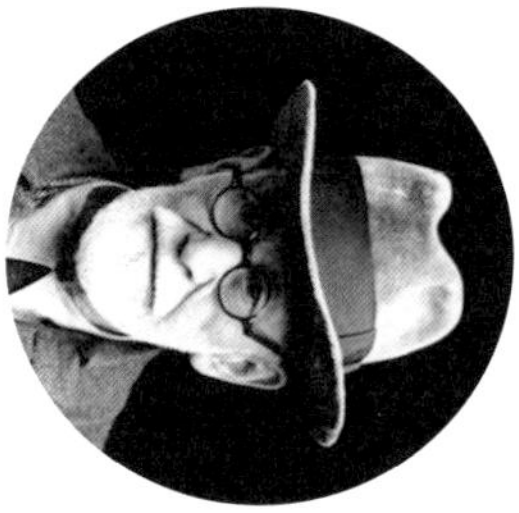

SALVADOR DALÍ
1904 – 1989, Spanish
painter, graphic artist,
writer, sculptor,
and stage designer

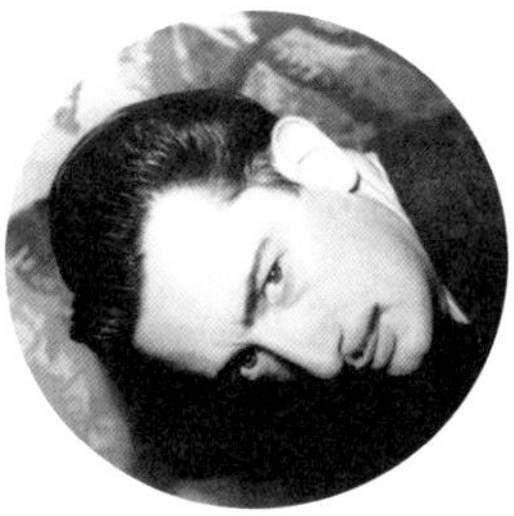

ANDRÉ BRETON
1896 – 1966,
French writer; the
most important
Surrealist theoretician

LUIS BUÑUEL
1900 – 1983,
Spanish-Mexican
filmmaker

ANA MARÍA DALÍ
1908 – 1989, Salvador
Dalí's sister, author

GALA ÉLUARD DALÍ
1894 – 1982, Salvador
Dalí's muse, wife,
and manager

EDWARD JAMES
1907 – 1984, British
multimillionaire,
art collector, poet,
patron of the arts,
and landscape artist

FEDERICO
GARCÍA LORCA
1898 – 1936, Spanish
poet and dramatist

SANTIAGO
RAMÓN Y CAJAL
1852 – 1934, Spanish
doctor and histologist,
recipient of the Nobel
Prize in Physiology

STEFAN ZWEIG
1881 – 1942, Austrian
writer and translator

Chapter Introductions:
Jaime Brihuega Sierra

Selection of Quotes:
Stephanie Auer
Eva Lorenzo

1

SALVADOR DALÍ'S EARLY YEARS

As the artist himself explains in his autobiography *The Secret Life of Salvador Dalí,* written in 1940/41 (→p. 21), his family environment as a child and adolescent—that is, the period between his birth in May 1904 and his move to Madrid in September 1922—was particularly conducive to the development of a complex personality.[1] His aloof father, Salvador Dalí Cusí, a notary from Figueres, always represented the paradigm of unrelenting authority, a powerful presence, whose morality and taboos had an enduring impact on Dalí's psyche (→p. 23). After the death of his mother, Felipa Domènech, when Dalí was just seventeen, his father married her sister, "La Tieta" Catalina. A woman who, for Dalí, could never compensate for the loss of his mother, which had affected him profoundly and in quite disturbing ways. His sister, Ana María, four years his junior, was closest to him within the family, and he cultivated an intense, complex relationship to her (→p. 26). This ambiance was compounded by the specter of a brother who had died at only twenty-two months, nine months before the birth of the future artist, and from whom he inherited the name Salvador. Dalí developed a curious imaginary relationship with the ghostly presence of this brother, which lasted for many years.[2]

The significance of this complex family situation is also apparent in many of Dalí's works. It can be seen in his early self-portraits, which depict him like someone suffering from an illness or as a young man whose gaze expresses introspection and mistrust. It also shows in the portraits of his father, consistently represented as a powerful, almost terrifying figure (→p. 29), and in the unsettling portraits of his sister, which seem charged with sinister connotations (→p. 27).

Yet, there are certain specific memories from his childhood and adolescence that provide most of the background to the artist's later works: for instance, his stay with his father near a mountain lake in the Pyrenees, which appears in numerous compositions after 1929; the stereoscopic images he had seen at school; the impression left on him by his classmate Burchaque's behind, occasionally provoking in him dizziness and conflicting sexual feelings; elements from Park Güell and other works by Antoni Gaudi and the Art Nouveau, whose forms were as flowing and capricious as a camembert and which were to become integral to his work after 1929; the landscapes of Cadaqués and the astonishing cliff formations of Cabo de Creus (→p. 25), whose memory inspired numerous double images; the shocking, disturbing, and obsessive image of his father in underpants, with his penis protruding through the open fly, an image that had etched itself irreversibly into the young Dalí's complicated sexuality; his ensuing attraction to the women and girls he met as a young man, including Julia, the adopted daughter of Ramón Pichot, a family friend whose Pointillist pictures held a particular fascination for him; the water stains on the ceiling of his elementary school, in which he was able to discern fascinating images; his crippling fear of grasshoppers—he even managed to perceive the shape of a grasshopper's head in that of a fish he had picked up in a pool as a child; his obsessive masturbatory experiences.[3] Also the numerous books he acquired one by one, especially those containing reproductions of paintings and sculptures—these constituted his first formative contacts with art history.

1 The most comprehensive documentation on this and other periods in the artist's life can be found in Ian Gibson, *La vida desaforada de Salvador Dalí* (Barcelona, 1998), pp. 33–86.
2 In his autobiography, however, Dalí writes: "My brother died three years prior to my birth at the age of seven from meningitis"; Salvador Dalí, "Vida Secreta" (1940–41), in Gibson 1998 (see note 1), p. 243.
3 According to various statements, recorded by Dalí's acquaintances Rafael Santos Torroella and Ian Gibson, masturbation was the only way Dalí could reach orgasm with his small penis (see Gibson 1998 [see note 1], p. 112). This gave rise to an atavistic anxiety about sexual failure as a result of a flaccid penis.

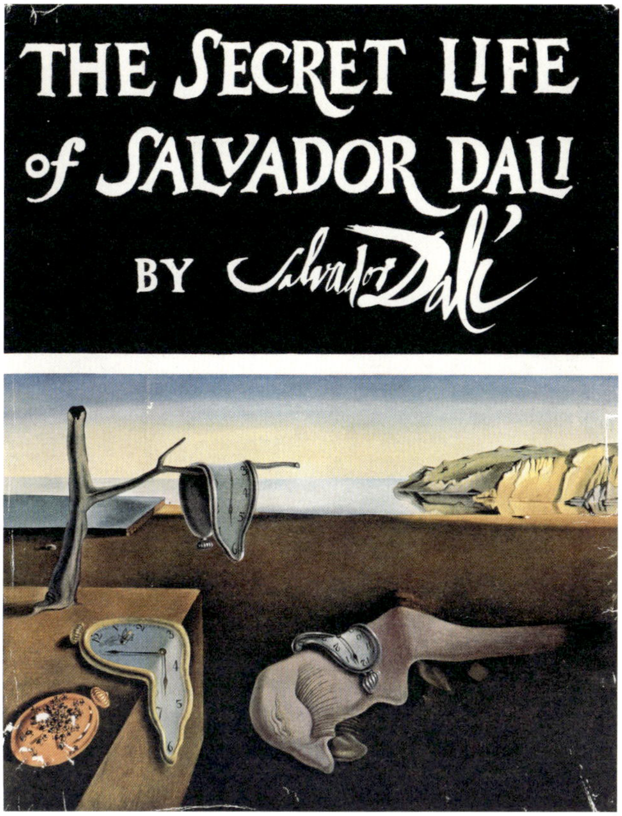

SALVADOR DALÍ, *The Secret Life of Salvador Dalí*
Translated by Haakon M. Chevalier
London 1942, book cover
Fundació Gala-Salvador Dalí, Figueres

[…] my brother died of meningitis, […] before I was born. […] My parents' despair was assuaged only by my own birth, but their misfortune still penetrated every cell of their bodies. […] I deeply experienced the persistence of his presence as both a trauma—a kind of alienation of affections—and a sense of being outdone.

— SALVADOR DALÍ, *The Unspeakable Confessions of Salvador Dalí as told to André Parinaud* (London, 1977), p. 12.

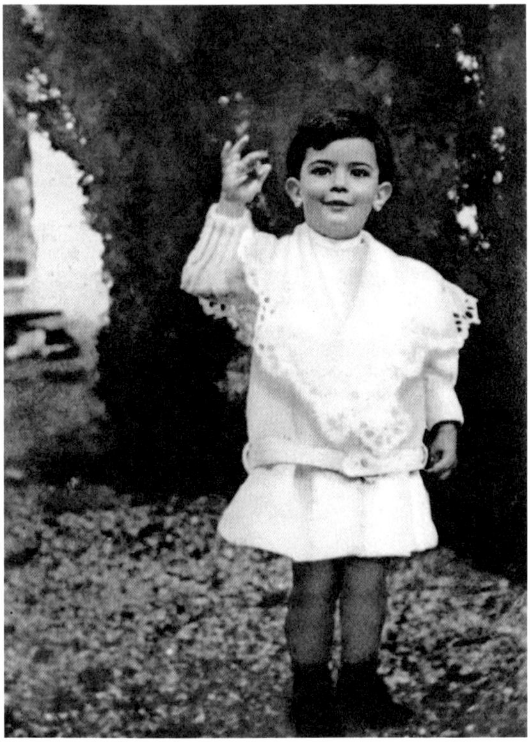

Salvador Dalí at the age of four, 1908
Fundació Gala-Salvador Dalí, Figueres

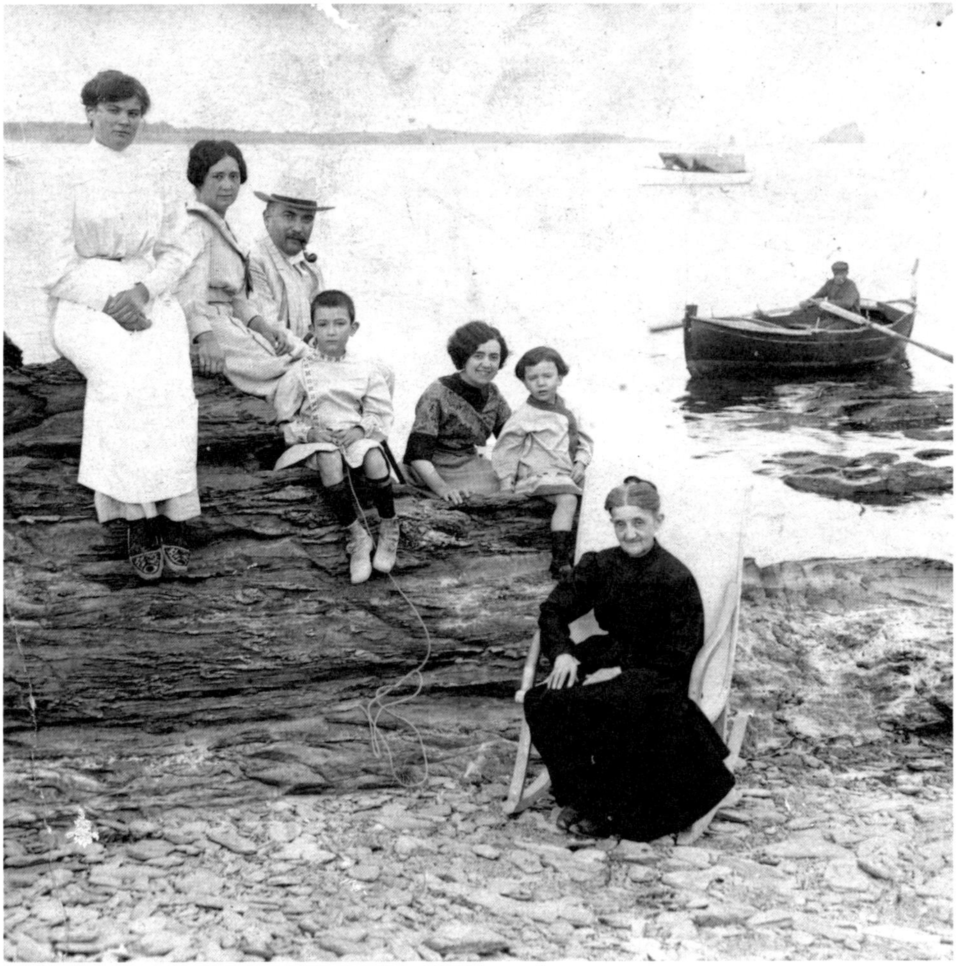

The Dalí family on the Llané beach, Cadaqués
(left to right: Aunt María Theresa, Dalí's mother, his
father, Salvador Dalí, his mother's sister Tieta,
his sister Ana María, and their grandmother Ana), c. 1910
Fundació Gala-Salvador Dalí, Figueres

Respected scholars (such as Santos Torroella or Ricard Mas) share the opinion that this work is probably a covert and metonymic portrait of Salvador Dalí's sister, Ana María (often depicted from behind by the artist). Emphasized by the pointing index finger, the buttocks most definitely play the starring role, linking the image to Dalí's recurrent sexual obsessions, which frequently revolved around incest and sodomy. These persisted in his later life, as reflected in Dalí's *Confesiones inconfesables* (*The Unspeakable Confessions*) as told to André Parinaud in 1973: "I surround myself with the most sublime arses imaginable. I get the most beautiful women to strip. I always say that through the arse the greatest of mysteries can be plumbed."
— JAIME BRIHUEGA SIERRA

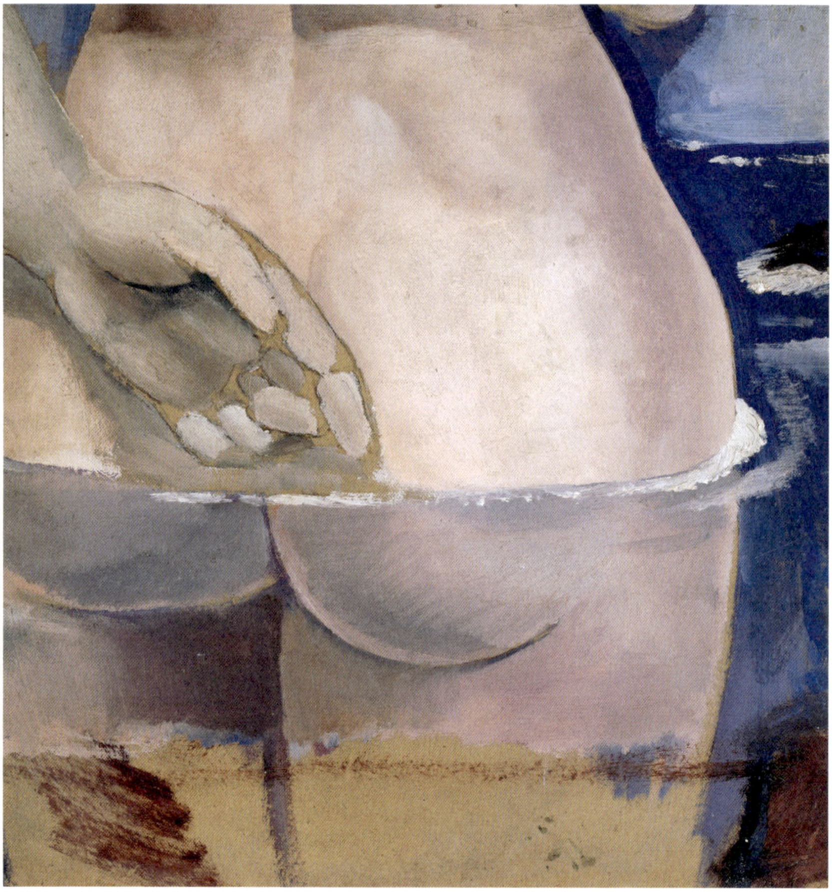

SALVADOR DALÍ, *Desnudo en el agua* (*Nude in the Water*), c. 1924, oil on cardboard, 50.5 × 47 cm
Museo Nacional Centro de Arte Reina Sofía, Madrid
Cat. no. P 160

[…] Cape Creus, which is exactly the epic spot where the mountains of the Pyrenees come down into the sea, in a grandiose geological delirium. […] there was also materialized, in the very corporeity of the granite, that principle of paranoiac metamorphosis which I have already several times called attention to in the course of this book. […] All the images capable of being suggested by the complexity of their innumerable irregularities appear successively and by turn as you change your position.
— SALVADOR DALÍ, *The Secret Life of Salvador Dalí* (New York, 1993), p. 304.

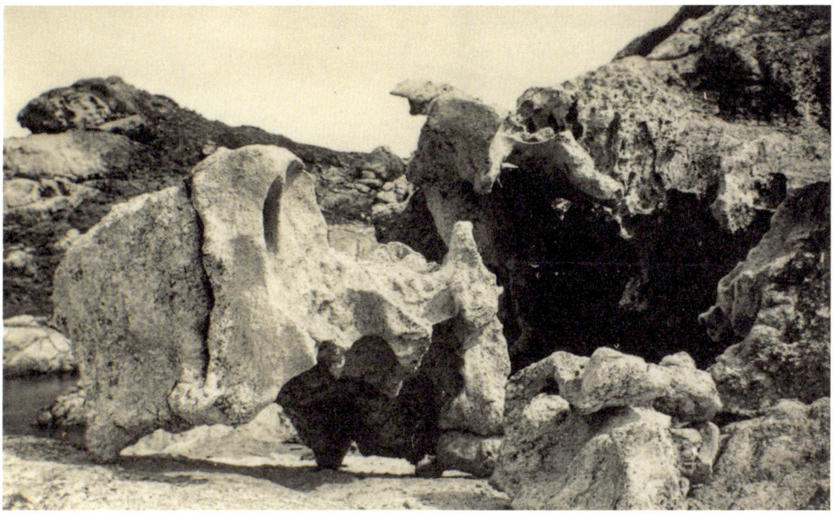

MAN RAY, *Rochers, Espagne* (cliffs near Cape Creus, Cadaqués, which frequently appear in Dalí's work, for example in *The Face of the Great Masturbator*, → fig. 12), 1933
Centre Pompidou—Musée national d'art moderne—Centre de création industrielle, Paris

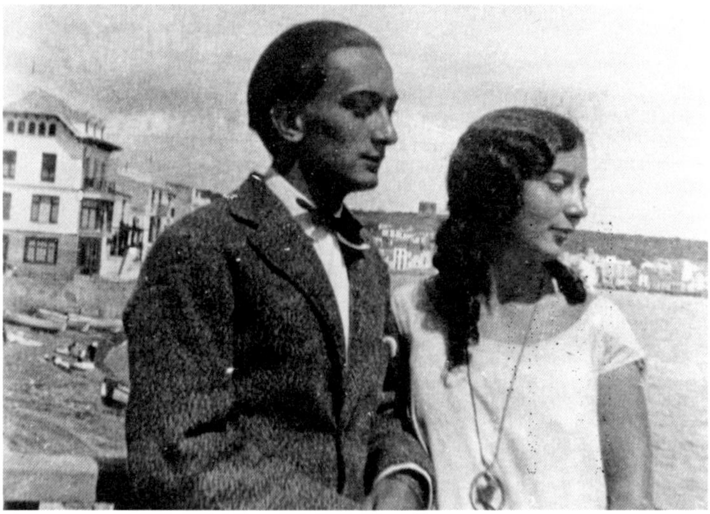

Salvador and his sister, Ana María, in Cadaqués, 1925
Fundació Gala-Salvador Dalí, Figueres

Within Dalí's complex family relationships, the one between the artist and his sister had been a tangled web of emotions and desires ever since adolescence, influenced by a deeper underlying ambiguity. Reading Freud helped Dalí accept this complexity and express it in his work. In fact, an abundance of portrayals of his sister exist—either explicit, more or less intentional, or metaphorical. These date from the early 1920s through to the mid-1950s, including many examples loaded with obsessive aspects, such as *Portrait of My Sister* (c. 1920) and *Young Virgin Auto-Sodomized by Her Own Chastity* (1954). The portrait shown here is a classic example of the figural style influenced by New Objectivity trends that flourished in Italy and Germany during this period. Its austere colors and meticulous, incisive brushwork imbue the image with an unsettling and enigmatic quality.

— JAIME BRIHUEGA SIERRA

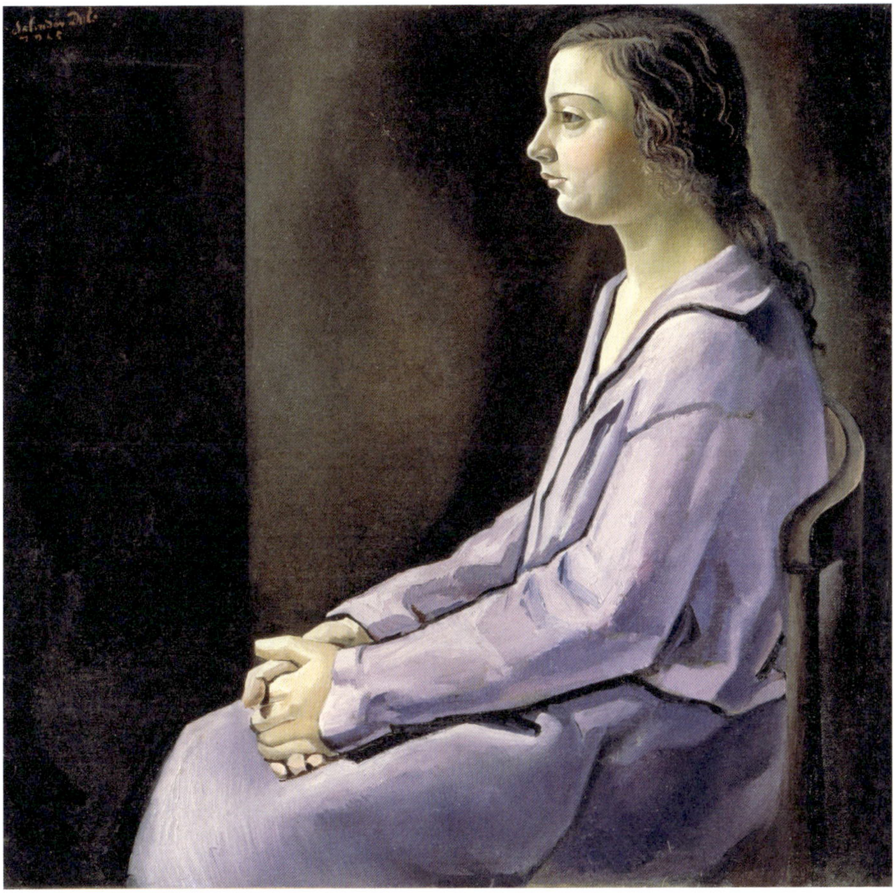

SALVADOR DALÍ, *Retrat de la meva germana* (*Portrait of My Sister*), 1925
Oil on canvas, 99 × 99 cm, Museo Nacional Centro de Arte Reina Sofía, Madrid, cat. no. P166

When my father got mad, the whole rambla of Figueras held its breath; his voice broke out of his office like a torrential stream carrying away everything before it in its path.
— SALVADOR DALÍ, *The Unspeakable Confessions of Salvador Dalí as told to André Parinaud* (London, 1977), p. 24.

In order for me to become Dalí, I had to immolate on the psychoanalytical altar my father Dalí y Cusí; shrink him as do the Java headhunters to the size of one of those celluloid toys that as a child I hammered to bits, and swallow him like the Eucharistic host so as to digest him and be nurtured by his substance and essence.
— SALVADOR DALÍ, *The Unspeakable Confessions of Salvador Dalí as told to André Parinaud* (London, 1977), p. 24.

My father [...] has never ceased being reborn in the mental projections I constantly make. He reappeared in the person of Picasso as well as in the lineaments of Stalin, admirable in strength and hardness, but devoid of terror or fear, without the shadow of any fascination to paralyze me. A Freudian hero par excellence, I freed myself of his guardianship, by battening on every cell of his self, and he became one of the motive forces of my genius.
— SALVADOR DALÍ, *The Unspeakable Confessions of Salvador Dalí as told to André Parinaud* (London, 1977), p. 31.

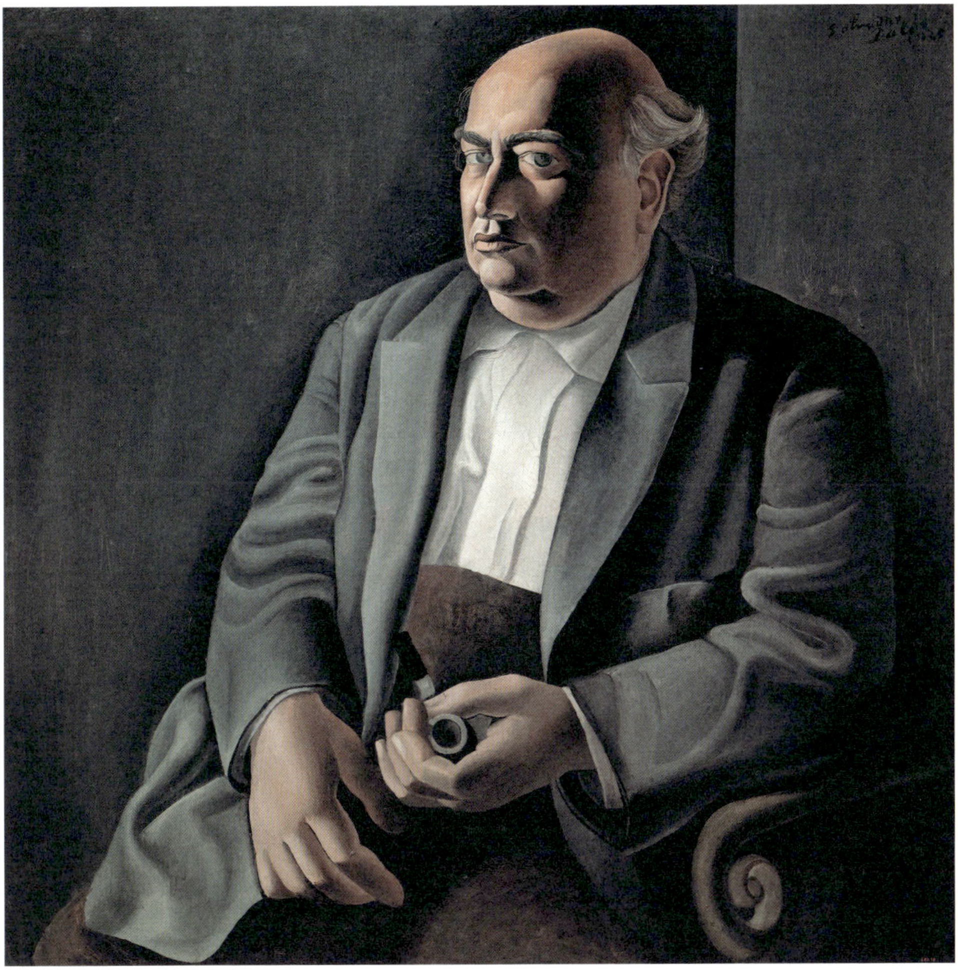

SALVADOR DALÍ, *Retrat del meu pare*
(*Portrait of My Father*), 1925, oil on canvas
104.5 × 104.5 cm, Museu Nacional d'Art de Catalunya,
Barcelona, cat. no. P 159

He had locked himself in, but I had seen him carry a platter piled high with the sea urchins he adores. I imagine him cracking them open in one movement and swallowing them with a sensuous enjoyment the more voluptuous for being savored privately.
— SALVADOR DALÍ, *The Unspeakable Confessions of Salvador Dalí as told to André Parinaud* (London, 1977), p. 25.

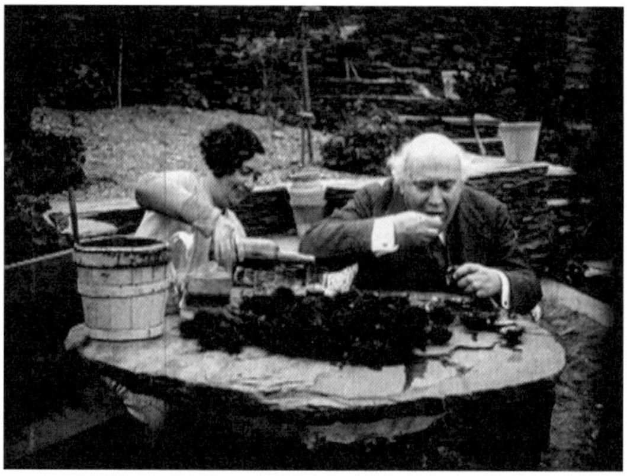

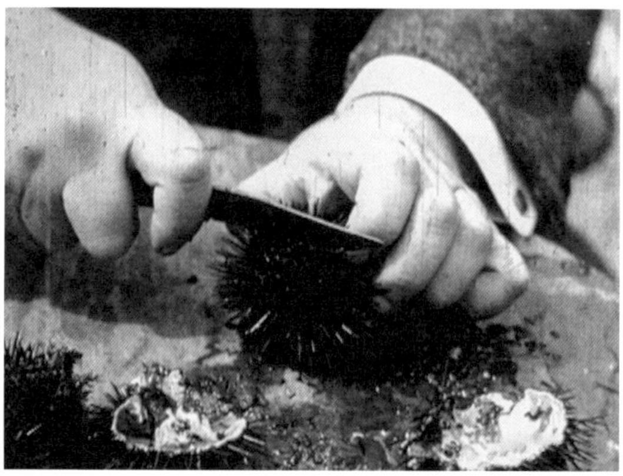

LUIS BUÑUEL, *Menjant garotes* (*Eating Sea Urchins*), 1930
Black-and-white silent film, 4 min.

Sea urchins have to be eaten as soon as harvested, and, if at all possible, from Cape Creus. They must be eaten, away from all and in full sunlight. Thus, after eating, the sun makes you sleepy and you feel great. Thought becomes fantasy, while about us the spiny, black, shiny shells move, and the sun runs its course.
— ANA MARÍA DALÍ, *Salvador Dalí visto por su hermana* (1949), unpublished translation by G. Boler and A. Norwood, 1998, p. 14.

To represent castration symbolically, the dream-work makes use of baldness, hair-cutting, falling out of teeth and decapitation. If one of the ordinary symbols for a penis occurs in a dream doubled or multiplied, it is to be regarded as a warding-off of castration.
— SIGMUND FREUD, *The Interpretation of Dreams* (1900), (London, 1953), p. 357.

A few days later I received a letter from my father notifying me of my irrevocable banishment from the bosom of my family. [...] When I received this letter, my first reaction was to cut off all my hair. But I did more than this—I had my head completely shaved. I went and buried the pile of my black hair in a hole I had dug on the beach for this purpose, and in which I interred at the same time the pile of empty shells of the urchins I had eaten at noon. Having done this I climbed up on a small hill from which one overlooks the whole village of Cadaques, and there, sitting under the olive trees, I spent two long hours contemplating that panorama of my childhood, of my adolescence, and of my present.
— SALVADOR DALÍ, *The Secret Life of Salvador Dalí* (New York, 1993), pp. 253–54.

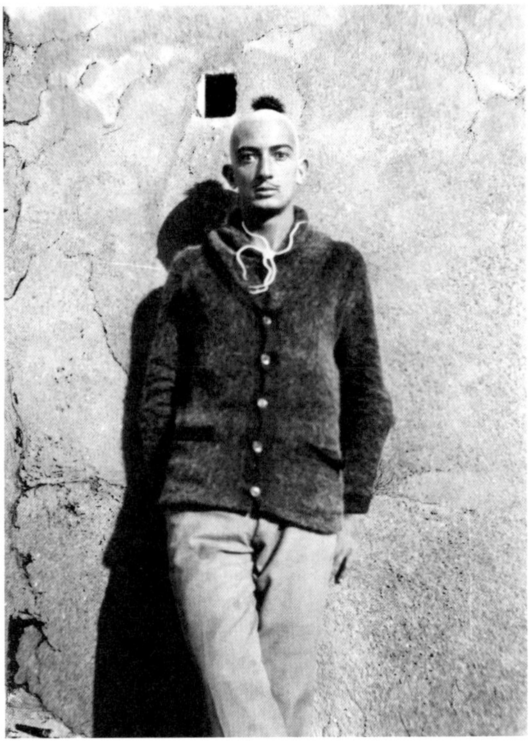

LUIS BUÑUEL, *Salvador Dalí*, 1929
Black-and-white photograph, 8.9 × 6.2 cm
Fundació Gala-Salvador Dalí, Figueres

When I arrived in Figueras, it was Christmas 1929. At first, all I could hear were angry shouts; then suddenly the door flew open and, purple with rage, Dalí's father threw his son out, calling him every name in the book. Dalí screamed back while his father pointed to him and swore that he hoped never to see that pig in his house again. The rage of the elder Dalí was perfectly understandable; it seems that on one of his paintings then at a show in Barcelona, Dalí had written—in black ink and large, sloppy letters—"I spit joyfully on my mother's portrait"!
— LUIS BUÑUEL, *My Last Breath* (Paris, 1994), p. 115.

2

READING FREUD: DALÍ AT THE MADRID RESIDENCIA DE ESTUDIANTES

After passing the entry exam at the Real Academia de Bellas Artes de San Fernando, Dalí moved to Madrid in September 1922, where he took up his quarters at the Residencia de Estudiantes (student halls) (→p. 37). He stayed there until his expulsion from the school in July 1926, after he had declared his examiners as incompetent.[1] During these four years, his artistic and intellectual personality emerged fully, and he aligned himself with the latest developments of the time. A decisive factor was his access, from 1926, to Sigmund Freud's work, published in Spanish translation by Biblioteca Nueva since 1922 (→p. 50), which led to his development of a visual poetics with Surrealist qualities.

The Residencia de Estudiantes was one of the most vibrant cultural centers of the era. A meeting place—whether as residents or visitors—of the intellectual, literary, artistic, and scientific elite of this period of Spanish culture, sometimes known as the "Spanish Silver Age," also including figures of international acclaim, such as Louis Aragon (who in 1925 gave a lecture about Surrealism[2]), H. G. Wells, Max Jacob, Howard Carter, G. K. Chesterton, Leo Frobenius, and Albert

Einstein. During this time, Dalí formed close friendships with the poet Federico García Lorca, the future filmmaker Luis Buñuel, and with José (Pepín) Bello, all of them fellow residents at the student halls (→p. 47). He also became acquainted with other important figures of the period, such as the poets Juan Ramón Jiménez and Rafael Alberti, the writers Ramón Gómez de la Serna and Guillermo de Torre, the painters Maruja Mallo and Rafael Barradas, the sculptor Alberto Sánchez, the philosopher José Ortega y Gasset, and many others.

Also living in the halls was the Medicine Nobel Prize winner Santiago Ramón y Cajal (→p. 58), whose histological studies, as well as the drawings by Yves Tanguy (→p. 75) and André Masson, were a major inspiration for the Surrealist drawings produced by Dalí and Lorca from 1926 (→pp. 61–73).

This was at a time when Madrid was gradually—albeit a little later than Barcelona—embracing Modernism and the avant-garde.[3] Already in 1915, Diego Rivera and María Blanchard had presented their Cubist works at exhibitions in the capital, followed from 1918 by the avant-garde literary movement of Ultraísmo, the nexus for most of the contemporary artistic developments then emerging in Madrid, such as Barradas's "Vibrationism" and "Clownism," the Expressionist woodcuts of Norah Borges and Francisco Bores, the Nabis aesthetic imported from Paris by Daniel Vázquez Díaz, later contributing to the formal language of Neo-Cubism, and Alberti's experiments in abstract painting.[4] All this was further fueled by the fact that Sonia and Robert Delaunay and the Poles Władysław Jahl and Marjan Paszkiewicz were also staying in Madrid at the time.

From 1922, movements gradually began to surface in Madrid that were linked to new trends prevailing in European modern art of the interwar years. A key role was played in this regard by cardboard sculptures, which resulted in Barradas's "Return to Order" after his Vibrationist and Clownist phase and which also found a devotee in the sculptor Alberto Sánchez.[5] This entire process culminated in the exhibition by the Society of Iberian Artists in 1925, marking the arrival of the avant-garde in Madrid and Dalí's assertion as an avant-garde artist.[6]

From this moment on and until his move to Paris in 1929, the numerous different components that had already characterized Dalí's work so far were supplemented by these new sources of inspiration, and Dalí showed a growing interest in the new avant-garde.

1 The two books by Rafael Santos Torroella (*Dalí residente* [Madrid, 1992] and *El primer Dalí: 1918–1929* [Madrid, 2005]) are essential to understanding this period, as is Juan José Lahuerta (ed.), *Dalí, Lorca y la Residencia de Estudiantes*, exh. cat., CaixaForum, Madrid (Madrid, 2010).

2 This lecture was perhaps the most impressive information Dalí and Lorca ever received about Surrealism.

3 The most comprehensive overview of the artistic activities encountered by Dalí on his arrival in Madrid can be found in the book by Isabel García, *Orígenes de las vanguardias artísticas en Madrid (1909–1922)* (Córdoba, 2005).

4 For an understanding of sculpture and the Ultraist movement, see Juan Manuel Bonet and Carlos Pérez, eds., *El ultraísmo y las artes plásticas*, exh. cat., Instituto Valenciano de Arte Moderno, Valencia (Valencia, 1996).

5 For an understanding of the works of Barradas and Alberto, see Jaime Brihuega and Concha Lomba, eds., *Barradas*, exh. cat., Centre Cultural Tecla Sala, L'Hospitalet de Llobregat (Zaragoza, 1992; revised edition: Madrid, 1993); ibid. *Alberto: 1895–1962*, exh. cat., Museo Nacional Centro de Arte Reina Sofía, Madrid; Museo de Santa Cruz, Toledo; Museu Nacional d'Art de Catalunya, Barcelona (Madrid, 2001).

6 For more on the exhibition by the Society of Iberian Artists, see Jaime Brihuega and Concha Lomba, eds., *La Sociedad de Artistas Ibéricos y el arte español de 1925*, exh. cat., Museo Nacional Centro de Arte Reina Sofía, Madrid; MNCARS—Museo de Bellas Artes de Bilbao (Madrid, 1995).

[…] I remained alone, settled in a very comfortable room in the Students' Residence [Residencia de Estudiantes], an exclusive place to which it required a certain influence to be admitted, and where the sons of the best Spanish families lived. I launched upon my studies at the Academy with the greatest determination. […] Sunday mornings I went to the Prado and made cubist sketch-plans of the composition of various paintings.

— SALVADOR DALÍ, *The Secret Life of Salvador Dalí* (New York, 1993), p. 159.

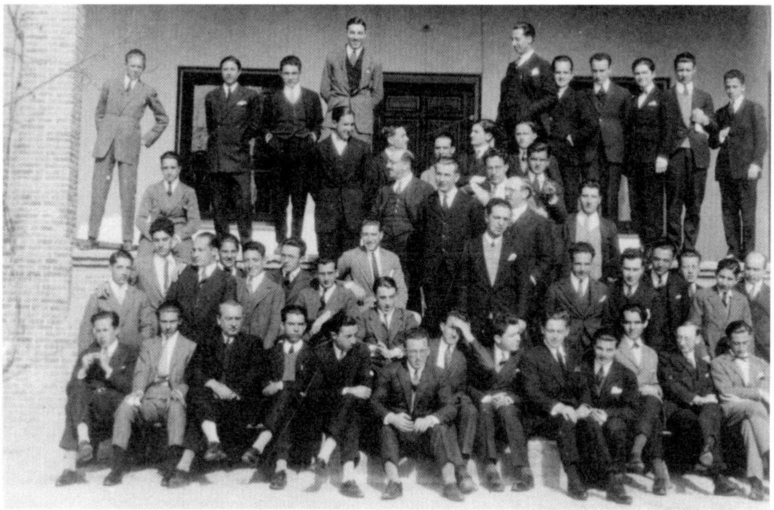

Students living in the "Transatlántico" building at the Residencia de Estudiantes. First row on the right: Federico García Lorca, León Sánchez Cuesta, and Salvador Dalí
Residencia de Estudiantes, Madrid

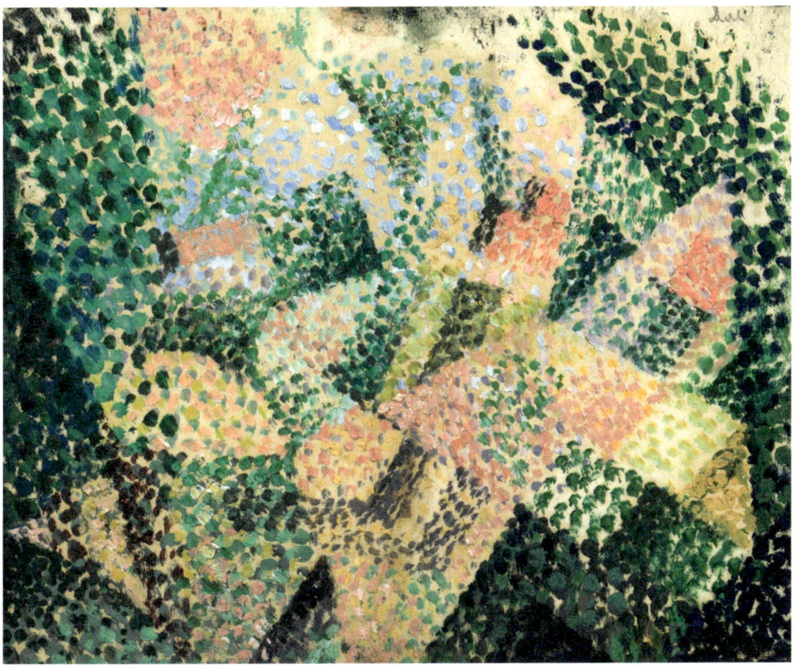

SALVADOR DALÍ, *Paisaje en Madrid* (Landscape of Madrid), 1922, oil on paper on cardboard 30.1 × 35.8 cm, Museo de Arte Contemporáneo, Madrid, cat. no. P 108

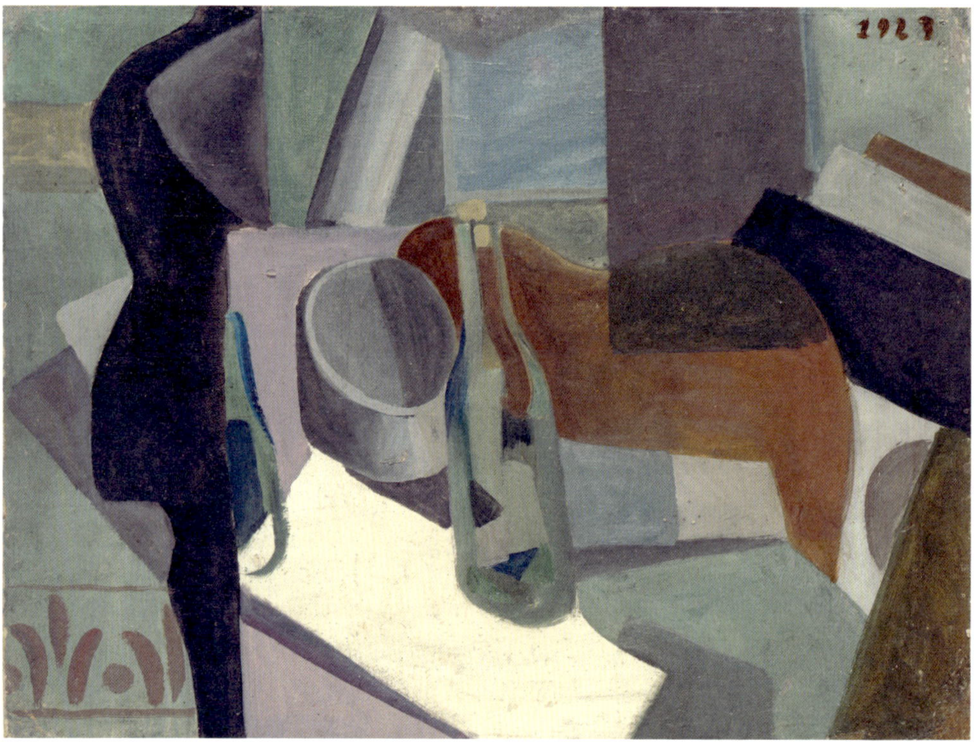

SALVADOR DALÍ, *Naturaleza muerta* (*Still Life*)
c. 1923, oil on cardboard, 50 × 56 cm
Museo Nacional Centro de Arte Reina Sofía, Madrid
Cat. no. P 123

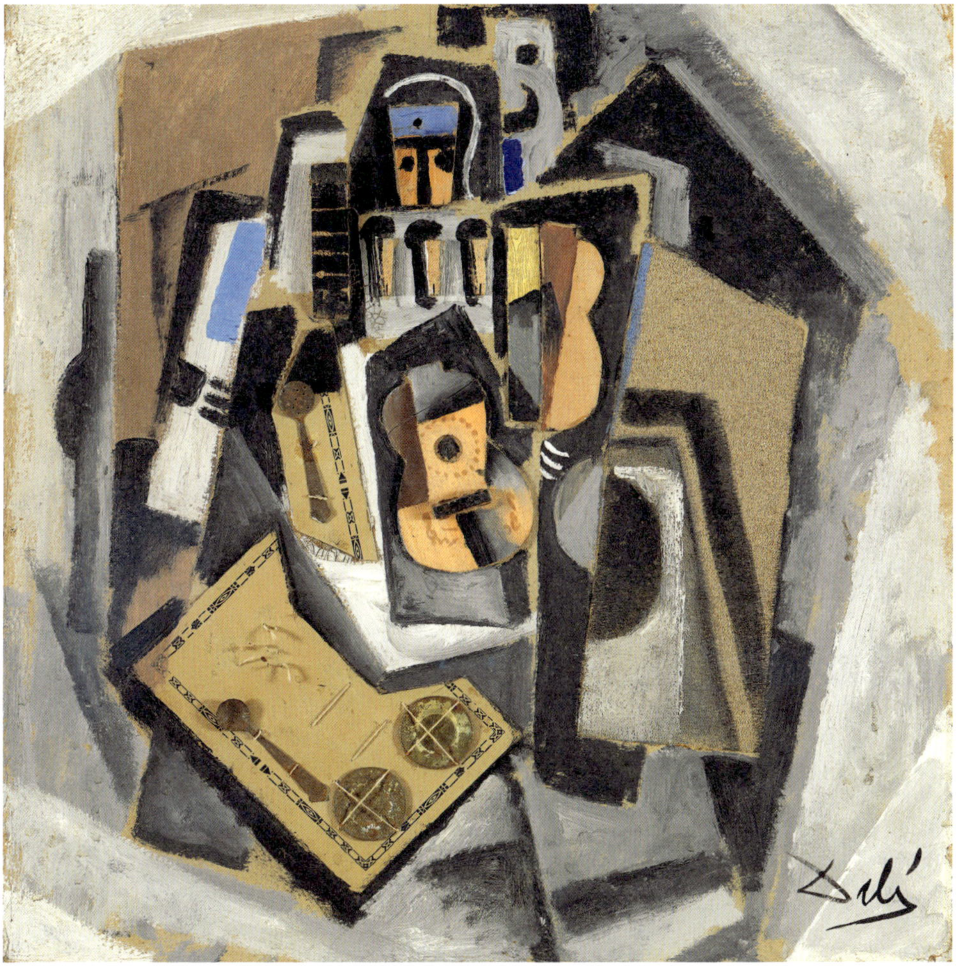

SALVADOR DALÍ, *Pierrot con guitarra* (*Pierrot with Guitar*), c. 1923, oil and collage on cardboard 54.5 × 52.3 cm, Museo Nacional Thyssen-Bornemisza, Madrid, cat. no. P 137

This is one of Dalí's first large-scale works. The monumental female figures and the young man show obvious connections to Picasso's Neoclassical phase, albeit with a pronounced geometric inflection. This is the formal language of New Objectivity, hailing from the interwar period, which is evident in Dalí's works from this period. Nevertheless, there are some elements that already hint at the pictorial vocabulary the artist adopted after his shift to a Surrealist poetics inspired by Freud's theories, elements that also link back to the complex relationship between Dalí and García Lorca at the time. Hence we see the severed head at the center of the composition, splitting into a succession of silhouettes and conveying the complexity of Dalí's inner world, while also alluding to García Lorca's features as well as to his own. Above this head stands a sexually ambiguous young man wearing a sailor's cap, clasping a flute—with phallic connotations—so tightly that the veins on his arm protrude with the exertion. An allusion that no doubt also applies to the two crossed fish in the foreground. Geometric cliffs recall the landscape of Cabo de Creus, which exerted such a profound influence on Dalí's childhood imagination. The shadow of the female figure's face on the right acts as a double image of this rocky landscape. And the shapes of the clouds, inspired by Mantegna's *Death of the Virgin*—so admired by the artist in the Prado—were to reappear frequently in Dalí's future work.
— JAIME BRIHUEGA SIERRA

They [students from the Residencia de Estudiantes] came all in a group to look at my paintings, and [...] their surprise knew no limits. That I should be a cubist painter was the last thing they would have thought of! They frankly admitted their former opinion of me, and unconditionally offered me their friendship.
— SALVADOR DALÍ, *The Secret Life of Salvador Dalí* (New York, 1993), p.176.

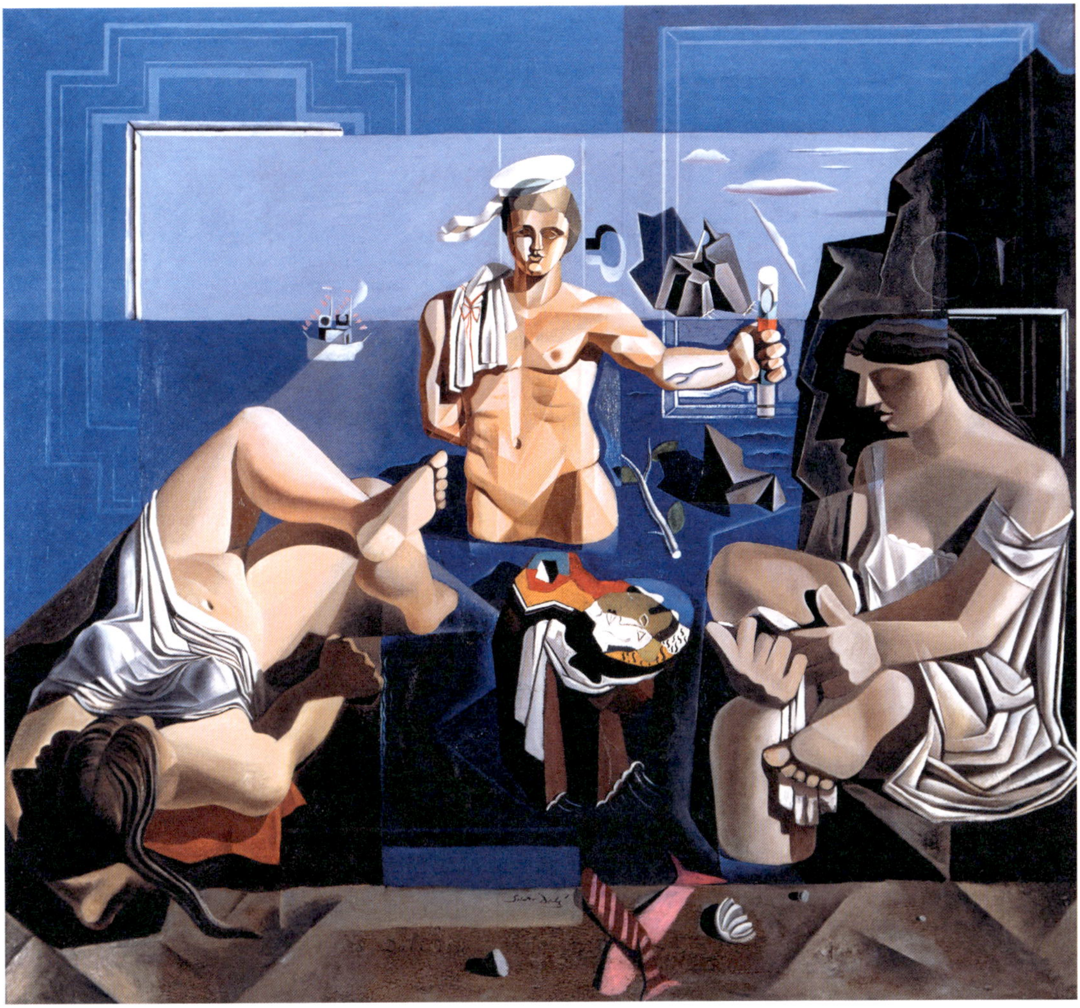

SALVADOR DALÍ, *Composició amb tres figures. "Acadèmia neocubista"* (*Composition with Three Figures. "Neo-cubist Academy"*), 1926, oil on canvas 190 × 200 cm, Museu de Montserrat, Barcelona, donated by Josefina Cusí, 1999, cat. no. P 171

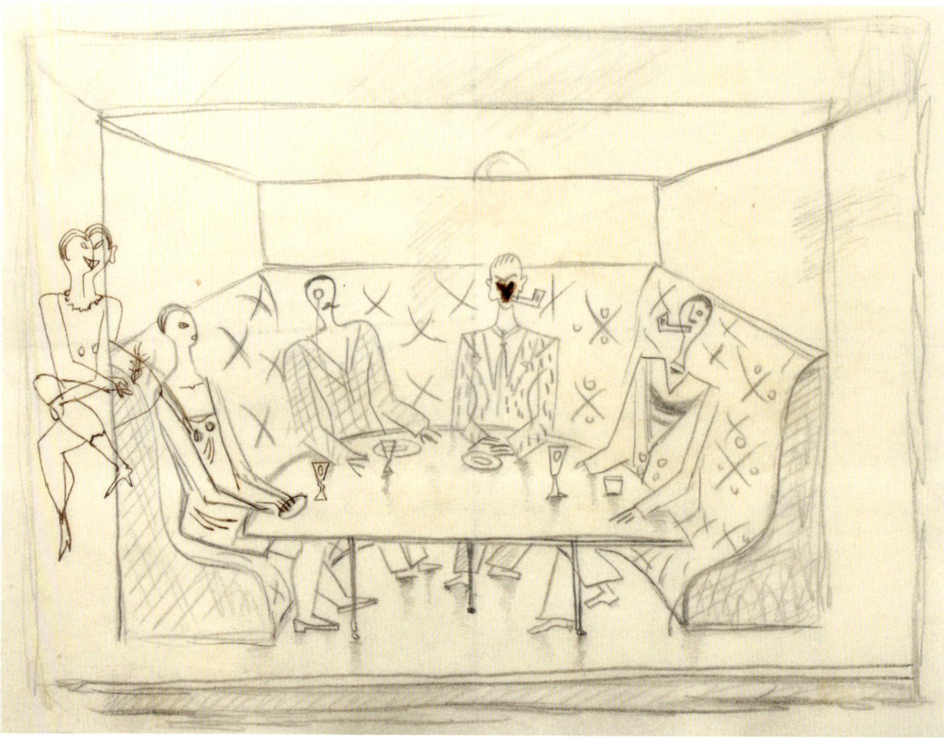

SALVADOR DALÍ, *Tertúlia en un cafè*, 1926
Pencil and ink on paper, 20.2 × 26.8 cm
Museu de Montserrat, Barcelona

I said a moment ago that the group which had just taken me so generously to its bosom was incapable of teaching me anything, and even as I said this I knew that it was not altogether true, since the group nevertheless taught me one thing, and it was precisely because of this thing that I remained in the group, and that I was going to continue to remain. They taught me how to go on a bender.
— SALVADOR DALÍ, *The Secret Life of Salvador Dalí* (New York, 1993), p. 177.

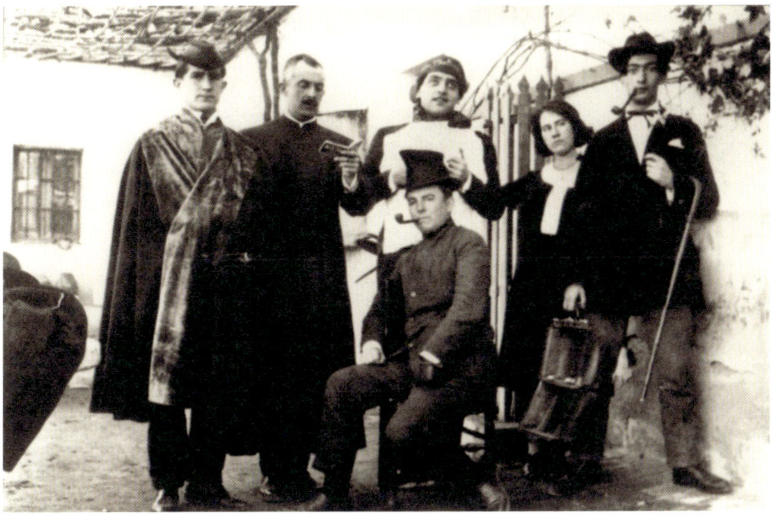

Meeting of the Order of Toledo at the Venta de Aires, Toledo (from left to right: José Bello, José Moreno Villa, Luis Buñuel, José María Hinojosa [seated], María Luisa González, and Salvador Dalí), 1924
Black-and-white photograph by Juan Vicens
Residencia de Estudiantes, Madrid

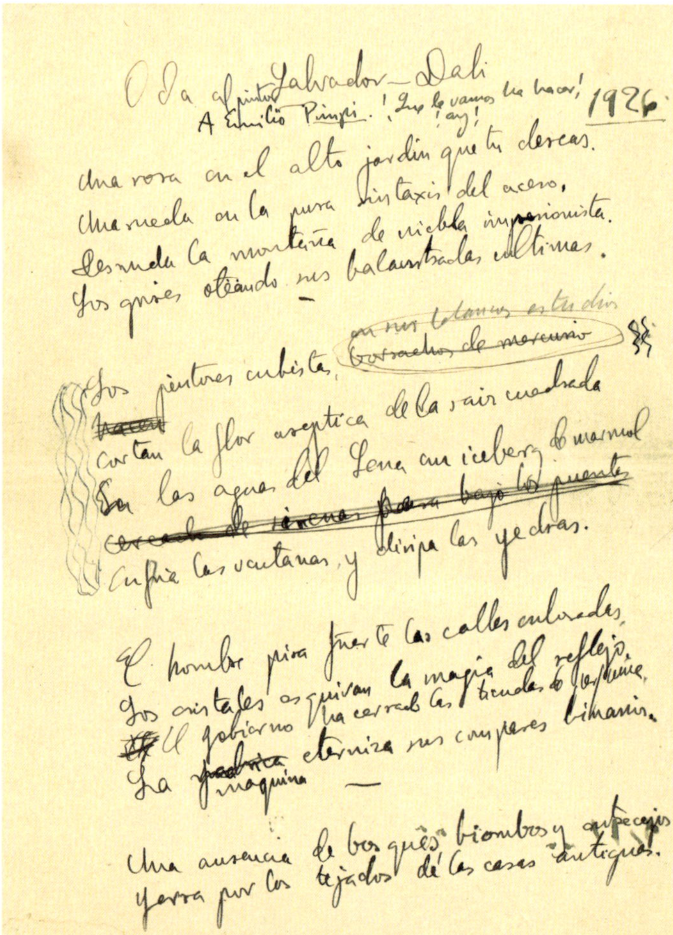

Oda al pintor Salvador Dalí 1926

Una rosa en el alto jardín que tú deseas.
Una rueda en la pura sintaxis del acero.
Desnuda la montaña de niebla impresionista.
Los grises oteando sus balaustradas últimas.

FEDERICO GARCIÁ LORCA, *Oda al pintor Salvador Dalí* (*Ode to the Painter Salvador Dalí*), 1926
Autograph, Fundación Federico García Lorca
Centro Federico García Lorca, Granada

I do not eulogize your imperfect adolescent brush
[...] but I extol your longings for the limited eternal.
— FEDERICO GARCIA LORCA, "Ode to Salvador Dalí," *The American Poetry Review*, vol. 14, no. 3, May/June 1989, p. 5.

When García Lorca tried to seduce me, I refused with distaste. But, now that I am growing older, I am a little more attracted to men. My voyeurism is extended to include them even with satisfaction. On condition that they have no beards, that they are very young, that they look like girls, and have long hair and angelic faces. To see a penis rise on a very supple, almost feminine body, is a delight to my eyes.
— SALVADOR DALÍ, quoted from *Louis Pauwels with Salvador Dalí, The Passions According to Dalí* (St. Petersburg, FL, 1985), p.155.

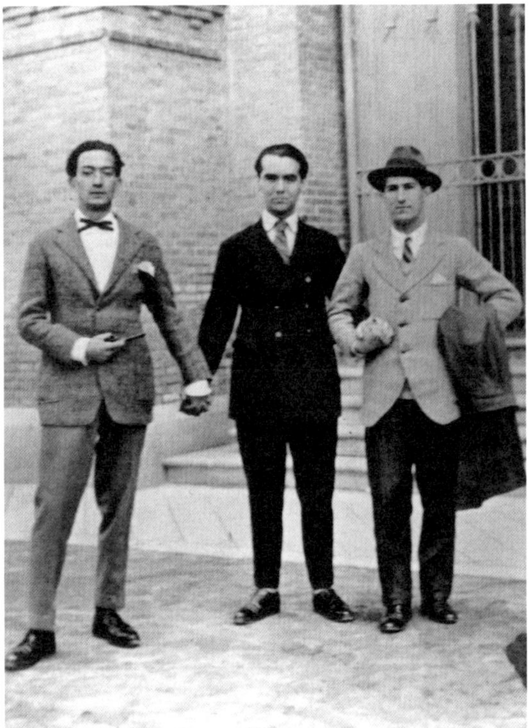

Salvador Dalí, Federico García Lorca,
and Pepin Bello in front of the
Museo Nacional de Ciencias Naturales, 1925
Fundación Federico García Lorca
Centro Federico García Lorca, Granada

Federico really pisses me off. I knew the boyfriend [Dalí] was a *putrefacto*, but Federico is even worse. [...] His rampant narcissism already made it difficult for him to have pure friendships. [...] Dalí is head-over-heels. He thinks he's a genius now, all puffed up by Federico's affections. He writes saying "Federico is better than ever. He's the real thing. His drawings are incredible [...]." I'd love to see him come over here and start again, away from García's perverse influence.
— LUIS BUÑUEL to Pepin Bello, September 5, 1927, quoted from *Luis Buñuel: A Life in Letters*, eds. Jo Evans and Breixo Viejo (New York, 2019), p. 22.

The other side of Saint Sebastian's magnifying glass corresponded to putrefaction. Everything seen through it was anguish, obscurity, and tenderness, even; tenderness, yet, because of the exquisite absence of spirit and naturalness.

Preceded by I don't know what lines by Dante, I got to see by and by the whole world of the putrefieds: cry-baby transcendental artists, removed from all clarity, cultivators of all germs, ignorant of the precision of the graduated double decimeter; [...].
— SALVADOR DALÍ, "San Sebastián: A Federico García Lorca," *L'amic de les arts*, Sitges, July 31, 1927, in *The Collected Writings of Salvador Dalí* (St. Petersburg, FL, 2017), p. 24.

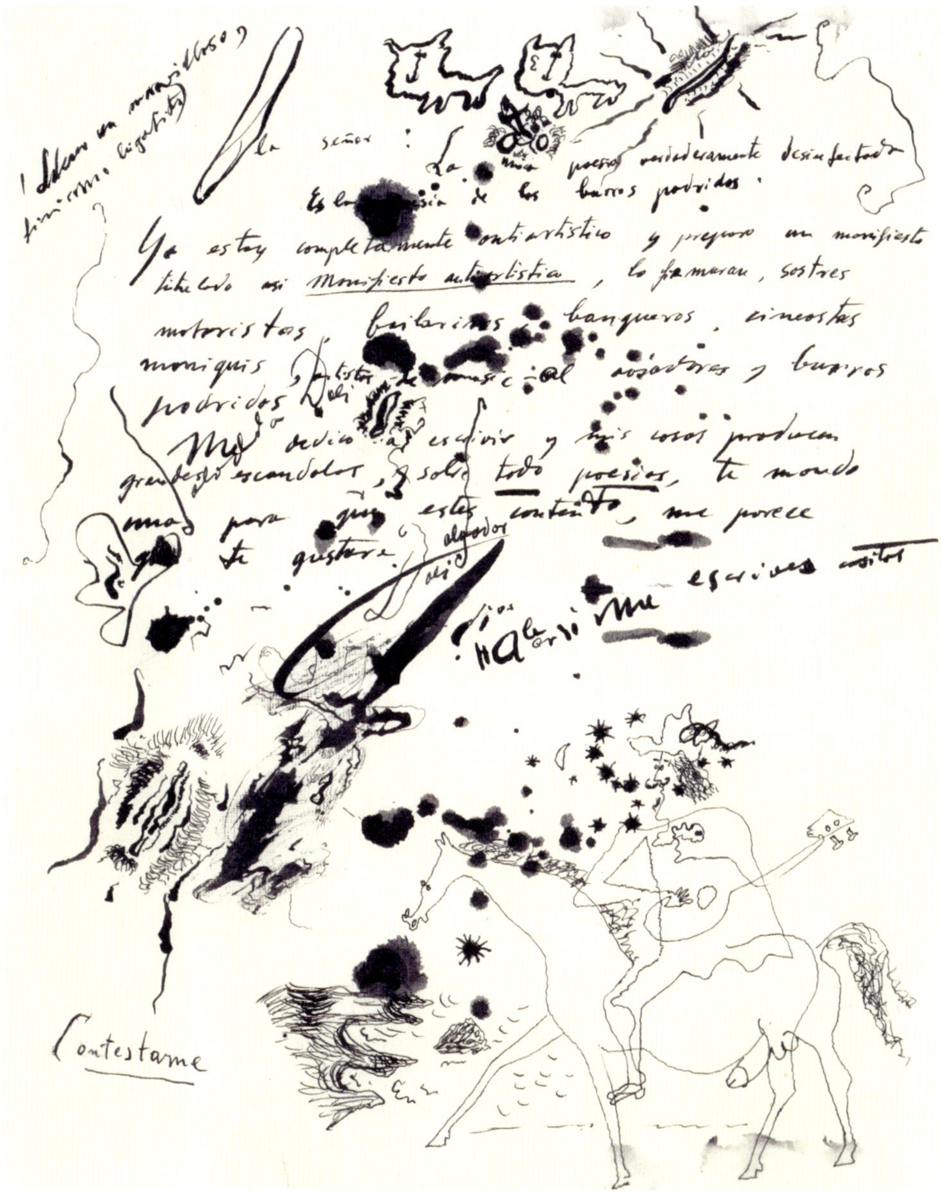

SALVADOR DALÍ, *Trovador ecuestre 2* (*Equestrian Troubadour 2*, from the series: *Putrefactos*)
1927, ink on paper, 20.8 × 16.5 cm, Museo Nacional Centro de Arte Reina Sofía, Madrid

At this period I had just begun to read Sigmund Freud's *Interpretation of Dreams.* This book presented itself to me as one of the capital discoveries in my life, and I was seized with a real vice of self-interpretation, not only of my dreams but of everything that happened to me, however accidental it might seem at first glance.
— SALVADOR DALÍ, *The Secret Life of Salvador Dalí* (New York, 1993), p. 198.

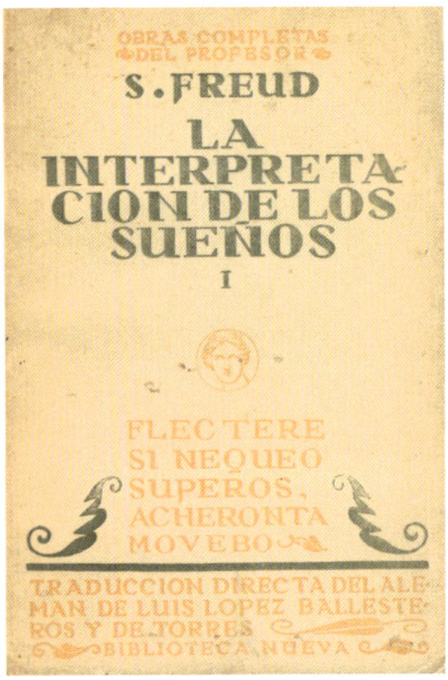

SIGMUND FREUD
La interpretación de los sueños I: Flectere si nequeo superos, acheronta movebo
Madrid 1923

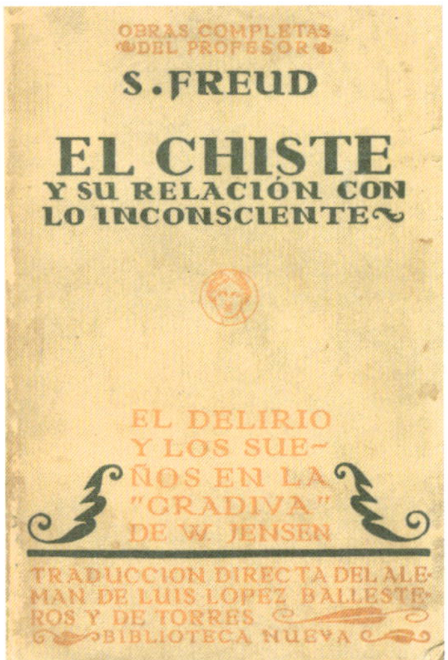

SIGMUND FREUD
El chiste y su relación con lo inconsciente: El delirio y los sueños en la "Gradiva" de W. Jensen, translated by Luis López-Ballesteros y de Torres, Madrid 1923

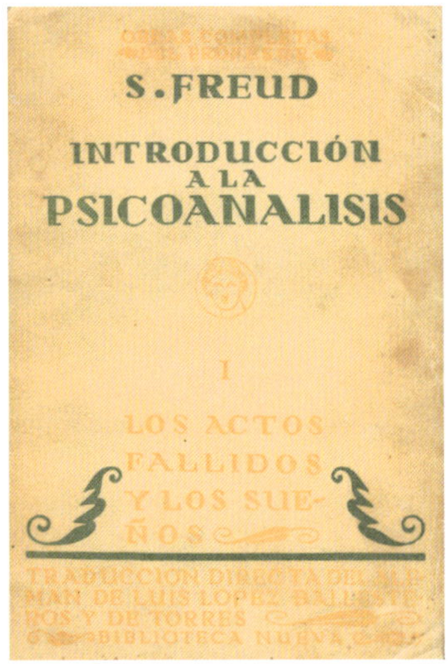

SIGMUND FREUD
Introducción a la psicoanálisis: I. Los actos fallidos y los sueños, translated by Luis López-Ballesteros y de Torres, Madrid 1923

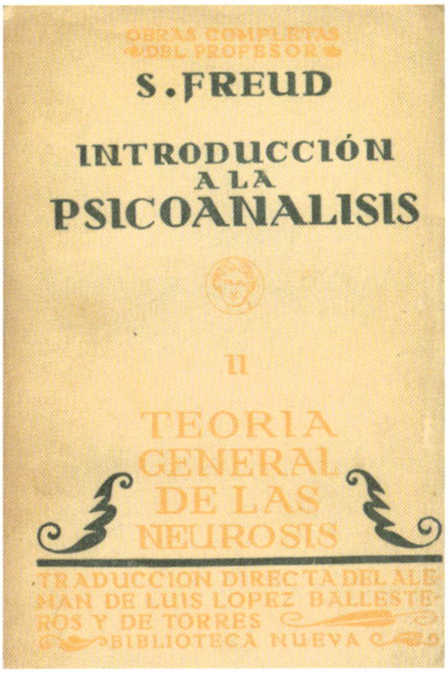

SIGMUND FREUD
Introducción a la psicoanálisis: II. Teoría general de las neurosis, translated by Luis López-Ballesteros y de Torres, Madrid 1923

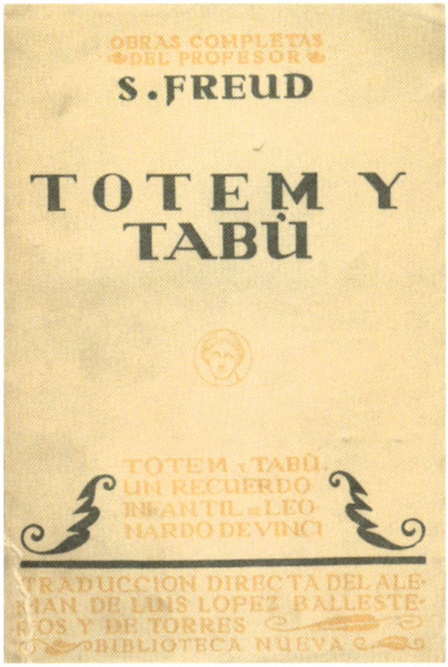

SIGMUND FREUD
Tótem y tabú: Un recuerdo infantil de Leonardo da Vinci
Translated by Luis López-Ballesteros y de Torres
Madrid 1923

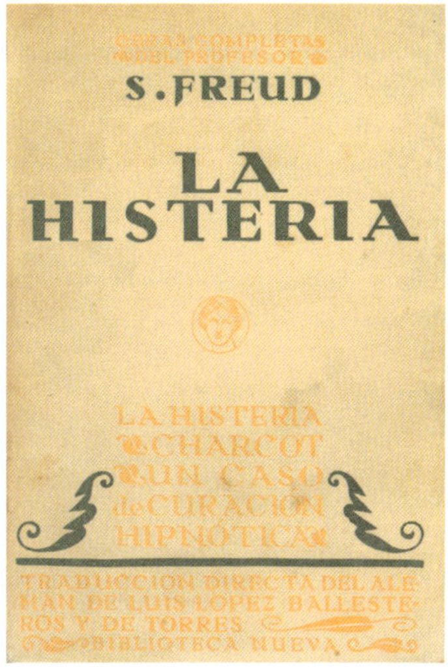

SIGMUND FREUD
La histeria: Charcot: Un caso de curación hipnótica
Translated by Luis López-Ballesteros y de Torres
Madrid 1925

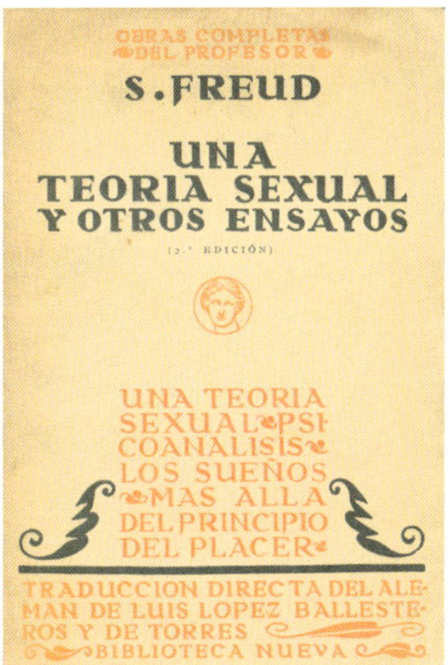

SIGMUND FREUD
Una teoría sexual y otros ensayos, translated by Luis López-Ballesteros y de Torres, Madrid 1929

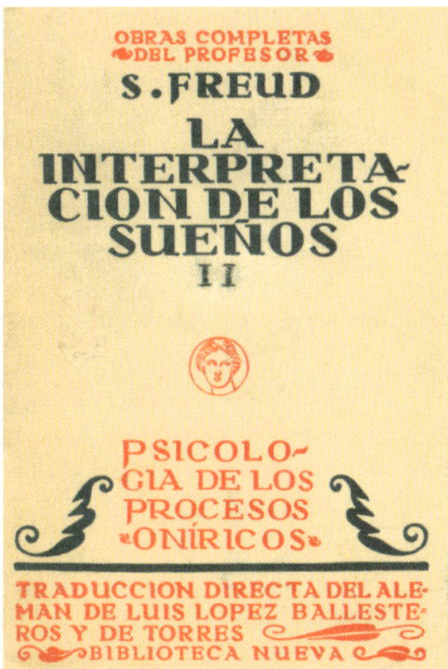

SIGMUND FREUD
La interpretacion de los sueños II: Psicología de los procesos oníricos, translated by Luis López-Ballesteros y de Torres, Madrid 1934

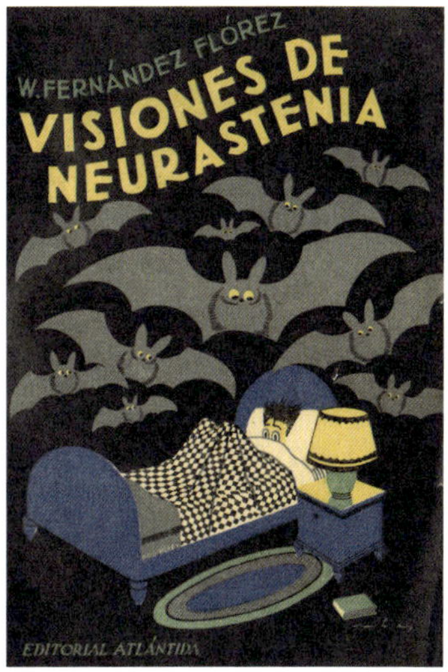

WENCESLAO FERNÁNDEZ FLÓREZ
Visiones de neurastenia
Madrid 1924

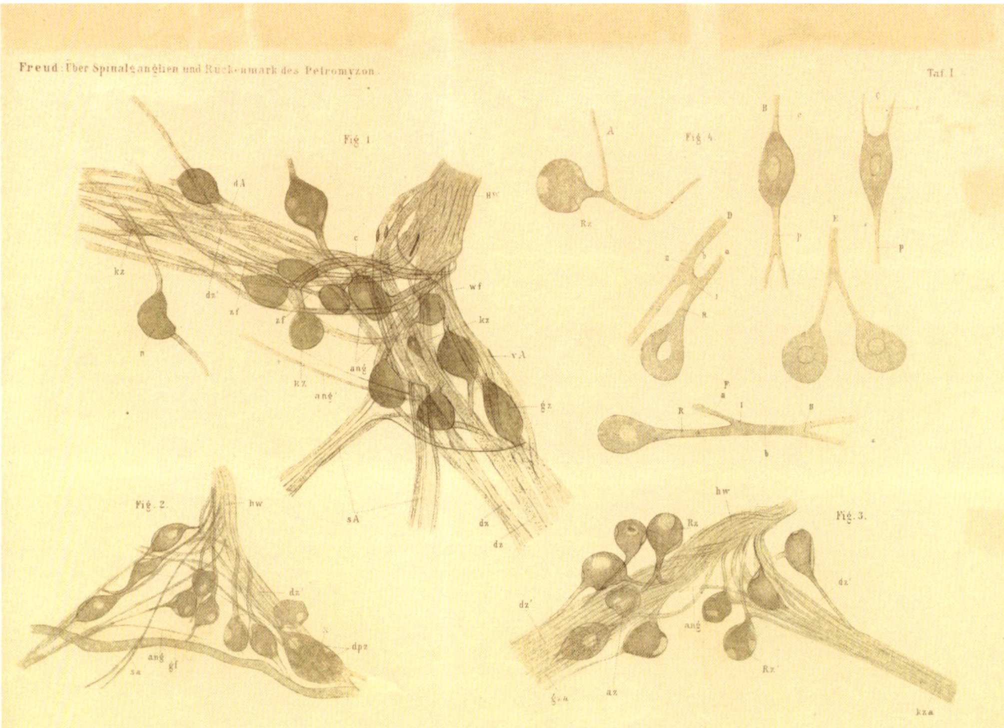

SIGMUND FREUD, "Über Spinalganglien
und Rückenmark des Petromyzon," 1878
From: *Sitzungsberichte der kaiserlichen Akademie der Wissenschaften (mathematisch-naturwissenschaftliche Classe)*, 3rd dept., vol. 78, pp. 81–167, plate II
Sigmund Freud Privatstiftung, Vienna

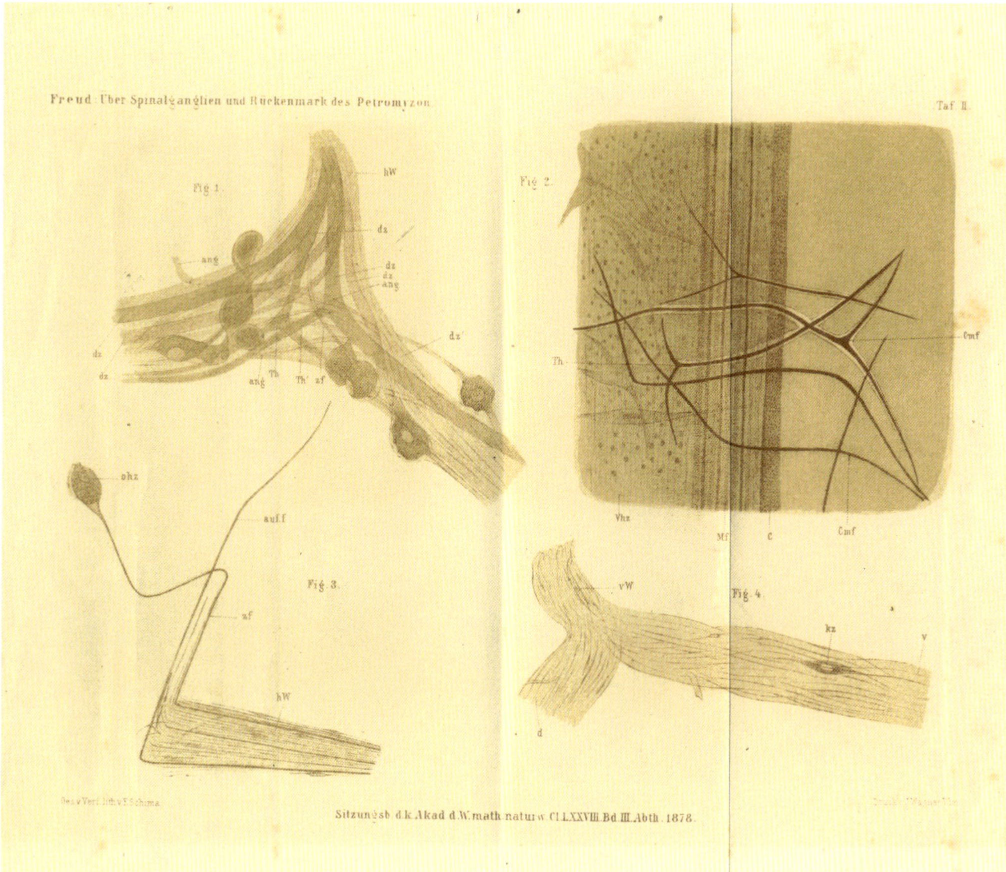

SIGMUND FREUD, "Über Spinalganglien
und Rückenmark des Petromyzon," 1878
From: *Sitzungsberichte der kaiserlichen Akademie der Wissenschaften (mathematisch-naturwissenschaftliche Classe)*, 3rd dept., vol. 78, pp. 81–167, plate I
Sigmund Freud Privatstiftung, Vienna

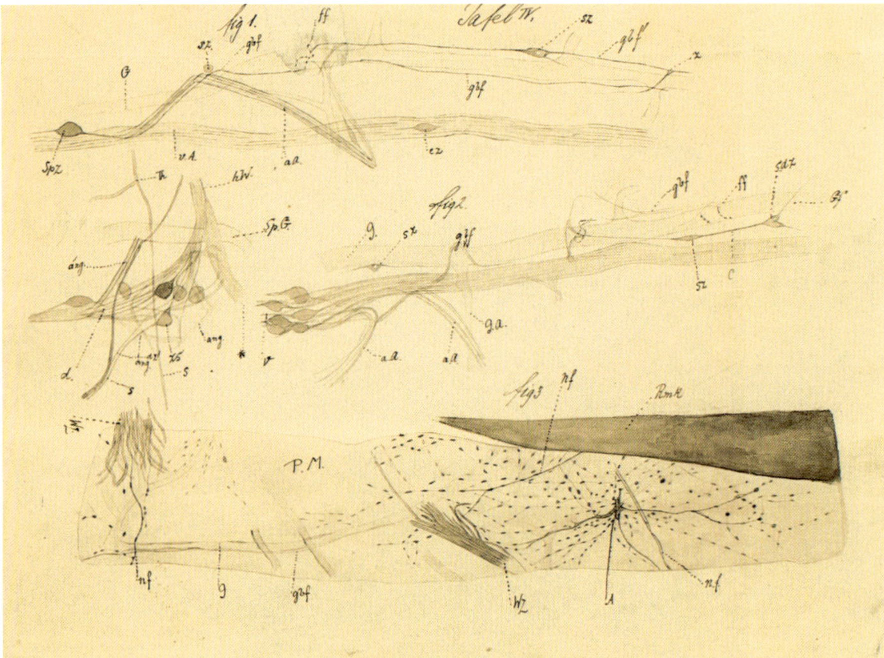

SIGMUND FREUD, *Spinal Ganglia and Spinal Cord of Petromyzon Fish (Ganglions spinaux et moelle épinière de la lamproie marine)*, 1878, ink on paper, 20.4 × 26.3 cm, Freud Museum London

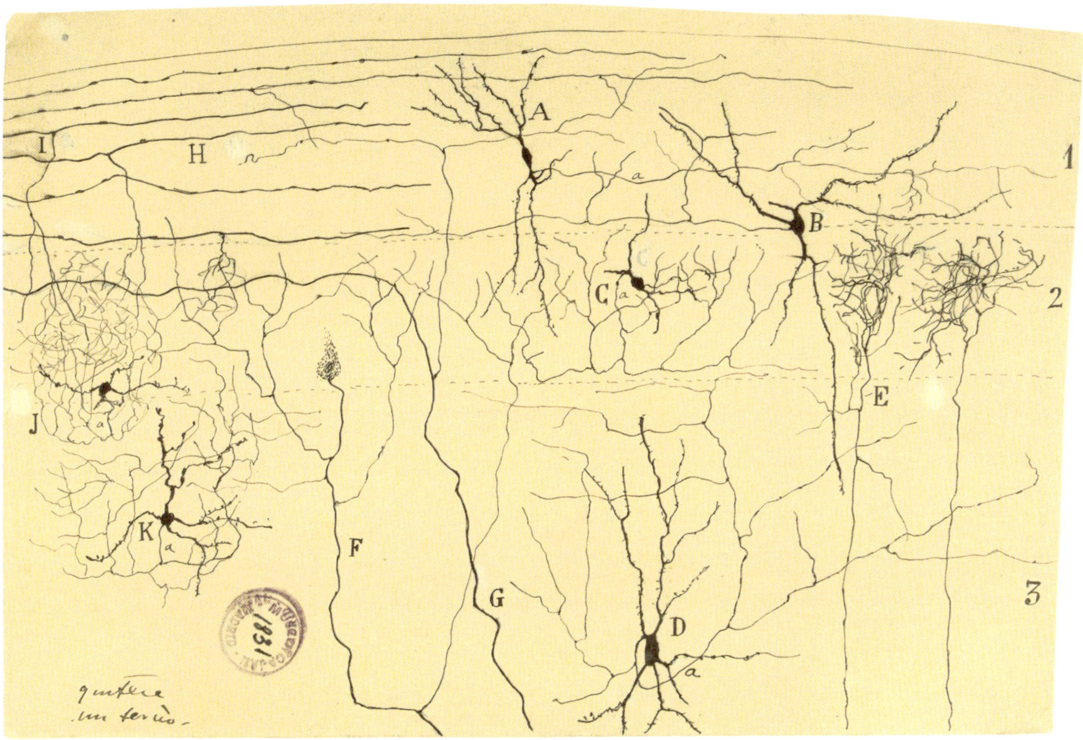

SANTIAGO RAMÓN Y CAJAL
Histological drawing: *Células de axón corto de la corteza esfeoidal olfativa* (*Short axons of the olfactory cells in the zone of the sphenoid bone*)
c. 1904, ink and pencil on paper, 16 × 22.7 cm
Instituto Cajal, CSIC, Madrid

Sleep releases within us an activity that defies the limits of time and space, but also of logic. And if we take Freud's famous theories seriously, the dream would also provide the greatest happiness, which would consist of making the dearest and most pleasing wishes come true.
— SANTIAGO RAMÓN Y CAJAL, *Charlas de café. Pensamientos, anécdotas y confidencias* (Madrid, 1922), pp. 82–83.

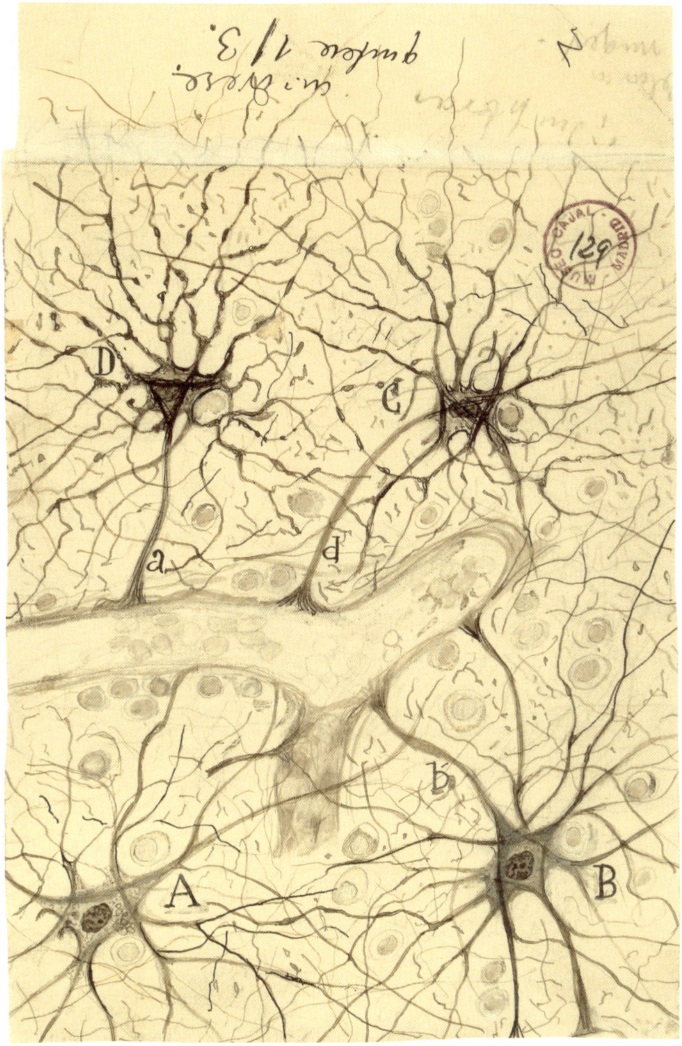

SANTIAGO RAMÓN Y CAJAL
Histological drawing: *Células neuróglias de la sustancia blanca del cerebro* (*Neuroglial cells of white matter in the brain*)
c. 1913, ink and pencil on paper, 20 × 12.7 cm
Instituto Cajal, CSIC, Madrid

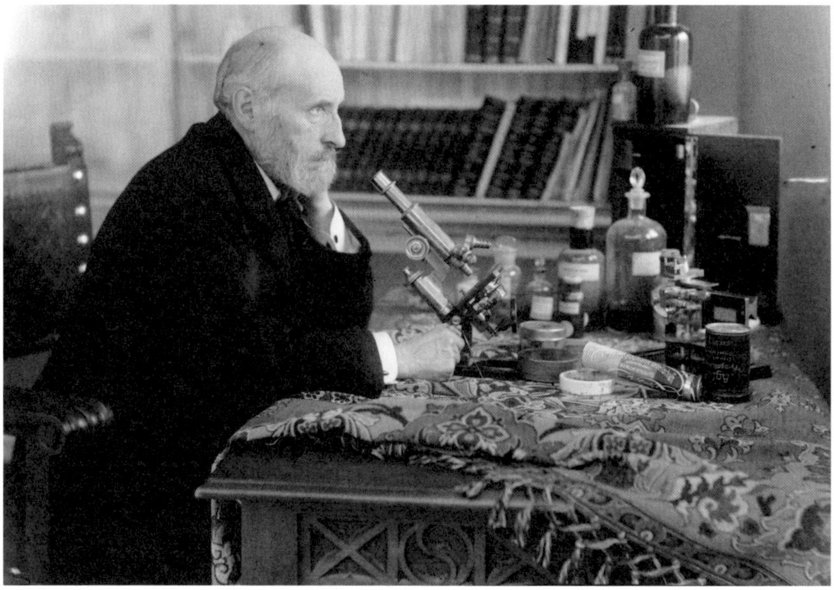

Santiago Ramón y Cajal at the microscope, 1920
Instituto Cajal, CSIC, Madrid

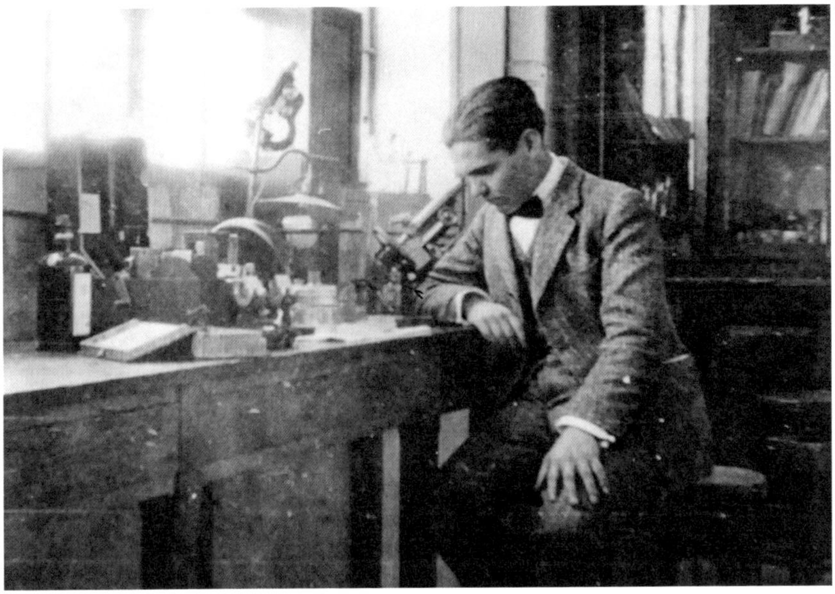

Federico Garciá Lorca at the microscope
at the Residencia de Estudiantes, 1924
Fundación Federico García Lorca
Centro Federico García Lorca, Granada

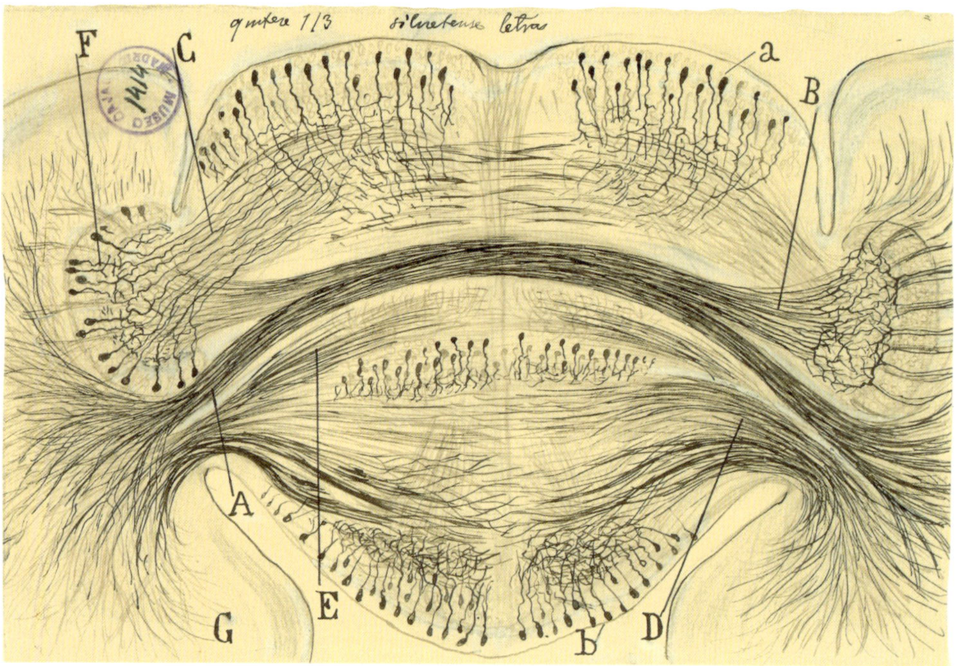

SANTIAGO RAMÓN Y CAJAL
Histological drawing: *Corte horizontal del centro cerebroide de sepia* (*Horizontal section through the midbrain of a cuttlefish*), c. 1917
Ink and pencil on paper, 13.1 × 19.2 cm
Instituto Cajal, CSIC, Madrid

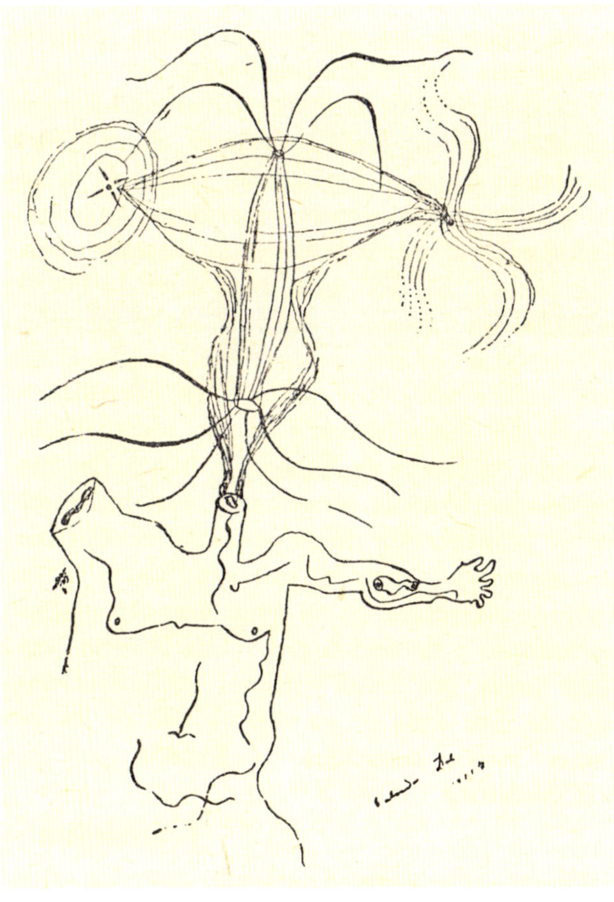

SALVADOR DALÍ, *Degollación de los Inocentes* (*Beheading of the Innocents*), 1928
From: *La Gaceta Literaria*, January 15, 1929

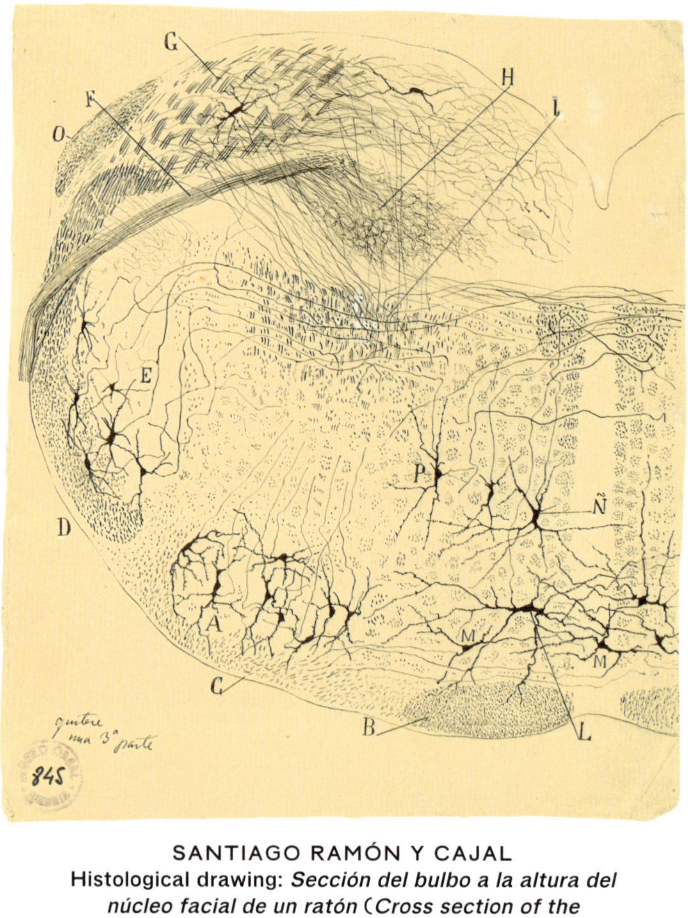

SANTIAGO RAMÓN Y CAJAL
Histological drawing: *Sección del bulbo a la altura del núcleo facial de un ratón* (*Cross section of the olfactory bulb of a mouse at the level of the facial nerve*)
c. 1898, ink and pencil on paper, 20 × 16.5 cm
Instituto Cajal, CSIC, Madrid

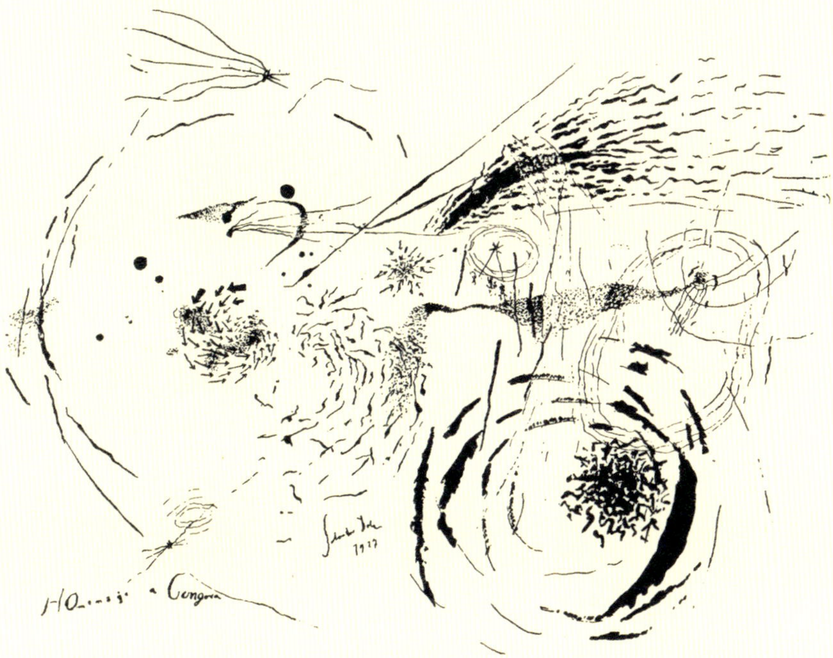

SALVADOR DALÍ, *Homenaje a Góngora*
(Homage to Góngora), 1927
From: *Litoral*, nos. 5/7, October 1927

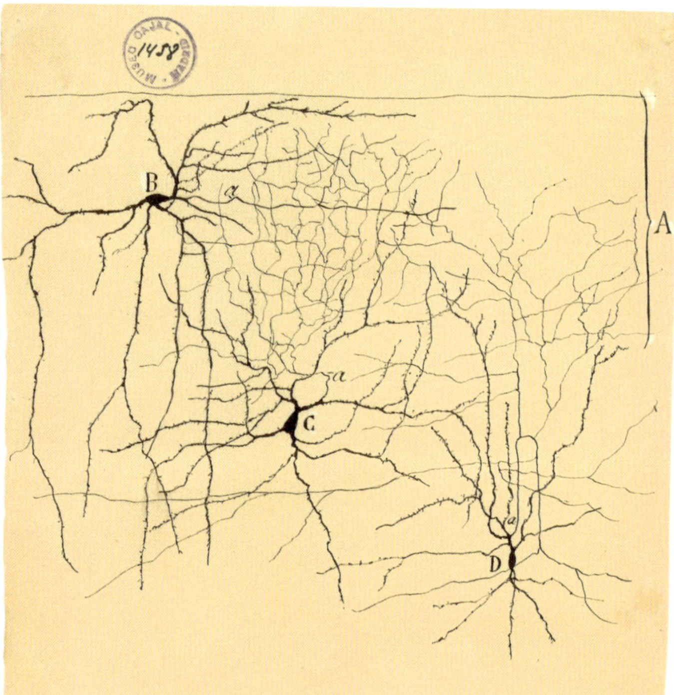

SANTIAGO RAMÓN Y CAJAL
Histological drawing: *Células de axón corto grandes de la circunvolución central anterior de niño de 25 días* (*Long and short axons from the cells of the anterior central gyrus of a 25-day-old infant*)
c. 1899, ink and pencil on paper, 16 × 17 cm
Instituto Cajal, CSIC, Madrid

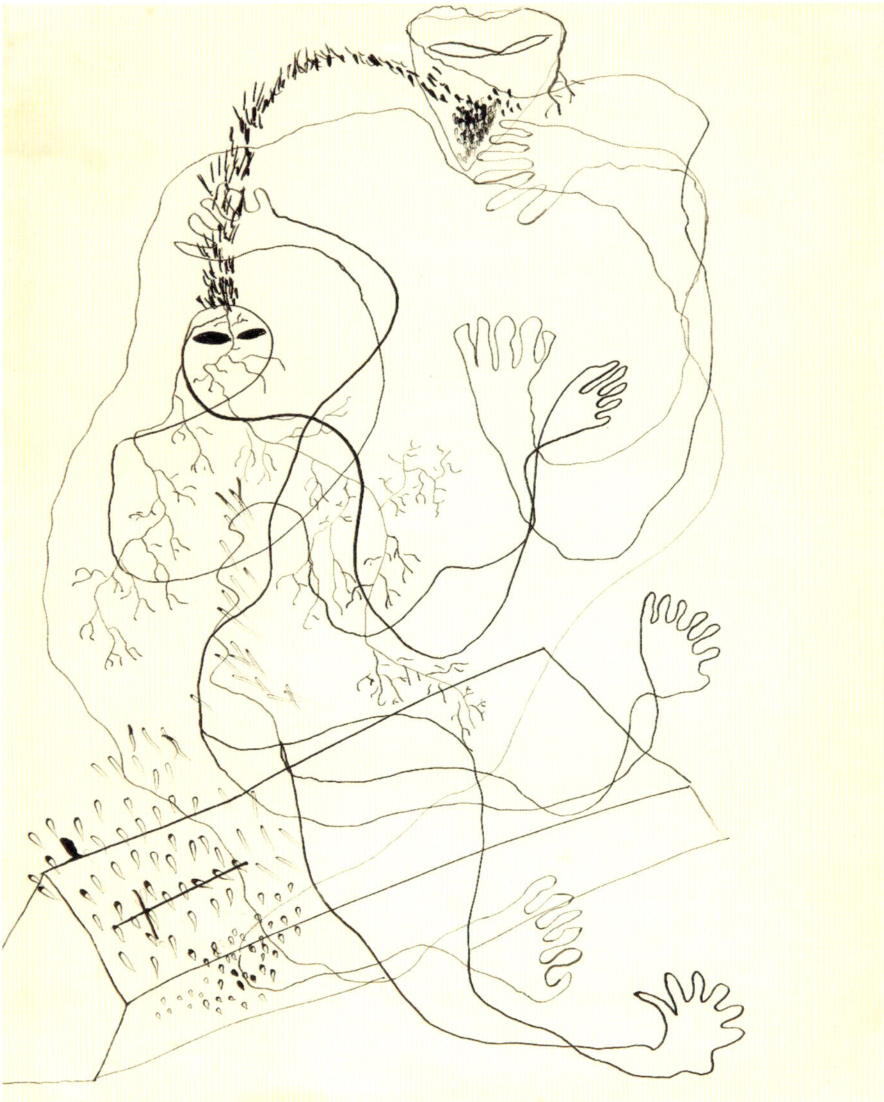

FEDERICO GARCIÁ LORCA, *Dos figuras sobre una tumba* (*Two Figures over a Tomb*)
c. 1929/31, ink on paper, 24.9 × 20.2 cm
Fundación Federico García Lorca
Centro Federico García Lorca, Granada

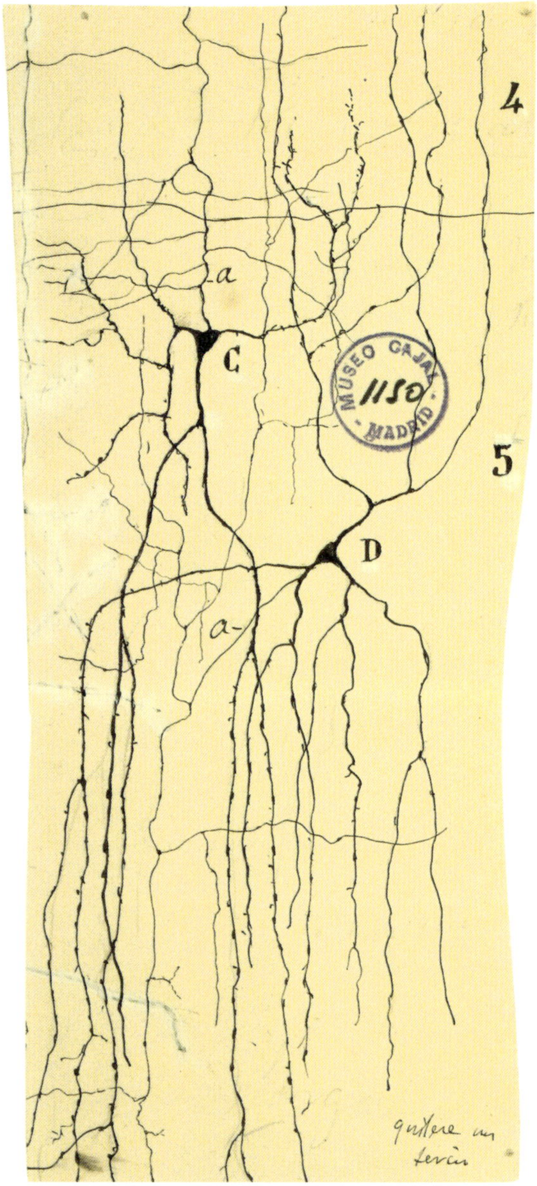

SANTIAGO RAMÓN Y CAJAL
Histological drawing: *Células de axón corto de la capa quinta de la corteza acústica humana* (*Short axons of the cells in layer 5 of the human auditory cortex*), c. 1900
Ink and pencil on paper, 17.6 × 7.1 cm
Instituto Cajal, CSIC, Madrid

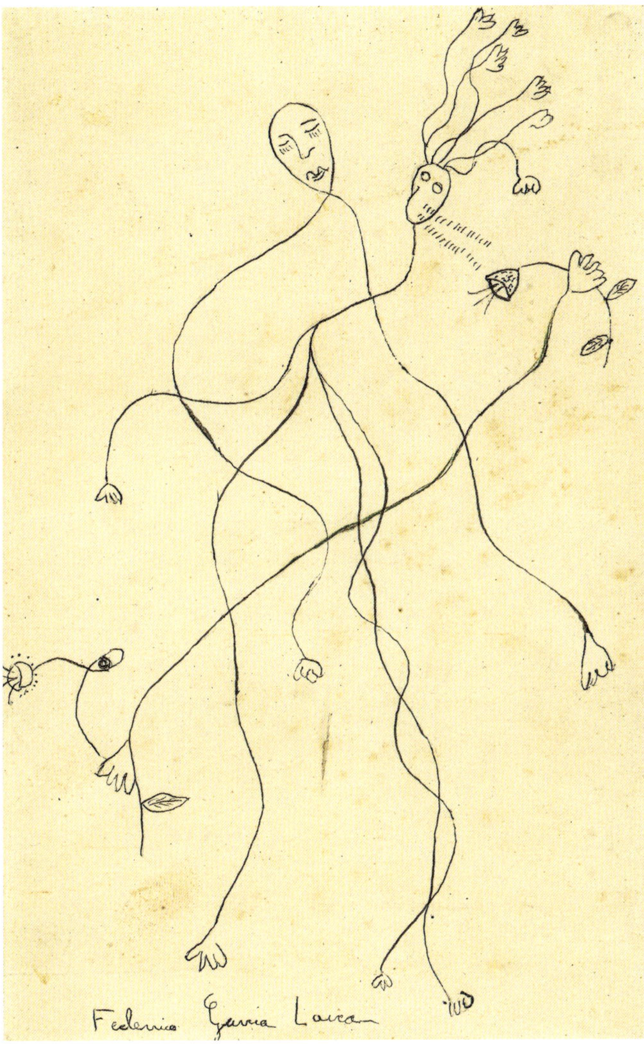

FEDERICO GARCÍA LORCA, *Sin título* (*Untitled*), 1928/30, ink on paper, 19.8 × 11.8 cm
Gregorio Prieto Foundation

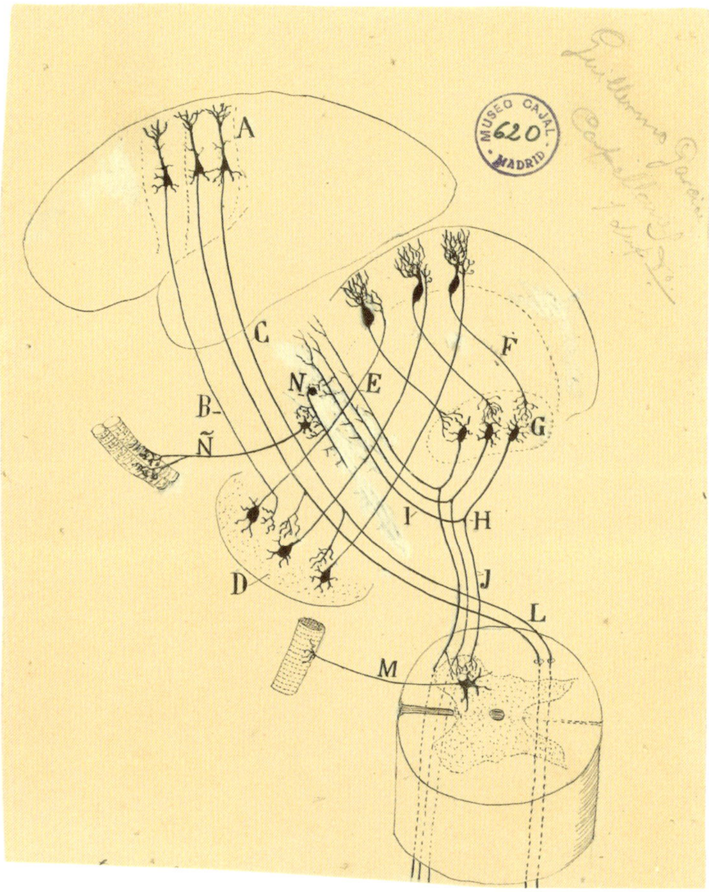

SANTIAGO RAMÓN Y CAJAL
Histological drawing: *Esquema de las vías motrices superiores e inferiores del cerebelo* (*Diagram of the upper and lower motor pathways of the cerebellum*), c. 1904
Ink and pencil on paper, 18.3 × 14.7 cm
Instituto Cajal, CSIC, Madrid

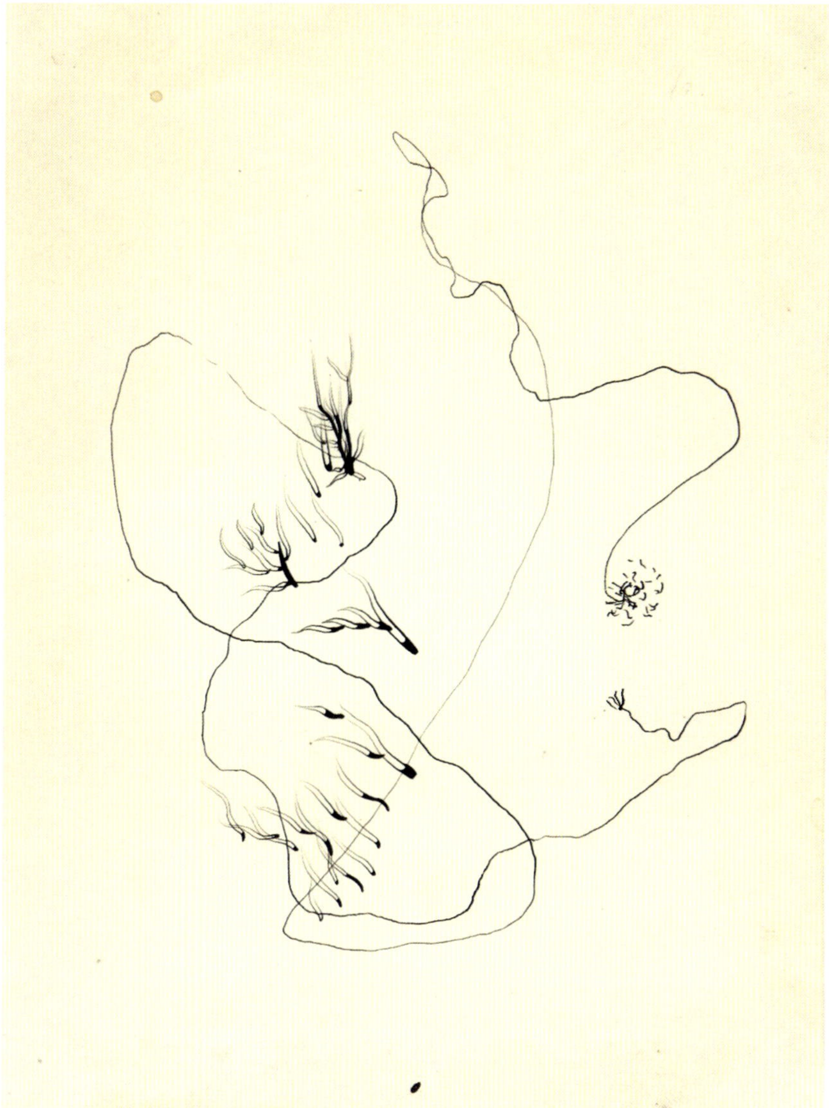

FEDERICO GARCIÁ LORCA, *Parque con linea envolvente* (*Park Enveloped by a Line*), 1935/36
Ink on paper, 22.6 × 16.5 cm
Fundación Federico García Lorca
Centro Federico García Lorca, Granada

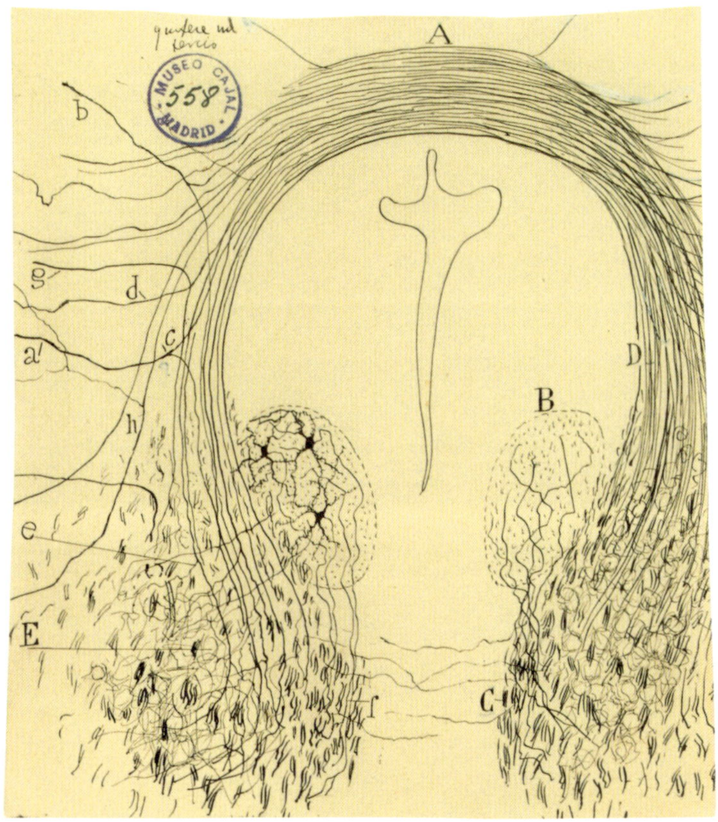

SANTIAGO RAMÓN Y CAJAL
Histological drawing: *Corte frontal de comisura posterior de gato* (*Frontal section through the posterior commissure of a cat*), c. 1903
Ink and pencil on paper, 15.2 × 13 cm
Instituto Cajal, CSIC, Madrid

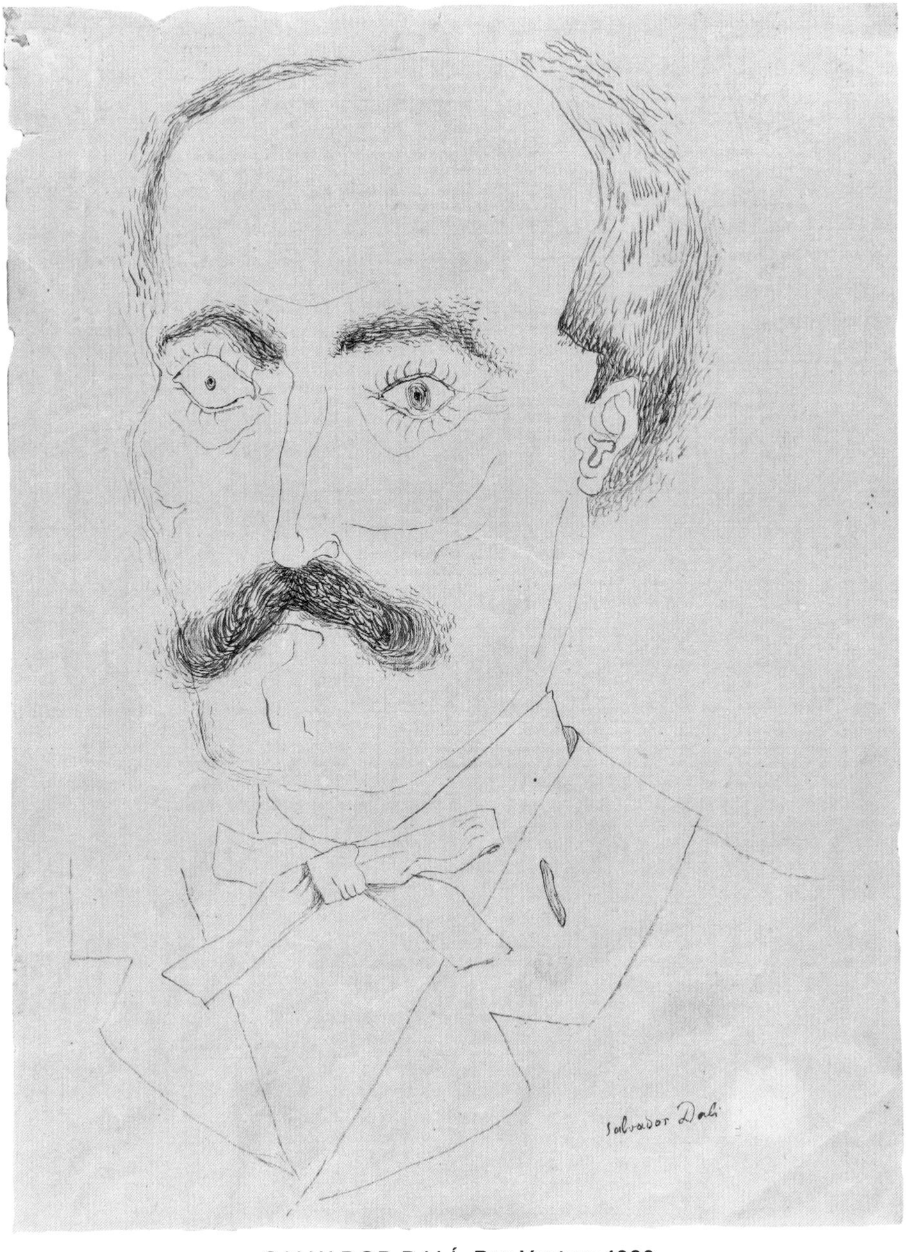

SALVADOR DALÍ, *Pep Ventura*, 1926
Ink on paper, 27 × 19 cm, Museu de Mataró

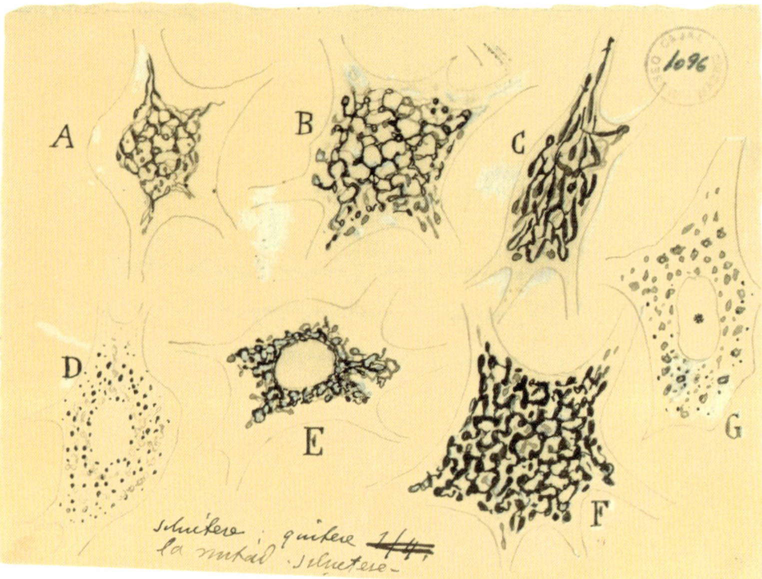

SANTIAGO RAMÓN Y CAJAL
Histological drawing: *Aparato reticular de Golgi en las neuronas motrices* (*Golgi apparatus of motor neurons*), c. 1914
Ink and pencil on paper, 12.7 × 16.1 cm
Instituto Cajal, CSIC, Madrid

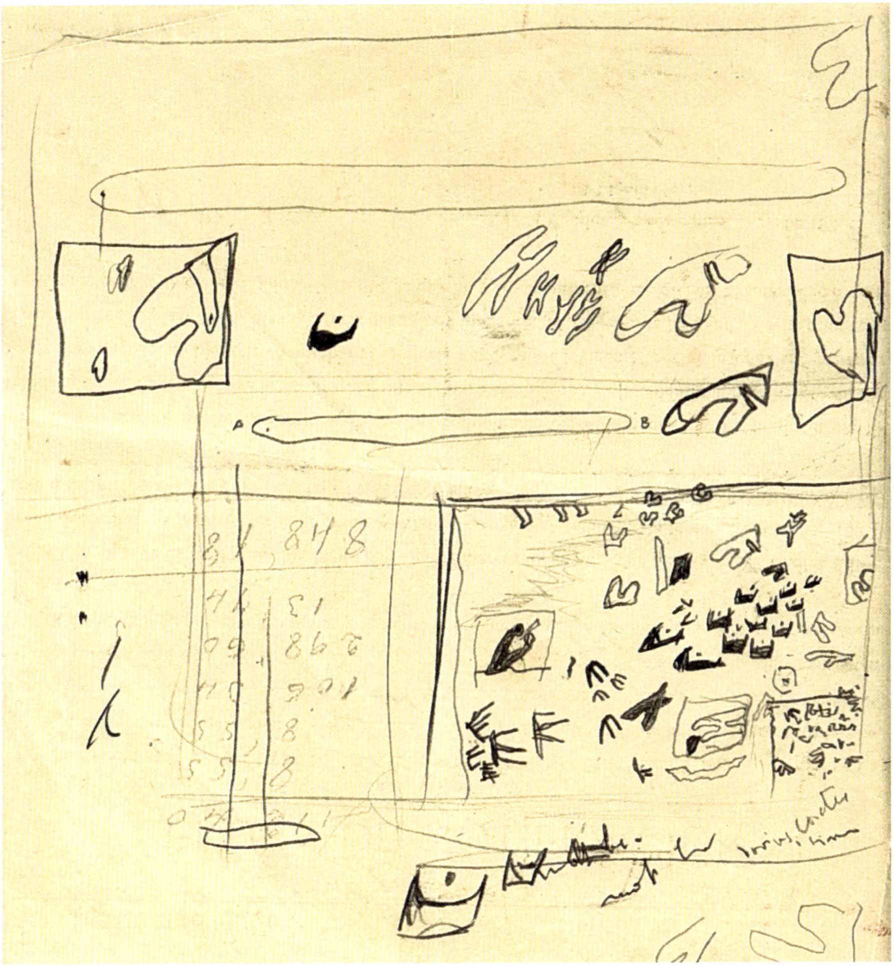

SALVADOR DALÍ, Sketch for *Pescadores al sol* (*Fishermen in the Sun*), 1928
Pencil on paper, 20 × 18 cm, Collection Pere Vehi

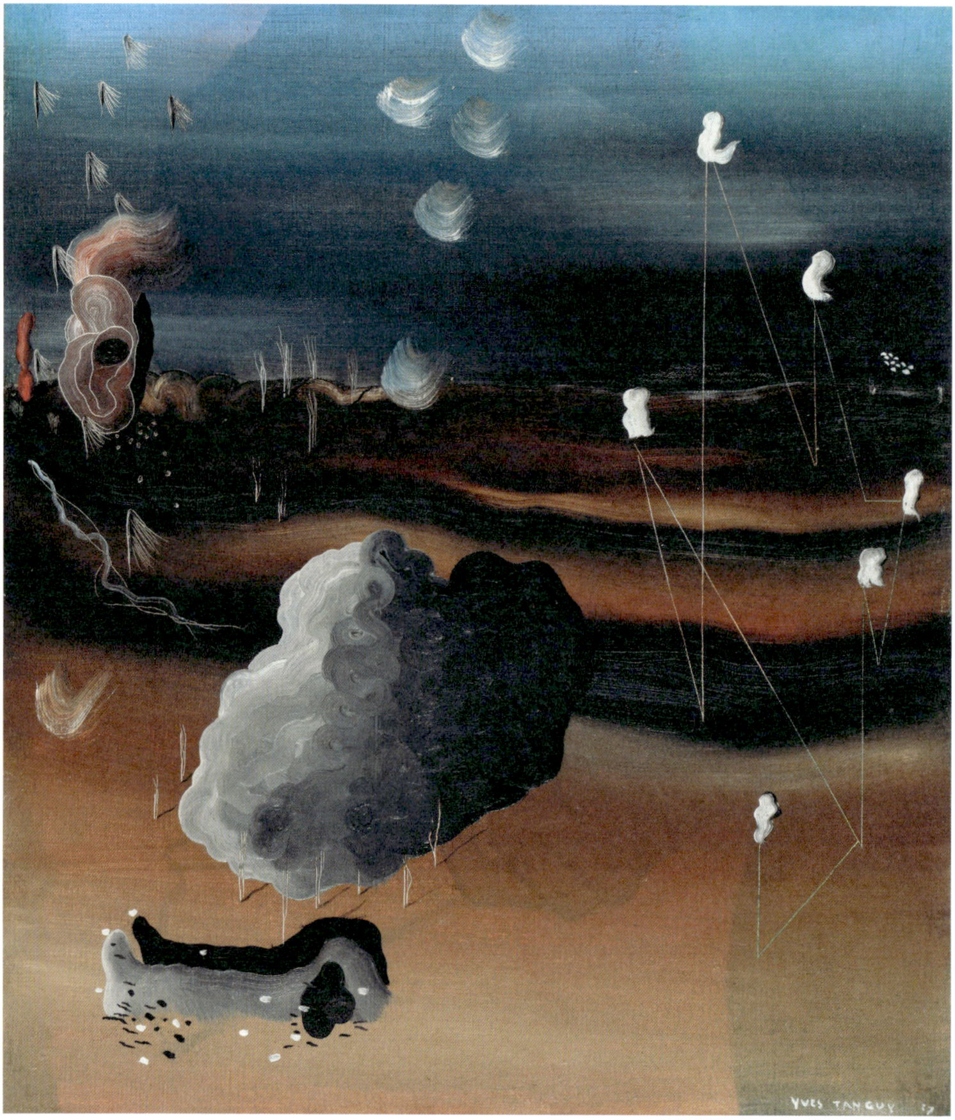

YVES TANGUY, *Quand on me fusillera*
(*When They Shoot Me*), 1927
Oil on canvas, 61 × 47 cm
Musée des Beaux-Arts de Brest

Yes, Yves Tanguy attains a new, soaring ecstasy, in which a violent purification tears all weakness from an unusually tender soul.
— SALVADOR DALÍ, "Nuevos límites de la pintura," *L'amic de les arts*, Sitges, February 29, April 30, May 31, 1928.

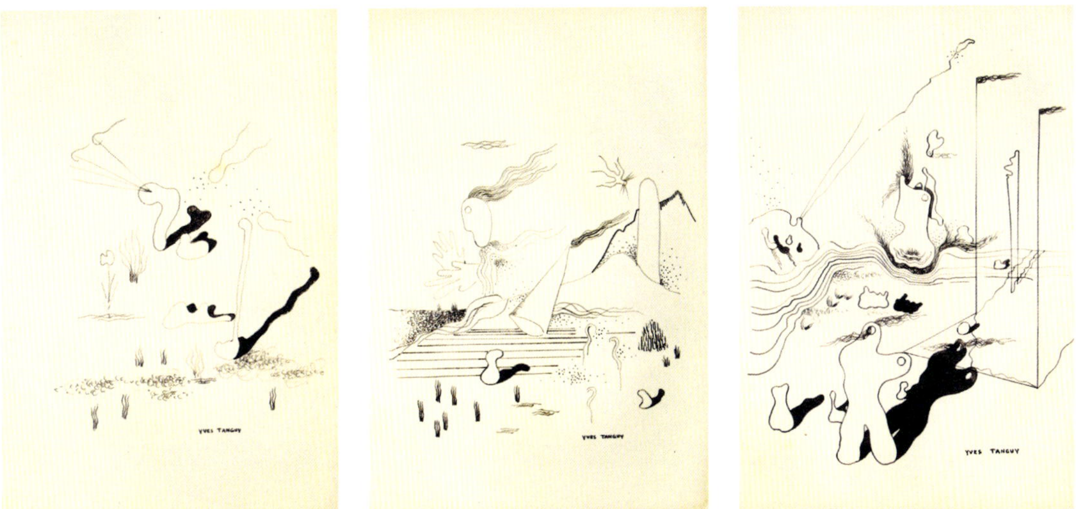

YVES TANGUY, Ilustrations for
René Bazin's *L'enseige de vaisseau Paul Henry*, 1926

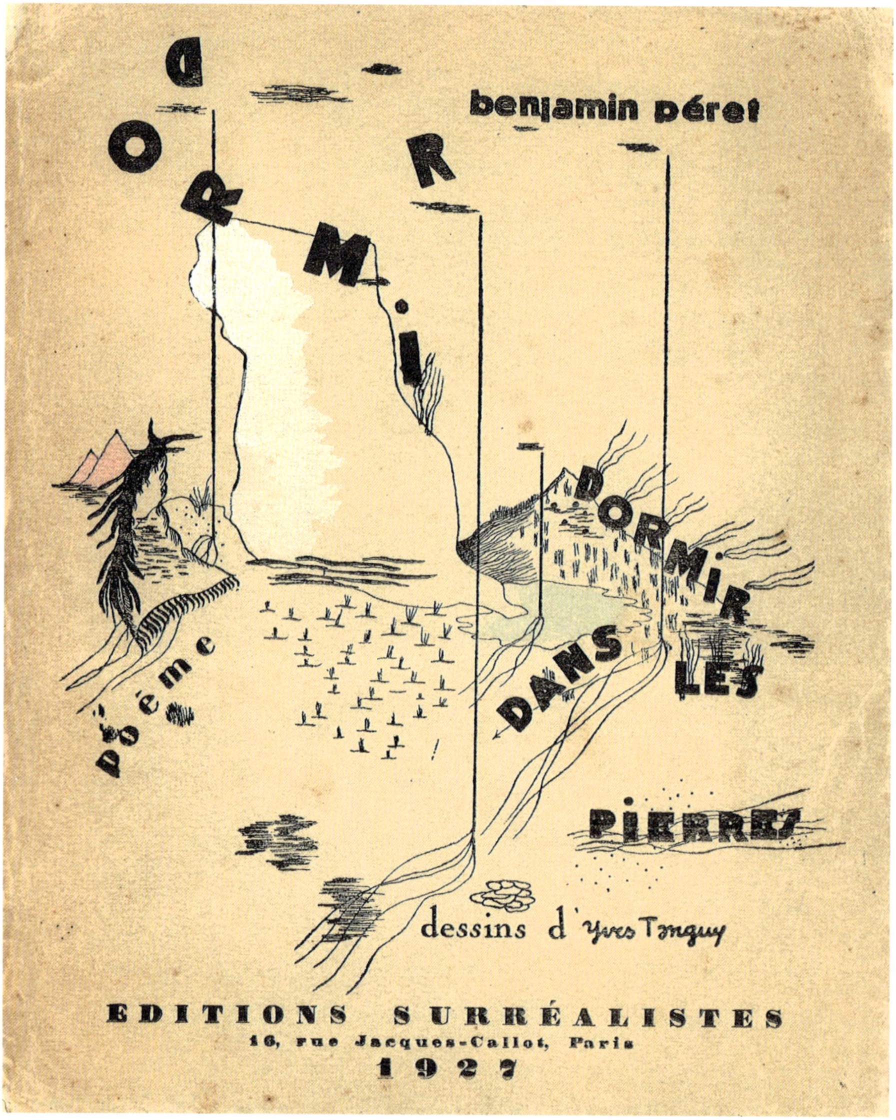

YVES TANGUY, Cover for
Benjamin Péret's *Dormir, dormir dans les pierres*, 1927
Galería de Osma, Madrid

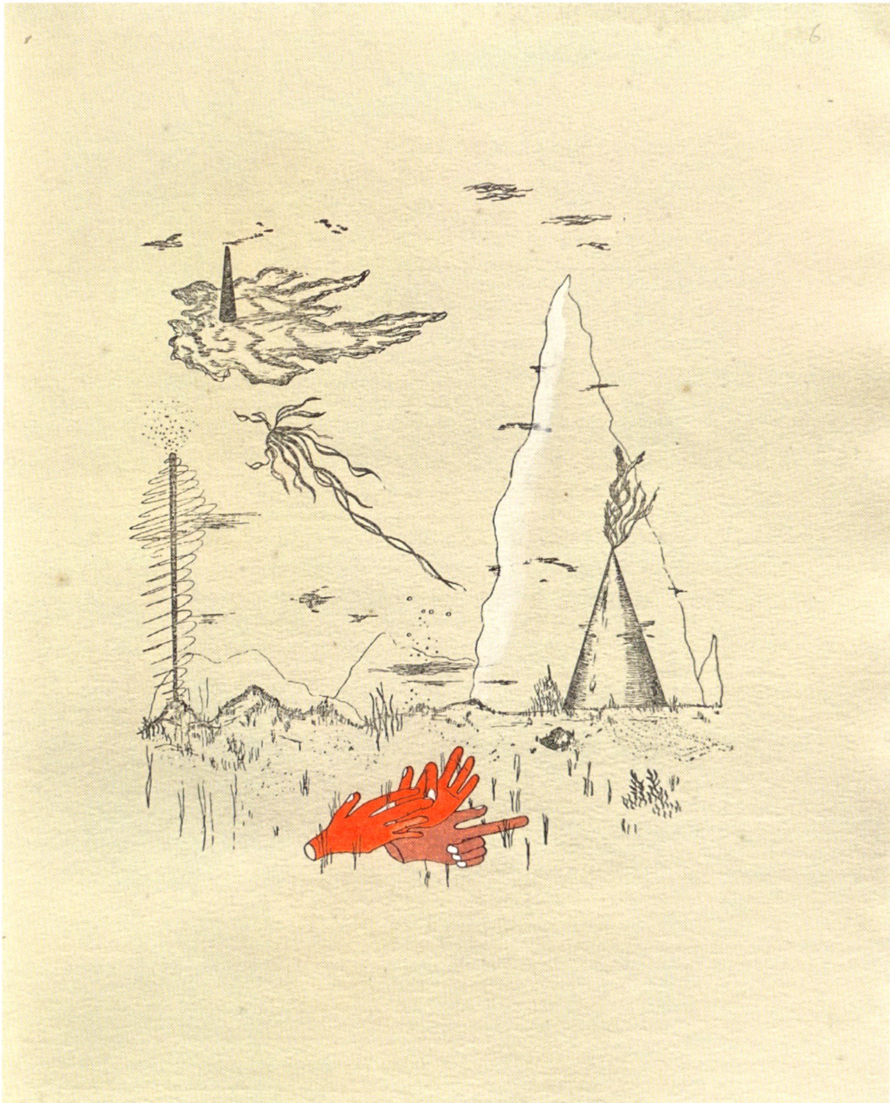

YVES TANGUY, Illustration for
Benjamin Péret's *Dormir, dormir dans les pierres*, 1927
Galería de Osma, Madrid

3

UNDER THE SPELL OF SURREALISM (1927–31)

As early as 1927, Dalí realized that the versatility of Surrealism offered a potential pathway for his own artistic and literary creations. In *Honey is Sweeter than Blood* (1927, P 194, →p. 83), a painting whose whereabouts are unknown and which is known only from old photographs, many of the elements are already apparent that were later to become typical of the formal language that brought him international renown. In 1927/28, his paintings show a convergence of influences from Giorgio de Chirico, Yves Tanguy, Max Ernst, René Magritte, and Jean Arp. However, this crossover of formal potentiality eventually came to an end, and his visual language consolidated in a singular direction, as can be seen in his emblematic work *Face of the Great Masturbator* (1929, P 235, →fig. 12).[10]

In 1929, Dalí traveled to Paris for the second time; here Joan Miró put him in contact with André Breton's Surrealist group (→p. 84). That same year, the film *Un chien andalou* (→p. 86), which he directed together with Luis Buñuel and which became the paradigm of Surrealist cinema, had its world premiere. In summer, Magritte and his wife, Buñuel, as well as Paul and Gala Éluard visited Dalí in Cadaqués. With the latter he developed an intense and complex relationship that lasted his whole life (→pp. 93–95).

In the years from 1927 to 1929, he produced important works revealing his penchant for the subconscious and showing the influences mentioned above, including *Futile Efforts* (1927–28, P 199), *The Spectral Cow* (1928, P 223), and *The Stinking Ass* (1928, P 225, →fig. 10). As early as 1929, the year he painted *Face of the Great Masturbator,* his Freudian imagery achieved formal and poetic independence in the revealing *The First Days of Spring* (1929, P 242), possibly containing a symbolic portrait of Freud, *Accommodations of Desire* (1929, P 239), *The Invisible Man* (1929–32, P 237, →fig. 62), *The Memory of the Woman-Child* (1929, P 236), and *The Lugubrious Game* (1929, P 232, →p. 91).

From this moment on, Dalí's presence on the international art scene increased steadily. In 1930, *L'âge d'or* (→p. 88), his second film with Buñuel, had its premiere, provoking great scandal and fierce attacks from far-right groups. Dalí published the illustrated book *La femme visible* (The Visible Woman) and the article "L'âne pourri,"[11] which was read with keen interest by a young Jacques Lacan, with whom he met. Little by little, Dalí laid down the foundations of what would later become his "paranoiac-critical method," a fundamental example of his association with Freudian psychoanalysis. In 1931, he exhibited at the Parisian gallery Pierre Colle and took part in the first Surrealist exhibition in the USA, held at the Wadsworth Atheneum in Hartford. He also published the book *L'amour et la mémoire* (Love and Memory).

After moving to Paris, Dalí painted new pictures in 1930/31 that confirmed unequivocally his identity as a Surrealist artist. *William Tell* (1930, P 254, →fig. 33), *Invisible Sleeping Woman Horse Lion* (1930, P 247), *Remorse* (1931, P 268, →p. 107), *The Hand. The Remorse of Conscience* (1930, P 251), *The Persistence of Memory* (1931, P 265), *Untitled. Woman Sleeping in a Landscape* (1931, P 269, →p. 101), and *Solitude* (1931, P 274, →p. 105) are all works demonstrating this development.

From 1927 to 1931, Dalí refined not only the formal characteristics but also the central themes of his future

paintings. The theme of sexual desire and its various manifestations—obsession, perversion, masturbation, moral ambiguities, and agonizing frustrations—have a particular significance in this. Gala became the epicenter of his personal universe. The world of dreams proved the perfect arena for the emergence of associations revealing the landscapes hidden in the inaccessible realm of the consciousness, some of them seemingly contradictory: Eros and Thanatos, joy and pain, attraction and revulsion, for example. His family conflicts, especially those with the figure of his father, unfolded into a veritable mythology surrounding William Tell. The "paranoiac" development of double images, with their ambiguous figurations, also played a significant role.

1 For a detailed analysis of this process see Fèlix Fanés, *Salvador Dalí: la construcción de la imagen, 1925–1930* (Barcelona, 1999).

2 Published in *Le Surréalisme au service de la révolution*, no. 1, July 1, 1930.

I began to run through the streets as fast as my legs would carry me. It astonished me that the people I passed were not more surprised at my running. [...] Peeved by this indifference, I embellished my run with more and more exalted leaps. [...] I further complicated my run with a marvelous cry. "Blood is sweeter than honey," [...]. But the word "honey" I shouted at the top of my lungs, and I pushed my leap as high and hard as I could. "Blood is sweeter than HONEY." And I leaped.
— SALVADOR DALÍ, *The Secret Life of Salvador Dalí* (New York, 1993), p.183.

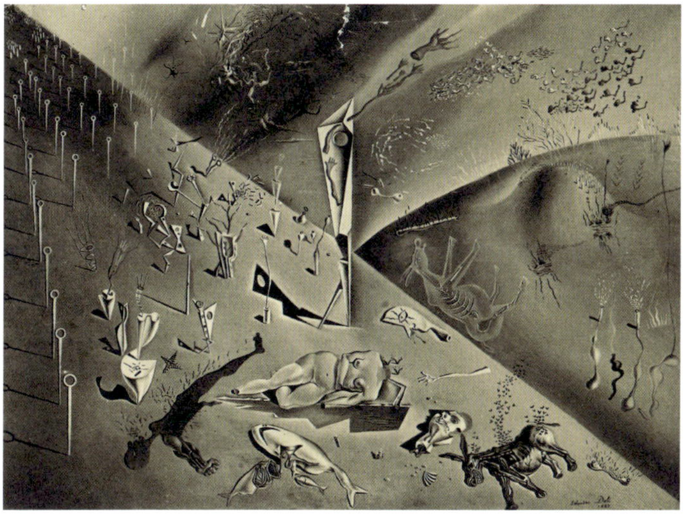

SALVADOR DALÍ, Photograph of the painting
La mel és més dolça que la sang
(*Honey Is Sweeter than Blood*), 1927
Oil on unknown support, measurements unknown
Whereabouts unknown
Fundación Federico García Lorca
Centro Federico García Lorca, Granada
Cat. no. P 194

At this time, Salvador painted *La mel és més dolça que la sang* (*Honey Is Sweeter than Blood*) in which there appears a decomposing donkey. According to Salvador that donkey seemed like a twig of roses.
— ANA MARÍA DALÍ, *Salvador Dalí visto por su hermana* (1949), adapted from an unpublished translation by G. Boler and A. Norwood, 1998, p. 53.

The Surrealist revolution has upheld the names of the Comte de Lautréamont, of Trotsky, of Freud, of the Marquis de Sade, of Heraclitus, of Uccello, etc.
— SALVADOR DALÍ, "The Moral Position of Surrealism," in *The Collected Writings of Salvador Dalí* (Cambridge/New York, 1998), p. 222.

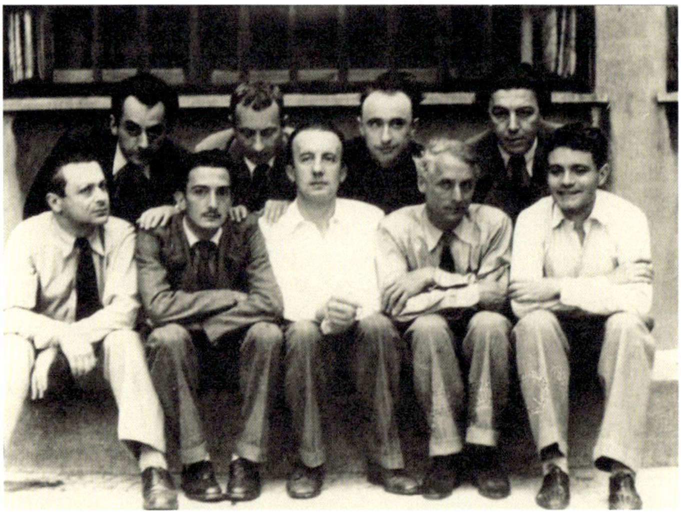

The Surrealists in a photograph taken at Maison Tzara (left to right: Tristan Tzara, Man Ray, Salvador Dalí, Hans Arp, Paul Éluard, Yves Tanguy, Max Ernst, André Breton, and René Crevel), c. 1930

SURREALISM, n. Psychic automatism in its pure state, by which one proposes to express—verbally, by means of the written word, or in any other manner—the actual functioning of thought. Dictated by thought, in the absence of any control exercised by reason, exempt from any aesthetic or moral concern.
— ANDRÉ BRETON, "Manifesto of Surrealism" (1924), *Manifestoes of Surrealism* (Ann Arbor, 1969), p. 26.

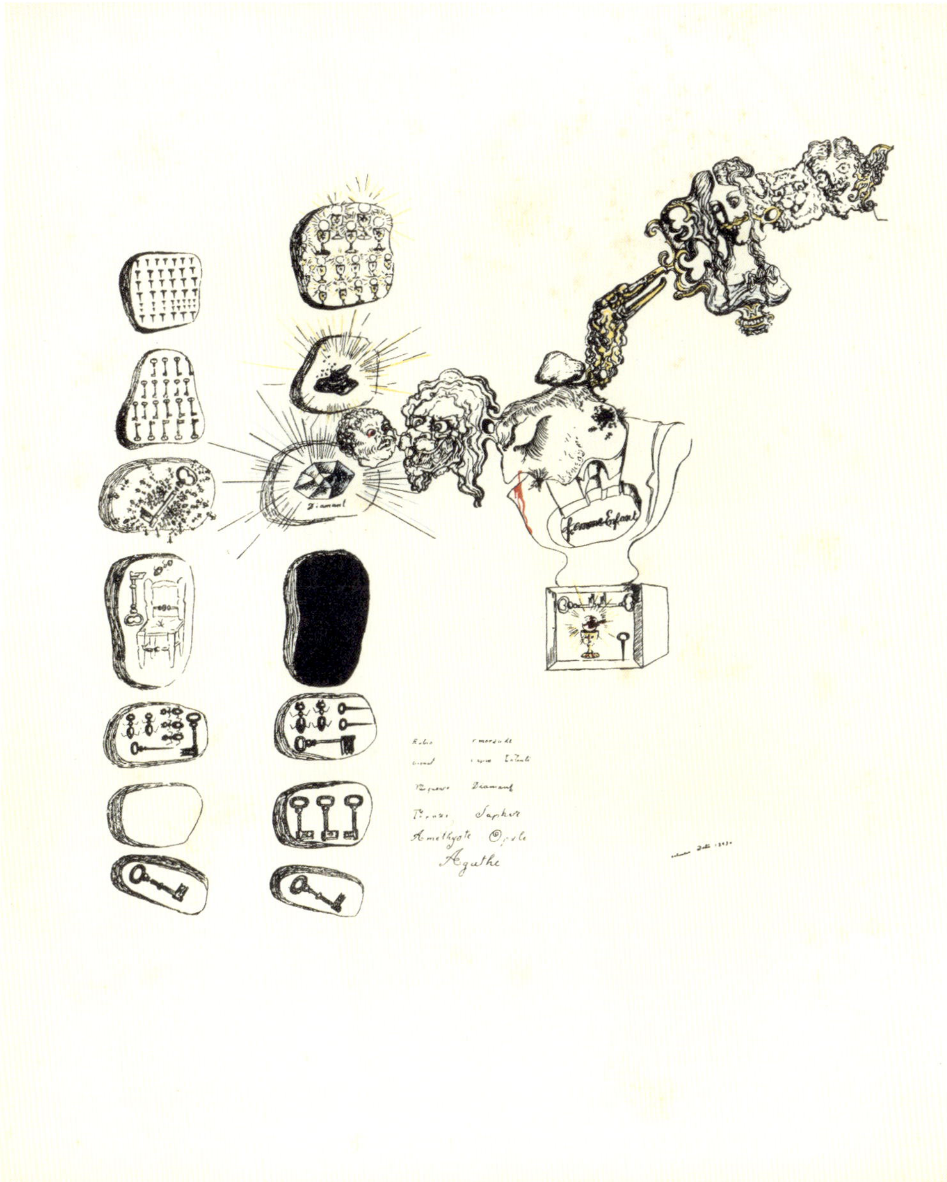

SALVADOR DALÍ, Frontispiece
for *Second manifeste du surréalisme*, 1930
Stencil print on paper, 28 × 22.5 cm
Museo Nacional Centro de Arte Reina Sofía,
Madrid

[...] I on the other hand, had just written a very short scenario which had the touch of genius, and which went completely counter to the contemporary cinema. [...] The scenario was written. I received a telegram from Buñuel announcing that he was coming to Figueras. He was immediately enthusiastic over my scenario, and we decided to work in collaboration to put it into shape. Together we worked out several secondary ideas, and also the title—it was going to be called *Le Chien Andalou*.
— SALVADOR DALÍ, *The Secret Life of Salvador Dalí* (New York, 1993), p. 206.

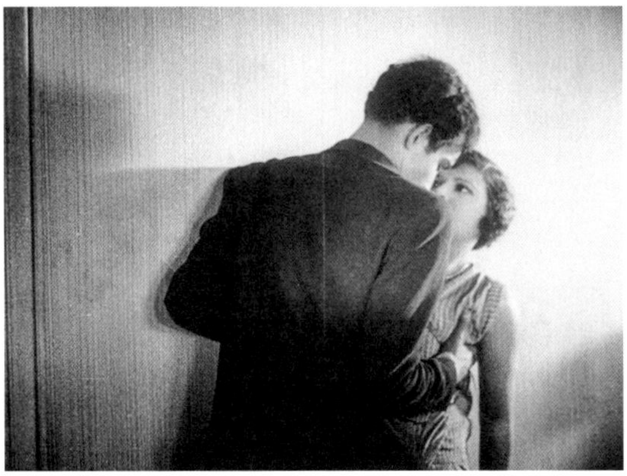

A few months later, I made *Un Chien andalou*, which came from an encounter between two dreams. When I arrived to spend a few days at Dalí's house in Figueras, I told him about a dream I'd had in which a long, tapering cloud sliced the moon in half, like a razor blade slicing through an eye. Dalí immediately told me that he'd seen a hand crawling with ants in a dream he'd had the previous night. "And what if we started right there and made a film?" he wondered aloud.
— LUIS BUÑUEL, *My Last Breath* (Paris, 1994), pp. 103–04.

Despite my hesitation, we soon found ourselves hard at work, and in less than a week we had a script. Our only rule was very simple: No idea or image that might lend itself to a rational explanation of any kind would be accepted. We had to open all doors to the irrational and keep only those images that surprised us, without trying to explain why.
— LUIS BUÑUEL, *My Last Breath* (Paris, 1994), pp. 104

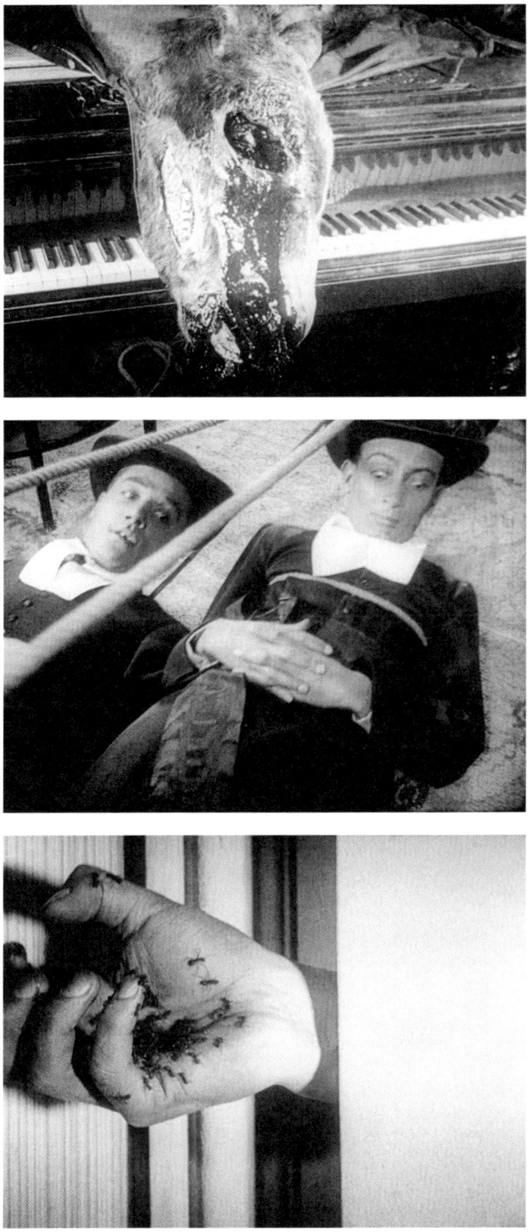

LUIS BUÑUEL, SALVADOR DALÍ
Un chien andalou, 1929
Black-and-white silent film, 16 min

Besides, my own heaven would always remain more violent and real than the ideal hell of *L'Age d'Or*, just as my classicism would one day be more surrealist than their romanticism! And my reactionary traditionalism more subversive than their abortive revolution.
— SALVADOR DALÍ, *The Secret Life of Salvador Dalí* (New York, 1993), p. 286.

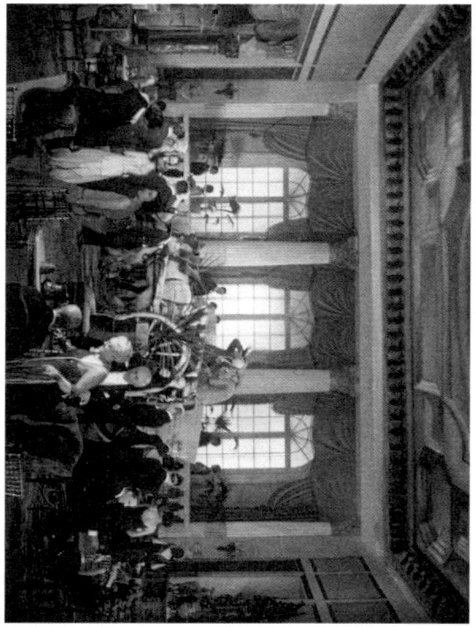

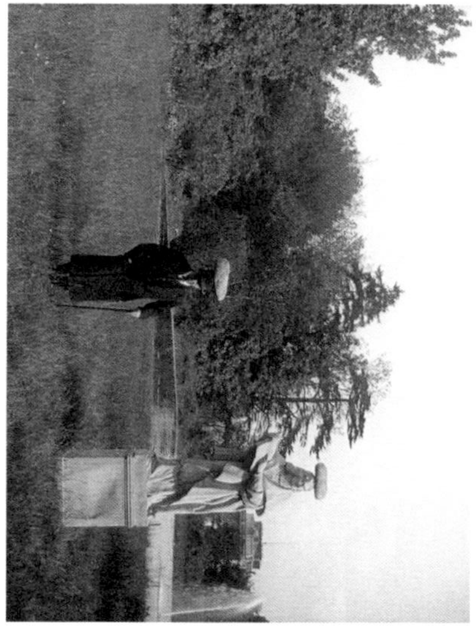

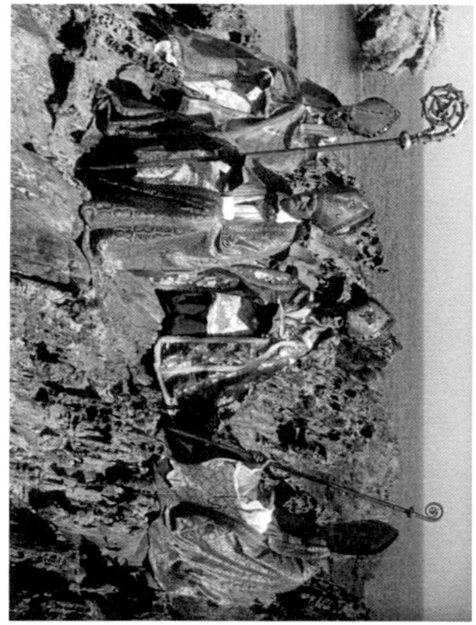

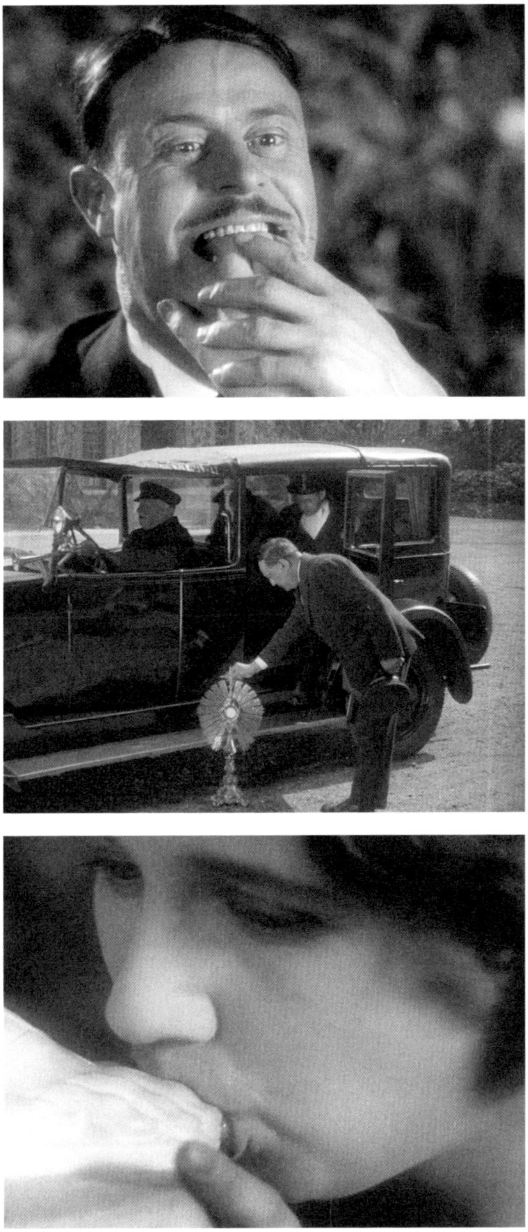

LUIS BUÑUEL, SALVADOR DALÍ
L'âge d'or, 1930, Black-and-white film, 35 mm, with sound, 1 h 3 min

The Lugubrious Game (1929) is one of those early works that combine a multitude of elements from Dalí's study of Freud's writings. It comprises a veritable inventory of obsessions, repressed desires, sexual frustrations, fear of breaking taboos, and so on. At its heart is the self-portrait of Dalí as the "great masturbator," accompanied by the dreaded image of a grasshopper, a slimy slug, viscera alluding to anatomical obsessions and fears (sex—swallowing, Eros—Thanatos), the conch shell recalling childhood joys on the beach, the masturbating hand, and an exploding brain, in which he combines many elements related to the above, in particular the finger of androgynous masturbation and the face of the bearded man representing the father figure, with a vagina in place of his mouth. The sculpture of the hermaphrodite, hiding her/his face and extending a giant hand while being masturbated by an ephebic man, accompanied by two lions alluding to physical desire, recalls de Chirico's enigmatic monuments, as does the anthropomorphic shadow on the floor in the foreground, which vaguely echoes the figure in various versions of Arnold Böcklin's *Isle of the Dead* (1880–86). The figure in the foreground, soiled with his own excrement, alludes to coprophilic impulses associated with the anal stages of psychological development, a theme reinforced by the other person embracing him, who inserts a finger into a kind of cranial sphincter.
— JAIME BRIHUEGA SIERRA

I, then, and only I was the true surrealist painter, at least according to the definition which its chief, André Breton, gave of surrealism. Nevertheless, when Breton saw this painting [Dalí is referring to *The Lugubrious Game*] he hesitated for a long time before its scatological elements—for in the picture appeared a figure seen from behind whose drawers were bespattered with excrement.
— SALVADOR DALÍ, *The Secret Life of Salvador Dalí* (New York, 1993), p. 254.

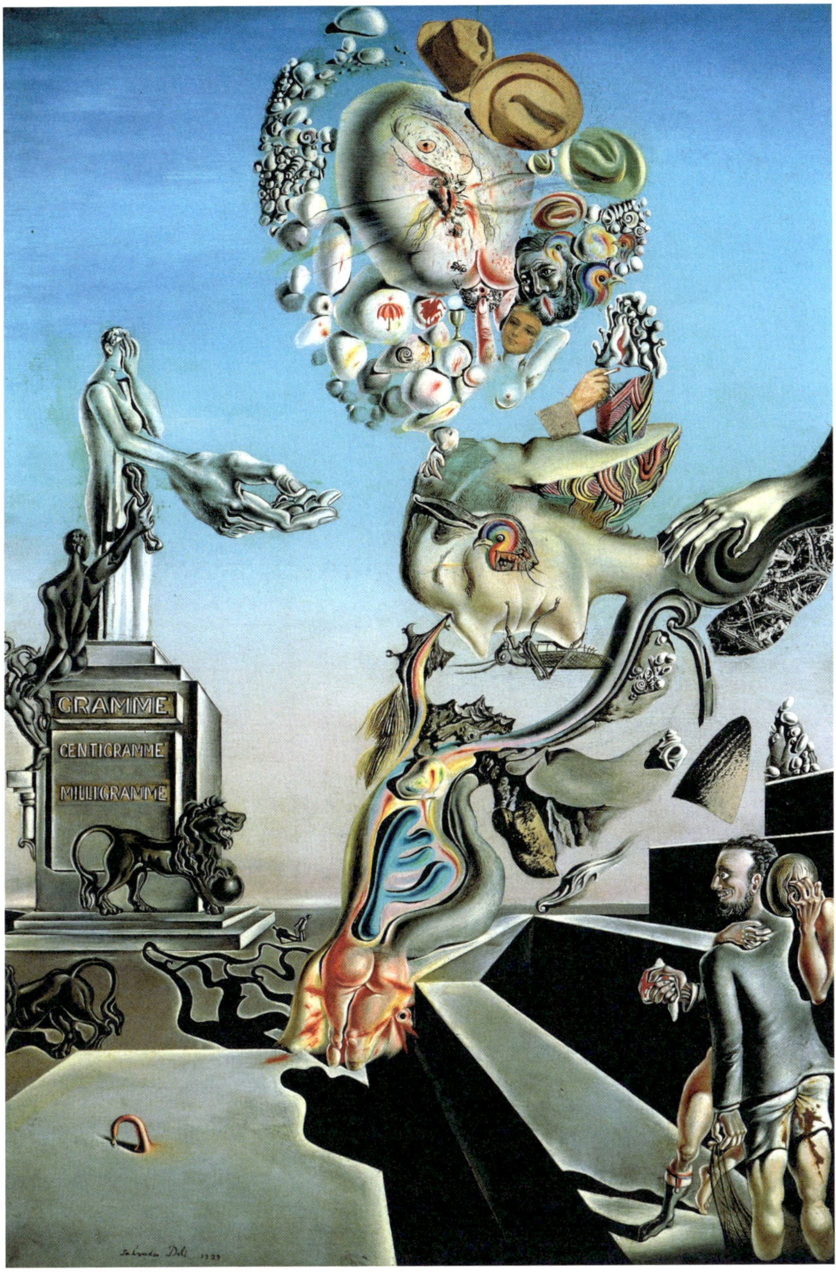

SALVADOR DALÍ, *Le jeu lugubre*
(*The Lugubrious Game*), 1929
Oil and collage on cardboard, 44.4 × 30.3 cm
Private collection, Switzerland
Cat. no. P 232

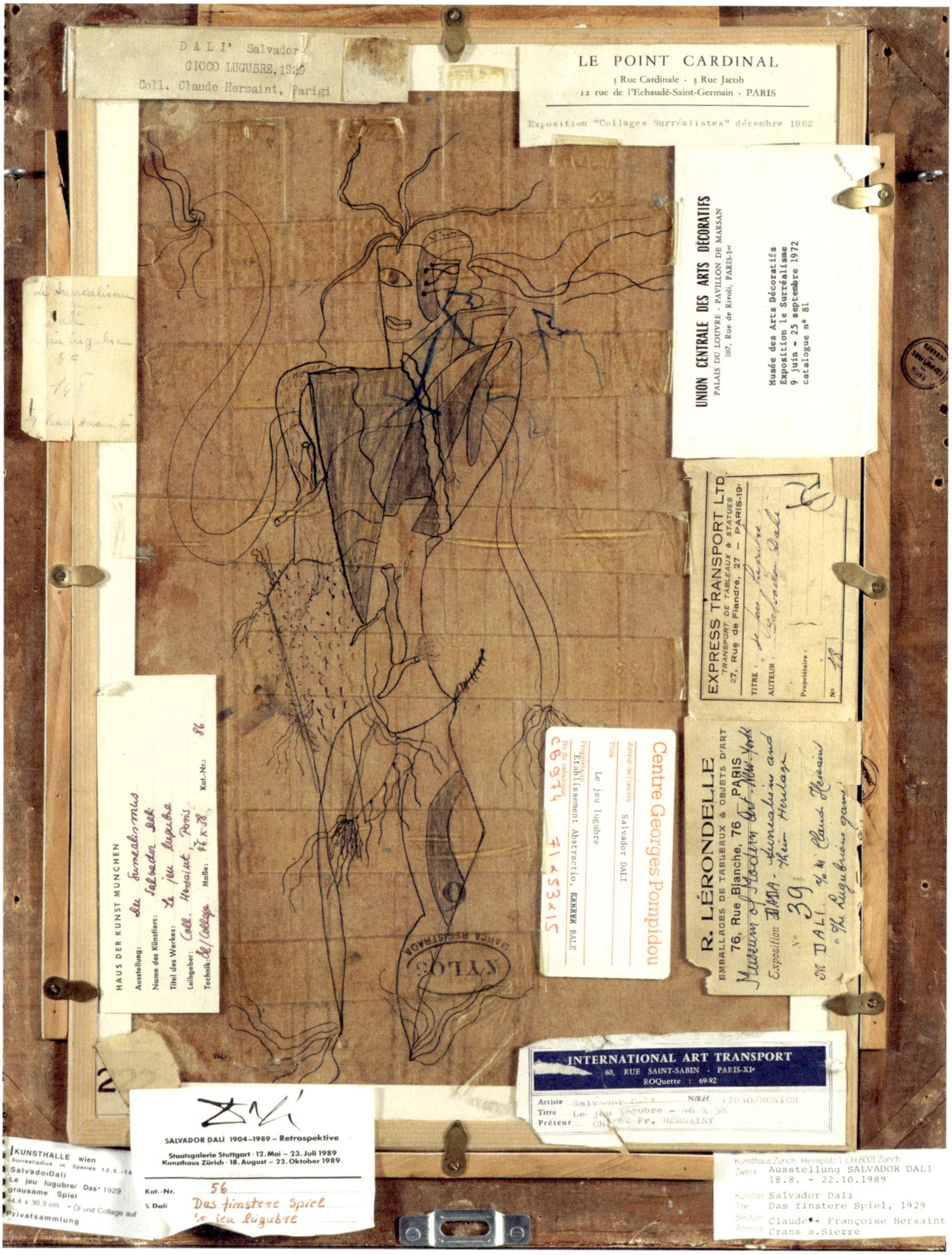

FEDERICO GARCIÁ LORCA, drawing
on the reverse of Salvador Dalí's *Le jeu lugubre*, 1929
Private collection, Switzerland

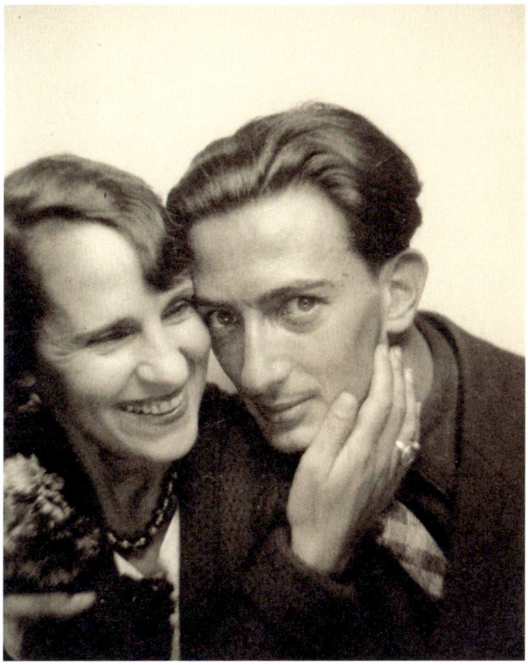

Self-portrait of Gala and Salvador Dalí
in a photo booth, c. 1929
Fundació Gala-Salvador Dalí, Figueres

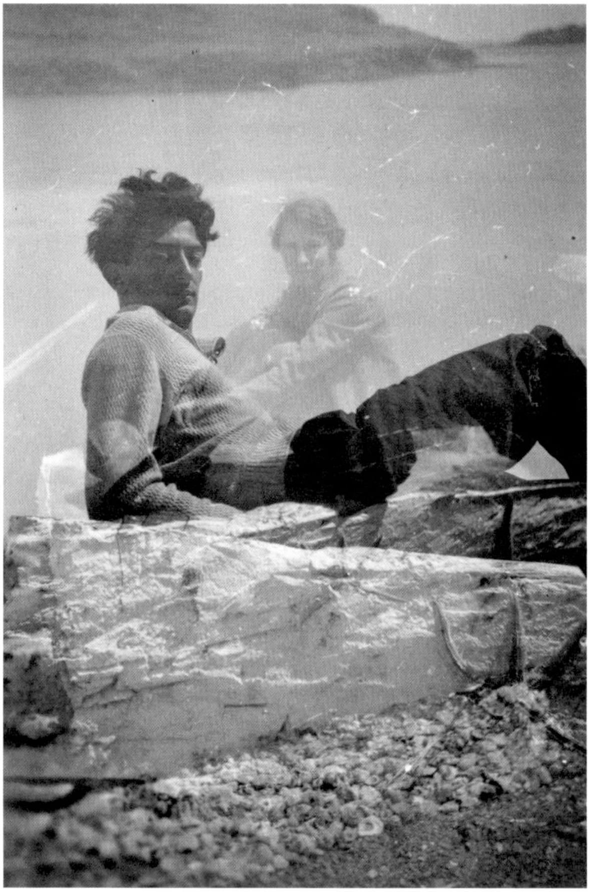

Salvador and Gala on the beach of Portlligat, 1930s
Fundació Gala-Salvador Dalí, Figueres

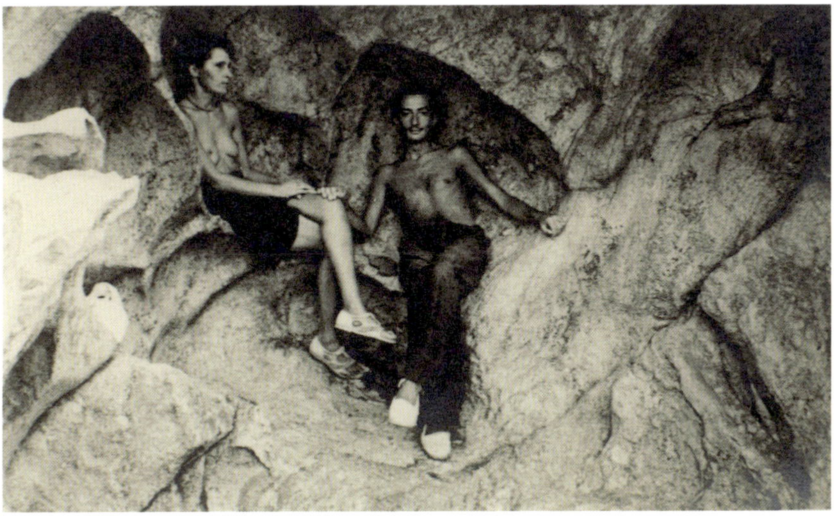

MAN RAY, *Gala et Dalí*, 1933
Centre Pompidou—Musée national d'art moderne—
Centre de création industrielle, Paris

Hard as a tiny pebble in the sea, / sensible as a loving and beloved woman, / passionate as a forsaken lover, / tender as the mother of an imperiled child, / sweet as a sick child, / silent as the heart of an infinite forest, / in love like a blind young animal, / cold as fruit in shadow, / strong as the branches of an ancient oak, / protective as a damp grotto, / innocent as an egg that has just hatched, / pure as a person receiving their Last Rites, / skillful as the vampire bee of the flowers, / agile as a root traversing rocky soil, / refreshing as the cool water of a fountain on a hot day.
— GALA DALÍ, *La vida secreta. Diario inédito* (Barcelona, 2011), p. 70.

La femme visible is the title of a book from 1930, in which Dalí first presented the key aspects of his "paranoiac-critical method." The drawing, dedicated to Paul Éluard, called *The Visible Woman: Chasing Butterflies* (1930) was intended as one of the illustrations for this book. Dalí has connected the figure of Gala with the awakening of adolescent sexuality, associated with desire, incest, pedophilia, feelings of guilt, and parental punishment, and encapsulates his theories in highly explicit images.
— JAIME BRIHUEGA SIERRA

In the early history of neurotics an important part is played by exposure to children of the opposite sex; in paranoia delusions of being observed while dressing and undressing are to be traced back to experiences of this kind; while among persons who have remained at the stage of perversion there is one class in which this infantile impulse has reached the pitch of a symptom—the class of "exhibitionists."
— SIGMUND FREUD, *The Interpretation of Dreams* (1900), (London, 1953), p. 244.

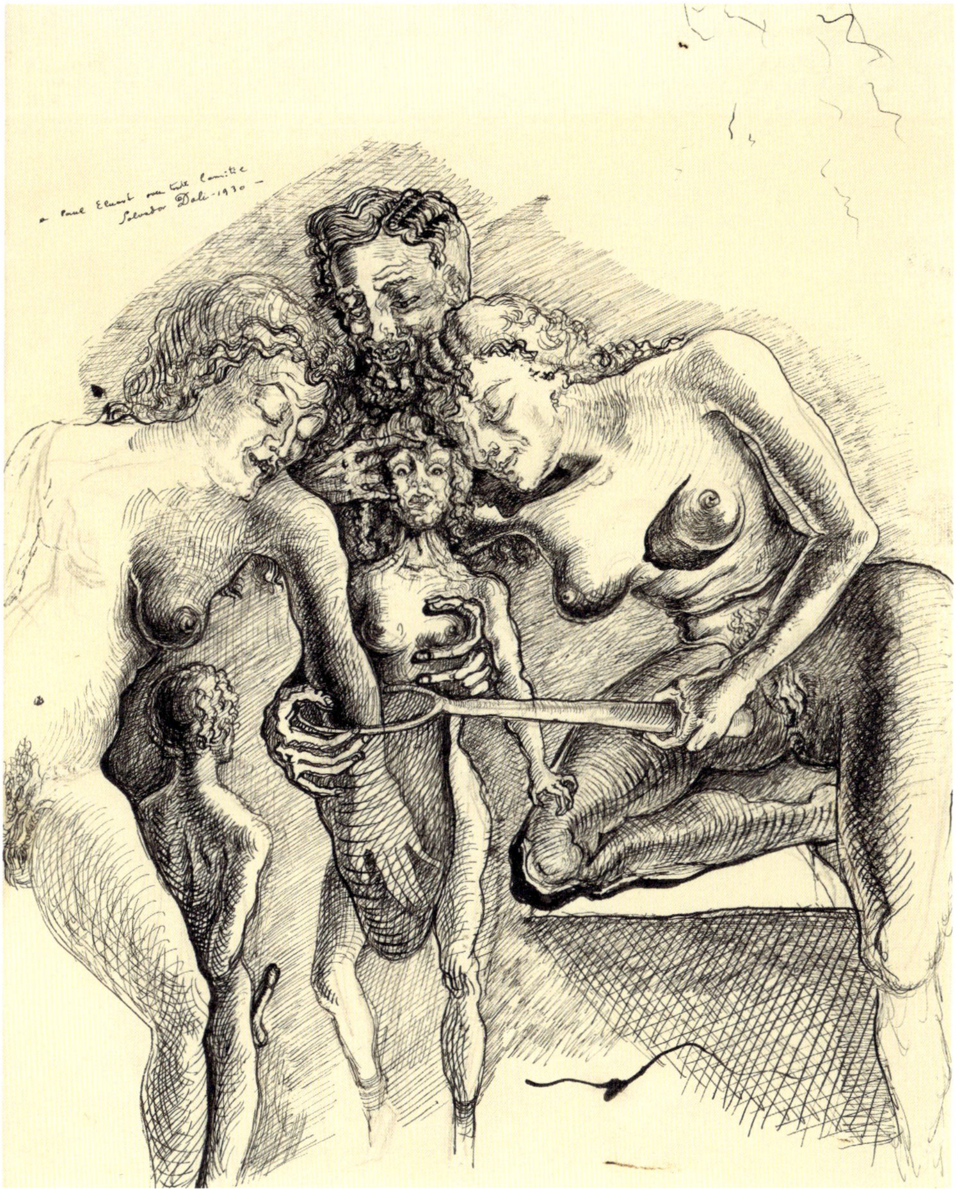

SALVADOR DALÍ, *La femme visible, La chasse aux papillons* (*The Visible Woman, Chasing Butterflies*), 1930, ink on paper on cardboard, 27.8 × 22 cm
Courtesy of Galerie Natalie Seroussi, Paris

The oil painting *The Invisible Man* (1929/32, → fig. 62), on display at the Museo Reina Sofía in Madrid, is one of the most eloquent examples of the double images typical of the paranoiac-critical method. It shows the figure of a man with his hands on a table, intermingled with a succession of different forms. The sketch for *The Invisible Man* (c. 1930), shown here, brings together many of these visual confusions, for this double image of a male figure incorporates superimposed motifs, such as the reverse of a female torso on a socle, a column, an anatomical depiction of the female reproductive organs linked to a lightbulb or testicles, and hands that echo those in a scene from Dalí and Luis Buñuel's film *Un chien andalou* (discussed only a few pages previously), as well as the hands of the blind man in the painting *La Saeta* (a song performed at processions during Holy Week; 1918, → fig. 60) by Julio Romero de Torres from Córdoba.
— JAIME BRIHUEGA SIERRA

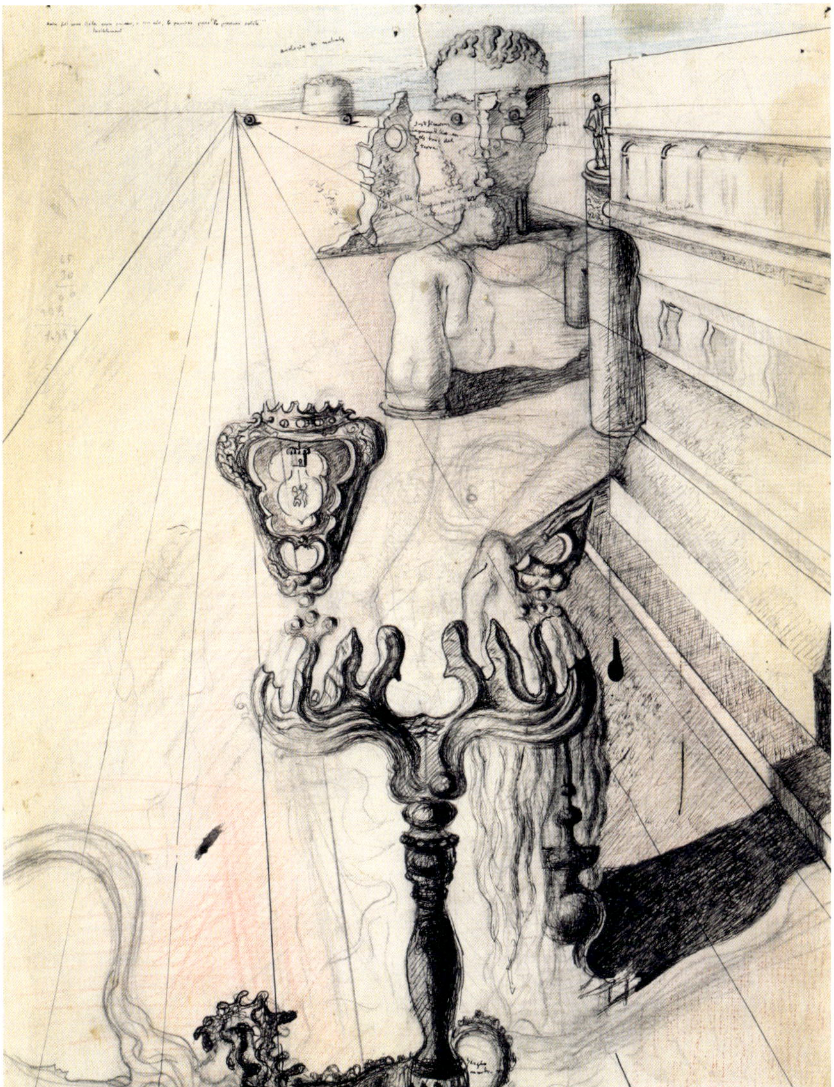

SALVADOR DALÍ, Sketch for
El hombre invisible (*The Invisible Man*), c. 1930
Graphite, colored pencil, and ink
on laid paper, 27.7 × 20.7 cm
Museo Nacional Centro de Arte Reina Sofía,
Madrid

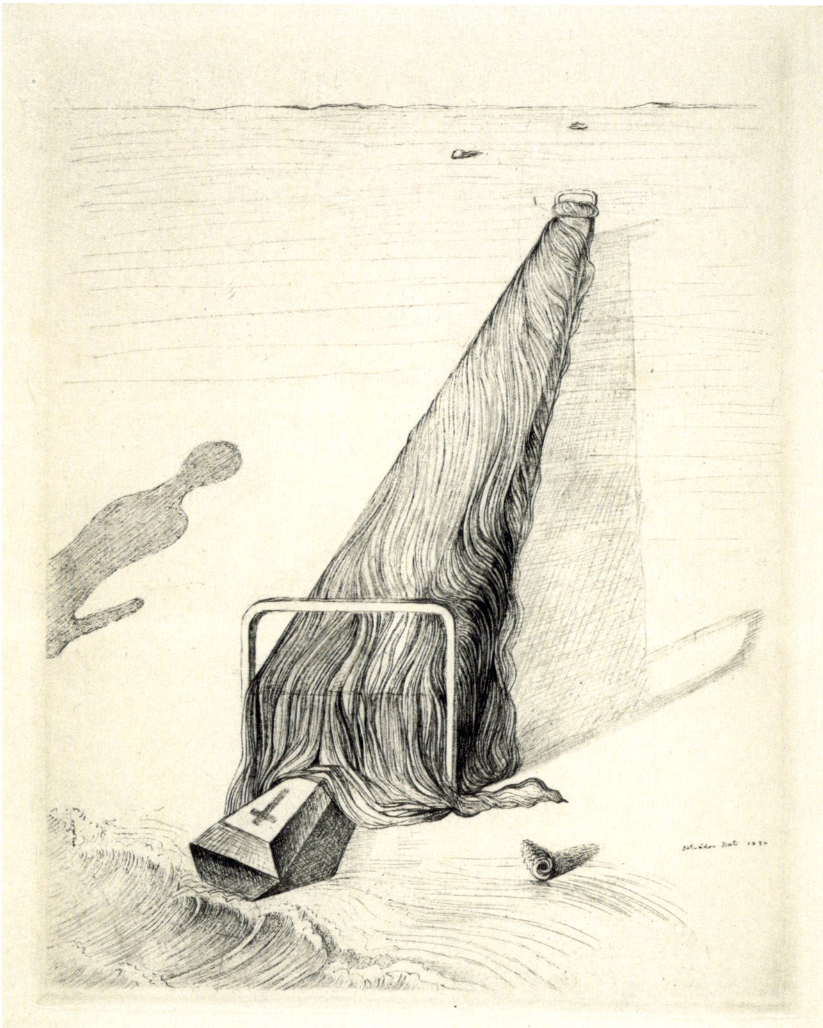

SALVADOR DALÍ, *Artine*, 1930
Heliogravure and etching
on Japan paper, 24 × 18.5 cm
Museo Nacional Centro de Arte Reina Sofía,
Madrid

In *Woman Sleeping in a Landscape* (1931), a work so obviously associated with Freudian thought, sleep is revealed as a state in which fears and desires surface that are kept hidden during waking hours, a troubled state, captured here with compelling eloquence. These phantoms emerge from the body of the sleeping woman, who is tenuously attached to the real world by a fragile string of pearls.
— JAIME BRIHUEGA SIERRA

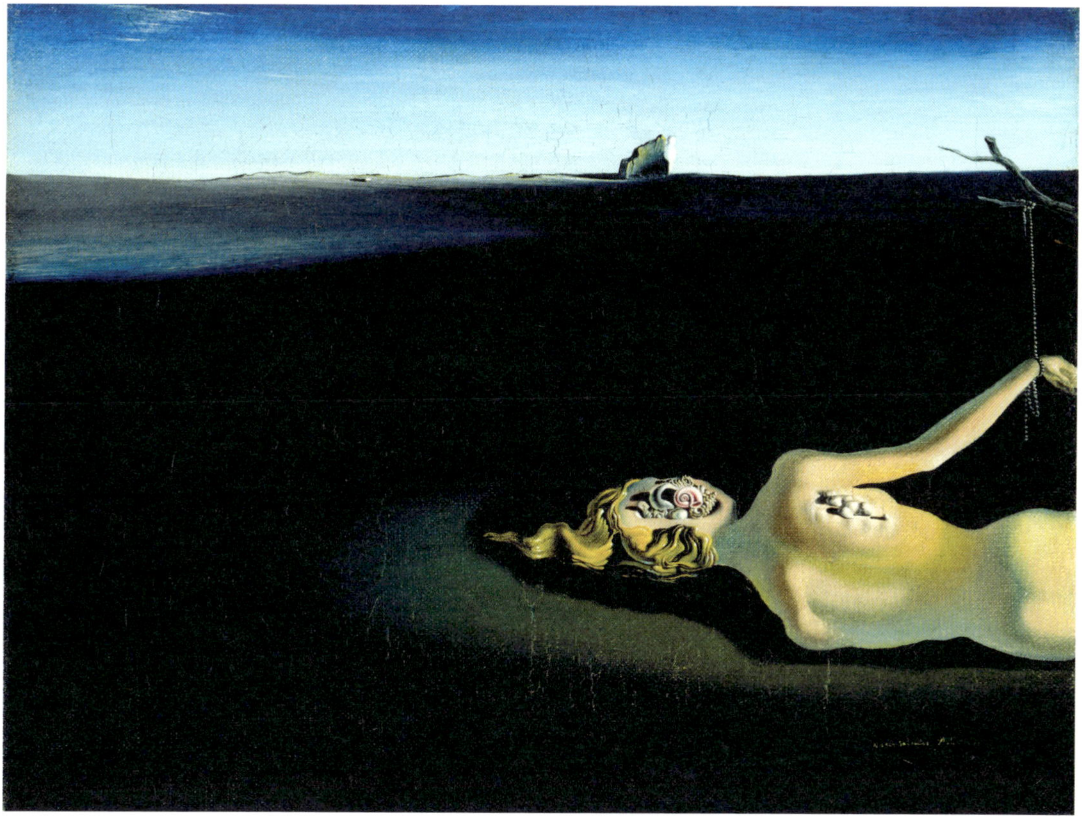

SALVADOR DALÍ, *Untitled. Woman Sleeping in a Landscape,* 1931
Oil on canvas, 27.2 × 35 cm
Peggy Guggenheim Collection, Venice
Cat. no. P 269

As already mentioned, the visual polysemy of double images is fundamental to the paranoiac-critical method. In *Fish Man* (1930), these double images clearly echo narratives that recur in other paintings and drawings from those years. An example is the monumental bust of a male figure, whose head, arranged around a central clock (time and memory), merges with a shoal of fish, his collarbone with a fetishistic high-heeled shoe. A phallic cypress, reminiscent of Böcklin's paintings (so often alluded to by Dalí), stands in a solitary landscape, which also includes the recurring motif of a high-heeled shoe, as well as a sphere referencing works by René Magritte and Max Ernst.
— JAIME BRIHUEGA SIERRA

The limb which is in the position in question may appear in the dream as an animal or monster, in which case a certain analogy is established between them.
— SIGMUND FREUD, *The Interpretation of Dreams* (1900), (London, 1953), p. 39.

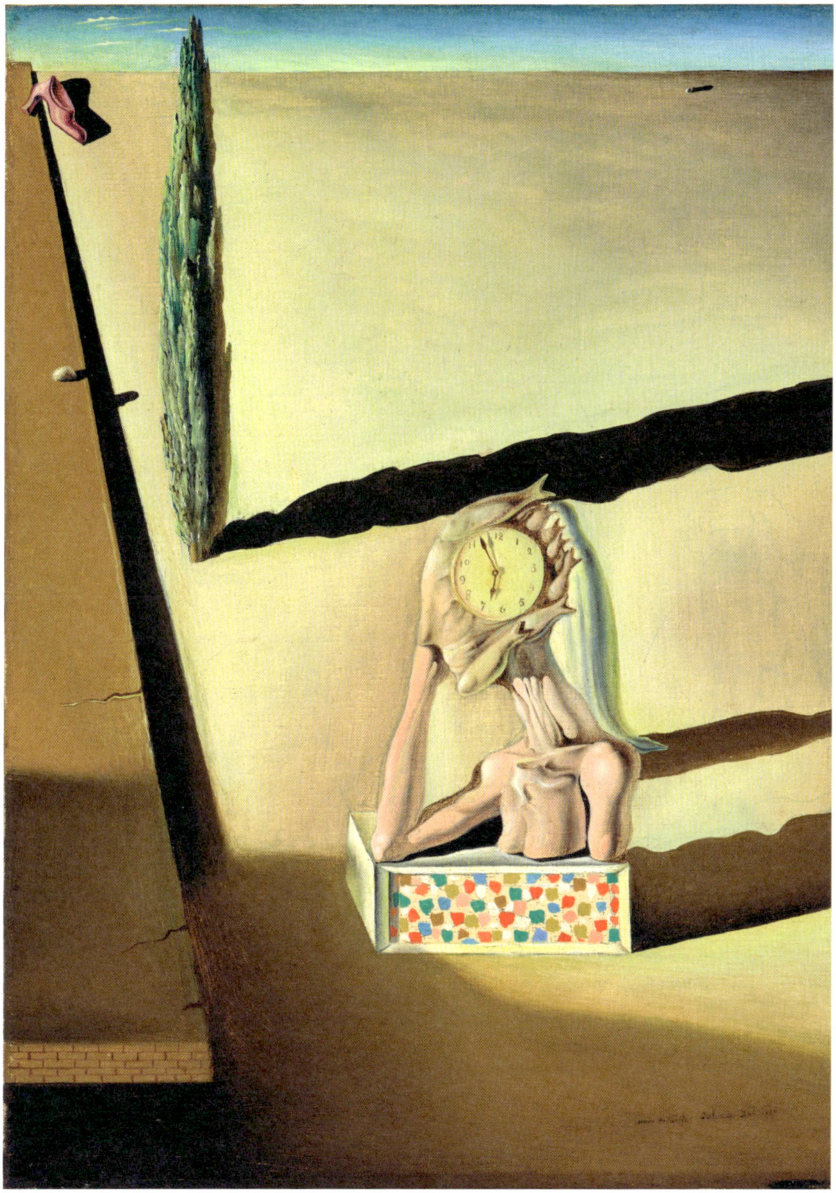

SALVADOR DALÍ, *Homme poisson* (*Fish Man*), 1930, oil on canvas, 26.7 × 19.1 cm Meadows Museum, Dallas, purchased with funds from the Meadows Foundation, Holly Bock, Doug Deason, Mrs. Eugen McDermott, Linda P. and William A. Custard, and Gwen and Richard Irwin, MM.2014.11, cat. no. P 383

Solitude (1931) as a title alludes to a feeling lodged in Dalí's memories from his childhood and adolescence. A mood of solitude and loneliness presides over this landscape, which is reminiscent of the Catalan coast often frequented by the painter in those years. Loneliness is expressed by the figure viewed from behind, seemingly merging with the rock, with the face of a classical bust on the back of its head. It is a face that also recalls the plaster casts so often depicted by Giorgio de Chirico. In this work, Dalí has clearly depicted an introspection that chimes with the Freudian narratives evident in many of the painter's compositions.
— JAIME BRIHUEGA SIERRA

She was a woman of the working classes and her back was turned to the dreamer. At last she turned round and gave him a terrible look so that he ran off in terror. The red flesh of the lower lids of her eyes could be seen standing out.
[...] Since the woman in the dream was standing in the same position as he had been in when he was micturating, it must have been a question of a micturating woman. This tallies with her terrible look and the *red flesh standing out*, which could only relate to the gaping of the genitals caused by stooping.
— SIGMUND FREUD, *The Interpretation of Dreams* (1900), (London, 1953), p. 201.

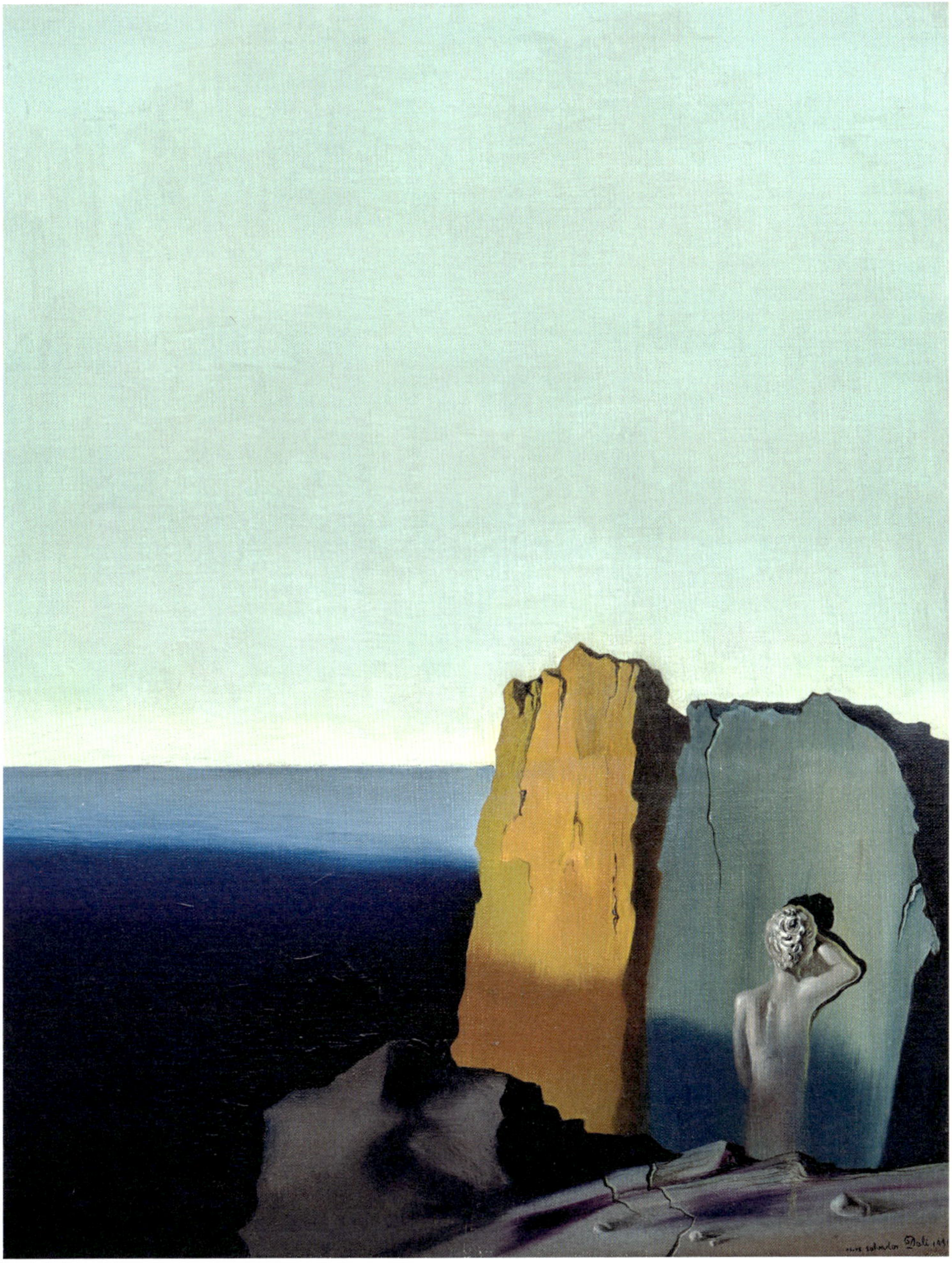

SALVADOR DALÍ, *La solitude* (*Solitude*)
1931, Oil on canvas, 35,2 × 27,2 cm
Wadsworth Atheneum, Hartford, CT, purchased through the gift of Henry and Walter Keney, 1932.218, cat. no. P 274

In *Remorse: Sphinx Embedded in the Sand* (1931), a feeling so often explored by Freud is evoked by a female bust buried in a desert landscape. Her shadow resembles a male figure. The woman's dress harbors the double images of a fetishistic high-heeled shoe and a cup with steaming contents, introducing sexual connotations to this feeling of remorse. The rock formations in the background recall the coast of Empordà, where Dalí spent his childhood and adolescence. The work thus clearly represents a psychoanalytic introspection.
— JAIME BRIHUEGA SIERRA

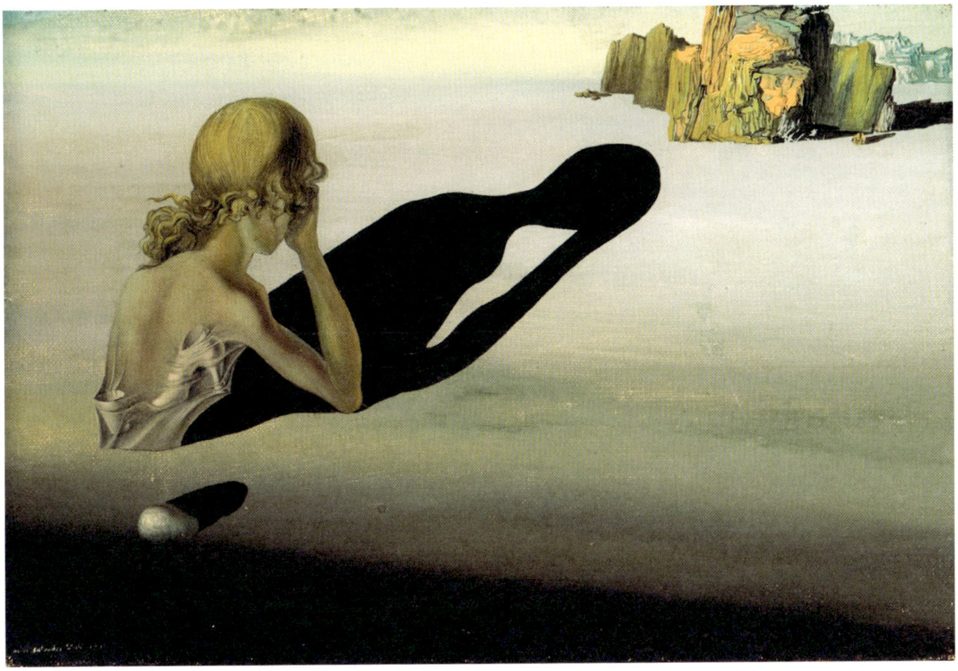

SALVADOR DALÍ, *Remorse: Sphinx Embedded in the Sand*, 1931, oil on canvas, 19 × 26.7 cm
Eli and Edythe Broad Art Museum,
Michigan State University, Gift of John Wolfram,
61.8, cat. no. P 268

4

THE DEVELOPMENT OF THE "PARANOIAC-CRITICAL METHOD" (1932–37)

Between 1932 and 1937, Dalí's public appearances became more frequent. In Paris, he exhibited his works numerous times, both in solo exhibitions (1932, 1933, and 1937), as well as in group exhibitions as part of the Surrealist group (1933 and 1936).

During this period, he also published essays laying down the theoretical foundations of his "paranoiac-critical method." The most important of these are *Babaouo,* (1932), the article "Nouvelles considérations générales sur le mécanisme du phénomène paranoïaque du point de vue surréaliste"[1] (published in 1932 in the magazine *Minotaure*)—in which he acknowledges his indebtedness to *De la psychose paranoïaque dans ses rapports avec la personnalité,* published by Lacan in the same year—and *La conquête de l'irrationnel* (1935). As early as 1937, he published the poem "Métamorphose de Narcisse" in Paris, which was also translated into English, putting into words the content of the eponymous painting, which he personally presented to Freud the following year (→ fig. 17).

Until his ultimate expulsion from the group in 1939, Dalí's

relationship with the Surrealists continued to be defined by episodes of crisis. His essay "Rêverie," published in 1931 in issue no. 4 of the magazine *Le surréalisme au service de la révolution,* for example, became the catalyst for Louis Aragon's break with the group. The essay, which was perceived as pornographic and immoral, was criticized by the Communist Party, although Breton, unlike Aragon, defended it in *Misère de la poésie* (1932). In January 1934, Breton sent a letter to Dalí,[2] accusing him of singing the praises of catastrophes that could cost human lives, and in particular of glorifying the person and racist thinking of Adolf Hitler. In the letter, Breton suggested that Dalí should take a step back, which he did—temporarily. His participation a few months later in the *Exposition du cinquantenaire* at the Salon des Indépendants at the Grand Palais in Paris, which the Surrealists had decided to boycott, implied a serious crisis with the group and effectively equated to his expulsion.

After marrying Gala in 1934, Dalí traveled to the United States for the first time. The following year he returned to Figueres, reconciling with his father with whom he had fallen out in 1929.

In spring 1937, Gala and Dalí spent some time in Zürs (→fig. 65) and set off for Vienna with the intention of meeting Freud in person, which they did not succeed in.[3] Nevertheless, Dalí's trip to Austria left a lasting impression on his work.[4] The Valluga and Roggspitze mountains, for example, feature in *Metamorphosis of Narcissus* (1937, P 455, →fig. 17) and Vienna's St. Canisius Church is depicted in the painting *City of Drawers* (1936, P 444, →fig. 5)—a clear allusion to Freud and his psychoanalysis—as well as elements from postcards acquired during his visit.

The works produced during this period, including *Myself at the Age of Ten When I was a Grasshopper Child (Castration Complex)* (c. 1933 P 208, →p. 135), *The Alert* (c. 1934, P 469, →p. 137), *West Side of the Isle of the Death (Reconstructed Compulsive Image After Böcklin)* (1934, P 391, →p. 133), and *Paranonïa* (c. 1935, P 422, →p. 131), testify to Dalí's impassioned attachment to Freud's intellectual world. One need only list the prevailing themes of those works: desire, guilt and remorse, dreams, time, fear, metamorphosis, cannibalism,

decay, terror, death, places of memory, double images and anamorphosis, repeated cross-references to Arnold Böcklin's *Isle of the Dead*, to Jean-François Millet's *Angelus* (→fig. 27), to Vermeer and the legend of William Tell, the supple viscosity of fried eggs, cutlets, boiled beans, the phallic associations of a stick of bread, drawers, soft architecture, fossilized cars and other objects, the piano equated to necrophilia, the harp, the skull, burning giraffes, monsters, Gala's omnipresence...

1 "New general considerations on the mechanism of the paranoiac phenomenon from the Surrealist point of view." This was the preface to the book *Le Mythe tragique de l'Angélus de Millet: Interprétation "paranoïaque-critique,"* which remained unpublished until 1963.
2 See Montse Aguer, "La incondicionalitat surrealista de Salvador Dalí a debat," in *L'Avenç*, no. 292, 2004, p. 92.
3 In *The Secret Life of Salvador Dalí*, Dalí discusses three trips to Vienna, where, while never succeeding in his aim to meet Freud, he always made time to see *The Art of Painting* by Vermeer at the Czernin Gallery of Paintings.
4 See Linus Klumpner, *Brennende Giraffen, die Greuel des Gebirges und kein Treffen mit Sigmund Freud: Salvador Dalí und Österreich*, master's thesis (Paris Lodron University of Salzburg, 2013.)

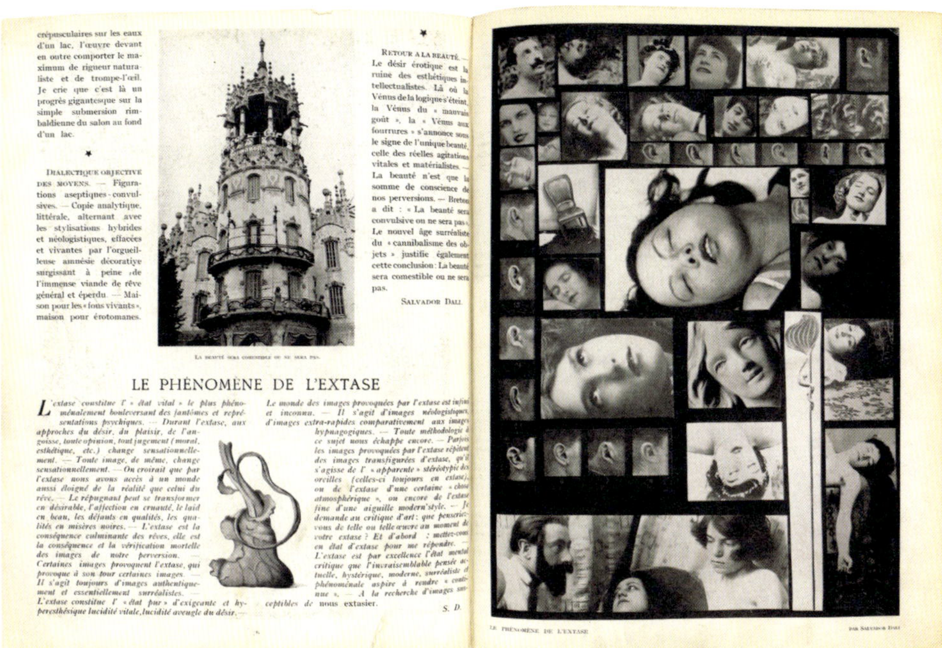
crépusculaires sur les eaux d'un lac, l'œuvre devant en outre comporter le maximum de rigueur naturaliste et de trompe-l'œil. Je crie que c'est là un progrès gigantesque sur la simple submersion rimbaldienne du salon au fond d'un lac.

*

DIALECTIQUE OBJECTIVE DES MOYENS. — Figurations aseptiques-convulsives. — Copie analytique, littérale, alternant avec les stylisations hybrides et néologistiques, effacées et vivantes par l'orgueilleuse amnésie décorative surgissant à peine de l'immense viande de rêve général et éperdu. — Maison pour les « fous vivants », maison pour érotomanes.

*

RETOUR A LA BEAUTÉ. — Le désir érotique est la ruine des esthétiques intellectualistes. Là où la Vénus de la logique s'éteint, la Vénus du « mauvais goût », la « Vénus aux fourrures » s'annonce sous le signe de l'unique beauté, celle des réelles agitations vitales et matérialistes. — La beauté n'est que la somme de conscience de nos perversions. — Breton a dit : « La beauté sera convulsive ou ne sera pas ». Le nouvel âge surréaliste du « cannibalisme des objets » justifie également cette conclusion : La beauté sera comestible ou ne sera pas.

SALVADOR DALI.

LA BEAUTÉ SERA COMESTIBLE OU NE SERA PAS.

LE PHÉNOMÈNE DE L'EXTASE

L'extase constitue l' « état vital » le plus phénoménalement bouleversant des fantômes et représentations psychiques. — Durant l'extase, aux approches du désir, du plaisir, de l'angoisse, toute opinion, tout jugement (moral, esthétique, etc.) change sensationnellement. — Toute image, de même, change sensationnellement. — On croirait que par l'extase nous avons accès à un monde aussi éloigné de la réalité que celui du rêve. — Le répugnant peut se transformer en désirable, l'affection en cruauté, le laid en beau, les défauts en qualités, les qualités en misères noires. — L'extase est la conséquence culminante des rêves, elle est la conséquence et la vérification mortelle des images de notre perversion. — Certaines images provoquent l'extase, qui provoque à son tour certaines images. — Il s'agit toujours d'images authentiquement et essentiellement surréalistes. — L'extase constitue l' « état pur » d'exigeante et hyperesthésique lucidité vitale, lucidité aveugle du désir. — Le monde des images provoquées par l'extase est infini et inconnu. — Il s'agit d'images néologistiques, d'images extra-rapides comparativement aux images hypnagogiques. — Toute méthodologie à ce sujet nous échappe encore. — Parfois les images provoquées par l'extase répètent des images transfigurées d'extase, qu'il s'agisse de l' « apparente » stéréotypie des oreilles (celles-ci toujours en extase), ou de l'extase d'une certaine « chose atmosphérique », ou encore de l'extase fine d'une aiguille modern'style. — Je demande au critique d'art : que penseriez-vous de telle ou telle œuvre au moment de votre extase ? Et d'abord : mettez-vous en état d'extase pour me répondre. — L'extase est par excellence l'état mental critique que l'invraisemblable pensée actuelle, hystérique, moderne, surréaliste et phénoménale aspire à rendre « continue ». — A la recherche d'images susceptibles de nous extasier.

S. D.

LE PHÉNOMÈNE DE L'EXTASE — PAR SALVADOR DALI

SALVADOR DALÍ, "Le phénomène de l'extase," 1933
From: *Minotaure*, nos. 3–4, 1933, pp. 76–77

One day in Paris I received a telephone call from a brilliant young psychiatrist. He had just read an article of mine in the review *Le Minotaure* on "The Inner Mechanism of Paranoiac Activity." He congratulated me and expressed his astonishment at the accuracy of my scientific knowledge of this subject, which was so generally misunderstood. He wished to see me to talk over this whole question. [...] At six o'clock sharp—the appointed time of our meeting—the doorbell rang. I hurriedly put away my copper, Jacques Lacan entered, and we immediately launched into a highly technical discussion.
— SALVADOR DALÍ, *The Secret Life of Salvador Dalí* (New York, 1993), pp. 17–18.

Lacan threw a scientific light on a phenomenon that is obscure to most of our contemporaries—the expression: paranoia—and gave it its true significance. Psychiatry, before Lacan, committed a vulgar error on this account by claiming that the systematization of paranoiac delirium developed "after the fact" and that this phenomenon was to be considered as a case of "reasoning madness." Lacan showed the contrary to be true: the delirium itself is a systematization. It is born systematic, an active element determined to orient reality around its line of force. It is the contrary of a dream or an automatism which remains passive [...] Paranoiac delirium asserts itself and conquers. Surrealist actions bring dream and automatism into the concrete; but paranoiac delirium is the very essence of Surrealism and needs only its own force.
— SALVADOR DALÍ, *The Unspeakable Confessions of Salvador Dalí as told to André Parinaud* (London, 1977), pp. 140–41.

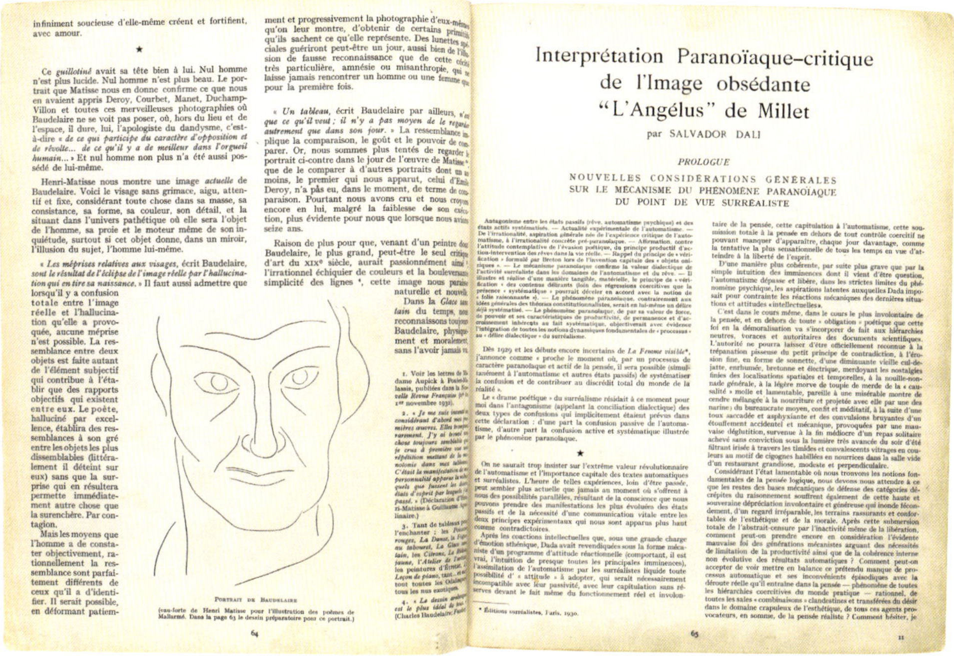

Interprétation Paranoïaque-critique de l'Image obsédante "L'Angélus" de Millet

par SALVADOR DALI

PROLOGUE

NOUVELLES CONSIDÉRATIONS GÉNÉRALES SUR LE MÉCANISME DU PHÉNOMÈNE PARANOÏAQUE DU POINT DE VUE SURRÉALISTE

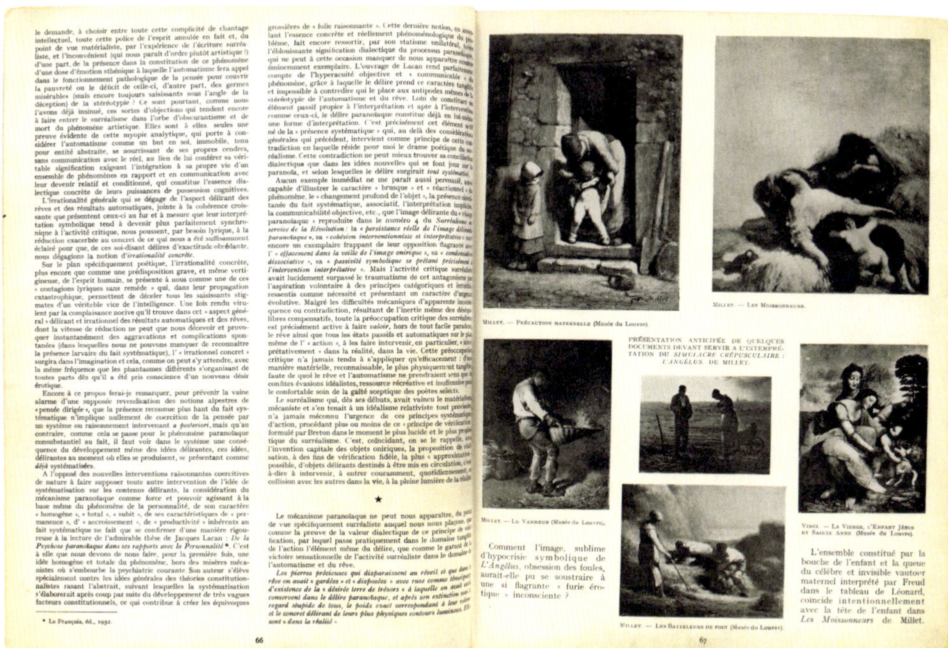

SALVADOR DALÍ, "Interprétation paranoïaque-critique de l'image obsédante 'L'Angelús' de Millet," 1933
From: *Minotaure*, no. 1, 1933, pp. 65–67

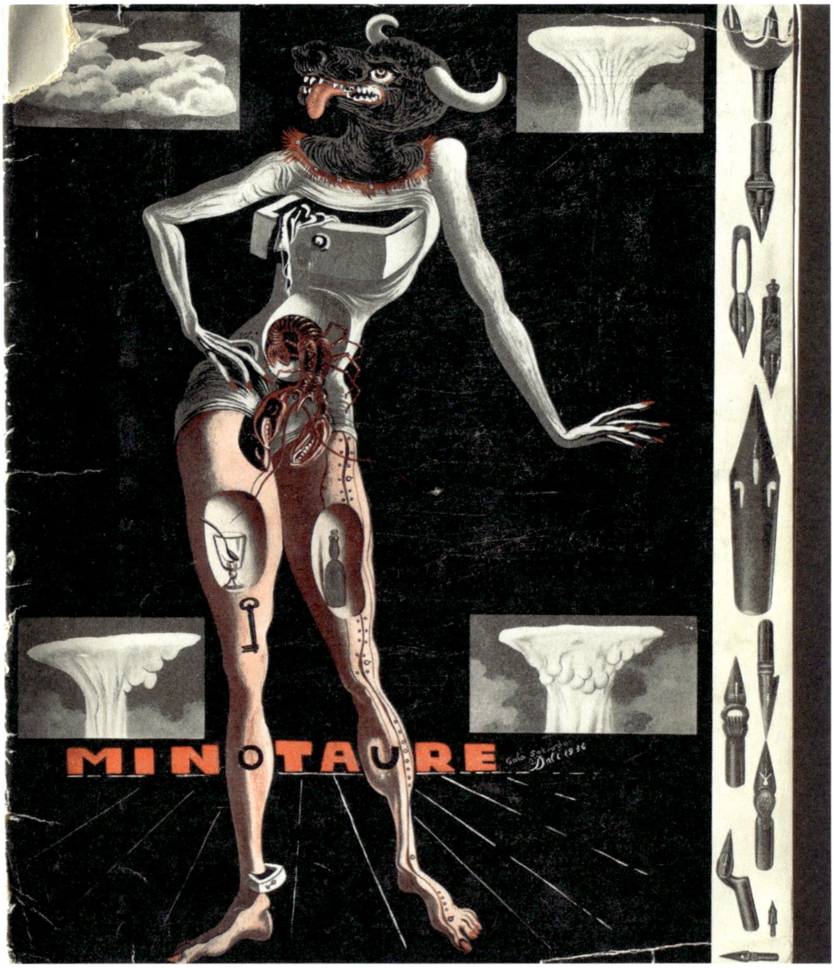

SALVADOR DALÍ, *Minotaure*, no. 8, 1936
Magazine cover

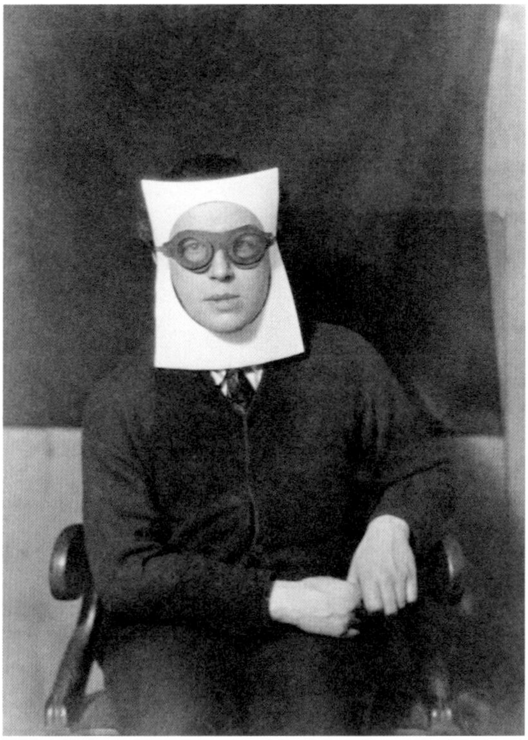

MAN RAY, *André Breton*, 1930
Man Ray Trust

Dalí has endowed surrealism with an instrument of primary importance, in particular the paranoiac-critical method, which has immediately shown itself capable of being applied with equal success to painting, poetry, the cinema, to the construction of typical surrealist objects, to fashions, to sculpture and even, if necessary, to all manner of exegesis.
— ANDRÉ BRETON, *What is Surrealism?* (1934), quoted from Eric Protter, *Painters on Painting* (New York, 1997), p. 240.

December 8, 1937 // Dear Sir, // Forgive me for the great delay in replying to your kind letter, addressed to my daughter, but intended for me. Given my age, you will not find it implausible that ill health was to blame. // I truly regret that I cannot fulfill your wish and submit an original contribution to your dream collection. For now, I must confess that I have nothing new to say about the dream. I ask you to note that the interpretation of dreams, which I call the "manifest" dream, has no interest for me. I was occupied with trying to find the "latent dream content," which can be discovered through analytical interpretation of the manifest dream. A collection of dreams without added associations, without knowledge of the circumstances under which they were dreamed, means nothing to me. I can hardly imagine what it could mean to anyone else. // It is conceivable that manifest dreams show all the multifariousness of our intellectual productions. For, according to Aristotle's unsurpassed insight, dreaming is no more than the continuation of our thoughts into the state of sleep. I can only add: modified by the psychological peculiarities of this state. // Yours faithfully // Freud

Freud had agreed to see me in Vienna in 1921 and, although the account I published of my visit in *Littérature* was rather derogatory (out of a regrettable sacrifice to the Dada spirit), he had the good grace not to hold it against me and to keep up our correspondence.
— ANDRÉ BRETON in a radio interview with André Parinaud, made between March and June 1952 for French radio, in André Breton, *Conversations: The Autobiography of Surrealism* (New York, 1993), p. 60.

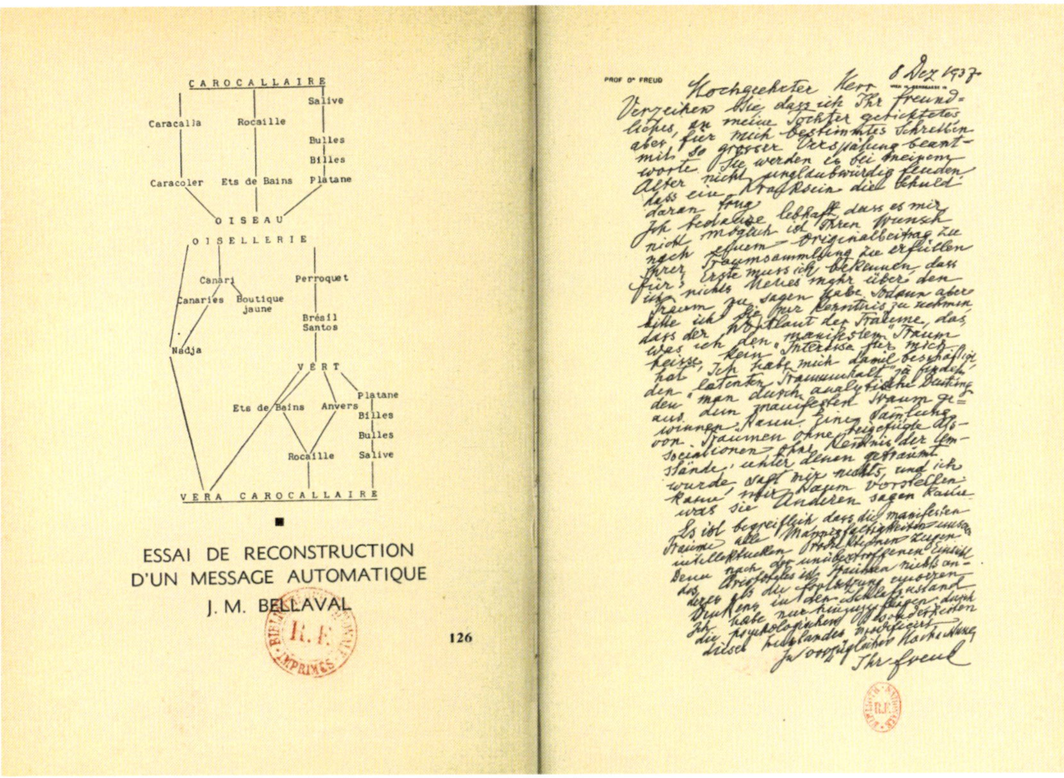

SIGMUND FREUD to André Breton,
December 8, 1937, from:
Trajectoire du rève no. 7, Cahiers G.L.M, Les textes & illustrations composant ce cahier consacré au rêve ont été assemblés par André Breton (Paris, 1938).

The high degree of narcissistic value which the penis possesses can appeal to the fact that that organ is a guarantee to its owner that he can be once more united to his mother—i.e. to a substitute for her—in the act of copulation. Being deprived of it amounts to a renewed separation from her, and this in its turn means being helplessly exposed to an unpleasurable tension due to instinctual need, as was the case at birth. But the need whose increase is feared is now a specific one belonging to the genital libido and is no longer an indeterminate one, as it was in the period of infancy. It may be added that for a man who is impotent (that is, who is inhibited by the threat of castration) the substitute for copulation is a phantasy of returning into his mother's womb.
— SIGMUND FREUD, "Inhibitions, Symptoms and Anxiety," (1926), in *The Standard Edition of Complete Psychological Works of Sigmund Freud*, vol. XX, p. 139.

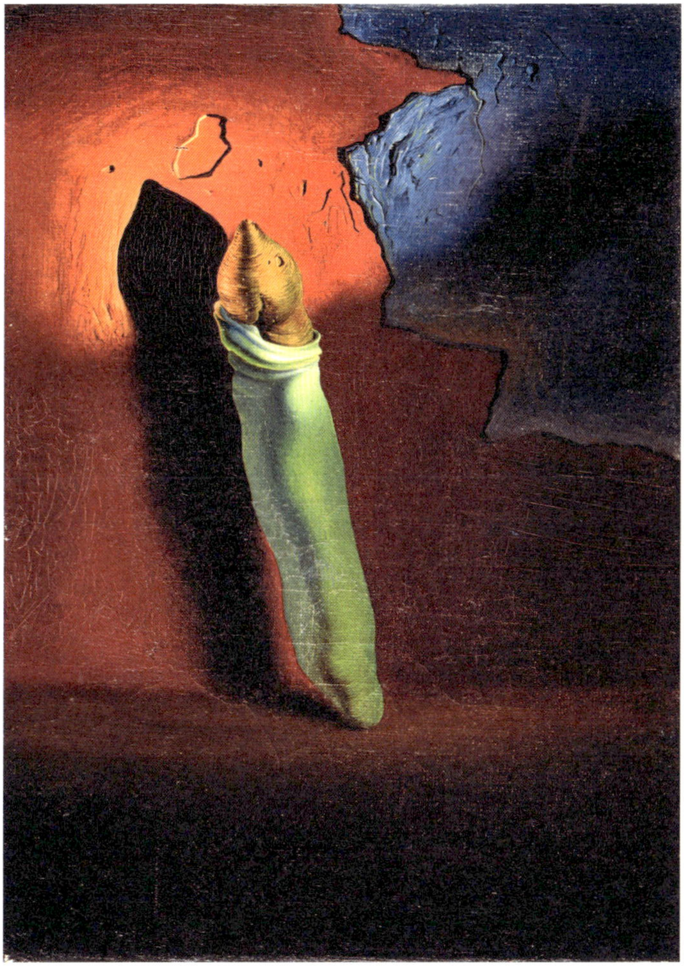

SALVADOR DALÍ, *Pa antropomorf*
(*Anthropomorphic Bread*), 1932
Oil on canvas, 24 × 16.5 cm, Town Hall of Figueres,
on permanent deposit
at the Fundació Gala-Salvador Dalí,
Figueres, cat. no. P 291

As in many of Dalí's paintings, the boldly erect cypress in *The Birth of Liquid Anguish* (1932) is an obviously phallic symbol. In other works this is represented by towers or loaves of bread. In this image, the cypress is also reminiscent of the trees in Arnold Böcklin's *Isle of the Dead*, a painting often referenced by Dalí and a work he associated with hallucinatory visions. The crumpled cloth calls to mind a bedsheet during restless dreams, while the jet of liquid alludes to nocturnal ejaculations, first experiences of sexual pleasure which, as a result of a repressive upbringing, are marred by oppressive pangs of guilt.
— JAIME BRIHUEGA SIERRA

All elongated objects, such as sticks, tree-trunks and umbrellas (the opening of these last being comparable to an erection) may stand for the male organ, as well as all long, sharp weapons, such as knives, daggers and pikes.
— SIGMUND FREUD, *The Interpretation of Dreams* (1900), (London, 1953), p. 354.

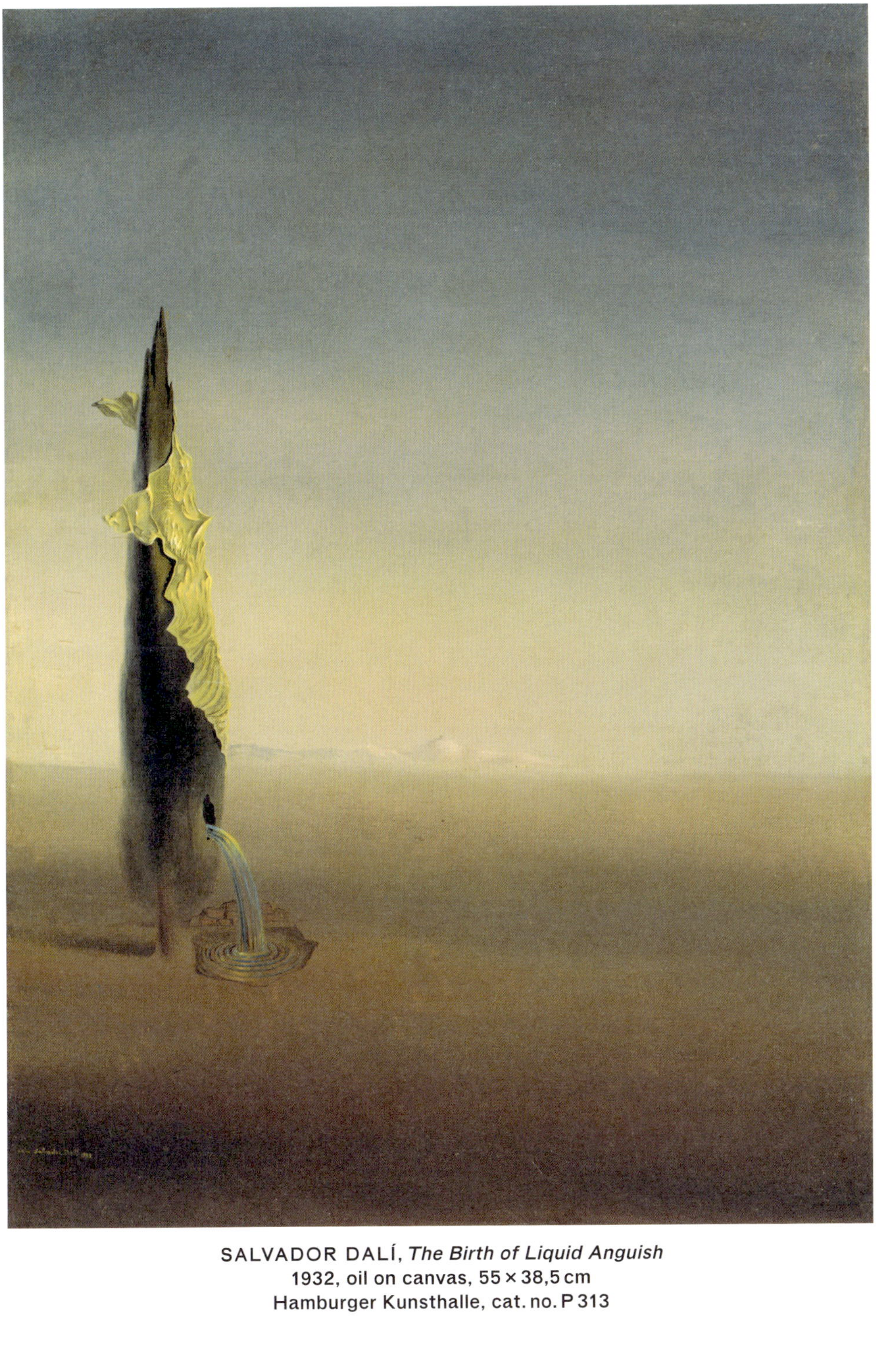

SALVADOR DALÍ, *The Birth of Liquid Anguish*
1932, oil on canvas, 55 × 38,5 cm
Hamburger Kunsthalle, cat. no. P 313

The historian Paloma Alarcó analyzed *Gradiva Rediscovers the Anthropomorphic Ruins. Retrospective Fantasy* (c. 1931–32) in the Museo Thyssen-Bornemisza's catalogue as follows: "Gradiva had entered Dalí's personal mythology in 1931, the year the French translation came out of Sigmund Freud's *Delusion and Dreams in Jensen's 'Gradiva,'* written in 1907. [...] Gradiva provided Freud with an archaeological metaphor for the analysis of repressed desire and immediately aroused the interest of the Surrealists, who regarded the novella as an expression of the power of dreams and desire over reality. The main character in Jensen's tale is a young archaeologist, Norbert Hanold, who is obsessed by the figure of a tunic-clad woman, Gradiva, he had seen in a classical relief. The young woman appears to him in dreams when Vesuvius is about to erupt in Pompeii, and when he visits the ruins of the ancient Italian town the same phantasmagorical figure appears to him on three occasions." Many of the elements from this narrative are present in the image.
— JAIME BRIHUEGA SIERRA

She said to me, "My little boy! We shall never leave each other." She was destined to be my Gradiva, "she who advances," my victory, my wife. But for this she had to cure me, and she did cure me!
— SALVADOR DALÍ, *The Secret Life of Salvador Dalí* (New York, 1993), p. 233.

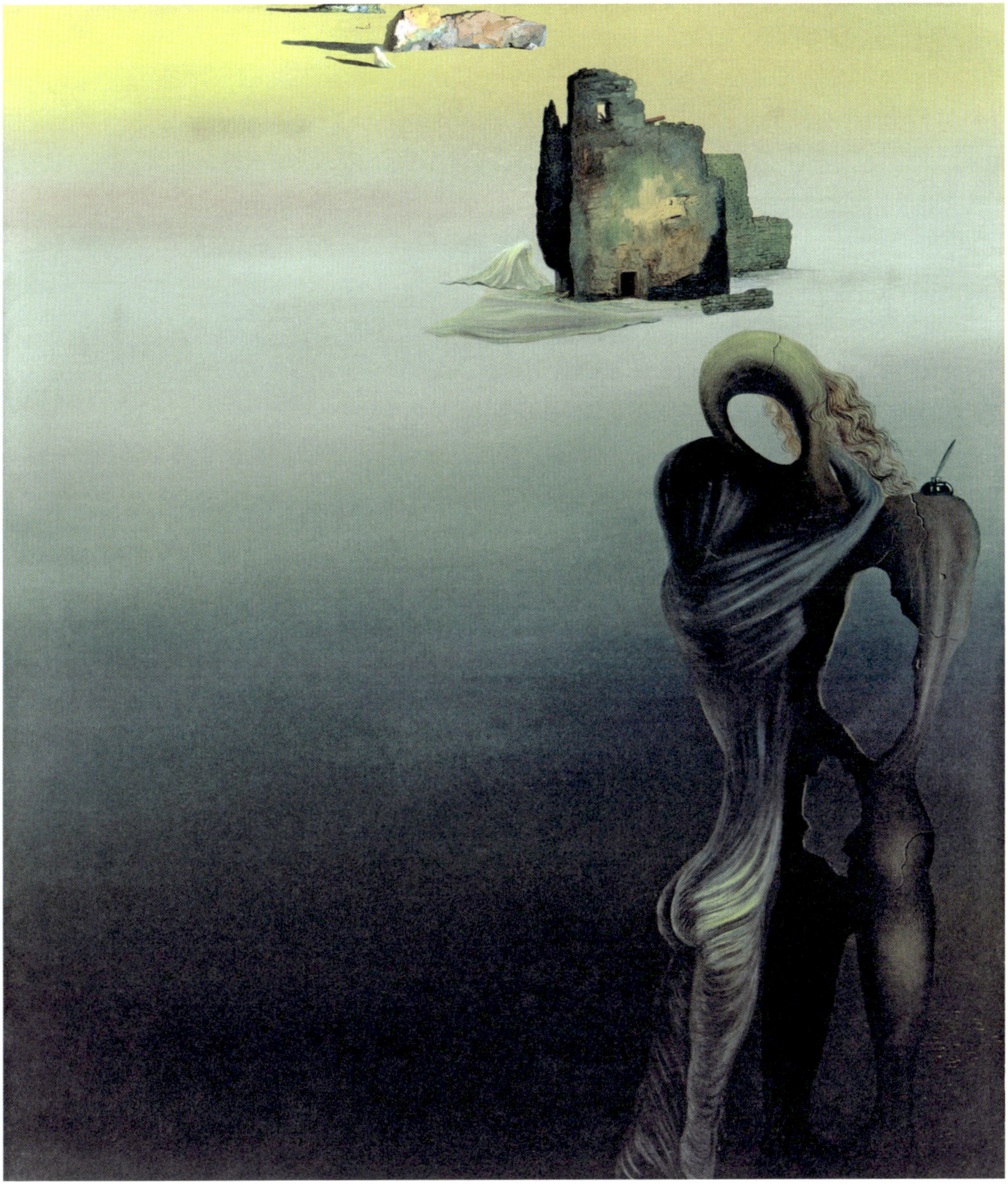

SALVADOR DALÍ, *Gradiva retrouve les ruines anthropomorphes (fantaisie rétrospective) (Gradiva Rediscovers the Anthropomorphic Ruins [Retrospective Fantasy])*, c. 1931/32
Oil on canvas, 65 × 54 cm
Museo Nacional Thyssen-Bornemisza, Madrid, cat. no. P 281

Concerning the factors of silence, solitude and darkness, we can only say that they are actually elements in the production of the infantile anxiety from which the majority of human beings have never become quite free.

— SIGMUND FREUD, "The Uncanny," (1919), in *The Standard Edition of Complete Psychological Works of Sigmund Freud*, p. 3701.

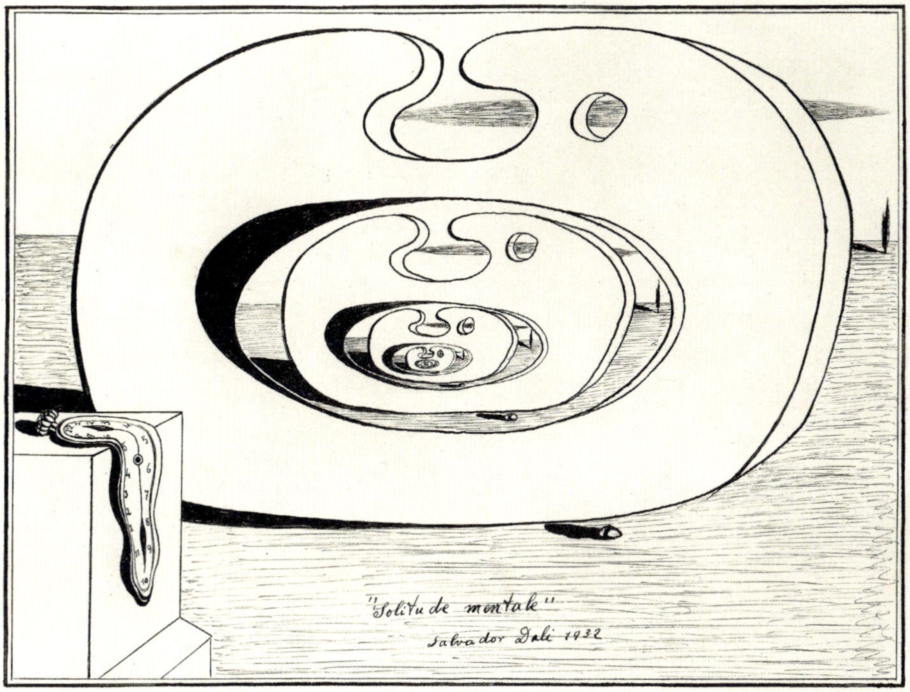

SALVADOR DALÍ, *Solitude Mentale*
(*Mental Solitude*), 1932
Ink on paper, 22.4 × 30.8 cm
Colecciones Fundación Mapfre

This drawing from 1934 is a preparatory sketch for the eponymous painting, dated 1936 in the Salvador Dalí catalogue raisonné, and now in the Philadelphia Museum of Art. It is a work that expresses the political tensions in Europe at the time. Almost all the elements that would later appear in the painting are already present in drawing no. 1: the head with its expression of intense pain, the mutilated figure, one hand squeezing a breast, the other scratching the ground, the bedside table upon which one arm rests, and the flaccid form, drooping over the soft extension of the figure's bottom. Dalí did, however, include one detail that would be omitted from the oil painting, namely the other strange female breast, protruding from the middle of one of the arms.
— JAIME BRIHUEGA SIERRA

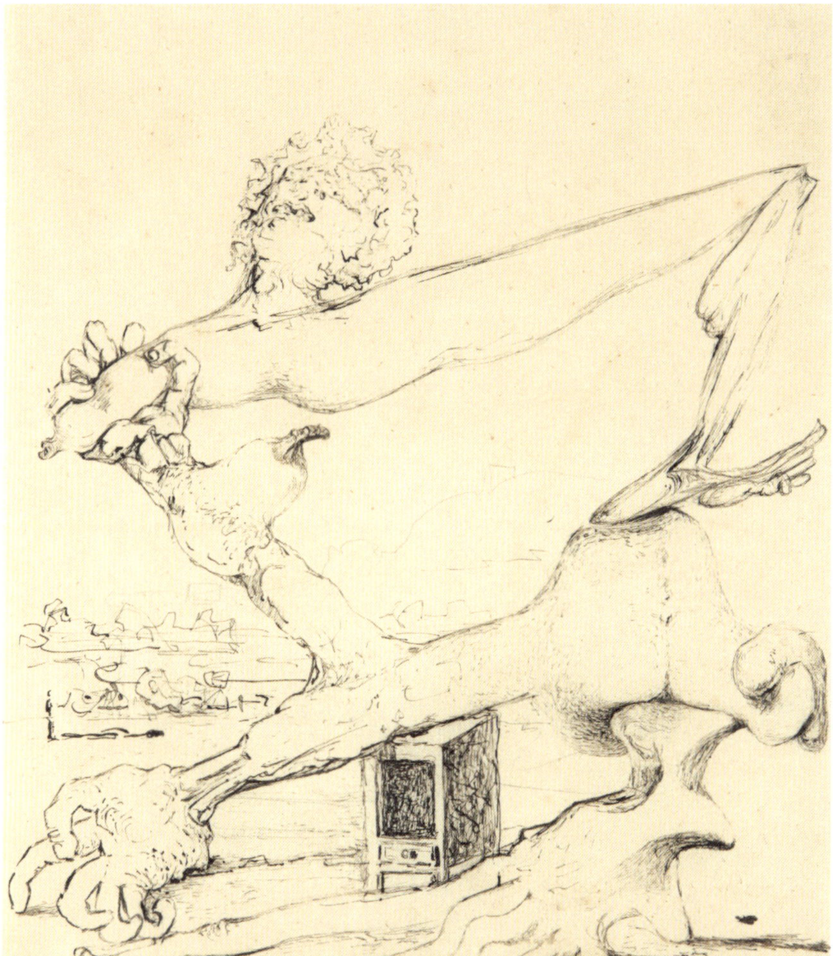

SALVADOR DALÍ, Sketch for
Soft Construction with Boiled Beans.
Premonition of Civil War 1
1934, pencil on paper, 22.7 × 17.7 cm
Asociación Colección Arte Contemporáneo—
Museo Patio Herreriano, Valladolid

It is to be noticed that even in paranoia, where the original state of things is restored, this reversal into a contrary is observed. The subject feels that he is no longer alone, he has no doubt that he is being observed, but the observers are “a lot of strangers” whose identity is left curiously vague.
— SIGMUND FREUD, *The Interpretation of Dreams* (1900), (London, 1953), p. 246.

I define the paranoia-critical method as a great art of playing upon all one's own inner contradictions with lucidity by causing others to experience the anxieties and ecstasies of one's life in such a way that it becomes gradually as essential to them as their own.
— SALVADOR DALÍ, *The Unspeakable Confessions of Salvador Dalí as told to André Parinaud* (London, 1977), p. 17.

The genius of paranoia-critical activity is to associate limp paranoia with tough criticism; the gooey with the sharp; force of life par excellence with mind; to reach the deepest intuition.
— SALVADOR DALÍ, *The Unspeakable Confessions of Salvador Dalí as told to André Parinaud* (London, 1977), p. 153.

The title *Paranonïa* (c. 1935) obviously alludes to Dalí's paranoiac-critical method. An expressive double image is therefore the focus of this work. The head of the female bust at the center of the composition is made up of a group of figures engaged in battle, reminiscent of Renaissance paintings. The pronounced linear perspective is a clear reference to the floorboards in de Chirico's images.
— JAIME BRIHUEGA SIERRA

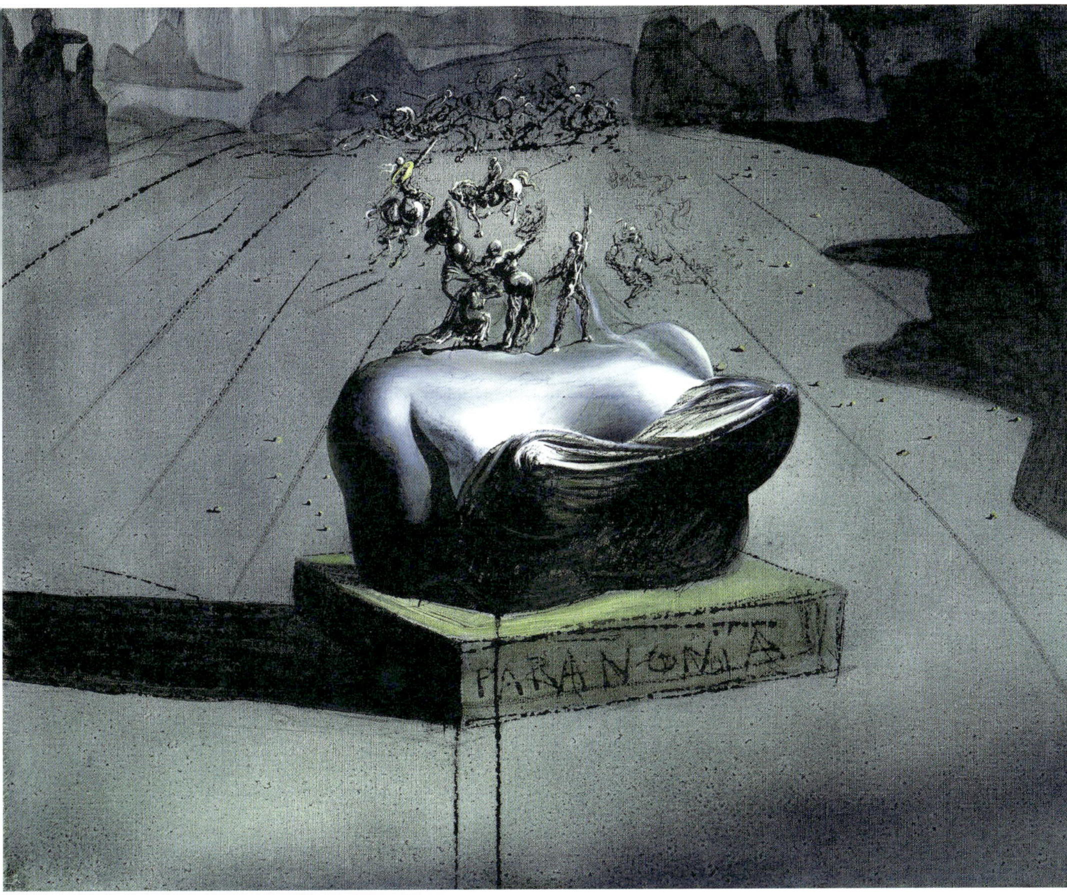

SALVADOR DALÍ, *Paranonïa*
c. 1935, oil on canvas, 38.1 × 46 cm
The Dalí Museum, Saint Petersburg (Florida)
Cat. no. P 422

Arnold Böcklin's *Isle of the Dead* in its various versions has always held a fascination, appealing to personalities as contrary as Hitler and Lenin. Furthermore, the work provides one of the most obvious connections between Freud and Dalí, as the former had a reproduction of Böcklin's painting in his office, while the latter referenced it on countless occasions in his pictures. ***West Side of the Isle of the Dead—Reconstructed Compulsive Image After Böcklin*** (1934) is one of the most explicit citations, as here Dalí is imagining an obsessive journey into the interior of this fictional island. The rugged cliffs with architectural remains, the cypresses referencing both death and phalli, as well as the phantasmagorical figure of the ferryman Charon, who seems to conceal an erection under his dark tunic, were chosen by Dalí as suitable elements from Böcklin's work to immerse the viewer in the dialectic of Eros and Thanatos.
— JAIME BRIHUEGA SIERRA

A man standing on a cliff in the middle of the sea, in the style of Böcklin.
— SIGMUND FREUD, *The Interpretation of Dreams* (1900), (London, 1953), p. 66.

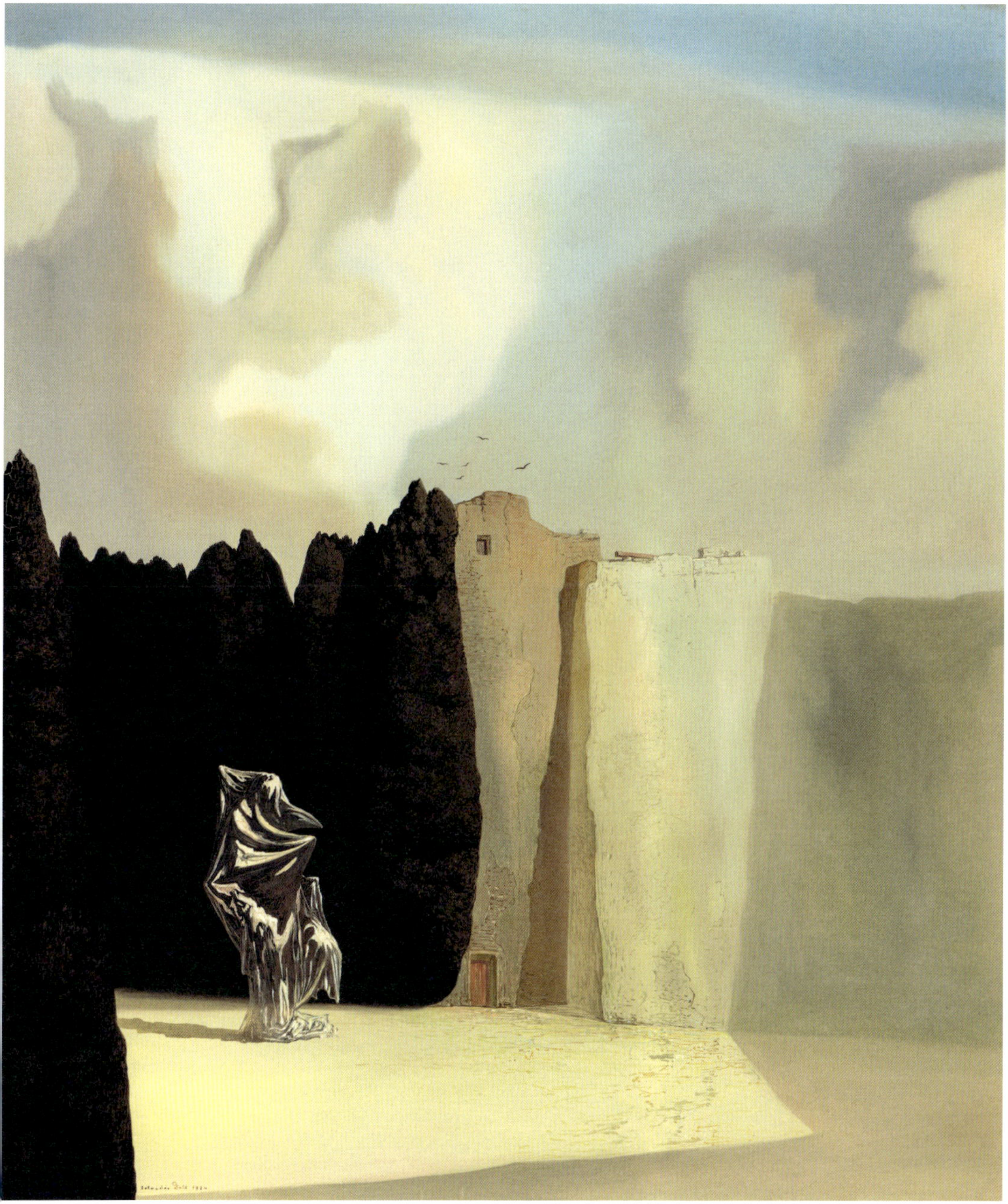

SALVADOR DALÍ, *Cour ouest de l'île des morts (obsession reconstitutive d'après Böcklin)* (*West Side of the Isle of the Dead [Reconstructed Compulsive Image After Böcklin]*)
1934, oil on canvas, 66 × 54.5 cm
ABANCA Art Collection, A Coruña, cat. no. P 391

Myself at the Age of Ten When I Was a Grasshopper Child (Castration Complex) (c. 1933). Freud's writings contain abundant references to the concept of the castration complex. In the title of this highly symbolic self-portrait, Dalí alludes to his phobia of grasshoppers, an insect he repeatedly includes in his self-portraits as the "great masturbator." The painting expresses the feelings of guilt associated with masturbation, which can lead to the aforementioned complex. The table and the boy's head have become deformed and elongated in a paranoiac allusion to an erect penis. The desolate setting—amid a semi-desert—is reminiscent of the landscapes from the artist's childhood.
— JAIME BRIHUEGA SIERRA

She told me that the piano was a *disgusting old box*, that it made an *ugly noise*, that it had been in her husband's possession before their marriage, and so on. But the key to the solution was only given by her words: "It's not worth while." [...] In the same way the "box" ["Kasten"] was a substitute for a "chest" ["Brustkasten"]; and the interpretation of the dream led us back at once to the time of her physical development at puberty, when she had begun to be dissatisfied by her figure.
— SIGMUND FREUD, *The Interpretation of Dreams* (1900), (London, 1953), p. 185–86.

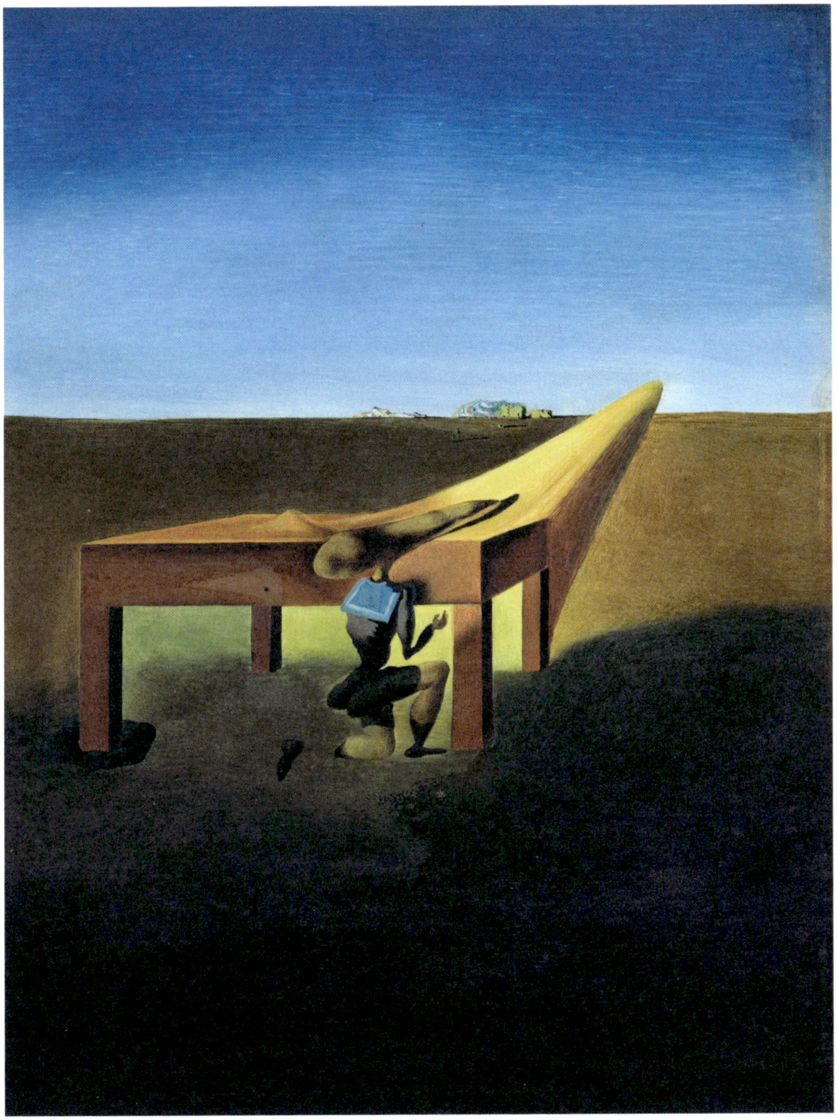

SALVADOR DALÍ, *Moi-même à 10 ans quand j'étais l'enfant-sauterelle (complexe de castration)* (*Myself at the Age of Ten When I Was a Grasshopper Child [Castration Complex]*), c. 1933, oil on wood, 21.9 × 16.2 cm
The Dalí Museum, Saint Petersburg (Florida)
Cat. no. P 208

The Alert (c. 1934) embodies the notion of fear and alarm in a Freudian sense. The protagonist in this undefined menace is an enigmatic figure concealed beneath a shroud in front of a peculiar building from which a phallic object protrudes, a wet cloth dangling from its top end. A strange, unidentified male figure advances from the distance toward these elements. In the foreground, a boggy landscape that seems to contain quicksand leads into the scene. Behind this we can see a sphere, a recurring element in Dalí's pictures.
— JAIME BRIHUEGA SIERRA

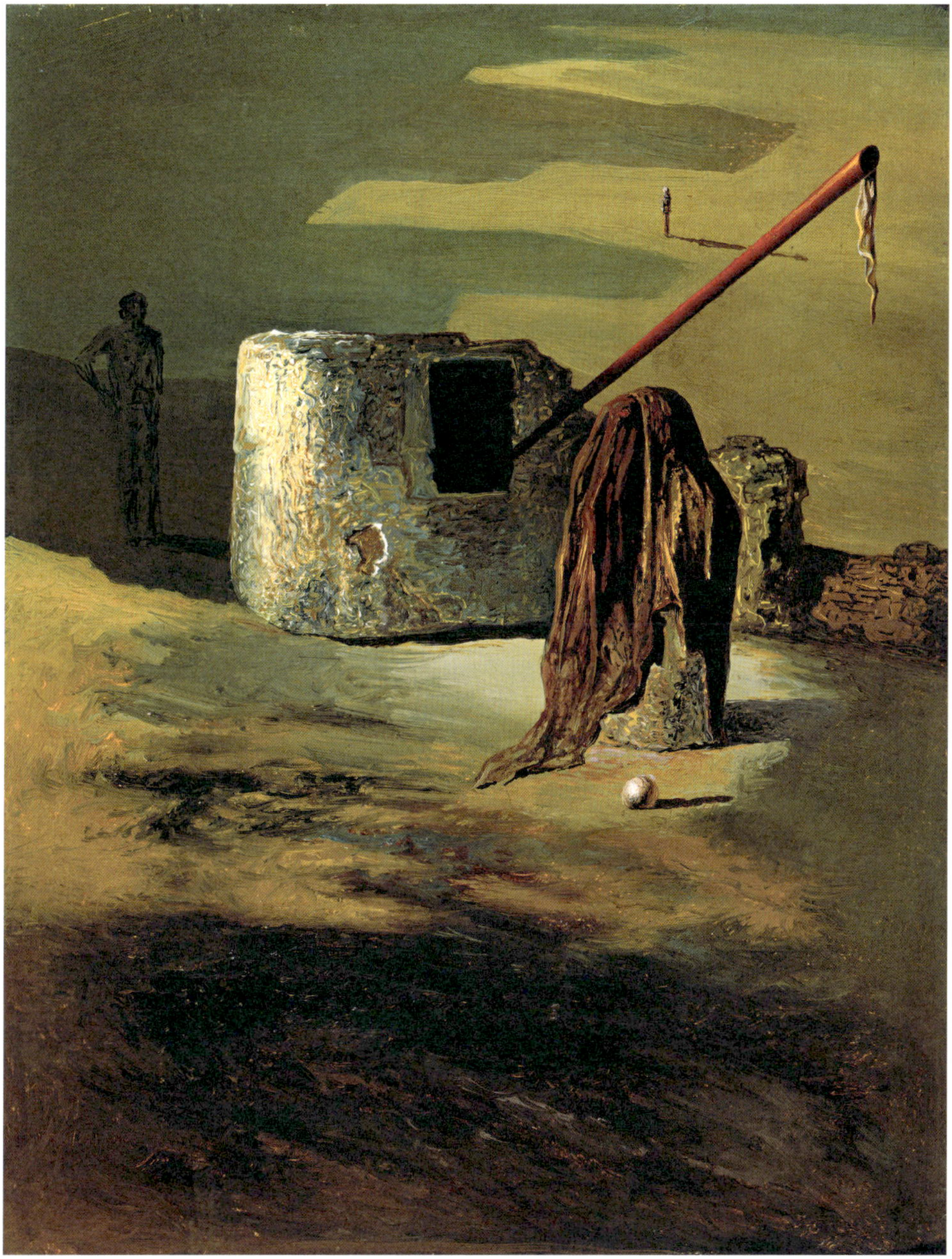

SALVADOR DALÍ, *The Alert*, c. 1934
Oil on wood, 24 × 18 cm
Ulla and Heiner Pietzsch Collection, Berlin
Cat. no. P 469

In the painting *Swans Reflecting Elephants* (1937) an elaborate double image dominates the scene as vividly as in *The Metamorphosis of Narcissus* (→ fig. 17), which was produced in the same year and was the painting Dalí showed to Freud at their meeting in London in 1938. A male figure turns his back on a lake out of which the trunks of dead trees rise. Three swans float on the lake's surface, their reflections morphing into three elephants walking along the shore. Rocky cliffs and clouds faintly hint at possible double images of animals and humans with disturbing fires flickering in their midst. In the foreground on the left, a complex figure combines visual allusions with organic elements reminiscent of snakes or elephant trunks.
— JAIME BRIHUEGA SIERRA

Imagination in dreams is without the power of conceptual speech. It is obliged to paint what it has to say pictorially, and, since there are no concepts to exercise an attenuating influence, it makes full and powerful use of the pictorial form.
— SIGMUND FREUD, *The Interpretation of Dreams* (1900), (London, 1953), p. 84.

What had been the camel's head now formed the comb [of the rooster], and the camel's lower lip which was already prominent had lengthened to become the beak.
— SALVADOR DALÍ, *The Secret Life of Salvador Dalí* (New York, 1993), p. 304.

While the fishermen rowed, and one saw these rocks at each monotonous stroke of the oars continually become metamorphosed, "become uninterruptedly something else," "change simulacra," as though they had been phantasmal quick-change artists of stone [...] Watching the "stirring" of the forms of those motionless rocks, I meditated on my own rocks, those of my thought.
— SALVADOR DALÍ, *The Secret Life of Salvador Dalí* (New York, 1993), p. 305.

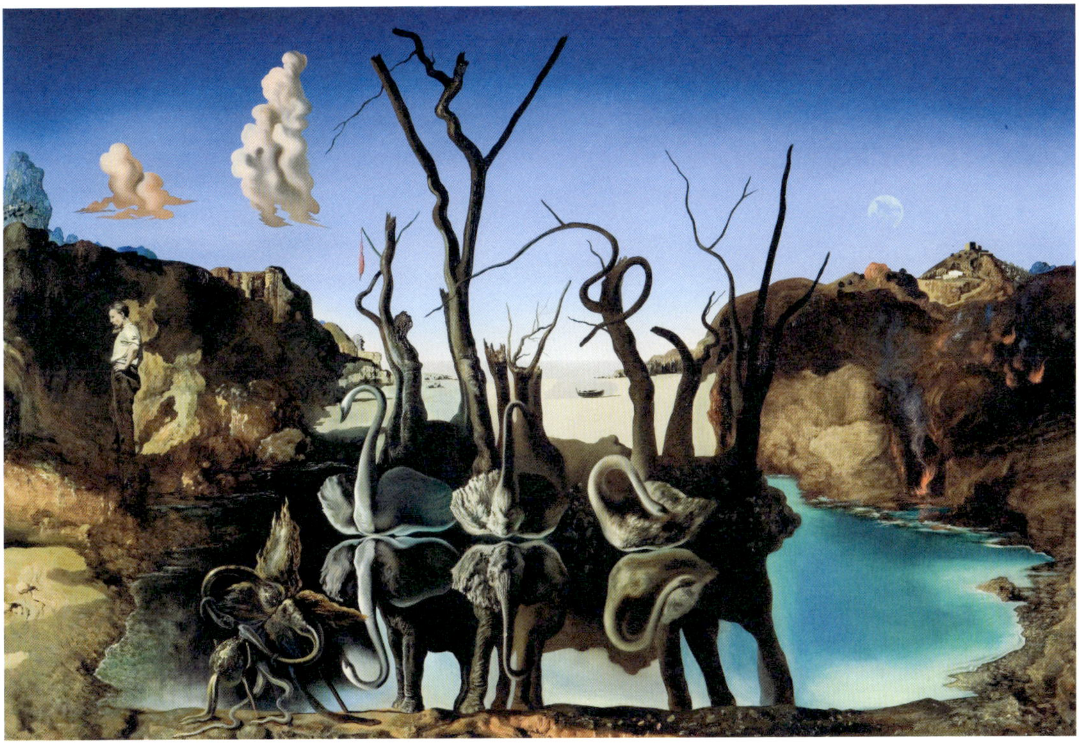

SALVADOR DALÍ, *Cisnes reflejando elefantes* (*Swans Reflecting Elephants*), 1937
Oil on canvas, 51 × 77 cm
Esther Grether Family Collection
Cat. no. P 454

5

LONDON 1938: DALÍ – FREUD – JAMES – ZWEIG

In January 1938, the *Exposition Internationale du Surréalisme*, organized by André Breton and Paul Éluard, opened in Paris. The entrance to the show featured Salvador Dalí's *Rainy Taxi* (→fig. 54). This was the last time that Dalí participated in the Surrealists' activities, and with the publication of Breton's article "Des tendences les plus récentes de la peinture surréaliste" the following year, Dalí's expulsion from the Surrealist group was final.[1]

In 1938, Dalí's work revolved around double images, references to Vermeer, and bedside drawers, while also being influenced by the political turmoil shaking Europe, the civil war in Spain, and the looming catastrophe of the war due to break out a year later. This is evident in works such as *Spain* (1938, P 468) or *Debris of an Automobile Giving Birth to a Blind Horse Biting a Telephone* (1938, P 463; inspired by Pablo Picasso's *Guernica*), but especially in pictures like *Imperial Violets* (1938, P 474) and *The Sublime Moment* (1938, P 472), already featuring the broken telephone and plate that would become key elements in *The Enigma of Hitler* (1939, P 475) and other paintings from 1939, the year André Breton ousted

Dalí from the Surrealist group, as mentioned before.

After several failed attempts to meet Freud in Vienna, the long-anticipated meeting finally took place.[2] Two weeks after Hitler's invasion of Austria on March 12, 1938, Freud was arrested in his apartment on Berggasse 19. On June 4, he, his wife, and daughter Anna managed to leave Austria, and two days later, after stopping over in Paris (→p. 152), he arrived in London, where he took up residence at 39 Elsworthy Road.

Dalí, who knew that Freud was in London, asked Edward James for his address, since Stefan Zweig, a close friend of the psychoanalyst who was also living in exile in London, had misplaced it. After locating the address, Zweig—at Dalí's behest—wrote three letters to Freud, requesting a meeting (→pp. 152–4). Contact was eventually made and James invited Dalí to London. The visit, which was attended by Dalí, Zweig, and James, took place on July 19 (→p. 159).

Dalí's description of this encounter in *The Secret Life of Salvador Dalí*[3] has a distinctly paranoid feel to it:

> "I was to meet Freud at last, in London. I was accompanied by the writer Stefan Zweig and by the poet Edward James. While I was crossing the old professor's yard I saw a bicycle leaning against the wall, and on the saddle, attached by a string, was a red rubber hot-water bottle which looked full of water, and on the back of the hot-water bottle walked a snail! The presence of that assortment seemed strange and inexplicable in the yard of Freud's house."[4]

Dalí took with him the picture *Metamorphosis of Narcissus* (1937, P 455, →fig. 17), an impressive example of his paranoiac-critical method, which Freud studied obligingly and attentively. During the meeting, Dalí drew a portrait of Freud (→p. 167). Two days after the visit, Freud wrote to Zweig, among other things, the following:

> "I really have reason to thank you for the introduction which brought me yesterday's visitors. For until then I was inclined to look upon surrealists, who have apparently chosen me for their patron saint, as absolute

(let us say 95 per cent, like alcohol) cranks. The young Spaniard, however, with his candid fanatical eyes and his undeniable technical mastery, has made me reconsider my opinion."[5]

1 In no. 12/13 of *Minotaure* magazine, May 12, 1939.
2 See Ian Gibson, *La vida desaforada de Salvador Dalí* (Barcelona, 1998), pp. 485–93.
3 Written 1940/41.
4 Salvador Dalí, *The Secret Life of Salvador Dalí*, translated by Haakon M. Chevalier (New York, 1993), p. 24.
5 Quoted from Ernst L. Freud, ed., *Letters of Sigmund Freud* (New York, 1960), Letter 303.

Later, when I saw the fruits of this folly threatening to clutter up my life, becoming so vigorous that it seemed as though they might deprive me of all the air I needed, then I rejected folly with violent kicks, and undertook a crusade to recover my "living-space"; and the slogan of this first moment—"The irrational for the sake of the irrational"—was one which I was to transform and canalize at the end of a year into that other slogan, which was already of Catholic essence—"The Conquest of the Irrational." So that the "Irrational" which, at the moment of which I am speaking, I was treating with all the honors and ceremonials due to a true divinity was a thing which I already completely rejected at the end of a year. And while profiting by the secrets I had torn from it, and which it had yielded to me, during the promiscuity of our relations, I set out with fury, stubbornness and heroism to try to conquer it, destroying it pitilessly as I progressed, and at the same time trying to pull the entire surrealist group along with me.

— SALVADOR DALÍ, *The Secret Life of Salvador Dalí* (New York, 1993), pp. 222–23.

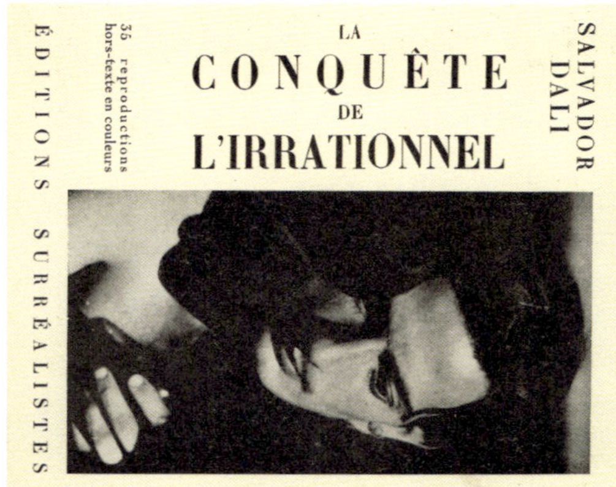

SALVADOR DALÍ, *La conquête de l'irrationnel*, Paris 1935, book cover
Fundació Gala-Salvador Dalí, Figueres

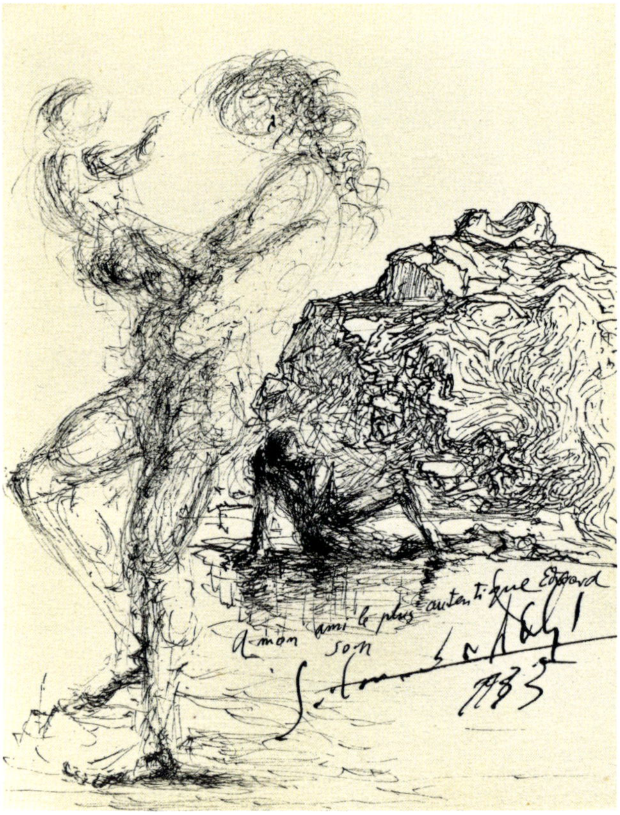

SALVADOR DALÍ, *La conquête de l'irrationnel* with a dedication and a drawing by Salvador Dalí, Paris 1935
West Dean College of Arts and Conservation

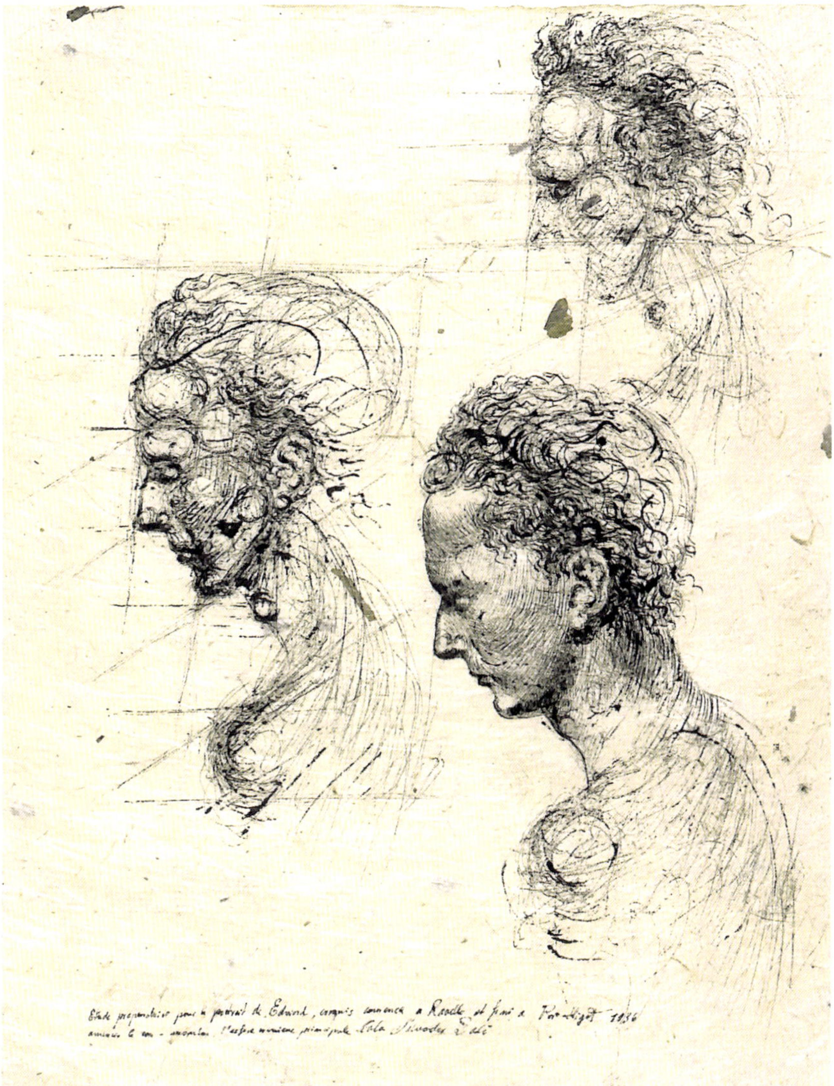

SALVADOR DALÍ, *Portrait Sketches of Edward James*, 1936
Pencil and ink on paper, 21 × 15.7 cm
West Dean College of Arts and Conservation

And Edward James, hummingbird poet, ordered aphrodisiac lobster-telephones, bought the best Dalís, and was naturally the richest.
— SALVADOR DALÍ, *The Secret Life of Salvador Dalí* (New York, 1993), p. 340.

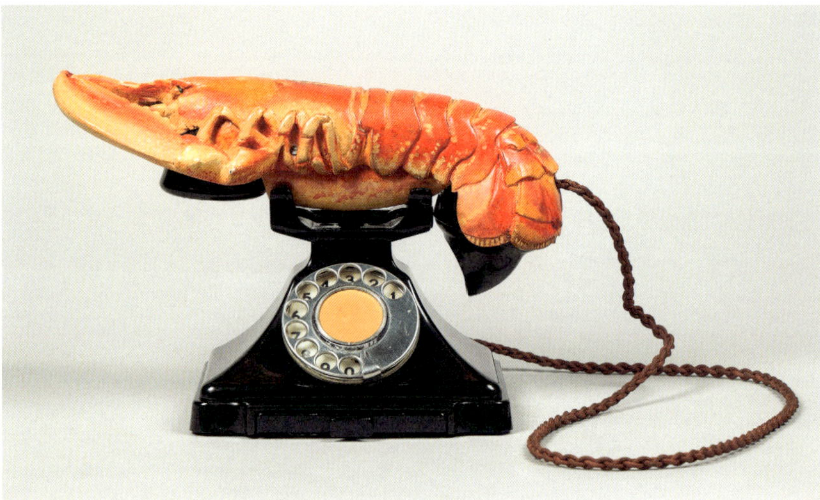

SALVADOR DALÍ, EDWARD JAMES
Lobster Telephone, 1938, steel, plaster, rubber, resin, and paper, 18 × 31 × 12.5 cm
West Dean College of Arts and Conservation

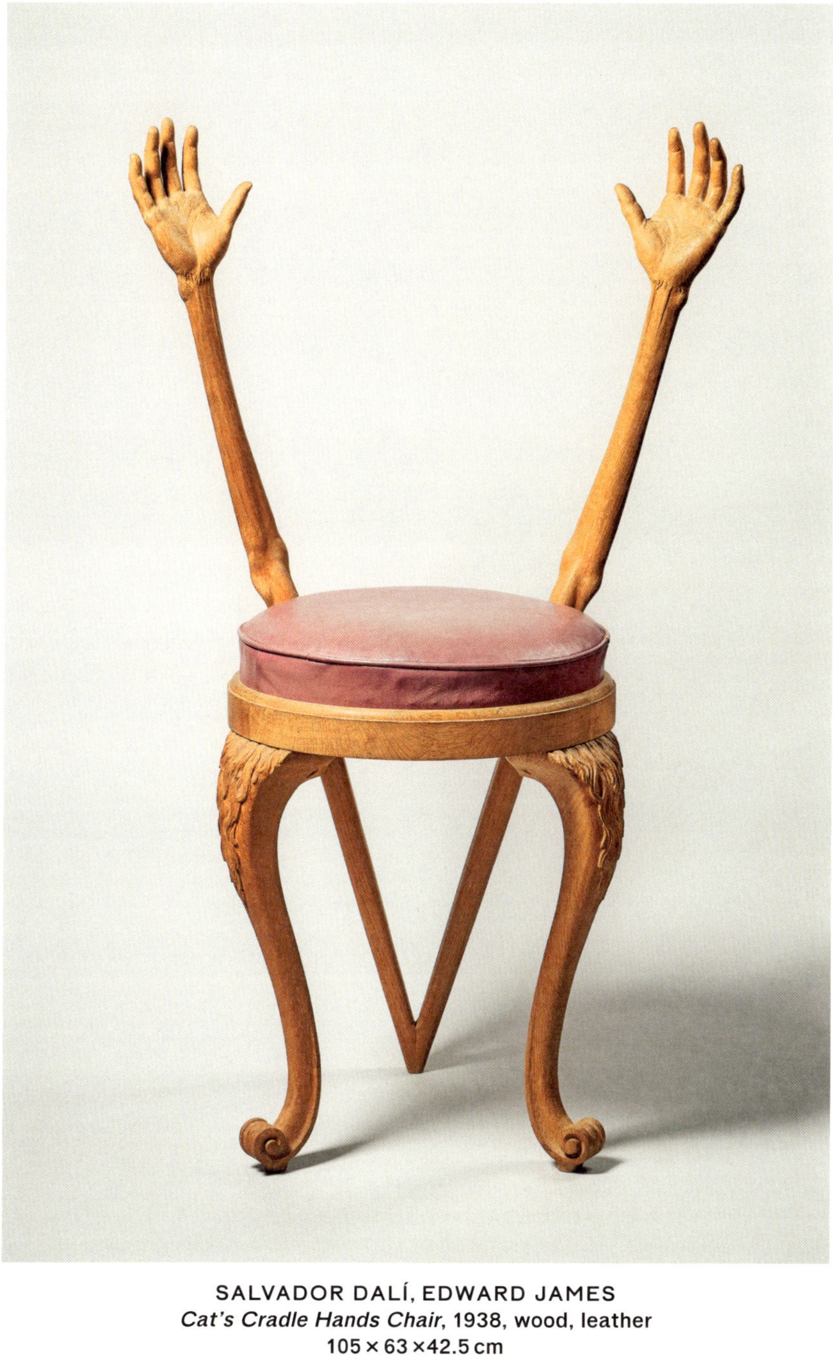

SALVADOR DALÍ, EDWARD JAMES
Cat's Cradle Hands Chair, 1938, wood, leather
105 × 63 × 42.5 cm
West Dean College of Arts and Conservation

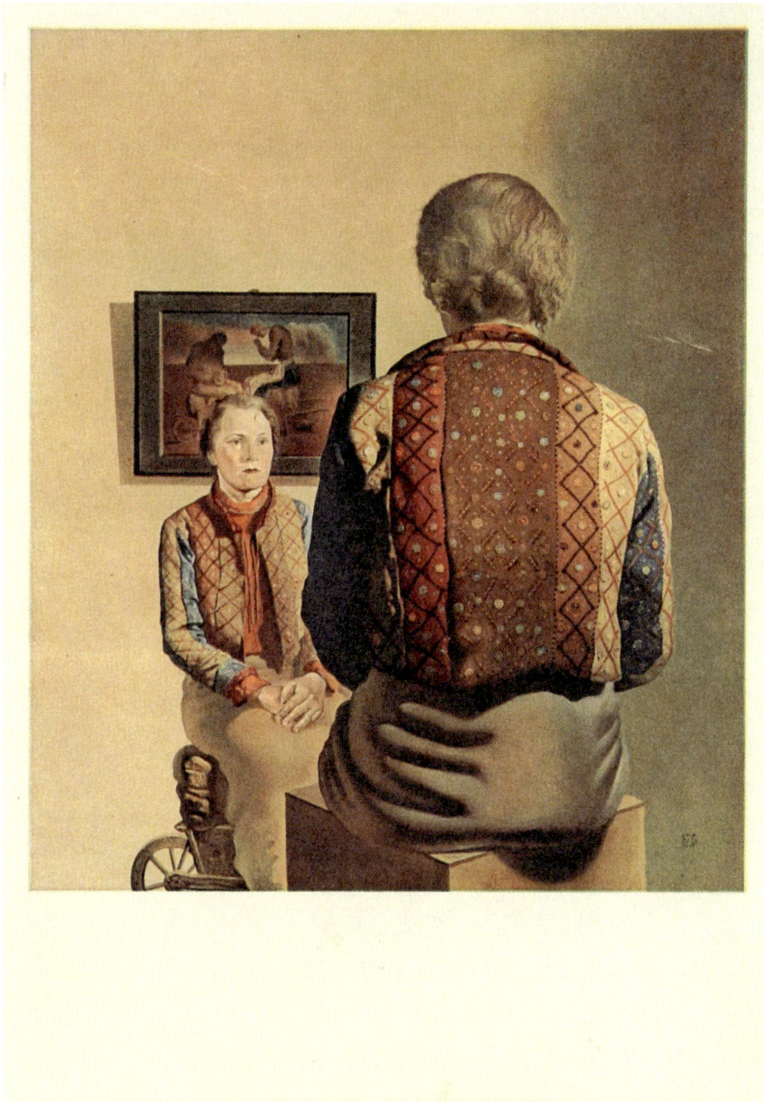

SALVADOR DALÍ, Postcard to Edward James
with a portrait of Gala Dalí, 1935
Front side, West Dean College of Arts
and Conservation

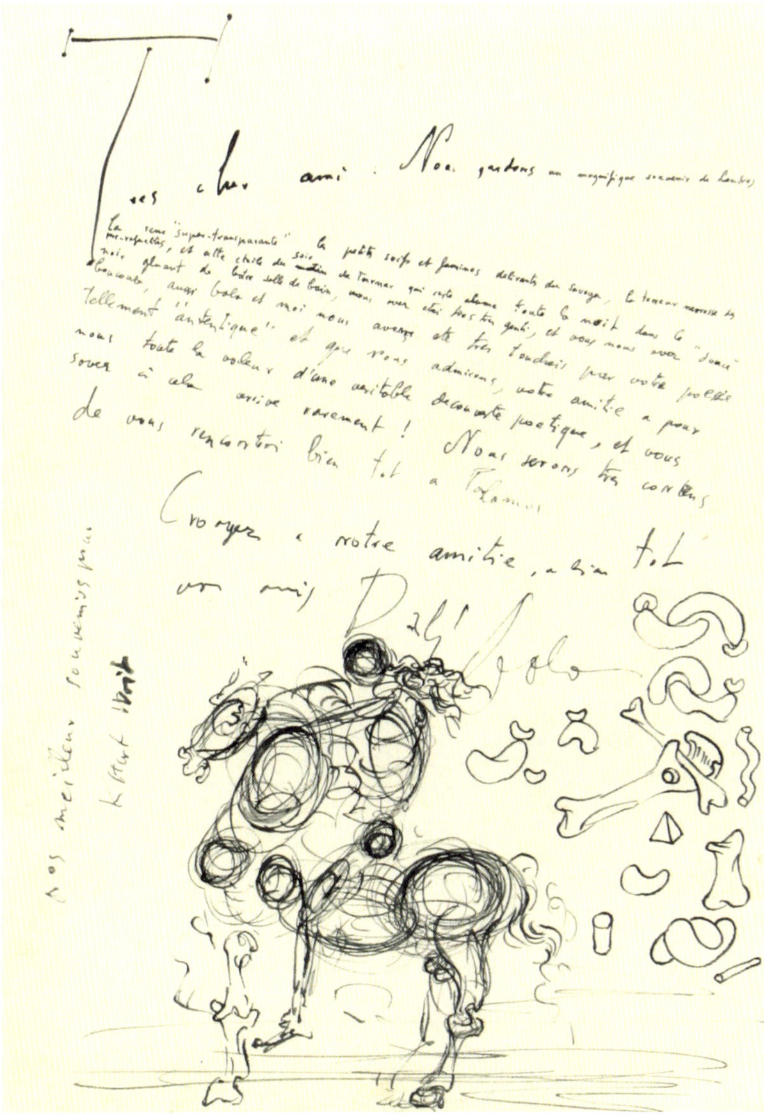

SALVADOR DALÍ, Postcard to Edward James
1935, reverse side, West Dean College of Arts
and Conservation

Several years after my last ineffectual attempt to meet Freud, I made a gastronomic excursion into the region of Sens in France. We started the dinner with snails [...] All of a sudden I saw a photograph of Professor Freud on the front page of a newspaper [...] I had just that instant discovered the morphological secret of Freud! Freud's cranium is a snail! [...] This discovery strongly influenced the portrait drawing which I later made from life, a year before his death.
— SALVADOR DALÍ, *The Secret Life of Salvador Dalí* (New York, 1993), p. 23.

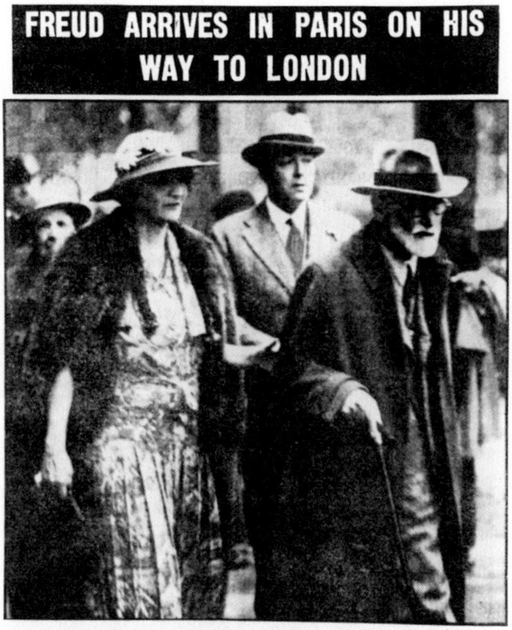

Martha Freud, Marie Bonaparte, William Bullitt, and Sigmund Freud. Arrival at Gare de l'Est, Paris, June 5, 1938

[about July 10, 1938] // Dear Professor, Salvador Dalí, the great painter, who is a fanatical admirer of your work, would like to see you and I know of nobody who could be more interesting to you. I love his work immensely, and would be happy if you could spend an hour with him. // Faithfully yours // Stefan Zweig
— STEFAN ZWEIG, translated from *Briefwechsel mit Hermann Bahr, Sigmund Freud, Rainer Maria Rilke und Arthur Schnitzler*, eds. Jeffrey B. Berlin et al. (Frankfurt am Main, 1987), p. 218.

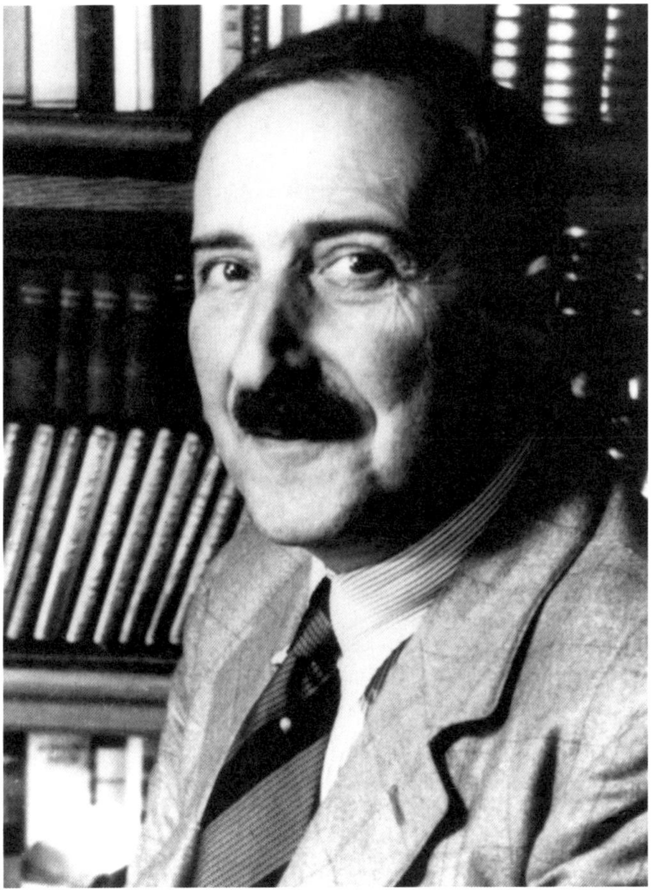

Stefan Zweig, London 1938

July 15, 1938 // Dear Professor! // My desire to see you again is intense, and now someone else is here next week who would so like to accompany me, one of your greatest admirers, who despite all his little follies, is perhaps the only genius of modern painting, Salvador Dalí, whose name and work you surely know. Unfortunately, he is here only for a few days, Monday and Tuesday, and I will take the liberty of phoning you on Monday morning, to see if we can visit you on one of these two days. […] // Your true and admiring friend // Stefan Zweig
— STEFAN ZWEIG, translated from *Briefwechsel mit Hermann Bahr, Sigmund Freud, Rainer Maria Rilke und Arthur Schnitzler*, eds. Jeffrey B. Berlin et al. (Frankfurt am Main, 1987), p. 218.

To Sigmund Freud // London, July 18, 1938. // Dear Herr Professor! // Just one more word of information. You know that I have always anxiously avoided bringing people to you, but tomorrow is truly an important exception. Salvador Dalí, in my opinion (strange as many of his works may appear), is the only painter of genius of our epoch, and the only one who will survive, a fanatic in his conviction, and the most faithful and most grateful disciple of your ideas among the artists. For years it has been the desire of this real genius to meet you. He says that he owes to you more in his art than to anybody else. And so we are coming tomorrow to see you, he and his wife. He would like to take this opportunity, during our discussion, to make a short portrait sketch of you, if possible. The real portraits he always does from memory, and from his inner Gestaltung. As a kind of legitimation, we are going to show you his last picture, in the possession of Mr. Edward James. [...] The picture is called "Narcissus" and has perhaps been created under your influence. [...] But I think that a man like yourself should once see the artist whom he has influenced like no other, and whom I have always considered a privilege to know and appreciate. [...] He is here from Paris for only two days (he is Catalan) and will not disturb our time together. I am only happy that you will once meet this perhaps greatest of your adepts. [...] The painting may surprise you at first, but I cannot imagine that it will not reveal to you the value of this artist. // Cordially and in deep admiration // Stefan Zweig // Salvador Dalí would of course have liked to show you his paintings at an exhibition here, but as we know you rarely or never go out, we are bringing this last and, as it seems to me, most beautiful opus, for you to see in your home.
— STEFAN ZWEIG, translated from *Briefwechsel mit Hermann Bahr, Sigmund Freud, Rainer Maria Rilke und Arthur Schnitzler*, eds. Jeffrey B. Berlin et al. (Frankfurt am Main, 1987), pp. 219–20.

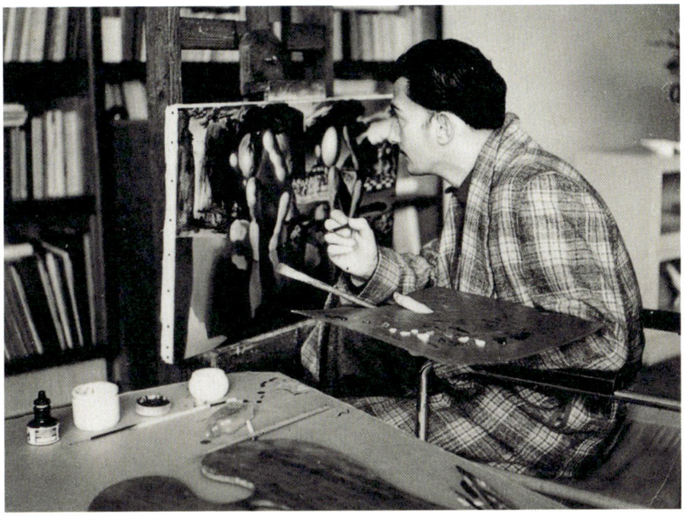

Salvador Dalí, working on his painting
The Metamorphosis of Narcissus (1937)
Fundació Gala-Salvador Dalí, Figueres

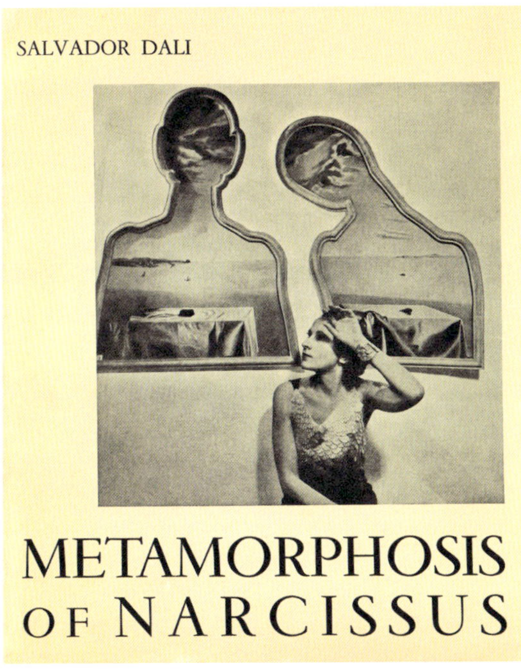

SALVADOR DALÍ, *Metamorphosis of Narcissus*
New York 1937, book cover
Fundació Gala-Salvador Dalí, Figueres

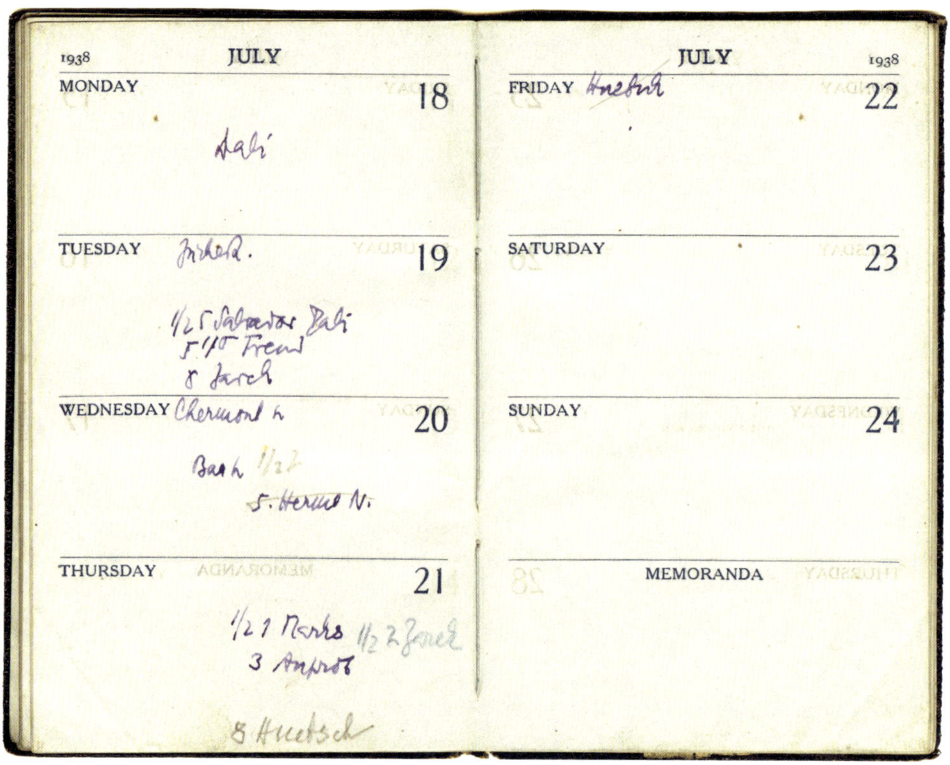

STEFAN ZWEIG, Diary, 1938
The Stefan Zweig Collection, Daniel A. Reed Library
Archives & Special Collections, State University
of New York at Fredonia

July 19, 1938 // Dear Professor, // I hope we did not disturb you for too long, but Salvador Dalí has already once traveled—in vain!—from Paris to Vienna to see you. / Edward James, the young man accompanying him, would certainly need psychoanalytical treatment. He is indecently rich by our standards and would very much like this treatment (Tilly Losch, his former wife, apparently could not cure him)—you only scared him a little by telling him it might stifle his literary work. But I think he will come to you himself one day! // All the best and in deep admiration // Your loyal friend Stefan Zweig
— STEFAN ZWEIG, translated from *Briefwechsel mit Hermann Bahr, Sigmund Freud, Rainer Maria Rilke und Arthur Schnitzler*, eds. Jeffrey B. Berlin et al. (Frankfurt am Main, 1987), pp. 219–20.

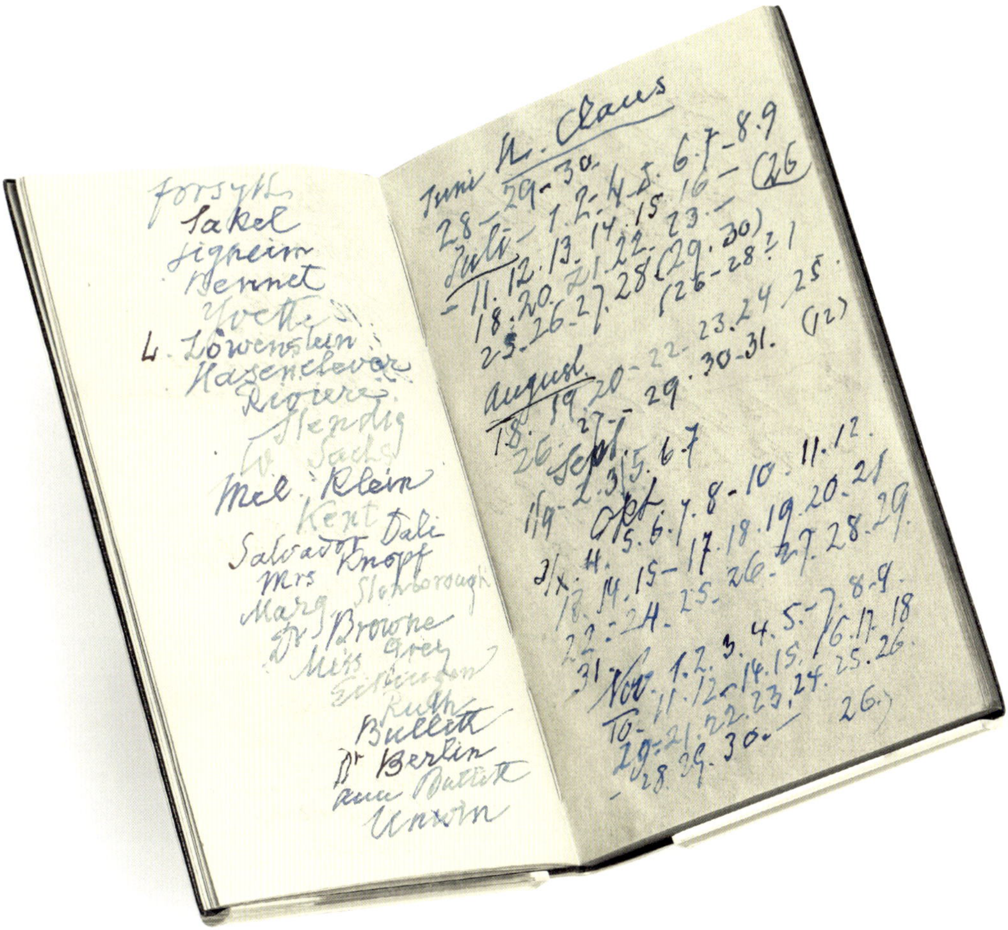

SIGMUND FREUD, Notebook with a list
of his guests, including Salvador Dalí, 1938/39
Freud Museum London

I was to meet Freud at last, in London. I was accompanied by the writer Stefan Zweig and by the poet Edward James. While I was crossing the old professor's yard I saw a bicycle leaning against the wall, and on the saddle, attached by a string, was a red rubber hot-water bottle which looked full of water, and on the back of the hot-water bottle walked a snail! The presence of that assortment seemed strange and inexplicable in the yard of Freud's house. Contrary to my hopes we spoke little, but we devoured each other with our eyes.

— SALVADOR DALÍ, *The Secret Life of Salvador Dalí* (New York, 1993), p. 24.

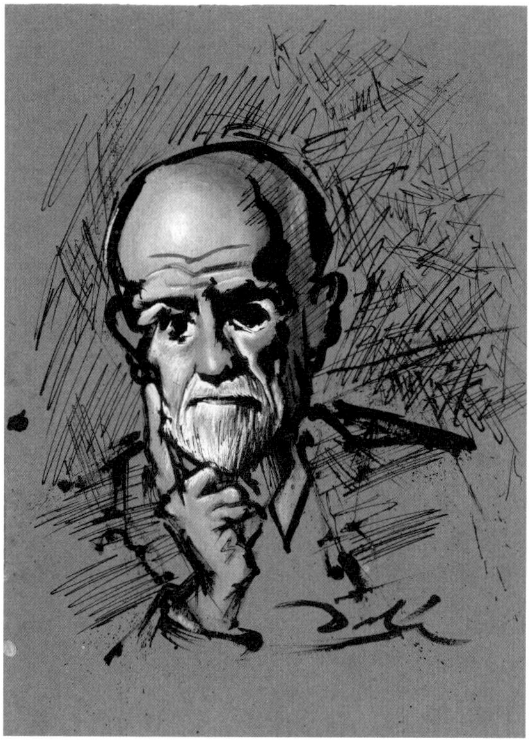

SALVADOR DALÍ, *Portrait of Sigmund Freud*, 1937, ink and gouache on paper, 35.1 × 25.5 cm
Fundació Gala-Salvador Dalí, Figueres

July 1938 // [...] / Tues 19/7 Deafness—Salvador Dalí / Sat 23/7 Dutch publishers / Tues 26/7 Martha 77 years / [...] Signed will / Thur 28/7 Completed house purchase.

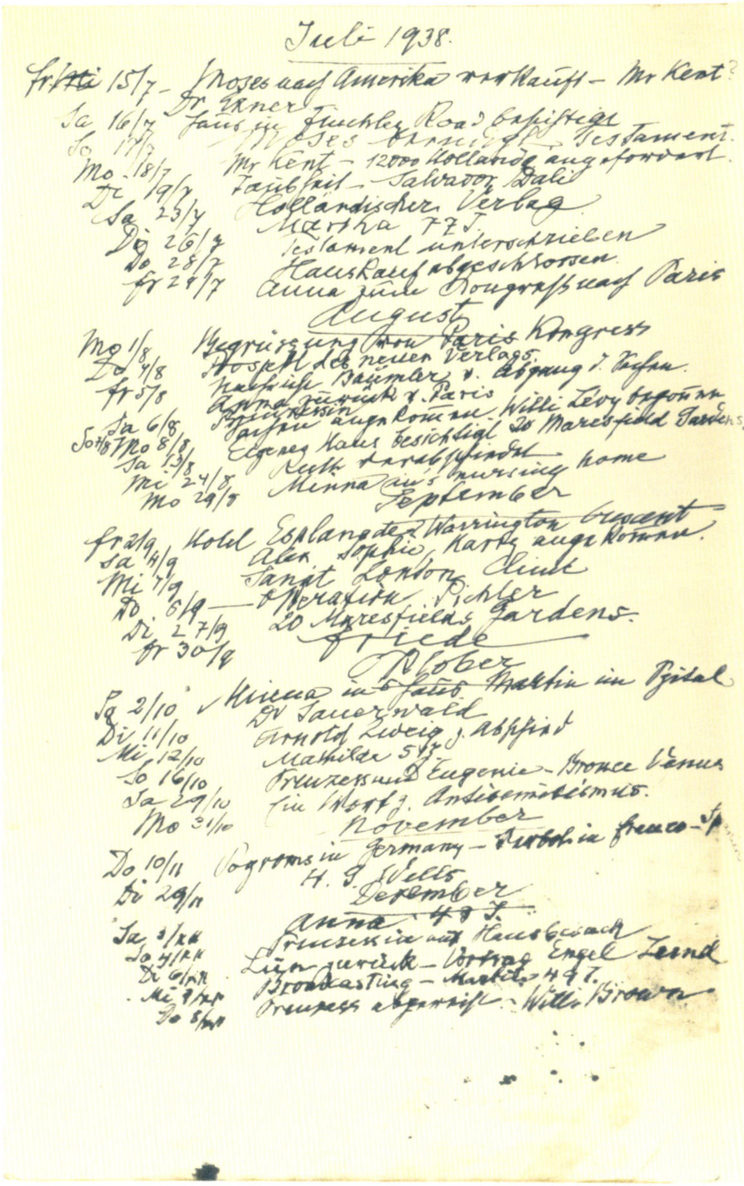

SIGMUND FREUD, diary entries in July 1938
Freud Museum London

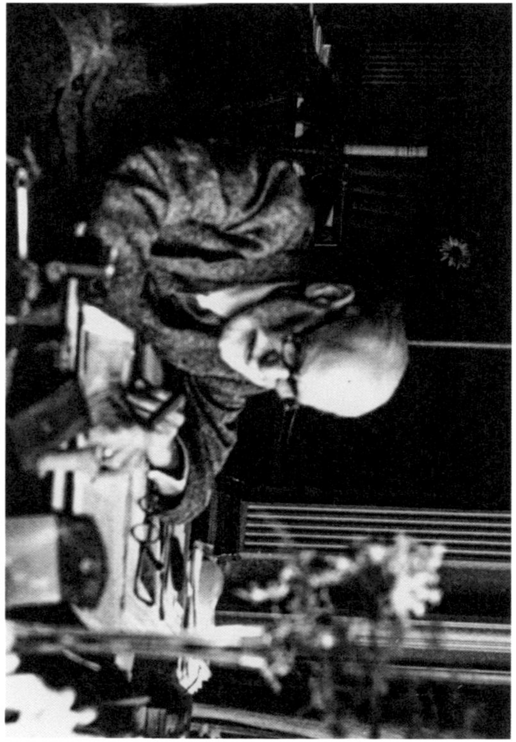

Freud knew nothing about me except my painting, which he admired, but suddenly I had the whim of trying to appear in his eyes as a kind of dandy of "universal intellectualism." I learned later that the effect I produced was exactly the opposite. Before leaving I wanted to give him a magazine containing an article I had written on paranoia. I therefore opened the magazine at the page of my text, begging him to read it if he had time. Freud continued to stare at me without paying the slightest attention to my magazine. Trying to interest him, I explained that it was not a surrealist diversion, but was really an ambitiously scientific article [...] Then, continuing to stare at me [...] Freud exclaimed, addressing Stefan Zweig, "I have never seen a more complete example of a Spaniard. What a fanatic!"
— SALVADOR DALÍ, *The Secret Life of Salvador Dalí* (New York, 1993), pp. 24–25.

The day I went to visit Sigmund Freud in his London exile, on the eve of his death, I understood [...] how many things were at last ended in Europe with the imminent end of his life. He said to me, "In classic paintings, I look for the subconscious—in a surrealist painting, for the conscious."
— SALVADOR DALÍ, *The Secret Life of Salvador Dalí* (New York, 1993), p. 397.

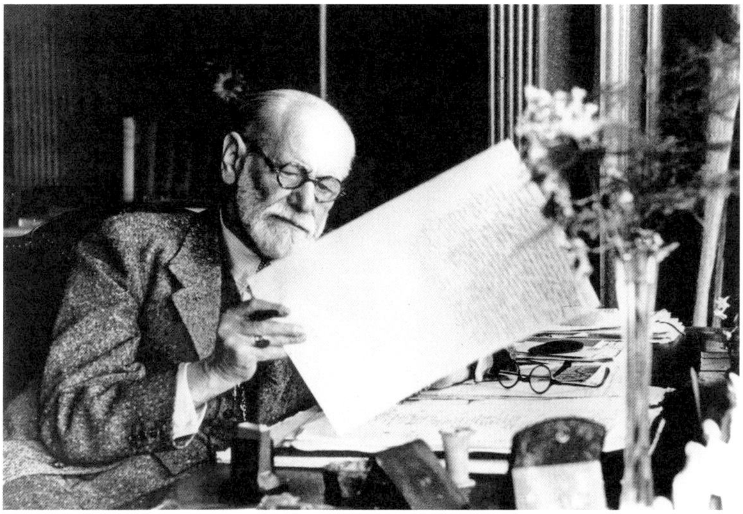

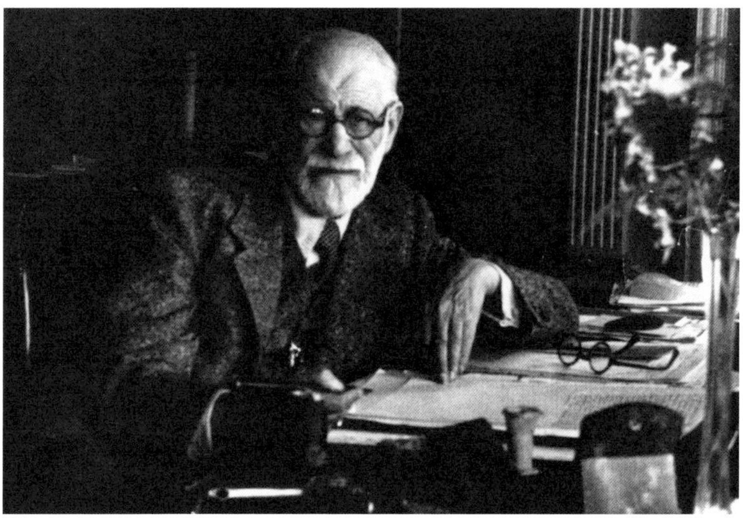

Sigmund Freud at his desk
on Elsworthy Road (Primrose Hill, London),
in the summer of 1938.
This is where the meeting between Freud
and Dalí took place.

July 20, 1938 // Dear Herr Doctor, // I really have reason to thank you for the introduction which brought me yesterday's visitors. For until then I was inclined to look upon surrealists, who have apparently chosen me for their patron saint, as absolute (let us say 95 per cent, like alcohol) cranks. The young Spaniard, however, with his candid fanatical eyes and his undeniable technical mastery, has made me reconsider my opinion. It would in fact be very interesting to investigate analytically how a picture like this came to be painted. From the critical point of view, it could still be maintained that the notion of art defies expansion as long as the quantitative proportion of unconscious material and pre-conscious treatment does not remain within definite limits. In any case, these are serious psychological problems. // As for the other visitor, I like putting obstacles in the path of a candidate in order to test the seriousness of his intention and increase his spirit of sacrifice. Psychoanalysis is like a woman who wants to be seduced but knows she will be underrated unless she offers resistance. If your Mr. J. takes too long thinking it over, he can go to someone else later on, to Jones or to my daughter. / I am told that on going away you left something behind—gloves etc. You realize that this means a promise to return. // Cordially Your Freud
— SIGMUND FREUD, quoted from *Letters of Sigmund Freud*, selected and edited by Ernst L. Freud (London, 1960), pp. 448–49.

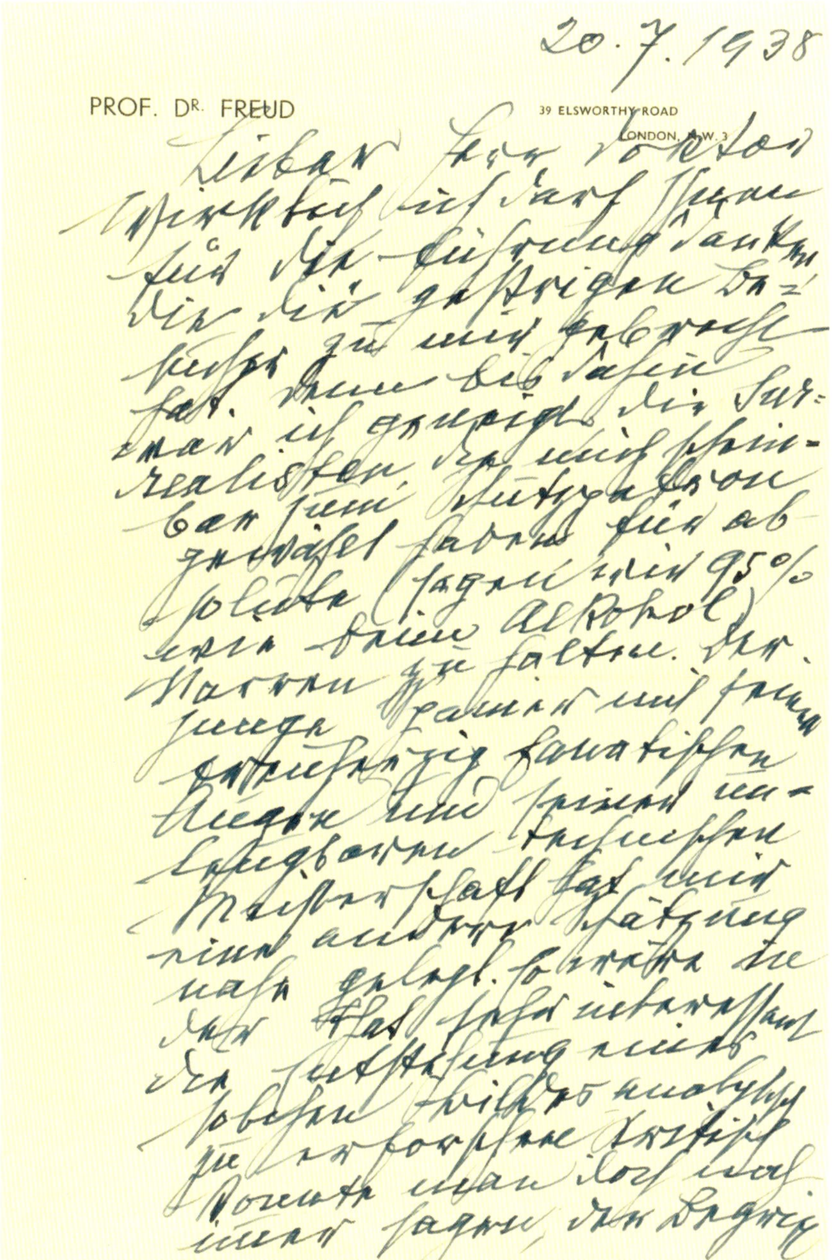

20.7.1938

PROF. DR. FREUD

39 ELSWORTHY ROAD
LONDON, N.W. 3

Lieber Herr Doktor

Wirklich ich darf Ihnen für die Anregung danken, die mir den gestrigen Besucher zu mir gebracht hat. Denn bis dahin war ich geneigt, die Surrealisten, die mich scheinbar zum Schutzpatron gewählt haben, für absolute (sagen wir 95% wie beim Alkohol) Narren zu halten. Der junge Spanier mit seinen treuherzig fanatischen Augen und seiner unleugbar technischen Meisterschaft hat mir eine andere Schätzung nahe gelegt. Es wäre in der Tat sehr interessant, die Entstehung eines solchen Bildes analytisch zu erforschen. Kritisch könnte man doch noch immer sagen, der Begriff

SIGMUND FREUD, Letter to Stefan Zweig
July 20, 1938, private collection,
Courtesy of Sotheby's, London

Dearest Christopher, // Here enclosed is a little page for you which deeply needs your help [...] // Yesterday, the afternoon after the ball, I went with Dalí to visit Dr. Freud. This was a very moving experience and a great deal more interesting than Audrey's party. But I have wasted so much time describing the former lesser incident that I have no space this evening left for the latter greater encounter. I must only add that Dr. Sigmund Freud, aged 82, is adorable. He is full of sparkle though a little baffled at moments by having newly become a bit deaf. He talked to me for a long while, during which Dalí sketched him hastily but accurately into a drawing book. Salvador was looking so inspired, his eyes were so blazing with excitement while he sketched the inventor of psycho-analysis, that the old man whispered in German to me and Stefan Zweig, who had introduced us: "That boy looks like a fanatic. Small wonder they have civil war in Spain if they look like that." // My fondest love to you both,
[EDWARD JAMES]

6.

A few mornings before Audrey had been very sly when Aunt Venetia had called on her. I had been present as she escorted round the house my aunt, of whom you know I personally am very fond; for, in order to get the darling old girl not to come, she had said or implied — by words to this effect — that, "there will be nobody but Peter's young racing friends and a lot of silly girls — I hope they will be tidy and not mess the place up for me. I really am an angel to allow my house to be used for his party!" and our Aunt Venetia had said: "Then I won't come if it is only that" and Audrey's Minor-bird from its cage had commented "Shut up!" In fact to all Aunt Venetia's comments that morning — which ranged from "How expensive your heating must be!" to "What a big lily bill you must have!" that Indian variety of parrot had snarled from its cage "Shut up!"

. . . .

Yesterday, the afternoon after the ball, I went with Dali to visit Dr. Freud. This was a very moving experience and a great deal more interesting than Audrey's party. But I have wasted so much time describing the former lesser incident that I have no space this evening left for the latter greater encounter. I must only add that Dr. Sigmund Freud, aged 82, is adorable. He is full of sparkle though a little baffled at moments by having newly become a bit deaf. He talked to me for a long while, during which Dali sketched him hastily but accurately into a drawing book. Salvador was looking so inspired, his eyes were so blazing with excitement while he sketched the inventor of psycho-analysis, that

EDWARD JAMES, Letter to Christopher Sykes
describing the meeting of Dalí and Freud (p. 6), 1938
West Dean College of Arts and Conservation

7.

the old man whispered in German to me and Stefan Zweig, who had introduced us: "That boy looks like a fanatic. Small wonder they have civil war in Spain if they look like that".

My fondest love to you both,

EDWARD JAMES, Letter to Christopher Sykes describing the meeting of Dalí and Freud (p. 7), 1938
West Dean College of Arts and Conservation

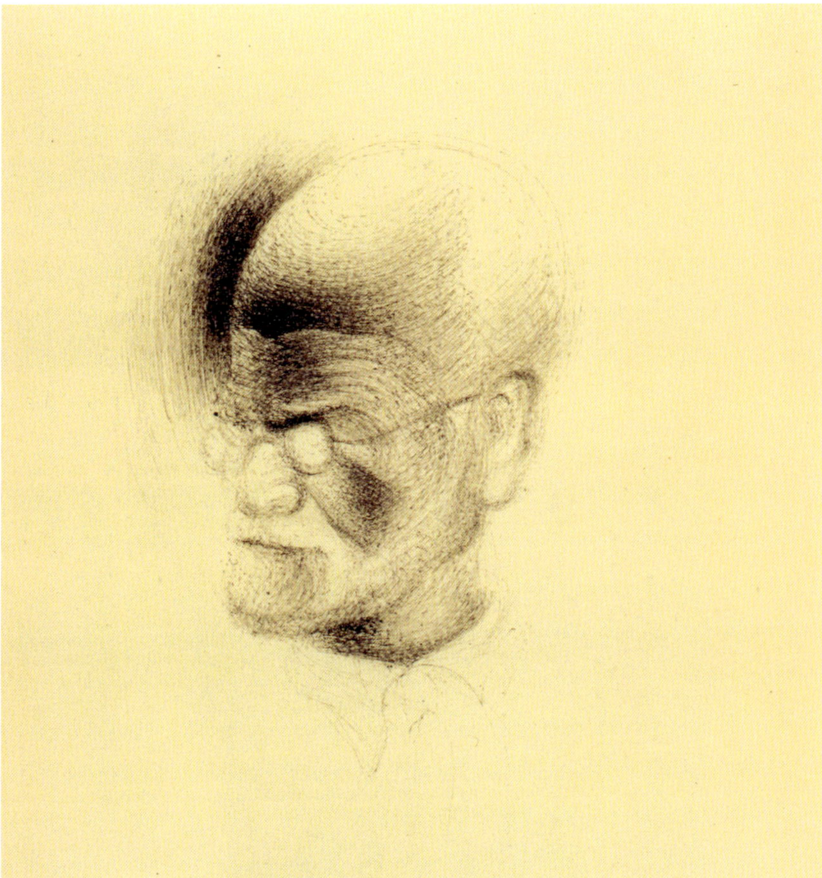

SALVADOR DALÍ, *Portrait of Sigmund Freud*
1938, ink on paper, 34.5 × 28 cm
Freud Museum London

Once, on one of my last visits to him, I took Salvador Dalí, in my view the most talented painter of the new generation, who venerated Freud. While I was talking to Freud, Dalí did a sketch of him. I never dared show it to Freud, because Dalí had prophetically shown death in his face.
— STEFAN ZWEIG, *The World of Yesterday* (London, 2009), p. 449.

ESSAYS

DALÍ – FREUD: ENCOUNTERS IN THE BACK ROOM OF CONSCIOUSNESS

Jaime Brihuega Sierra

In his early readings of Freud, Salvador Dalí found explanations for many of the fantasies, obsessions, desires, and anxieties which had pursued him since childhood. As a consequence, he started developing a system of visual symbols to translate and gain access to that inner world. His affiliation with the group of French Surrealists acted as a form of intensifier, contributing to his international fame. In 1930 he met Jacques Lacan, who was interested in an article Dalí had published in the journal *Le surréalisme au service de la révolution* and whose work inspired Dalí to develop a theory he later called the "paranoiac-critical method." Still, Dalí had already resolved to seek out the man who had furnished him with the best arguments for his imaginary world: Sigmund Freud. After several unsuccessful attempts to visit him in Vienna the meeting finally took place—brokered by Stefan Zweig and Edward James—while Freud was in exile in London.

This exhibition comprises pictures, sculptures, photographs, books, journals, letters, and other documents demonstrating the intense relationship between the oeuvre and personality of Salvador Dalí on the one hand and the writings of Sigmund Freud on the other. Although, as already mentioned, a face-to-face meeting between the two did not take place until 1938, Dalí already had access to translations of Freud's work in the early 1920s while living in the student halls in Madrid, where he had formed a close relationship with Federico García Lorca and Luis Buñuel. From 1926, connections between Dalí's work and the poetics of Surrealism become recognizable, and this is also when key elements from Freudian literature begin to shape many of the paintings that were to define Dalí's oeuvre.

PHYSIOLOGY, PSYCHOANALYSIS, AND ITS INFLUENCE ON THE FORMATION OF DALÍ'S IMAGINARY WORLD, AS REALIZED IN WORKS SUCH AS *FACE OF THE GREAT MASTURBATOR* AND *THE LUGUBRIOUS GAME*

> "At this period I had just begun to read Sigmund Freud's *Interpretation of Dreams*. This book presented itself to me as one of the capital discoveries in my life, and I was seized with a real vice of self-interpretation, not only of my dreams but of everything that happened to me, however accidental it might seem at first glance."[1]

Since Dalí's childhood, the reality that surrounded him was continuously being reconstructed in his mind. This created a parallel world, in which his fantasies, obsessions, and unfulfilled desires took form. It was also a place where the meaning of objects and forms multiplied and nestled into the deepest corners of his mind, giving rise to memories that then gradually resurfaced throughout his life and were transformed under the influence of new perceptions.[2] Thus, in the early 1920s, as he was introduced to Freud's books one by one,[3] Dalí discovered in these a guiding principle that enabled him to give expression to this internal universe he had created. From then on he was constantly engaged in a kind of mental game with distorted mirrors, whose manifestations he then captured on canvas in a visual language that gradually crystallized into a vocabulary and, eventually, a recurring code.

Particularly striking is Dalí's remarkable ability to assimilate the visual languages he encountered and make them his own. Practically from the beginning of his artistic career in the late 1910s, Dalí was responsive to movements such as Impressionism and its progeny, which ushered in a contemporary artistic renaissance. This was accompanied by a process of aesthetic and semiotic adaptation that became increasingly ambitious and complex. A development that reached its zenith in 1929, when he moved to Paris, already equipped with a firmly established visual language—a visual language that brought him international renown and is exemplified in *Face of the Great Masturbator* (1929, P 235, →fig. 12) and *The Lugubrious Game* (1929, P 232, →p. 91).[4] Many years later, already in his mature years, Dalí also made extensive use of appropriation, through which he symbolically assumed the personality of other artists.[5]

DALÍ IN THE RESIDENCIA DE ESTUDIANTES IN MADRID, 1922–26

In 1922 Dalí moved into the Residencia de Estudiantes in Madrid, where he remained until his expulsion from the Academia de Bellas Artes de San Fernando in 1926. During this period, and in the time he subsequently spent in Catalonia, before moving to Paris in 1929, Dalí's work came under the influence of various movements of the Spanish and international avant-garde, before his visual language finally consolidated in 1929.

The influence of Barradas's "Clownist" works, which had already left traces in some drawings, remained strong (→figs. 6 and 7). Similarly, his Ultraist illustrations and the general Expressionist aesthetics, as typified by the woodcuts illustrating Ultraist journals, also exerted a clear influence. In other works, new components emerged, drawing from Italian Futurism or even the paintings of Marcel Janco. In some works meanwhile, such as *Landscape of Madrid* (c. 1922, P 108, →p. 39), the key references are clearly derived from the Futurist paintings of Balla, Severini, and Russolo.[6]

1922 also heralded a change in direction from all that had gone before, giving Dalí the opportunity to advance his figurative skills. This can be seen in a series of meticulously executed still lifes, which, while referencing typical sources of the nascent Modernism, also tie in with the broad spectrum of modern poetics associated with the "Return to Order." In almost all of the aforementioned still lifes Cézanne's influence is undoubtedly most prominent (as evidenced by the pivotal role he now plays in the artistic development of Noucentisme); however, they also exhibit a certain receptiveness to the restoration of figurative mimesis (often by means of the still life genre), as already practiced by Pablo Picasso, the group surrounding the magazine *Valori Plastici* (Severini, Felice Casorati, Ardengo Soffici, Roberto Melli, Francesco Trombadori), and André Derain. In all of this one must not forget the transcendental neofigurative preamble laid down by the influential work of Giorgio de Chirico and the cardboard sculptures developed by Barradas in summer 1922.

1923 was a year of transition for Dalí. The majority of elements from contemporary visual art had already been integrated in his work. Thenceforth, however, he would be using these in a much more conscious, controlled way than in previous years, which had been characterized, above all, by the bedazzlement of the neophyte.

The connection that had developed, especially after 1923, between the works of Salvador Dalí and those of Josep de Togores, Joaquim Sunyer, and other representatives of what is often referred to as "Noucentist Mediterraneanism"[7] has been pointed out repeatedly. It must be emphasized, however, that this connection was cultivated entirely deliberately by Dalí, and that a surprising fusion was occurring between visual aspects of the ongoing Catalan project of promoting a national artistic identity and several new directions in international Modernism. In all of these paintings, Cézanne's presence is channeled, invariably, through a hybridization with the works of Joaquim Sunyer from the early 1910s. Consequently, a fruitful relationship emerged, linking Dalí's works and those created by Togores

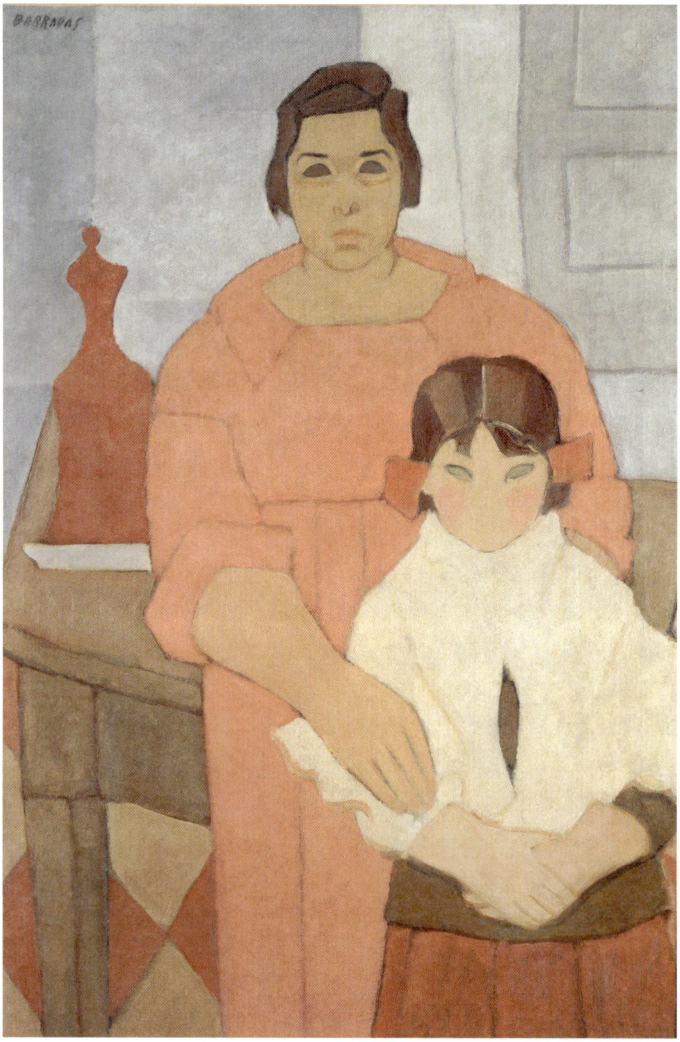

fig. 6
RAFAEL BARRADAS, *Pilar y Antoñita*
(*Pilar an Antoñita*), c. 1922
Museo Nacional Centro de Arte Reina Sofía,
Madrid

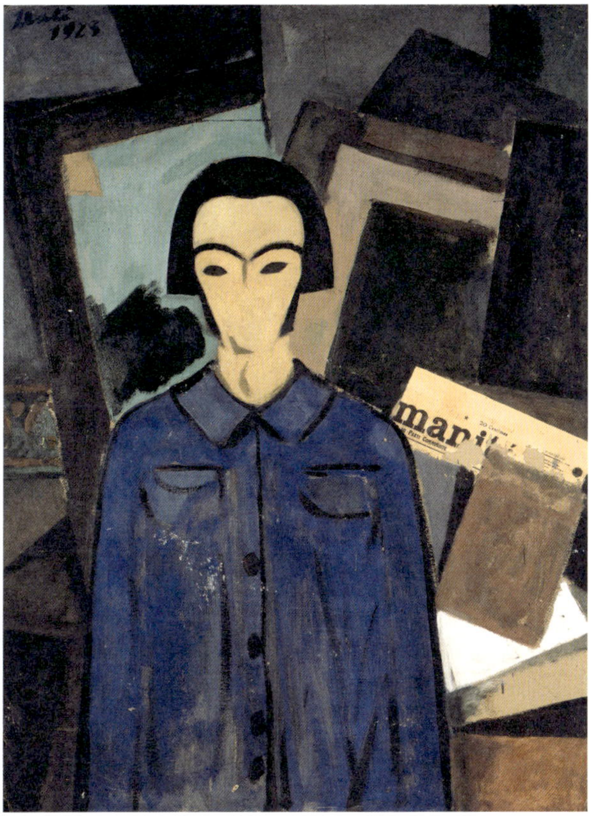

fig. 7
SALVADOR DALÍ, *Self-Portrait with "L'Humanité"*
1923, Figueres Town Hall, on permanent loan
at the Fundació Gala-Salvador Dalí, Figueres
Cat. no. P 113

between 1916 and the early 1920s. Successively we discover, in line with the logic of "concentric spheres of influence," that Dalí also drew on several early works by Joan Miró[8] and other Noucentist artists.

Dalí, fully aware of this cyclical formal ambivalence, thus embarked on—or even instrumentalized—a double game that would stay with him throughout his life. A pirouette with which to navigate the pitfalls of the tricky dialogue between timeless Catalan identity and modern cosmopolitanism. An—at times strategically opportunistic, at others ironically provocative—double game that was, in fact, an—at times strategically opportunistic, at others ironically provocative—strategy, but at times also unavoidable for him in a schizophrenic way.

Thus far, we have explored the oeuvre of the young Dalí by maintaining a literal interpretation of the metaphorical "alloying" of outside influences, behind whose apparent external coherence the origins of their components are easy to identify, since the majority of their original attributes remain essentially unchanged—and this transparency is intended by the painter. Once we consider his works created after 1924, however, the situation changes fundamentally. Although Dalí sustained this dynamic of intermixture and hybridization for a further five years, his artistic results underwent a form of "transmigration" in terms of their creative components. A metamorphosis that liberated the forms from their original semiotic roots and altered their meaning, which now was no longer a simple semantic accessory to their primary components. This opened up unexpected and unusual perspectives for the reception of such works in the artistic imagination of the era.

It can generally be said that, at this point in the genesis of art on the Iberian peninsula, artistic reception and acceptance, not just in the case of Dalí, but also of cultural centers such as Madrid, was no longer just a landing strip for the latest trends in international Modernism. By the end of the first quarter of the twentieth century, aesthetic reception—which in the Spanish capital had hitherto been purely passive (in contrast to Catalonia, which at the time was in uproar due to Noucentism)—gradually underwent a transformation owing to an increasingly active hermeneutic interpretation, as a result of which successive perspectives of renewal achieved relative autonomy from their sources. Thus the new contributions that were gradually assimilated from the outside influenced a landscape increasingly thought capable of "bringing in its own harvest." One only has to read texts written by the most progressive (and, above all, "most well-informed") voices in art criticism of the time to assess the plausibility of such claims.

His sister, his father, friends, again and again Federico García Lorca, familiar landscapes, dreams, obsessions, memories, neurotic visions… and many other elements emerging from Dalí's subjective imagination and personal life story were now constantly merging with the objective narratives of his paintings. Thus began the impassioned promiscuity between subject and object so typical of Dalí's poetics. Here we touch upon another crucial aspect in understanding the "new" Dalí, an artist who hereafter proved himself to be "master" of his own artistic development.

In 1924 and 1925 Dalí's visual language oscillated between diverse registers, which can be roughly divided into two groups:

A. Works that can be explicitly categorized as "novel figurative representations." The various manifestations constituting this group basically include the extensive domain of the "Return to Order" and "Neoclassicisms" that crystallized in Paris and other international centers, the Italian aesthetics of Pittura Metafisica and the group forming around *Valori Plastici*, and the new wave of German figurative painting, which subsequently spawned Magical Realism and New Objectivity. Also in evidence within these "novel figurative representations," is the influence of the Neoclassical Picasso.

B. The second group, in direct succession to Cubism, comprises a number of works that can be subdivided into those connected to the cubo-metaphysical aesthetics of *Valori Plastici* and those following the Purist model, as represented by *L'esprit nouveau*. Occasionally, works in this group belong to both movements. Here, too, art historians have already recognized the key forerunners in Picasso, Gris,

Amédée Ozenfant, Charles-Édouard Jeanneret, Morandi, and others. To these names others can be added, such as Soffici, de Chirico, and Carrà.

THE FLOURISHING OF 1926

From 1926, a number of new possibilities open up in Dalí's painting. *Depart. "Homage to Fox Newsreel"* (1926, P 154, → fig. 8), a work Dalí showed to Picasso in April 1926 during his brief visit to Paris, comprises a veritable compendium of the "receptive – prospective" tension accumulating in this moment of transition. Within the iconographic figure of a prostitute with a sailor splayed across her abdomen—a reference to the Byzantine *Theotokos* (god-bearer)—this picture combines Neoclassical elements from Picasso's art with influences from the seascapes of Severini, with toys and perforated angles (or anamorphic metaphors) from Giorgio de Chirico, and the disconcerting restlessness of the ice-cold, mathematically structured figurations of several artists from the group around *Valori Plastici.* Despite all of this, already present in the bottom right of the painting, as noted by Rafael Santos Torroella some time ago, is the prophetic, monolithic twinned crystal of cylinders and inverted, perforated pyramids that was to take center stage in some of 1927's most significant works of Dalinian Surrealism.

Similar elements and visual "premonitions" are also present in profusion in the exceptional *Composition with Three Figures. "Neo-cubist Academy"* (1926, P 171, → p. 43), which Santos Torroella also considered emblematic for this year of transition, and in which themes like the decapitated head and the lip-shaped clouds already emerge—as does the penis flute and the fish with its phallic connotations. It marks a moment in Dalí's development that he described in a letter as follows: "Now it is a return to the living, as opposed to the mechanical, and an acceptance of instinct and the most penetrating lyricism, always conditioned by intelligence and calculation."[9]

There are works from this period which, without abandoning figuration, already depart in other directions,

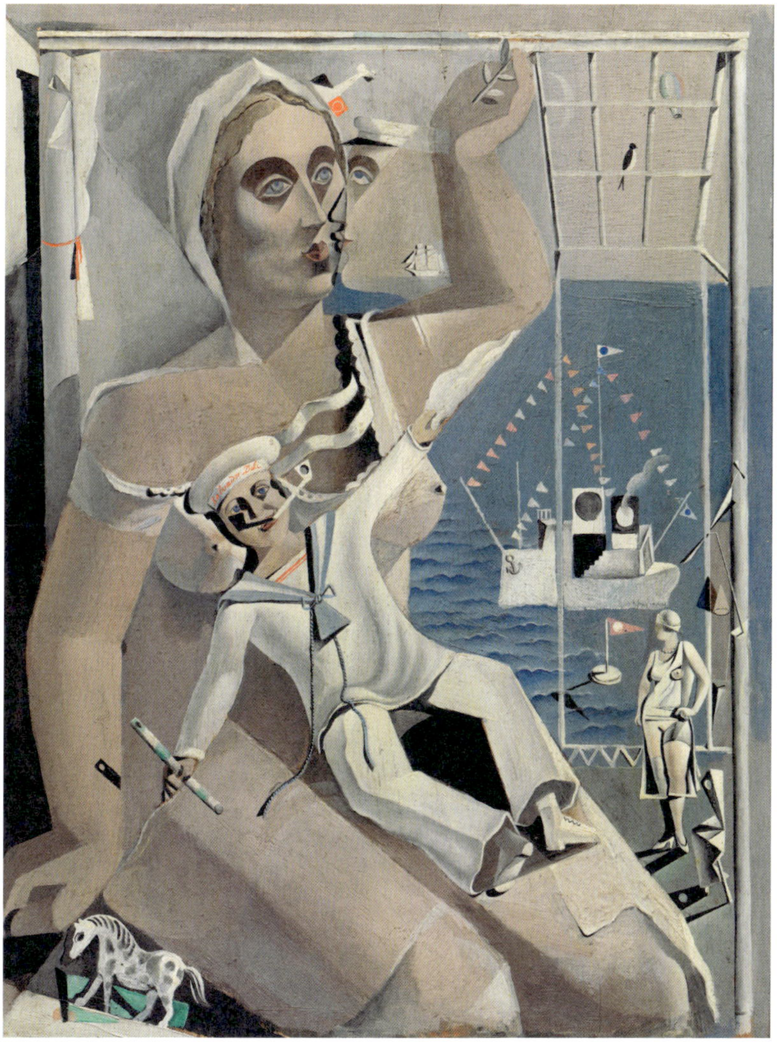

fig. 8
SALVADOR DALÍ, *Depart. "Homenatge al Noticiari Fox"* (*Depart. "Homage to Fox Newsreel"*)
1926, private collection, cat. no. P 154

signaling with absolute precision the adoption of Picasso's highly geometric Neoclassicism. However, they also foreshadow bathing in the sea as a scenario of erotic fantasy.

Dalí was very aware of the developments in Picasso's painting. Alongside the diverse variations of his Neoclassical figuration, up until 1925, Picasso had retained a monumental Cubism rich with connotations as the underlying principle of his pictorial universe. Perhaps it was for this very reason that, from 1926, Dalí established a new register, which he ascribed to the general framework of this second direction. I am referring to the large Cubist-inspired compositions painted by Picasso between 1921 and 1925; works that to some extent arose from his experience as a set designer, which gifted him his "decorative" approach to real space, but were also the result of a certain reconnection with a Matisse-style Mediterranean sensibility.

However, to fully understand 1926 as a genuine prelude to Dalí's Surrealism, it is sufficient to consider several drawings from this time, which serve as links between the illustrations for the book *Libro de los putrefactos* from the year 1925 and the distinctly Surrealist drawings of 1927. In these drawings, the influence of Miró, Yves Tanguy, and even of several neurological illustrations by Santiago Ramón y Cajal is easy to identify.[10]

CAJAL, LORCA, DALÍ, TANGUY

> "Because we are so happy, today we will go to the beach, bursting the most painful fibers of our physiology and lacerating the weakest pulse of our membranes, while the surface is inflamed by small apparatuses and sharp corals. If we contract the nerves and press our fingertips onto our pupils, we will feel the veins explode in guttural joy and our blood pressure soar under a thousand noises with each new injury [...]."[11]

The critical point in this moment of transition to a thoroughly Surrealist focus—in addition to the significant influence of psychology and Freudian psychoanalysis—

is the spectacle of visual physiology revealed to Dalí in the drawings of Santiago Ramón y Cajal. This became the second pillar upon which this new poetic course could be developed.

Let me describe this complex, well-documented situation with the help of a fictitious story:[12]

AN APOCRYPHAL STORY: DALÍ AND LORCA'S PERAMBULATIONS OF THE MAPS OF BODY AND SOUL

One eye to the microscope and the other on the paper, his mind absorbed in the endeavor of maintaining a strict yet simultaneously expressive correspondence between what is seen and what is drawn—for what is drawn must serve to picture what has been seen. It is thus that Cajal traveled across the landscapes of the nerve tissue, mapping it. He took a path already trodden by other scientists since the mid-nineteenth century, who had likewise sketched landscapes of thought, and he followed this path to its end.[13]

Once Cajal's drawings had been printed and published they were presented to a scientific audience; this was a few decades before the end of the nineteenth century, the same century in which Goya, Füssli, Blake, Friedrich, Turner, Moreau, Redon, and others had also dreamed in their own way of venturing into the impenetrable landscapes of the soul.

When, in 1906, Cajal was awarded the Nobel Prize, this mapping of the tissues as representations of the landscapes of the soul extended beyond the purely scientific, advancing into regions of the collective imagination frequented by far larger cultural circles. Thus, a number of artists and their imaginary worlds were also inspired by these drawings.

To see and touch the corporeality of the soul up close; to have at your disposal maps that enable you to travel through the landscapes of your innermost thoughts—a chimera as old as the world itself. A chimera, which the artists who had joined the ranks of Surrealism in one form or another adopted as their primary objective. Not even the question—ultimately proving to be pivotal—about the feasibility of a Surrealist visual language with which to navigate the back rooms of consciousness like on a ship of boundless freedom, could suppress the uncontrollable desire for such a journey.

Psychic automatism: this seemed to be the most successful method. Enabling the deepest waters of human consciousness to flow from words and lines emanating from an involuntary stream. This seemed to be the shortest route to penetrating the soul, and it was also the route that Masson and Tanguy embarked upon before anyone else. And, although they realized to some degree that pure psychic automatism was an unattainable utopia, they at least let their hands be guided by inspiration (in the romantic sense).

Yet, at the same time, it was inevitable that these hands would also work through the concepts that had been accumulated in the individual and collective consciousness. Thus, within this imaginary world, they found themselves—intentionally or not—back before the credible image that histology had produced of the organs of thought. They stumbled upon a palpable anatomy of the soul, in which, surely, its most intimate secrets must be inscribed. Perhaps it was in this simple fashion, that is, through the obvious association of ideas, that the first traces of this formal analogy between automatic drawing and the histological illustrations of the nervous system emerged. Of all these illustrations, those by Cajal had already gained worldwide fame.

When, after 1926, Lorca and Dalí, equipped with Freud's writings, eclipsed the ironic frivolity of *Los putrefactos*[14] and set out to sate the deep and uncontrollable desire instilled in them by their visits to the literary and artistic places that Surrealism had spawned, all the pieces of the puzzle now lay scattered on the table before them. On the one hand, the dazzling radiance of Cajal and his drawings, only meters away from their rooms in the student halls, a radiance that was consistently reaffirmed by the systematic work of the histological team of Pio del Río Hortega. On the other hand, the drawings of Tanguy and Masson, which they encountered in French books and publications.[15] And, furthermore, the occasional realization that Max Ernst had already explored the human anatomy in the early days of Surrealist sculpture.

Thus it happened that some molecules in Dalí's drawings emerged almost spontaneously. Neurites, axons, hairy strands, mucosal folds, capillary networks, numbers, arrows, fibrous rivulets, cellular metaphors, chromosome shapes… An entire pictorial lexicon, evolving alongside the other elements that were driving the transformation of his visual poetics at this time.[16] Similar visual clues can be observed in Dalí's work until 1929, while in Lorca's work they appeared with particular intensity until 1928, and more sporadically until 1936.

Once this "Hypnerotomachia anatómica" had begun to flourish, it became a prominent force (in a lead or supporting role) in the visual vocabulary of Spanish and international Surrealism. And for those engaged in the exploration of the labyrinth of dreams, or the chimera of gesture that is freed from the constraints of logic, it always remained present.

The moral of this fictional story is that, curiously, Cajal became the inadvertent creator of a formal correspondence (which later morphed into a very specific harmony), connecting, by virtue of various mechanisms for transmitting forms, Tanguy, Masson, (occasionally) Miró, Lorca, Dalí, and several other Spanish artists, such as Nicolás de Lekuona or the young Manuel Viola.

Cajal's drawings were very well-known at the time, having been published in numerous books and illustrated articles in scientific journals. The most widely published was the book *Textura del sistema nervioso del hombre y de los vertebrados* (*Texture of the Nervous System of Man and Vertebrates*; Madrid, 1897–1904), an extended edition with almost five hundred illustrations, which had been translated into French in 1911. Undoubtedly, both Lorca and Dalí (who, along with other students of various disciplines living at the Residencia de Estudiantes in Madrid, were right next to the laboratory of Pío del Río Hortega) had access to these publications and would have met Cajal in 1926 at the Residencia de Estudiantes.

Careful examination of the corpus of Cajal's histological drawings reveals the surprising intensity of his influence, not just on fragments of many of Dalí and Lorca's drawings, but also on some of their compositional approaches. By way of confirmation of this—to give just one overwhelmingly compelling example—one might note that both the morphological elements and the composition of such an emblematic drawing as *Homage to Góngora* (→p. 63)[17] can be related with astonishing precision to *Sección del bulbo a la altura del núcleo facial de un ratón* (*Cross section of the bulb of a mouse at the level of the facial nerve*, →p. 62), a drawing produced by Cajal at around 1895. The same can also be said of Dalí's drawing *Decapitation of the Innocents* (→p. 61),[18] which in a way picks up on another drawing by Cajal: *Corte horizontal del centro cerebroide de la sepia* (*Horizontal section through the midbrain of a cuttlefish*; c. 1917, →p. 60).

All of this demonstrates that, in its beginnings, the Surrealist pictorial language of Dalí and Lorca, which is synonymous with the very root of Spanish Surrealism, went hand in hand with psychiatry and physiology.

THE EMERGENCE OF DALINIAN SURREALISM, 1927–29

Even so, 1927 was the year in which Salvador Dalí's Surrealist painting fully blossomed. This flowering continued—in intensified form and in diverse articulations—throughout 1928. Eventually, by 1929, his Surrealism embraced the dominant direction of a pictorial language, as expressed most coherently and explicitly in works like *Face of the Great Masturbator* (1929, P 235, →fig. 12) or *The Lugubrious Game* (1929, P 232, →p. 91), which represent the paradigm of Dalí's painterly identity. As this moment of "linguistic normalization" occurs, one can clearly see how, in the years 1927 and 1928, different formal orientations exist alongside one another to a relevant degree. In these, a broad spectrum of artistic references is expressed, along with the palpable polyphony of poetic attributions that accompanies such diversity.[19]

The formal focal points of Dalí's Surrealism during its early years of 1927 and 1928 can once again be illustrated—in a highly simplified way—through a number of significant work groups. Groups that within themselves are continuously linked to one another via numerous cross references.

A. The most obvious attempts at "automatic drawing," as practiced by international Surrealism for several years. Belonging to a parallel register—yet already comprising more "controlled" pictorial elements strongly reminiscent of Miró and Tanguy—are the drawings that illustrate Spanish avant-garde magazines.

B. Works belonging to the collected experiments, which in 1927 and 1928 formed the essential core of what would later become the "mature" pictorial language of 1929. These include *Honey is Sweeter than Blood* (1927, P194, →p.83), an old photo of which is on display in the exhibition,[20] *Apparatus and Hand* (1927, P195, →fig. 9), *Futile Efforts* (1927–28, P199), *Inaugural Gooseflesh* (1928, P221), *Female Nude* (1928, P202), *Bathers* (1928, P203), *Woman-Animal Symbiosis* (1928, P226), and *Two Figures on a Beach. Unsatisfied Desires* (1928, P204). The latter four represent a subgroup in which the technique of assemblage, borrowed from the rich tradition of historical avant-garde, plays a key role.

Within a figurative space designed according to the principles of Renaissance perspective, the aforementioned works already bring together the elements constituting the essence of Dalí's Surrealist imagination. De Chirico and Tanguy undoubtedly form the backbone for this perspective, with its relentless horizons and opaque-blue skies, but so, too, does Miró's work from the first half of the 1920s; not forgetting the Flemish artists from the fifteenth century, Mantegna, Bosch, Patinir, or, more generally, the collection

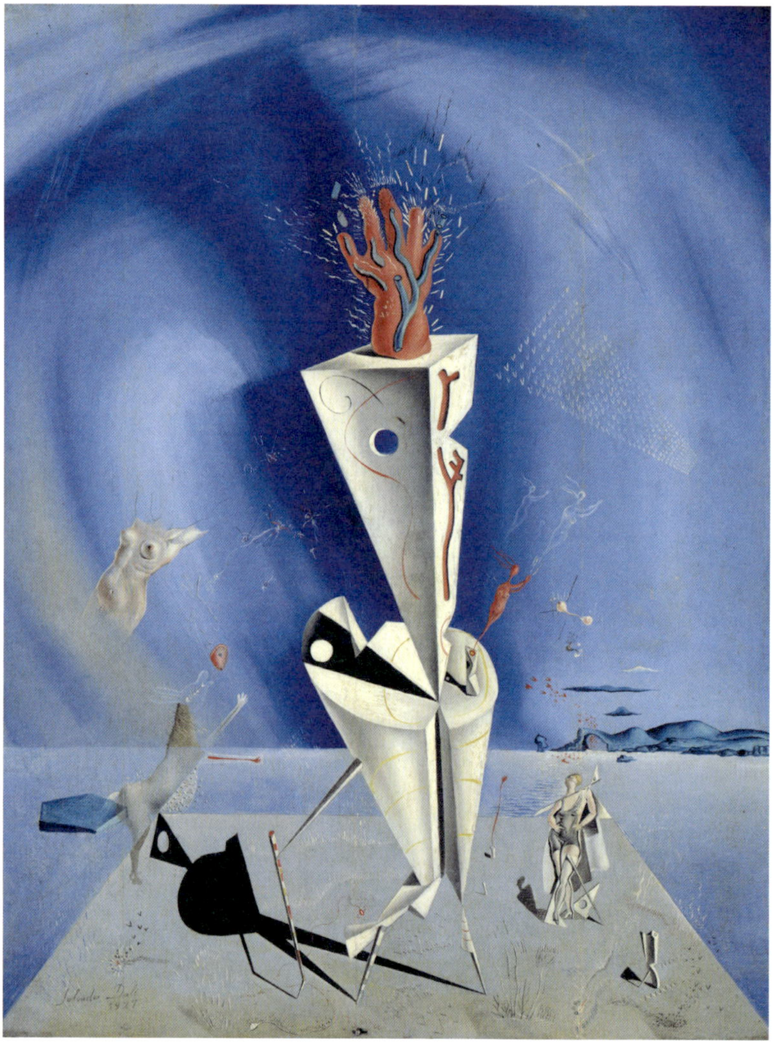

fig. 9
SALVADOR DALÍ, *Aparell i mà*
(*Apparatus and Hand*), 1927
The Dalí Museum, Saint Petersburg (Florida)
Cat. no. P 195

of Mannerist paintings, which, being on display at the Museo del Prado, were easily recalled.

Those rooms contain the broad repertoire of elements whose meanings are generally the subject of countless studies on the Dalinian universe. Yet, rather than focusing on the retrospective and prospective semantics of such an imaginary world, we should instead sketch out their respective pictorial genealogies: from 1926 onward, we increasingly encounter those geometrical monoliths (the precursors of which can be found in the works of de Chirico, Carrà, Picasso, Léger, Picabia, Duchamp, and Ernst); mutilated human bodies, severed hands and heads (originating from Ernst, de Chirico, Picasso, Man Ray, Magritte, and—surprisingly—Julio Romero de Torres, among others); phallic elements (including onanistic fingers) or anovaginal ones (Masson, Miró, Ernst, Tanguy, and others, including Julio Romero de Torres); venous systems, the circulatory system, and dendritic configurations (Tanguy, Masson, Ernst, Magritte, Cajal, and others); decomposed elements or those transforming through decay (for the most part copied from Max Ernst); pointed elements, nailed into the ground or into flesh (also originating from Max Ernst); various types of abstract elements (the references here are innumerable, extending as far as Wassily Kandinsky and Paul Klee); and, finally, a considerable number of biomorphic elements, some more, some less figurative, which are, in fact, none other than the foundations for his well-known soft forms (already partly showing in the "clouds—lips—viscous fluids—breads" of 1926. These soft forms, which Dalí himself once compared to a camembert, have their direct origin in Picasso, Arp, Tanguy, Constantin Brancusi, Ernst, Masson, Miró ...).

C. Although representing an isolated episode that was only reactivated in fragments in his later oeuvre, a series of works appeared in 1928 depicting the figure of a decomposed, spectral, or metamorphic animal, not merely as part of a perspective scenario, but as an essential semantic or formal symbol. The poetic-visual core of this group, consisting partly of fragments from earlier groups of works (with which they are naturally connected), is expressed in paintings such as *The Wounded Bird* (1928, P 219), *Bird...Fish* (c. 1928, P 218), *Thumb, Beach, Moon and Decaying Bird* (1928, P 220), *Bird* (c. 1928, P 222), *Rotting Bird* (c. 1928, P 201), *The Spectral Cow* (1928, P 223), and *The Stinking Ass* (1928, P 225, → fig. 10).

D. Another direction, both beginning and ending in 1928, is also represented by a group of works that is directly influenced by the biomorphic abstractions of Arp and Miró. I am referring here to paintings such as *Anthropomorphic Beach (present state)* (1928, P 209), *Female Nude* (1928, P 206), *Fishermen in the Sun* (1928, P 214), *Abstract Composition* (c. 1928, P 213), *Fishermen's Wives in Cadaqués* (1928, P 216, → fig. 11), *Four Fishermen's Wives in Cadaqués* (c. 1928, P 216), and *Female Figure and Male Figure on a Beach* (1928, P 215). This group comprises works in the anti-art spirit of Dadaism, but which also have strong links with the formal and semantic background of the other groups.

A CRUCIAL TURNING POINT IN DALÍ'S WORK, 1929

This brings us to the year 1929. For Salvador Dalí this was a year of transition between Catalonia and Paris, where he lived from April.[21] It was also the crucial year of the start of his relationship with Gala Éluard, whom he met in Figueres that summer and who would become his lifelong muse and lover, embracing him like a womb, offering sanctuary from his primal anxieties. This was therefore also the moment when Dalí's pictorial language found maturity, when his universe finally consolidated, culminating in ten works that brought their creator international fame. These ten paintings, all of which are entered in the catalogue raisonné of the Fundació Gala-Salvador Dalí under the year 1929, are: *Face of the Great Masturbator* (1929, P 235), *Portrait of Paul Éluard* (1929, P 233), *The Enigma of Desire or Ma mère, ma mère, ma mère* (1929, P 238), *The Invisible Man* (1929–32, P 237, → fig. 62), *Accommodations of Desire* (1929, P 239), *A Man of Unhealthy Complexion Listening to the Sound of the Sea* (1929, P 240), *Illuminated Pleasures* (1929, P 241, → fig. 20),

The First Days of Spring (1929, P 242), *The Memory of the Woman-Child* (1929, P 236), and the extraordinary work *The Lugubrious Game* (1929, P 232).

Thereafter, the Freudian key elements are clearly on display—cited almost literally—and subsequently appear in numerous works until 1945, and even in some from his later oeuvre.

In fact, all of them are, more or less obviously, Freudian self-portraits by Dalí. Much has been written about the person depicted in *Face of the Great Masturbator* (1929, P 235, →fig. 12).[22] Here the painter assumes the form of a soft, sleeping head[23] haunted by anxieties and sexual obsessions that are embodied by the grasshopper, its abdomen covered in ants, the calla lily with its phallic stamen, the lion's tongue embodying desire, the female bust (an allusion to Gala) with the promise of fellatio, the small figures suggesting contrition and incomplete sexual intercourse, the cork, stone, snail, and egg forming a vertical, totemic, phallic series, the fishhook, from which a flaccid shape suggesting impotence is suspended, and the network of veins signifying the blood pressure of desire, and so on. In the form of this amoeba-like self-portrait one may also sense the direct influence of a section from the left panel of the triptych *The Garden of Earthly Delights* by Hieronymous Bosch (1503–15, Prado, Madrid), or, indeed, a rock formation from the Cap de Creus.[24] The sleeping figure is repeated in *The Lugubrious Game* (→p. 91), *Portrait of Paul Éluard* (P 233), and *The Enigma of Desire or Ma mère, ma mère, ma mère* (P 238, →fig. 13).

The intensity of his sexual desires is expressed in the lion's head, which functions as a form of self-portrait and which—with the exception of *The First Days of Spring* (P 242), a picture perhaps featuring a symbolic portrait of Freud—also appears in all his other paintings from 1929.

Beyond that, however, all of the remaining elements belonging to the group of paintings from this year relate to Dalí's own personality, which he interprets in a Freudian sense. A simple list of the most noteworthy elements speaks for itself and suggests motifs that, until his meeting with Freud in 1938—the year that marks the endpoint of this

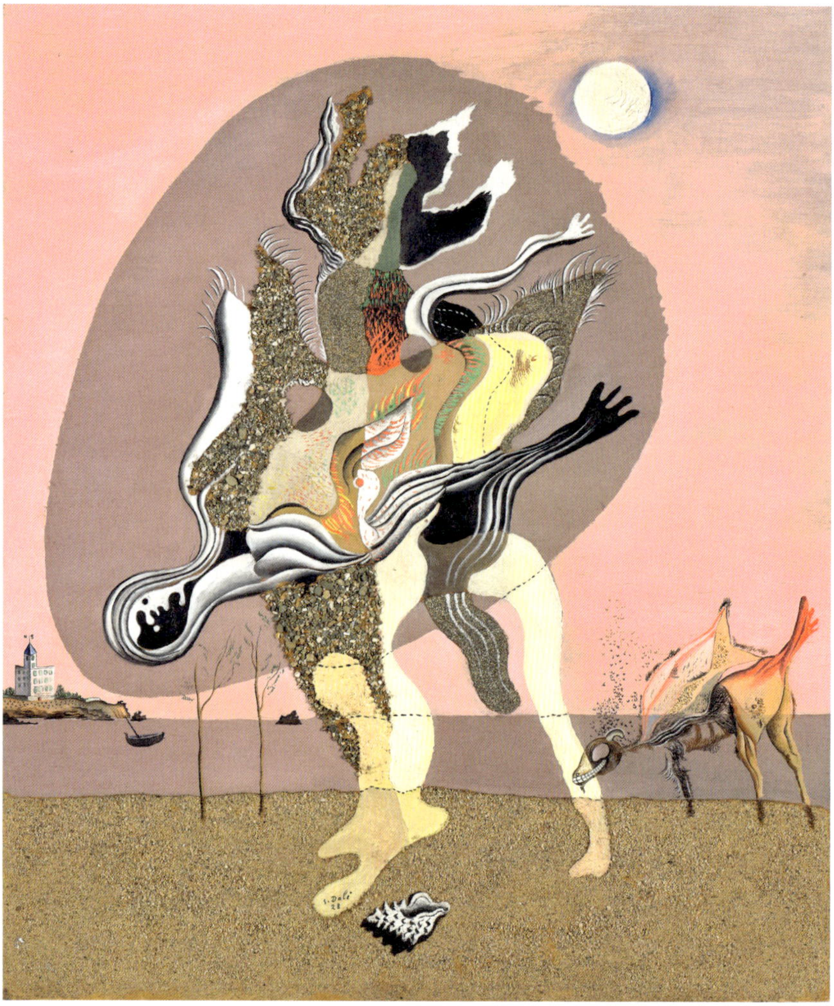

fig. 10
SALVADOR DALÍ, *L'âne pourri*
(*The Stinking Ass*), 1928
Centre Pompidou—Musée national d'art moderne—
Centre de création industrielle, Paris
Cat. no. P 225

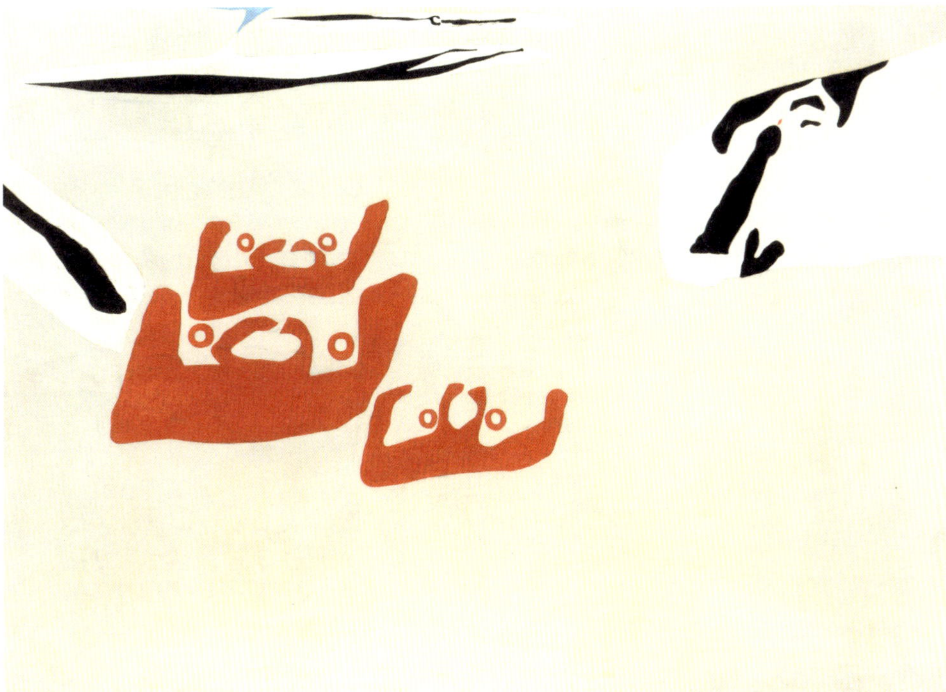

fig. 11
SALVADOR DALÍ, *Cuatro mujeres de pescadores en Cadaqués* (*Four Fishermen's Wives in Cadaqués*), c. 1928, Museo Nacional Centro de Arte Reina Sofía, Madrid, cat. no. P 216

exhibition—are repeated continually throughout his oeuvre: the masturbating hand; the fingers, naturally phallic in their form and their ability to explore all of the body's orifices; egg-shaped objects that are in the process of opening or bursting, pouring forth desires and secret obsessions; bearded faces, always alluding to the image of patriarchal authority, and male statues with outstretched arms, their faces (as in de Chirico) remaining hidden; unequivocally scatological forms and references; snails that recall sexual organs as well as the beach, where sexual desires are aroused; shapes reminiscent of entrails or wombs, with allusions both to anatomical hallucinations and to death and putrefaction; vertical monuments with phallic connotations; female busts and torsos embodying desires and anxieties; double images, like the one in which the figure of a woman is overlaid with a horse, or where the skeleton of an abandoned boat represents a human figure, or rocks that appear like human heads; family groups loaded with complex connotations; gestures expressing shame, and much more. *The Lugubrious Game* (1929, P 232), to give one example, contains a veritable catalogue of these elements.

THE "PARANOIAC-CRITICAL METHOD" AND THE UNFOLDING OF THE FREUDIAN IMAGINARY WORLD: FROM *THE LUGUBRIOUS GAME* TO *METAMORPHOSIS OF NARCISSUS*

The repertoire of paintings influenced by Freud that Dalí produced after 1929, including *Face of the Great Masturbator* (1929, P 235) and *The Lugubrious Game*, as well as *Metamorphosis of Narcissus* (1937, P 455, →fig. 17), which he presented to Freud at their meeting in London in 1938, is exceptionally varied. During this period Dalí also created the paranoiac-critical method as theoretical basis for these artistic outcomes. From then on, paintings of a Freudian nature formed an integral part of his oeuvre.

Dalí spent several years developing his paranoiac-critical method.[25] In 1930 he published the book *La femme visible*[26] and the article "L'âne pourri,"[27] which sparked such fascination in the young Lacan that he resolved to meet its author. Over the following years, one by one, Dalí laid down the foundation stones of his method, which fundamentally illustrates his connection to Freudian psychoanalysis. He did this in various essays,[28] the most significant being the article "Nuevas consideraciones generales sobre el mecanismo del fenómeno paranoico desde el punto de vista surrealista"[29]—in which he confesses his indebtedness to *De la psychose paranoïaque dans ses rapports avec la personnalité,*[30] a book published by Lacan in the same year—and the essay "La conquête de l'irrationnel."[31]

The essence of this theoretical incursion by Dalí is his view of paranoia as a "state of grace," enabling the artist to associate forms and objects with meanings that extend beyond their superficial appearance. Something that transcends the limits of what Giorgio de Chirico had already linked with the perception of the "sinister" background of objects. A peculiarity of critical paranoia is the perception of "double images," in which two different visible meanings are rooted in the same form. Beyond that, however, paranoiac-critical thought and its resultant practice can also act as a connector if they induce similar mental states in the observer to those experienced by the painting's creator.

Between 1929 and 1938, the year of Dalí's meeting with Freud in London, the works in the artist's oeuvre that demonstrate a Freudian influence not only intensify, but gradually coalesce into a veritable repertoire, a kind of vocabulary of symbols that, to the same degree that it evolves into its own universe of references, also becomes increasingly self-referential. If, then, the observer forms a link between their own individual mental state and one of these paintings, they do so not directly, but by means of a language that, through its repetition, has already become embedded in the collective artistic memory. This continues to increase with the widespread dissemination of Dalí's work until the end of the Second World War. After this point the paintings' Freudian expression is gradually superseded by the personal mythos of this ever-changing artist.

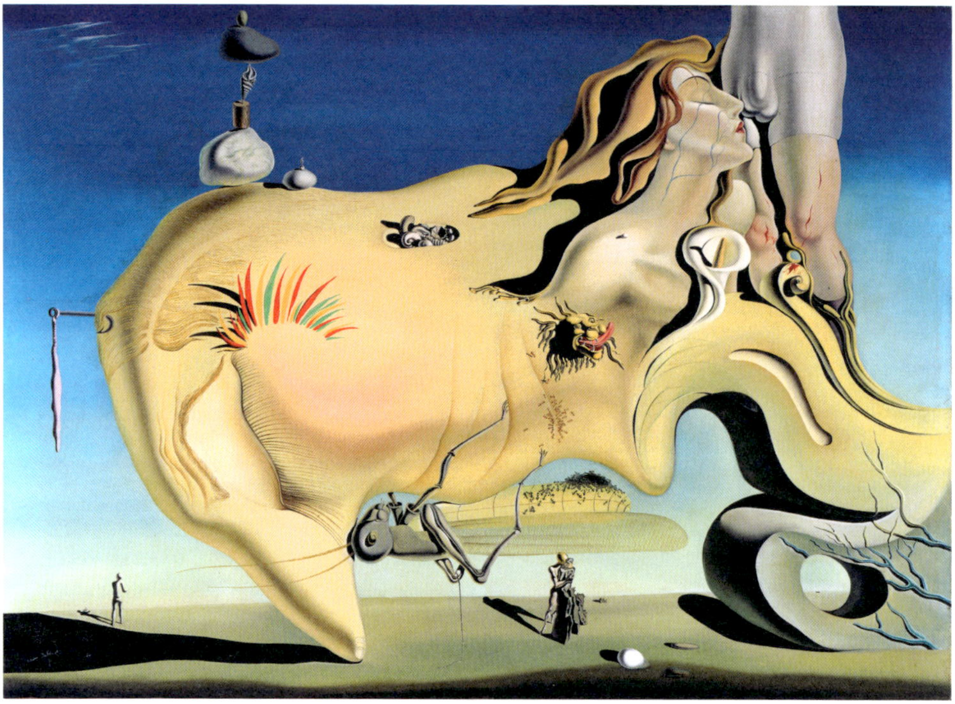

fig. 12
SALVADOR DALÍ, *Visage du Grand Masturbateur* (*Face of the Great Masturbator*), 1929
Museo Nacional Centro de Arte Reina Sofía, Madrid, cat. no. P 235

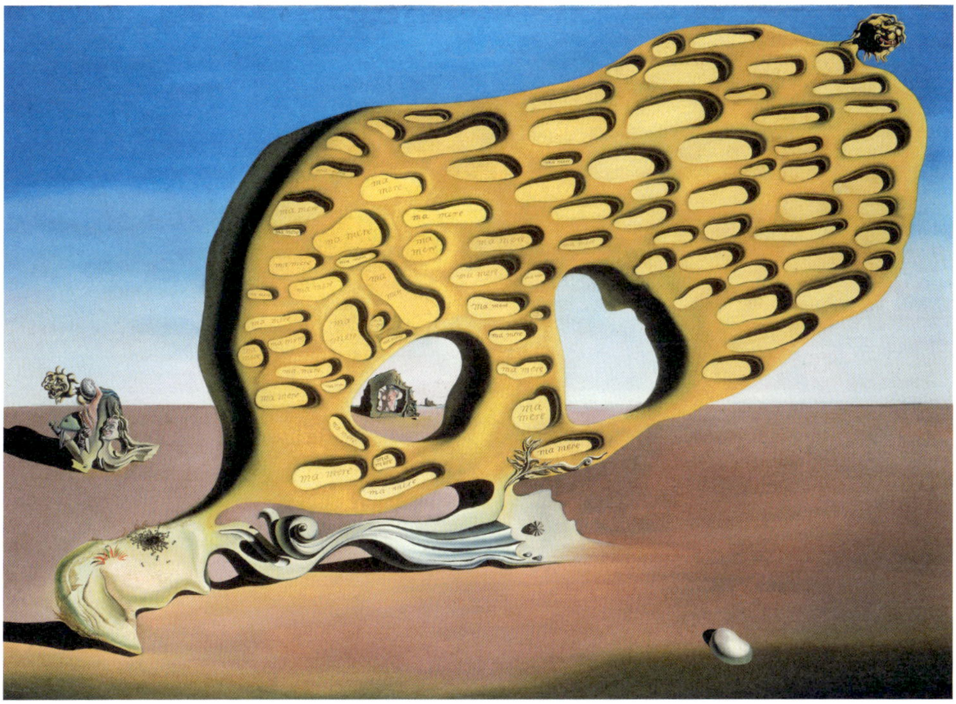

fig. 13
SALVADOR DALÍ, *El enigma del deseo o Ma mère, ma mère, ma mère (The Enigma of Desire or Ma mère, ma mère, ma mère)*, 1929
Bayerische Staatsgemäldesammlungen, Sammlung Moderne Kunst, Pinakothek der Moderne, Munich, cat. no. P 238

On display in this exhibition is a collection of paintings and drawings by Dalí from the years 1929 to 1937 that exemplify just how effective the paranoiac-critical method was in forging a connection between Dalí's painting and Freud's writing.

1 Salvador Dalí, *The Secret Life of Salvador Dalí*, translated by Haakon M. Chevalier (New York, 1993), p. 167. Here Dalí is referring to the period between 1922 and 1926, when he lived at the Residencia de Estudiantes in Madrid.

2 See the subheadings in *The Secret Life of Salvador Dalí*: "False Childhood Memories" and "True Childhood Memories" (ibid. pp. 35–111).

3 See Rafael Santos Torroella, *La miel es más dulce que la sangre: las épocas lorquiana y freudiana de Salvador Dalí* (Barcelona, 1984), pp. 31–32.

4 I refer to pictures and sculptures by Dalí using the dates and numbers in the catalogue raisonné of the Fundació Gala-Salvador Dalí. I have provided an extensive treatment of the development of Dali's pictorial language prior to 1929 in "Aspersor de aleaciones: genealogía y proyección del lenguaje daliniano en el contexto español," in *Huellas Dalinianas*, exh. cat., Museo Nacional Centro de Arte Reina Sofía, Madrid; Artium, Vitoria-Gasteiz (Madrid, 2004), pp. 15–65.

5 Jaime Brihuega, "En la piel de los otros: contaminaciones y canibalismo icónicos en Salvador Dalí," in *Estudios de historia del arte en honor de Tomás Llorens* (Madrid, 2007), pp. 167–78.

6 Dalí is known to have owned a book by Umberto Boccioni, *Pittura e scultura futuriste* (Milan, 1914), an elaborately illustrated work, which Dalí had annotated with sketches and graphic notes. See also Santos Torroella, 1984 (see note 3), p. 23.

7 See selected studies and images in *El noucentisme: un projecte de modernitat*, exh. cat., Centre de Cultura Contemporània de Barcelona (Barcelona, 1994); Fèlix Fanés, *Salvador Dalí: The Construction of the Image, 1925–1930* (New Haven, 2007), pp. 19–20.

8 For example, *Montroig, la iglesia y el pueblo* (*Church and the Village of Montroig*; 1919, private collection, Mallorca).

9 Santos Torroella 1984 (see note 3), pp. 69–77. The unpublished letter containing this quotation can be found in this study.

10 Santiago Ramón y Cajal was a Spanish histologist and pathologist who received the Nobel Prize for Medicine in 1906 alongside Camillo Golgi. From the end of the nineteenth century, he published drawings of nerve tissue, which he had studied under a microscope. In 1926 Cajal stayed at the Madrid Residencia de Estudiantes.

11 *Salvador Dalí: poesía, prosa, teatro y cine*, vol. 3 (Barcelona, 2004), pp. 176–77.

12 I wrote a monograph on this topic in "Hipnerotomachia anatómica," in *Fisiología de los sueños: Cajal, Tanguy, Lorca Dalí...*, exh. cat., Edificio Paraninfo de la Universidad de Zaragoza (Zaragoza, 2015), pp. 13–42.

13 Deiters, Butzke, Gerlach, Meynert, Golgi, Denisenko, Luys, Maestre de San Juan, Retzius, Dogiel, Kölliker, Sala, Held, Dejerine, Apáthy, Arnold, Dogiel, Nissl... See Javier de Felipe, Henry Markram, and Jorge Wagensberg, eds., *Paisajes neuronales: homenaje a Santiago Ramón y Cajal* (Madrid, 2007), pp. 101–02.

14 Santos Torroella 1984 (see note 3), pp. 31–32.

15 This refers to magazines such as *L'esprit nouveau, Cahiers d'art, L'art d'aujourd'hui...*, and *La révolution surréaliste*; issues 7 (June 15, 1926), 8 (December 1, 1926), and, particularly, 9–10 (October 1, 1927) in the following year featured pictures by Yves Tanguy showing the emergence of lines reminiscent of histological or biological illustrations. One year previously, in issue 2 of the same magazine (February 15, 1925), an automatic drawing by André Masson was published, featuring the same stylistic elements of the visual correspondence discussed here. Dalí and Lorca may also have had access to issue 26 of *La revue européenne* (April 1, 1925), featuring a portrait of Benjamin Péret by Masson, which shared several similarities with the neurological drawings of Cajal. Yet, this poetic empathy with histological microscope images of the nervous system became strikingly evident from the moment the two young residents were able to study *Dormir, dormir dans les pierres* by Benjamin Péret (Paris, 1927), which was illustrated with fourteen of Tanguy's drawings.

16 I am once more referring to the collection of aesthetic sources on which Lorca and Dalí were able to draw and which are described so comprehensively by Juan José Lahuerta in his essays for the exhibition catalogue *Dalí, Lorca y la Residencia de Estudiantes*, exh. cat., Caixa Forum, Madrid (Madrid, 2010).

17 Illustration in the magazine *Litoral*, October 1927.

18 Published in *La gaceta literaria*, January 15, 1929.

19 The visible references central to the visual and poetic admixtures of this complex prelude to Dalí's Surrealist language, developing between 1927 and 1928, have been thoroughly and comprehensively researched by art historians such as Dawn Ades, Rafael Santos Torroella, Fèlix Fanés, Ian Gibson, Juan José Lahuerta, Haim Finkelstein, Juan Antonio Ramírez, and Karin von Maur. As primary sources these authors cite, almost unanimously, de Chirico, Miró, Tanguy, Hans Arp, Max Ernst, Masson, Picasso, Man Ray, Fernand Léger, Le Corbusier, Marcel Duchamp, Francis Picabia, and others, alongside non-contemporary artists such as Hieronymus Bosch, Pieter Bruegel the Elder, Andrea Mantegna, and Joachim Patinir. The aforementioned scholars were also able to pinpoint quite clearly and precisely those models definitively belonging to the previously discussed linguistic form, which began during 1929. The spectrum of visual sources is therefore broad, well-substantiated, and sufficiently well-known to allow me to merely provide a brief, systematic summary while introducing some previously neglected themes.

20 The catalogue raisonné of the Fundació Gala-Salvador Dalí lists the following study for the year 1926: *Study for "Honey is Sweeter than Blood"* (1926, P 185).

21 See Ian Gibson, *La vida desaforada de Salvador Dalí* (Barcelona, 1998), pp. 259–60.

22 Torroella 1984 (see note 3), pp. 47–63, dedicates an entire chapter to him.

23 A preliminary stage of this self-portrait in the form of a (in this instance decapitated) head can be seen in the photograph of the lost painting *Honey is Sweeter than Blood* (→ p. 83) already mentioned. This painting also features Lorca's picture of a head.

24 Fanés 2007 (see note 7), p. 92–93.

25 See Jesús Lázaro Docio, *El método paranoico-crítico de Salvador Dalí: de la realidad subjetiva a la objetiva realidad (1927–1937)*, doctoral thesis, Madrid, 2001.

26 Paris 1930.

27 Published in *Le surréalisme au service de la révolution*, no. 1, July 1, 1930.

28 They were all summarized by Dalí in *OUI* (Paris, 1971).

29 In *Minotaure*, June 1933. This was the preface to the book *Interprétation paranoïaque-critique de l'image obsédante 'L'Angélus' de Millet*, which remained unpublished until 1963.

30 Jacques Lacan, *De la psychose paranoïaque dans ses rapports avec la personnalité* (Paris, 1932).

31 Paris 1935.

DALÍ'S FREUD: A CASE STUDY

Robert Lubar Messeri

In his eccentric autobiography of 1942, *The Secret Life*, Salvador Dalí recounts a series of failed encounters and imaginary meetings with the father of psychoanalysis, Sigmund Freud:

> "My three voyages to Vienna were exactly like three drops of water which lacked the reflections to make them glitter. On each of these voyages I did exactly the same things: in the morning I went to see the Vermeer in the Czernin Collection, and in the afternoon I did *not* go to visit Freud because I invariably learned that he was out of town for reasons of health.
>
> I remember with a gentle melancholy spending those afternoons walking haphazardly along the streets of Austria's ancient capital. The chocolate tart, which I would hurriedly eat between the short intervals of going from one antiquary to another, had a slightly bitter taste resulting from the antiquities I saw and accentuated by the mockery of the meeting which never took place. In the evening I held long and exhaustive imaginary

conversations with Freud; he even came home with me once and stayed all night clinging to the curtains of my room in the Hotel Sacher."[1]

Dalí's narrative is permeated by the wistful air of presentment, heavily perfumed by unfulfilled wishes and failed expectations. As the artist wanders the streets of Vienna, he experiences the melancholy of absence, the loss of the father. Things come to fill the space of that emptiness, mundane sites are laden with significance, and desire is sublimated in the rich flavor of a chocolate tart, only to be introjected as fantasy and consigned to the realm of the imaginary.

Then, at long last, there is the epiphany. As the specter of war casts its ominous shadow over Europe, Dalí meets the exiled Dr. Freud in London. But first, some more disclosures. "Several years after my last ineffectual attempt to meet Freud," Dalí writes, "I made a gastronomic excursion into the region of Sens in France. We started the dinner with snails, one of my favorite dishes. The conversation turned to Edgar Allan Poe, a magnificent theme while savoring snails, and concerned itself particularly with a recently published book by the Princess of Greece, Marie Bonaparte, which is a psychoanalytical study of Poe. All of a sudden I saw a photograph of Professor Freud on the front page of a newspaper which someone beside me was reading. I immediately had one brought to me and read that the exiled Freud had just arrived in Paris. We had not yet recovered from the effect of this news when I uttered a loud cry. I had just that instant discovered the morphological secret of Freud! Freud's cranium is a snail! His brain is in the form of a spiral—to be extracted with a needle! This discovery strongly influenced the portrait drawing [→fig. 14] which I later made from life, a year before his death."[2]

Upon learning the news of Freud's arrival at his final destination in London, on June 6th, 1938, Dalí contacted Freud's friend, the Austrian writer Stefan Zweig, in the hope of arranging an audience with the psychoanalyst. On July 18th, Zweig wrote to Freud:

> "Salvador Dalí, in my opinion (strange [!] as many of his works may appear), is the only painter of *genius* of our epoch, and the only one who will survive, a fanatic in his conviction, and the most faithful and most grateful disciple of your ideas among the artists. For years it has been the desire of this real genius to meet you. He says that he owes to you more in his art than to anybody else. And so we are coming tomorrow to see you, he and his wife. He would like to take this opportunity, during our discussion, to make a short portrait sketch of you, if possible. The real portraits he always does from memory, and from his inner *Gestaltung*. As a kind of legitimation, we are going to show you his last picture, in the possession of Mr. Edward James."[3]

Aside from the portrait session, we have only a partial record of what transpired during that short meeting. Dalí's maecenas, Edward James, wrote to Christopher Sykes on July 20th, the day after the meeting with Freud, which James attended, to give his account of the events: "Salvador was looking so inspired, his eyes were so blazing with excitement while he sketched the inventor of psychoanalysis, that the old man whispered in German: 'That boy looks like a fanatic. Small wonder they have civil war in Spain if they look like that.'"[4]

Nevertheless, Freud appears to have held the young painter in high regard. That same day he wrote to Zweig: "I really have reason to thank you for the introduction which brought me yesterday's visitors. For until then I was inclined to look upon surrealists, who have apparently chosen me for their patron saint, as absolute (let us say 95 per cent, like alcohol) cranks. The young Spaniard, however, with his candid fanatical eyes and his undeniable technical mastery, has made me reconsider my opinion."[5]

In many respects, Dalí's meeting with Freud represented a curiously empty conclusion. If Freud, according to Dalí, dismissed the degree of conscious elaboration in Surrealism's psychoanalytic narratives, Dalí based his entire "paranoiac-critical method" on the idea of a "delirium of interpretation," which he explained in numerous articles and justified with

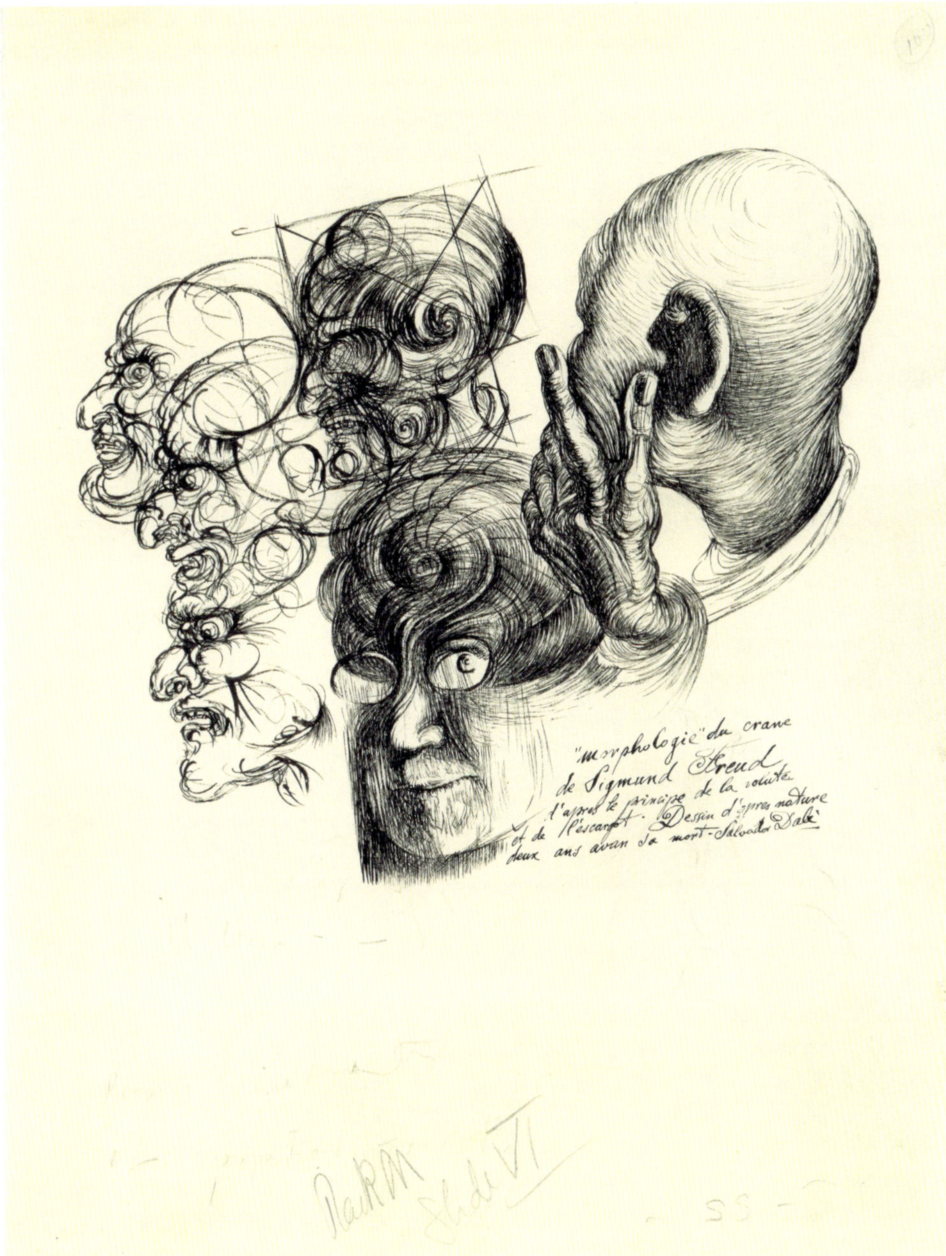

fig. 14
SALVADOR DALÍ, *Morphology of the Skull of Sigmund Freud*, c. 1939/41
Fundació Gala-Salvador Dalí, Figueres

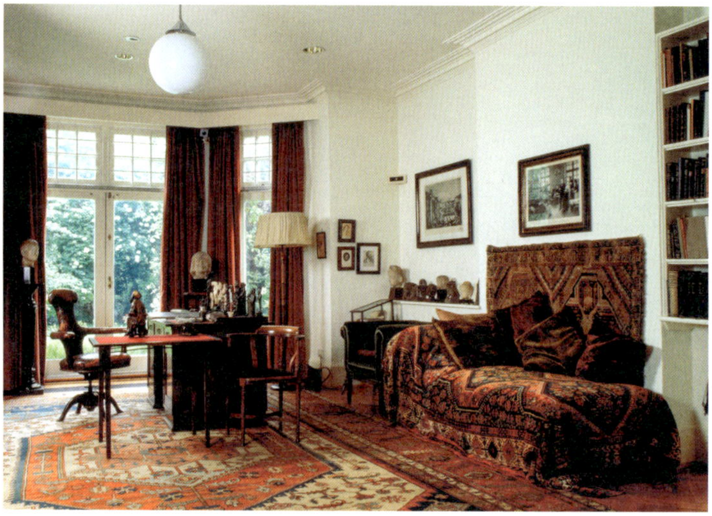

fig. 15
Sigmund Freud's study at his house in London with the famous couch, which he had shipped over from Berggasse 19

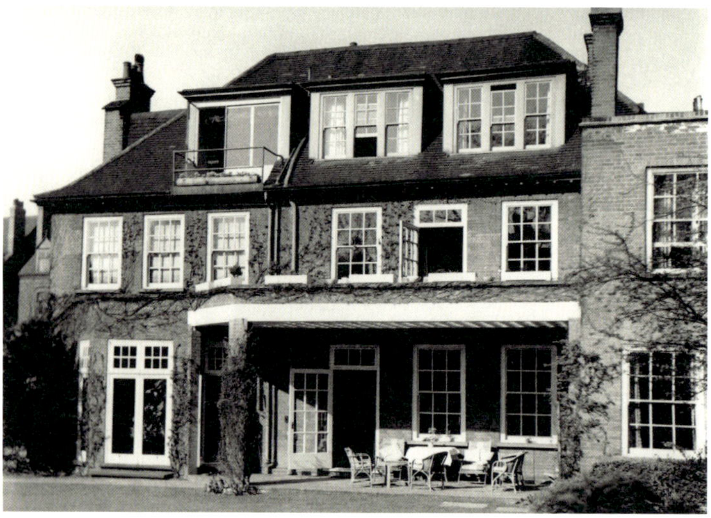

fig. 16
Sigmund Freud's house at 20, Maresfield Gardens, London, c. 1940

the celebrated comment: "The only difference between me and a madman is that I am *not* mad." Dalí remarked in *The Secret Life* that, upon reading the Spanish translation of Freud's *Interpretation of Dreams* while a student in Madrid in the mid-1920s, he was "seized with a real vice of self-interpretation."[6] Indeed, Dalí's "breakthrough" Surrealist dreamscapes of 1929 stage the subject of psychoanalysis in ways that may appear patently obvious, but are in fact deeply coded. As Dawn Ades has astutely observed, "[...] what makes the paintings of 1929–30 so extraordinary is the way they hold in balance a real neurotic fear which is clearly very powerful, and a knowing use of psychology textbooks."[7] In effect, Dalí works both sides of the psychoanalytic couch, assuming the role of analyst and analysand in his artistic practice.

Freud, however, appears to have found Dalí disingenuous. In *The Secret Life,* Dalí recalls that at the time of their meeting he tried to interest Freud in an article he had written on paranoia, seeking recognition from the doctor. "I explained," Dalí writes, "that it was not a surrealist diversion, but was really an ambitiously scientific article, and I repeated the title, pointing to it at the same time with my finger. Before his imperturbable indifference, my voice became involuntarily sharper and more insistent."[8] Indeed, as Dalí spoke, Freud observed the young Spaniard with a penetrating gaze, initially more interested in the man than in Salvador Dalí the writer, theorist, and artist. Dalí, it appears, had now taken *his* place on the analyst's couch (→fig. 15).

At stake in Dalí's encounter with Freud, as he critically interpellates it in the narrative, is the question of ego identity, as the artist describes a scopic encounter that is filled with admiration and anxiety. The authorial voice of the speaking subject—Dalí in the first person—serves to anchor the ego's sliding identifications, as Dalí's dialogue with Freud represents a demand for recognition by the other.

There is much more to this anecdote than meets the eye, but it immediately alerts us to the kind of psychic transference that transpired during Dalí's interview with Freud, the archetypal father figure for the young painter. As Dalí did not speak English or German, and Freud, who was suffering from cancer of the mouth, found it difficult to speak at all, the gaze assumed a particular intensity in their encounter. Dalí reminisced in *The Secret Life*: "Contrary to my hopes we spoke little, but *we devoured each other with our eyes*. Freud knew nothing about me except my painting, which he admired, but suddenly I had the whim of trying to appear in his eyes as a kind of dandy of 'universal intellectualism.' I learned later that the effect I produced was exactly the opposite."[9] There is, to be sure, something deeply unsettling about Dalí's description of this scopic exchange, and here the metaphor of edibility, transmitted through the anecdote about the eating of snails in Sens—in other words, the catalytic moment leading up to Dalí's fourth, successful attempt to meet Freud—assumes special relevance. Upon entering Freud's yard, Dalí notices a bicycle with a red rubber hot-water bottle hanging from the saddle, on the back of which a snail is attached. The anecdote connects the two moments in the narrative framing the meeting with Freud, but it also serves a symbolic function. Aside from its folkloric, gastronomic, and cultural associations for Dalí, the snail is a bisexual animal whose somewhat amorphous form is protected by an exoskeleton, a kind of armor of sorts, that can only be pierced by a needle. The snail, in this sense, might be thought of as an apt metaphor for the ego, its defensive shield protecting a self that is constantly embattled. But the bisexual status of the animal lends itself to another interpretation, inasmuch as Dalí's reference to the red water bottle elicits a moment *prior* to both the formation of self and the constitution of sexual identity, when the child suckles at its mother's breast in a state of jubilant unity with the primordial object of desire.

In this light, Dalí's description of Freud's garden inscribes the constitution of the ego, perpetually under siege, in relation to an *anterior* moment of polymorphous perversity within the mother/child dyad to which the subject *qua* subject can never return. It is therefore no wonder that, confronted with Freud's penetrating gaze as a kind of assault on the ego, Dalí, a notorious narcissist, responded by blinding the father symbolically (that is to say, in representation): Freud's blank, bespectacled eyes cannot return the artist's gaze and, in the process, pierce the shield of the ego (→p. 167).

In psychoanalytic terms, narcissism is the latent subject of Dalí's encounter with Freud, and it is hardly casual that the painting Dalí brought with him to show his mentor was the recently completed *Metamorphosis of Narcissus* (P 455, →fig. 17), which Edward James owned. In his letter to Stefan Zweig of July 20th, Freud commented on the painting and the question of its manifest psychoanalytic content: "It would in fact be very interesting to investigate analytically how a picture like this came to be painted. From the critical point of view, it could still be maintained that the notion of art defies expansion as long as the quantitative proportion of unconscious material and preconscious treatment does not remain within definite limits. In any case these are serious psychological problems."[10] If Narcissus, in other words, was self-deluded, Freud seemed to suggest that Dalí was all too knowing. More importantly, Freud's comment concerning the limits of psychoanalytic interpretations of works of art resulted from a lifetime of thinking about the relation of psychoanalysis to cultural criticism, a subject which particularly preoccupied him at this time, as he worked on his late, great text, *Moses and Monotheism*. As early as September 13, 1908, on the occasion of a visit to London's National Portrait Gallery, Freud jotted down some "Notes on Faces and Men," in which he was curiously reticent about dynamic psychological typologies for the mind/body relationship: "Face is race, family and constitutional predisposition," he wrote, in a throwback to nineteenth century positivist notions about racial and geographic determinism. By 1910, however, Freud advanced a theory of artistic formation in his groundbreaking, highly speculative, and now largely discredited essay, "Leonardo da Vinci and a Memory of His Childhood," a text that was to have a considerable impact on Dalí's art and writings.

Freud's aim in the essay was to sketch the broad contours of Leonardo's "mental and intellectual development" as reflected in his art. It was decidedly *not* his intention to advance a general theory of creativity. As he stated in a 1928 essay "Dostoevsky and Parricide": "Before the problem of the creative artist analysis must, alas, lay down its arms."[11] Already in 1909, in a letter to Carl Gustav Jung, Freud had asserted that, "the domain of biography, too, must become ours [...] the riddle of Leonardo da Vinci's character has suddenly become transparent to me. That, then, would be the first step in biography."[12] With this task in mind, Freud considered what he perceived to be two key events in Leonardo's life: his adult experience of painting that most enigmatic of all works, *Mona Lisa*, and Leonardo's record, in his notebooks, of a childhood screen memory it evoked: that of the infant Leonardo, lying in his cradle, vulnerable to the advances of a vulture who swoops down, opens the child's mouth and strikes his lips repeatedly with its tail. Noting that in Egyptian hieroglyphics vulture signifies "mother," Freud interpreted Leonardo's predicament as that of a fatherless (illegitimate) child, who is coddled by his bereft mother, and who in turn represses his love for her by assuming her position; that is to say, by identifying with her: "The violence of the caresses, to which his phantasy of the vulture points, was only too natural," Freud writes, "the poor forsaken mother had to give vent to all her memories of the caresses she had enjoyed as well as her longing for new ones; and she was forced to do so not only to compensate herself for having no husband, but also to compensate her child for having no father to fondle him. So, like all unsatisfied mothers, she took her little son in place of her husband, and by the too early maturing of his erotism robbed him of a part of his masculinity."

In Freud's reading, Leonardo's predicament is that of all homosexual men, compounded in this case by the fact that Leonardo's father later married a young woman of higher social standing named Albiera, who became the child's second mother, a triangular family relationship that Freud argued is reflected in Leonardo's *Virgin and Child with Saint Anne* (1501–19, → fig. 18). And, as if the story of the vulture—an animal known for its strong maternal instincts—were not "proof" enough of Leonardo's identification with his mother, Freud noted in a 1919 edition of his text that his friend, the Swiss minister and lay analyst Oskar Pfister, had

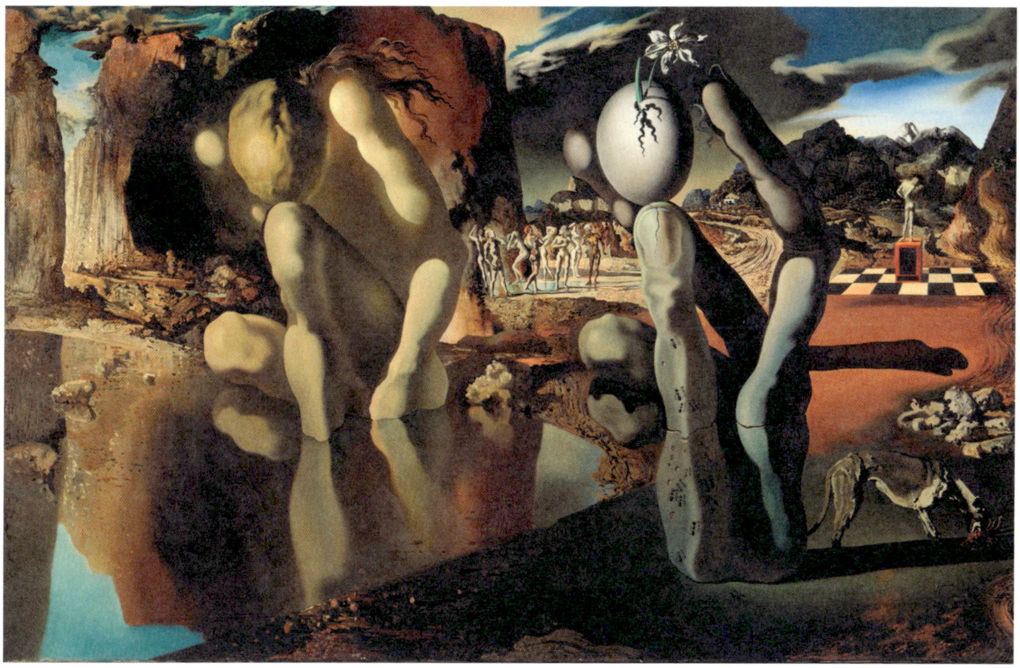

fig. 17
SALVADOR DALÍ, *Métamorphose de Narcisse*
(*Metamorphosis of Narcissus*), 1937
Tate Modern, London, cat. no. P 455

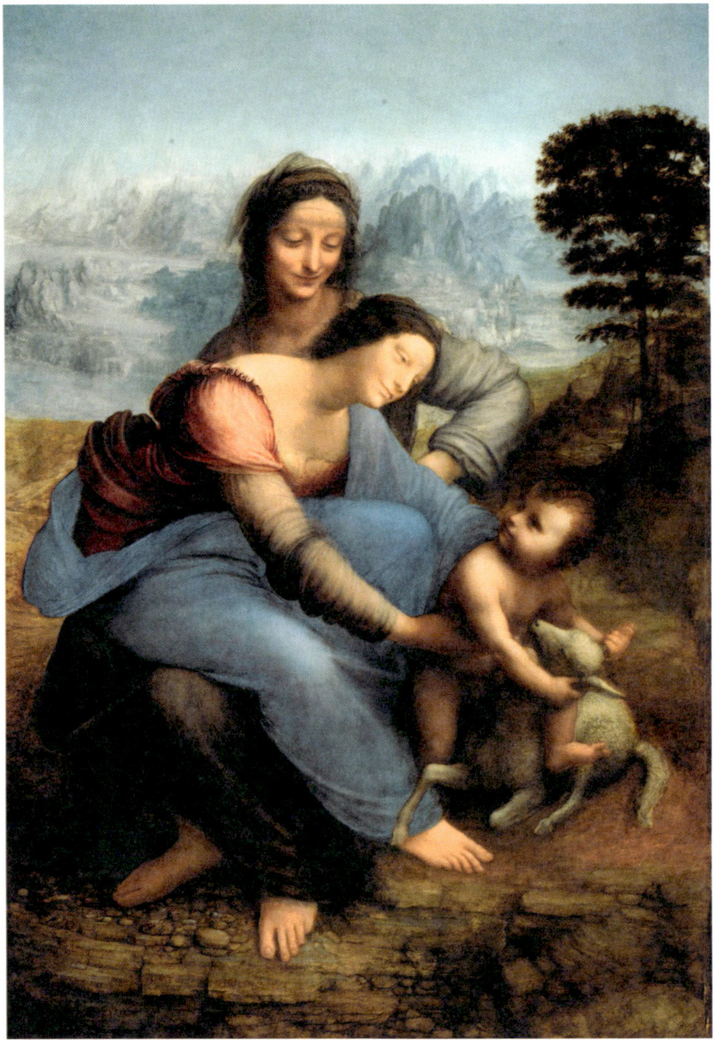

fig. 18
LEONARDO DA VINCI, *The Virgin and Child with Saint Anne*, 1501–19, Louvre, Paris

discerned the actual contours of the vulture in Leonardo's great painting, which he reproduced as a schematic diagram in his 1913 study *The Psychoanalytic Method*, as did Freud in the 1919 re-edition of his essay.[14]

As is well known, Freud's entire interpretation of Leonardo's screen memory was based on little more than inferences he had drawn from the scant biographical evidence available and from Leonardo's surviving works of art. As for the vulture anecdote on which the interpretation largely rests, it is unlikely that Freud's source was Leonardo's *Notebooks*, but, rather, it came to him by way of the German edition of Dimitri Merejkowski's historical novel *The Romance of Leonardo da Vinci*, in which the Italian word *nibbio*, meaning "kite," was mistranslated as "vulture." Add to this the fact that the story of a bird of prey entering the mouth of a child was, as Meyer Schapiro has brilliantly argued, a well-worn trope for the sources of inspiration and creativity in the literature of Leonardo's day, and Freud's interpretation of the artist's homosexual fantasy of fellatio filtered through a memory of nursing, collapses like a house of cards, as Freud himself recognized.[15]

Yet, however much Freud later confessed to select friends that his much-esteemed Leonardo essay was a largely fictional account, his analysis contained many far-reaching implications for his emerging theory of homosexual narcissism. "In all our homosexual cases," Freud writes, "the subjects had had a very intense erotic attachment to a female person, as a rule their mother, during the first period of childhood, which is afterwards forgotten; this attachment was evoked or encouraged by too much tenderness on the part of the mother herself, and further reinforced by the small part played by the father during their childhood." The child subsequently "represses his love for his mother: he puts himself in her place, identifies himself with her, and takes his own person as a model in whose likeness he chooses the new objects of his love. In this way he has become a homosexual. What he has in fact done is to slip back to auto-erotism: for the boys whom he now loves as he grows up are after all only substitutive figures and revivals of himself in childhood—boys whom he loves in the way in which his mother loved *him* when he was a child." Freud then makes the startling observation that the boy "finds the objects of his love along the path of narcissism."[16] Four years later, Freud would develop this theory in his controversial essay "On Narcissism," in which he reconsidered his earlier view that ego drives are separate from sexual drives.

There is no question that at the time of his meeting with Freud, Dalí was fully conversant with the Leonardo essay. In *The Font* of 1930 (P 248, →fig. 19), the vulture appears as an extravagant appendage emerging from the neck of a male figure who kneels in an apparent act of fellatio; his standing partner hides his face in shame before the image of a fantastic chalice and host in the middle-ground, a symbol of the censoring superego. Presiding over the scene is a pitcher in the form of a self-portrait head of the artist. Elsewhere, Dalí figured the terms of homosexual narcissism symbolically. Thus, the bicycle in Freud's garden serves an emblematic function within Dalí's literary portrait in relation to the constitution of sexual identity and sexual object choice. Not only is the cyclist represented in miniature in *Illuminated Pleasures* (1929, P 241, →fig. 20), where Dalí had invoked the primal scene as the moment of sexual identity formation—the image of two hands wielding a bloody knife in the lower left foreground is an explicit reference to the trauma of symbolic castration that is figured elsewhere in the painting—but he makes a notable appearance in *Un chien andalou* of the same year. In one notorious sequence, the male protagonist, portrayed by Pierre Batcheff, falls off his bicycle in the street as his female paramour observes with horror from her apartment window.

The bicycle suggests a host of symbolic meanings, from the idea of "spinning one's wheels" in an act of auto-eroticism, to sexual impotence and the failure to achieve heterosexual intercourse. In this light it is significant that the cyclist is dressed in what are described as "frilly"—that is to say, feminine—clothes, for the sequence that follows plays explicitly on the theme of gendered difference (→fig. 21).

The point here is not to suggest a transparent relation between Dalí's art and life, but, rather, to underscore the

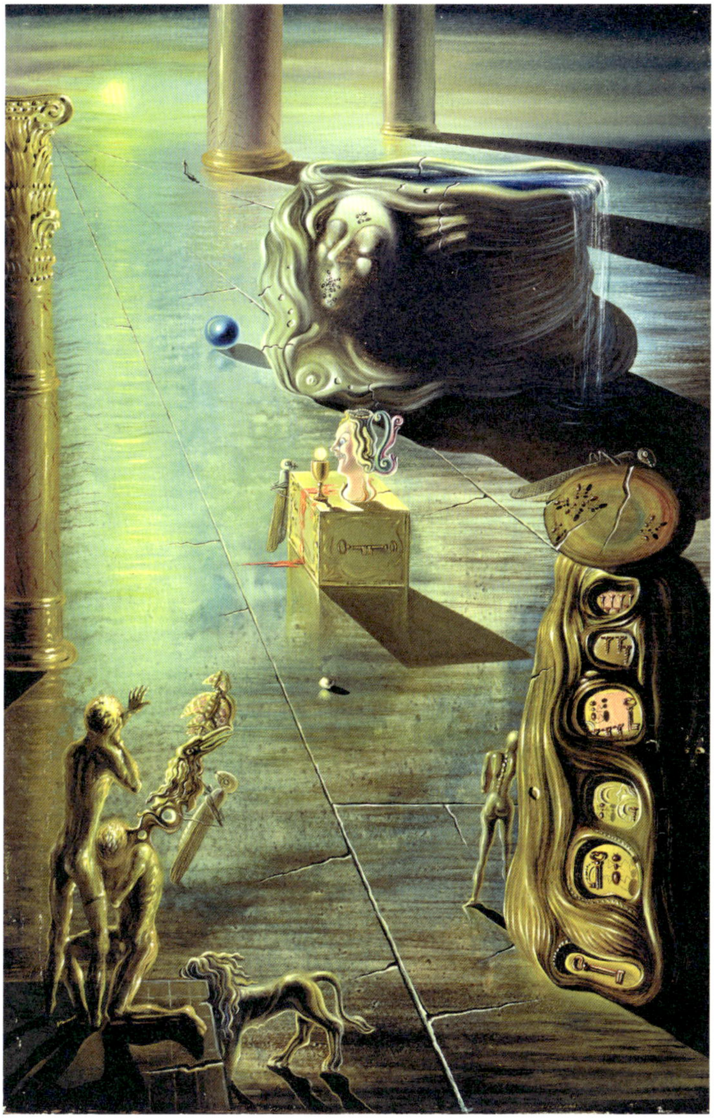

fig. 19
SALVADOR DALÍ, *The Font*, 1930
The Dalí Museum, Saint Petersburg (Florida)
Cat. no. P 248

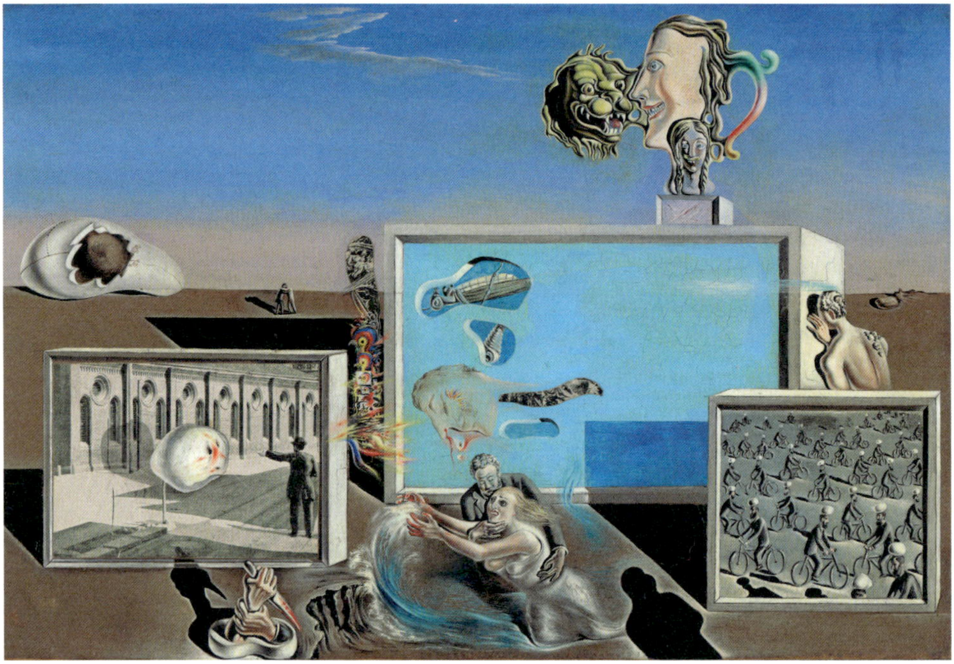

fig. 20
SALVADOR DALÍ, *Les plaisirs illuminés*
(*Illuminated Pleasures*), 1929
Museum of Modern Art, New York,
The Sidney and Harriet Janis Collection, 1967
Cat. no. P 241

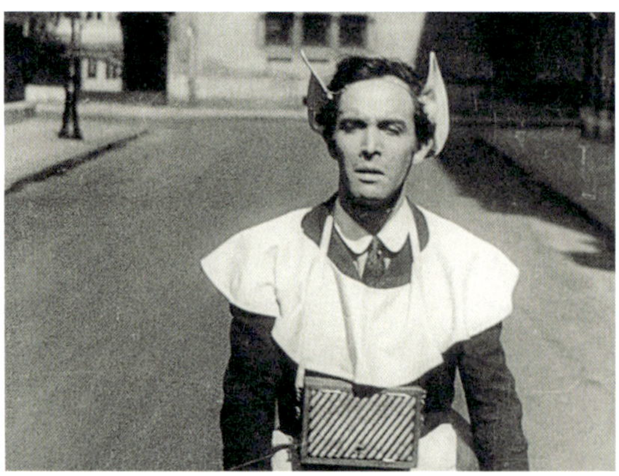

fig. 21
LUIS BUÑUEL, SALVADOR DALÍ
Un chien andalou, 1929

ways in which he staged the heterosexual ideal as a psychoanalytic construction—a social myth of sorts. If Dalí can be said to have lived that ideal in his mature relationship with Gala, he did so in a performative rather than a mimetic sense. Dalí self-consciously exaggerated the terms of compulsory heterosexuality in his life and work, restaging the Freudian concept of homosexual narcissism as parody.[17] In *The Tragic Myth of Millet's Angelus*, an elaborate paranoiac-critical text he largely conceived in the early 1930s, Dalí goes so far as to read the Oedipal drama *against the grain* of Freud's Leonardo essay.[18] Pondering the popular status of Jean-François Millet's *Angelus* (→fig. 27) as an object of pious veneration and serial reproduction in mass culture, Dalí asks rhetorically: "How could the *Angelus*, sublime image of symbolic hypocrisy and obsession of crowds, have been capable of unleashing such a flagrant, unconscious *erotic fury*?"[19] In analyzing his own obsessive responses to the image, Dalí embarks on a series of extended interpretations, finding concrete proof of the latent content of the painting in the cultural imaginary. Peeling away layers of cultural accretion one by one, and adopting the archaeological metaphor for psychoanalysis, first employed by Freud in his 1907 essay "Delusion and Dream in Jensen's *Gradiva*," Dalí exposes the core of an unresolved Oedipal conflict beneath the ruins of Millet's iconic image. The painting, in Dalí's elaborate literary exegesis and in his corresponding visual production, is the site of predatory sexual aggression: the male peasant is dwarfed by his mantis-like companion—the domineering woman par excellence—and, together, the couple stands before the site of their dead child's grave, marked by the wheelbarrow. In other words, the wife has symbolically castrated the husband and devoured their child.

Now, as it turns out, *The Tragic Myth of Millet's Angelus*, included among its illustrations Leonardo's *Virgin and Child with St. Anne*, precisely the image Freud had discussed in relation to Leonardo's homosexual narcissism. Elsewhere in *The Tragic Myth*, Dalí makes an oblique reference to the vulture story in the form of a "false memory" of his own mother "sucking" and "devouring" his penis as an infant, presumably the "source" of his adult impotence, which is only cured by the appearance of Gala, "the resources of [whose] love," he writes, "surpass[ed] in vital intuition the most subtle advances of psychoanalytic treatments."[20] In other words, Dalí passes from a stage of homosexual narcissism to that of mature object love in this apocryphal tale of psychosexual development. There is, however, a notable difference in Dalí's method: whereas Freud was interested in the biographical facts of Leonardo's life as reflected in his art, Dalí was primarily interested in the status of psychoanalysis as an interpretative system through which he could restage the trajectory of his own sexual development. In the process, he held a critical mirror to Freud's psycho-biographical method.

Freud, of course, got the point, as his comment to Stefan Zweig about the "quantitative relation of unconscious material and pre-conscious elaboration" in Dalí's *Metamorphosis of Narcissus* makes patently clear. If Freud saw the biographical facts of Leonardo's life mirrored in his art, Dalí reversed the terms of the argument, using psychoanalytic theory to construct an elaborate, and largely mythic, biographical persona. One might even go so far as to say that Dalí's Freudian narratives, like his literary texts, involve rhetorical structures that *undermine* the psychoanalytic method, simultaneously staging its subject *and* object. Thus, in the eponymous poem Dalí conceived as a literary pendant to *Metamorphosis of Narcissus,* Gala arrives just in time to rescue the artist from self-love and restore him to a state of "normative" heterosexuality, thereby reinscribing narcissism, to quote David Lomas, "as a transitional phase in a developmental schema that reaches its socially acceptable terminus in mature object love."[21] Yet a residue of doubt remains, one that Freud found sufficiently interesting to consider Dalí's painting as a complex historical and social text. And no wonder, for that doubt, perhaps, belonged to Freud himself.

In a letter to his friend the psychiatrist Sándor Ferenczi, dated October 6, 1910—that is to say, just five months after the Leonardo essay appeared in print—Freud discussed his own homosexuality as a passing phase in the constitution of his ego identity: "since the case of Fliess, with whose overcoming you just saw me occupied, this need has died out in me. A piece of homosexual charge has been withdrawn and utilized for the enlargement of my own ego. I have succeeded where the paranoiac fails."[22] Several authors have suggested that the emotional intimacy the young Freud had with the physician Wilhelm Fliess, with whom he had been in close contact since 1887, may have had a physical dimension. But the question of physical intimacy between the two men is far less important than Freud's view that homosexuality must be sublimated in order for the subject to overcome the narcissistic cathexis and achieve mature object love. What is particularly surprising in Freud's letter, however, is his association of homosexuality with paranoia, that is to say, with internalized guilt and the foreclosure of the emancipated social self, an issue he would explore in his case study of Daniel Schreber. And, as he had written to Jung in 1908, "My erstwhile friend Fliess developed a beautiful paranoia after he had disposed of his inclination, certainly not slight, toward me."[23] Of course, today Freud's association of adult homosexual narcissism with guilt and self-loathing rings hollow, but in the context of Victorian sexual mores and his own conflicted relationship with Wilhelm Fliess, it provided the dual biographical and autobiographical materials for a complex interpretation of the development of sexuality and the constitution of subjectivity, an interpretation that conditioned his reading of Leonardo's life and work, which Dalí, through an ingenious act of critical inversion, dismantled in his own myth of sexual maturation, the painting *Metamorphosis of Narcissus.*

Beyond the question of manifest content and biographical transparency, Freud recognized that what Dalí had staged in his art and writings was the subject of psychoanalysis itself—its aims, explanatory methods, and its literary, as opposed to its purely scientific, foundations. In the face of such arresting evidence, what could the good doctor do but gaze intently at his young disciple, in whose eyes, like Narcissus before a pool of water, he saw his own distorted reflection.

This text was first published in: Robert S. Lubar, "El Freud de Dalí," in Dawn Ades, ed., *Dalí, un creador disidente,* Barcelona, 2004, pp. 317–31.

1 Salvador Dalí, *The Secret Life of Salvador Dalí*, translated. by Haakon M. Chevalier (New York, 1942), p. 23.

2 Ibid., p. 23.

3 Ernst L. Freud, ed., *Letters of Sigmund Freud 1873–1939* (London, 1961), p. 233.

4 Cited in Ian Gibson, *The Shameful Life of Salvador Dalí* (London, 1997), p. 383.

5 Ernst L. Freud, ed., *Letters of Sigmund Freud* (New York, 1960), Letter 303.

6 Salvador Dalí, *The Secret Life* (see note 1), p.167, n. I.

7 Dawn Ades, *Dalí* (New York, 1982).

8 Salvador Dalí, *The Secret Life* (see note 1), p. 25.

9 Salvador Dalí, *The Secret Life* (see note 1), p. 24.

10 Ernst L. Freud, ed., *Letters of Sigmund Freud*, Letter 303.

11 James Strachey, ed., *Standard Edition of the Complete Psychological Works of Sigmund Freud*, pp. 153–92, p. 177.

12 Peter Gay, *Freud: A Life for our Time* (New York and London, 1988), p. 268.

13 Sigmund Freud, "Leonardo da Vinci and a Memory of His Childhood," reprinted in Peter Gay, *The Freud Reader* (New York and London, 1989/1995), p. 470.

14 In this 1919 addendum to his essay, Freud noted: "A remarkable discovery has been made in the Louvre picture by Oskar Pfister, which is of undeniable interest, even if one may not feel inclined to accept it without reserve. In Mary's curiously arranged and rather confusing drapery he has discovered the *outline of a vulture* and he interprets it as an *unconscious picture puzzle*." For the full citation, see James Strachey's edition of Freud's essay (New York and London, 1964/1980), pp.74–75.

15 Meyer Schapiro, "Freud and Leonardo: An Art Historical Study," in Meyer Schapiro, *Theory and Philosophy of Art: Style, Artist, and Society* (New York, 1994), pp. 153–92.

16 Freud, "Leonardo da Vinci and a Memory of his Childhood" (see note 13), pp. 562–63.

17 For a discussion, see David Vilaseca, *The Apocryphal Subject: Masochism, Identification, and Paranoia in Salvador Dalí's Autobiographical Writings* (New York, 1995).

18 See, for example, David Lomas's discussion in *The Haunted Self: Surrealism, Psychoanalysis, Subjectivity* (New Haven and London, 2000), pp. 152–54.

19 Salvador Dalí, *The Tragic Myth of Millet's Angelus* (St. Petersburg, Florida, 1986).

20 Ibid., p. 77, as discussed by Ian Gibson in *The Shameful Life* (see note 4), p. 312.

21 David Lomas, *The Haunted Self* (see note 18), p. 184.

22 Cited in Peter Gay, *Freud: A Life*, (see note 12), p. 275.

23 Ibid., p. 274.

FROM FREUDIAN UTOPIA *TO* PSÍQUICA RECREATIVA

Agustín Sánchez Vidal

The evolution of cinematography and psychoanalysis ran in parallel. The Lumière brothers presented their invention in 1895, the same year in which Sigmund Freud and Josef Breuer published *Studies on Hysteria*. The rapid development of these two innovations facilitated the encounter between them, and, by 1925, the producer Samuel Goldwyn was offering Freud the impressive fee of 100,000 dollars to act as consultant on a film about Anthony and Cleopatra. The psychologist, however, turned down the offer.

Yet his refusal did not prevent the launch of two film projects about mental illness and the treatment methods proposed by him. The first, conceived in Vienna by Adolf Josef Storfer and Siegfried Bernfeld, was never completed. The other, *Secrets of a Soul* (Georg Wilhelm Pabst, 1926), was filmed in Berlin with the collaboration of the psychoanalysts Hanns Sachs and Karl Abraham. Although Freud refused to give his approval to his two students for this project—he did not consider the medium of cinema to be capable of adequately handling such complex theories—the filming continued.

The leading role was played by Werner Krauss, who had already played a psychiatrist in *The Cabinet of Dr. Caligari* (Robert Wiene, 1920). In *Secrets of a Soul* he plays the biochemist Dr. Fellman. One day, as he is whetting his razor, his wife asks him to trim some hair on the back of her neck. Just as he is about to start, a neighbor is heard screaming in another house, where a woman has just been decapitated. The startled Fellman nicks his wife in the neck and is traumatized into associating sharp objects with uncontrollable impulses. This opening scene anticipates the notorious opening scene of *Un chien andalou* (*An Andalusian Dog*, Luis Buñuel, 1929) and assigns an important role to the razor, which is revisited in *Spellbound* (Alfred Hitchcock, 1945). The plot of the latter is very similar to that of Pabst's film and contains a dream sequence by Salvador Dalí, in which Buñuel's slit eyeball scene recurs (→figs. 22–24).

At the start of the year in which *Secrets of a Soul* was filmed, Buñuel moved to Paris, three months after the publication of the first *Manifesto of Surrealism* in October 1924. In the French capital he became acquainted with the world of cinema and was initially planning a film about Goya and then a more avant-garde project, based on a screenplay by Ramón de la Serna. In early 1929, Dalí suggested the short film *Un chien andalou*, portraying the full gamut of youthful fantasies, first and foremost desire and its limits, sex and death.

Buñuel later confirmed that these images were derived from an amalgamation of one of his dreams (the eyeball being slit while a cloud passes slowly over the moon, →fig. 25) and one of Dalí's (a hand swarming with ants). Most of them had already been used previously, however. The cut eyeball, for example, appears in Dalí's text "Mi amiga y la playa" (My friend and the beach; 1927). And the idea is already hinted at in his *Portrait of Luis Buñuel* (1924, P 141, →fig. 26), today in the Museo Reina Sofía in Madrid, in which a long cloud threatens to cover Buñuel's right eye.

The same could be said of the decomposed donkeys, which play a prominent role in *Honey is Sweeter than Blood* (1927, P 194, →p. 83), *Futile Efforts* (1927–28, P 199), and *The Stinking Ass* (1928, P 225, →fig. 10). Jan Vermeer's

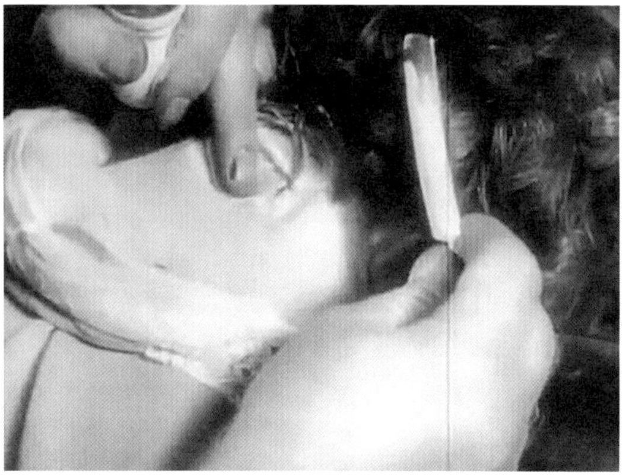

fig. 22
WERNER PABST
Secrets of a Soul, 1926

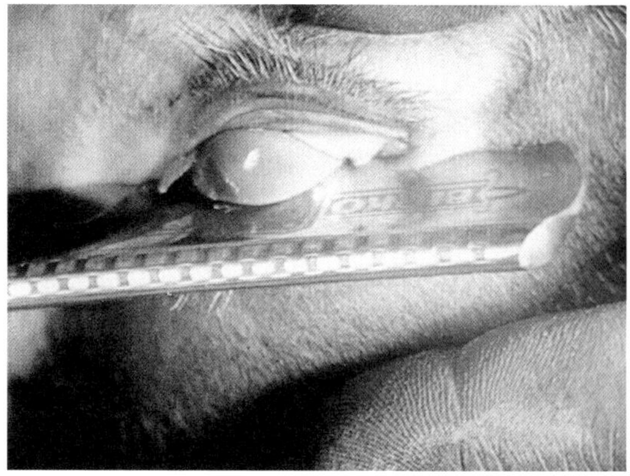

fig. 23
LUIS BUÑUEL, SALVADOR DALÍ
Un chien andalou, 1929

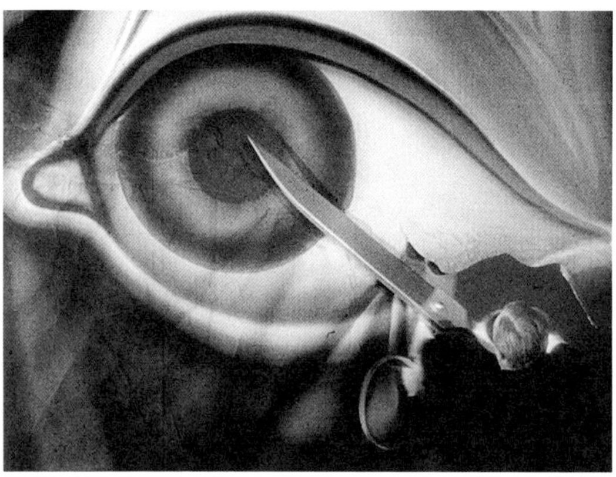

fig. 24
ALFRED HITCHCOCK
Spellbound, 1945

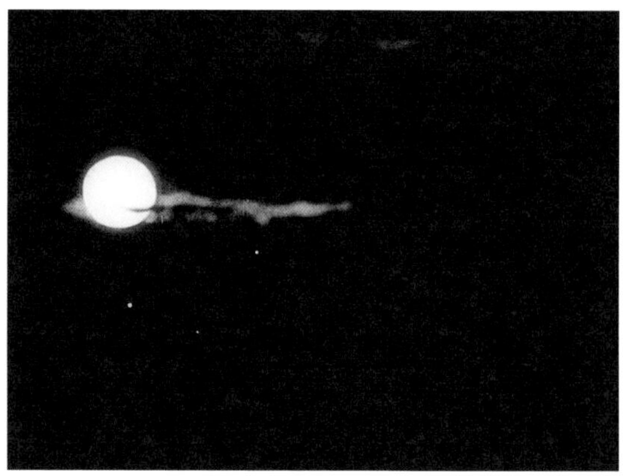

fig. 25
LUIS BUÑUEL, SALVADOR DALÍ
Un chien andalou, 1929

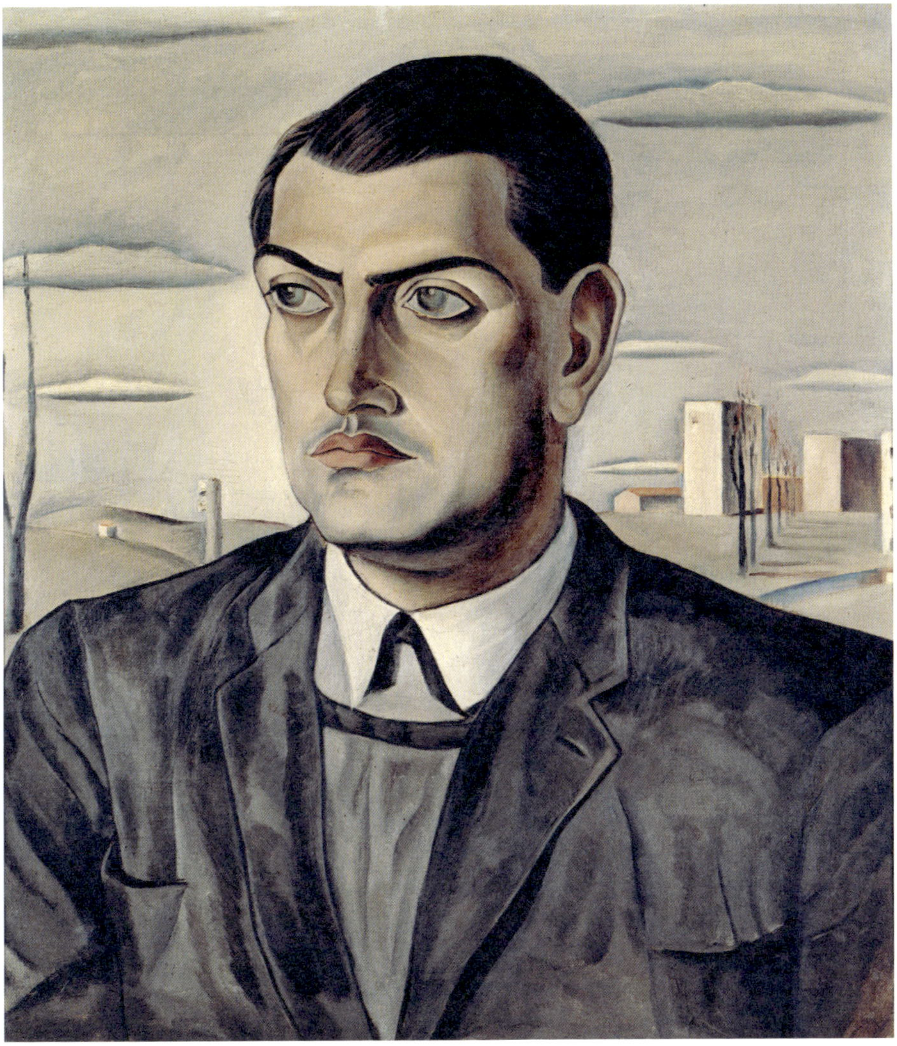

fig. 26
SALVADOR DALÍ, *Retrato de Luis Buñuel*
(*Portrait of Luis Buñuel*), 1924
Museo Nacional Centro de Arte Reina Sofía,
Madrid, cat. no. P 141

The Lacemaker, meanwhile, is cited directly in *Un chien andalou* and is referenced in Dalí's earlier paintings, such as *Girl from Figueres* (1926, P 189), while Jean-François Millet's *Angelus* (→fig. 27) is paraphrased at the end of the film (→fig. 28).

Most interesting from a structural point of view, however, is that these and other images represent a kind of "paranoid association," which in Dalí's case references the recurrent delirious associations of Lidia de Cadaqués, a fisherwoman who was able to construct obsessive connections between entirely different events. For example, she would read two separate books, which she had borrowed from Picasso, as though they were the first and second part of one and the same work.

The same phenomenon is at work in the film *Un chien andalou*, in which independent works are continually presented in such a way that they inevitably form a sequence. Of particular significance here are works that show an injured or amputated hand (→fig. 29), such as *The Difficult Crossing* (1926) or *One Night Museum* (1927, →fig. 30) by René Magritte. Or the scene where the main protagonist is reading a book while the young man talking to her is watching a swarm of ants on his hand (→fig. 31). This composition again links two pictures by the Belgian artist, *The Submissive Reader* and *The Mysterious Suspicion* (→fig. 32), both from 1928. Equally, the theme of recurrent sexual harassment had already been used by Magritte that same year in his painting *The Titanic Days*.[1]

No less significant are the iconographic references to insects, such as the African death's-head hawkmoth or the praying mantis. The former is superimposed on the film's main protagonist in an alternating montage, so that the moth's thorax, which shows the image of a skull, replaces the girl's face. This Freudian connection between Eros and Thanatos is inspired by the same moth that is being shown to a girl by the shepherd in the painting *The Hireling Shepherd* (1851) by the English Pre-Raphaelite William Holman Hunt.[2]

The same concept underlies the final image of *Un chien andalou*. The position of the man and the woman calls to mind the figures in Millet's *Angelus* (→fig. 27). Later, Dalí made even more explicit reference to Millet's painting with his curtain for the ballet *Tristan fou* choreographed by Léonide Massine, which premiered in New York in 1944. Once again, eroticism and death are inextricably linked, the woman's pose here resembling that of a female praying mantis, which devours the male after mating. The picture anticipates the interpretation the artist was to develop further in his book *The Tragic Myth of Millet's Angelus.* In this, he established the basis for his "paranoiac-critical method," using Freud's 1910 essay "Leonardo da Vinci, A Memory of His Childhood" as his starting point.

The reference to Eros and Thanatos is further emphasized in *Un chien andalou* and *L'âge d'or* (*Age of Gold,* 1930) through the use of the "Prelude" and "Liebestod" from Wagner's opera *Tristan and Isolde.* Half a century before Freud, the composer anticipated—better than any of his contemporaries—the significant role of the psyche in mythology, such as the story of Oedipus, which later led to the statement that "all the mature Wagner operas except *The Mastersingers* are like animated textbooks of psychoanalysis."[3]

The smooth collaboration between Buñuel and Dalí in *Un chien andalou* was not repeated in their next work, *L'âge d'or.* In summer 1929 Dalí met Gala, which led to a rift with his father. This and other circumstances explain the continuities and the differences between the two films. To a certain extent, the second film represented a departure from the individual and adolescent perspective of the earlier short film and added a social and more mature dimension. In addition to having read the French entomologist Jean-Henri Fabre and Freud's theories, a new decisive influence here were the writings of the Marquis de Sade. *L'âge d'or* starts out as a documentary about scorpions, written by Fabre, and ends with the staging of a quote from *The 120 Days of Sodom,* 1785.

L'âge d'or is more "narrative" than *Un chien andalou* and is no longer reliant on the "paranoiac association" of a series of (largely painterly) images, but rather on the overlapping of different blocks of film in a form of collage. Added to this

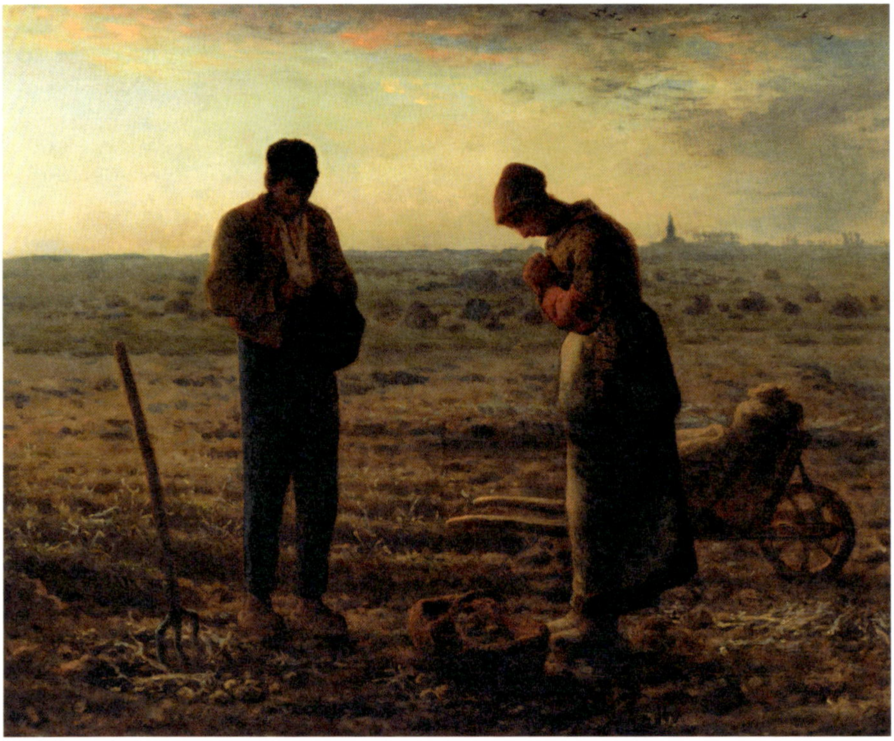

fig. 27
JEAN-FRANÇOIS MILLET, *L'Angélus*
(*The Angelus*), 1857–59
Musée d'Orsay, Paris

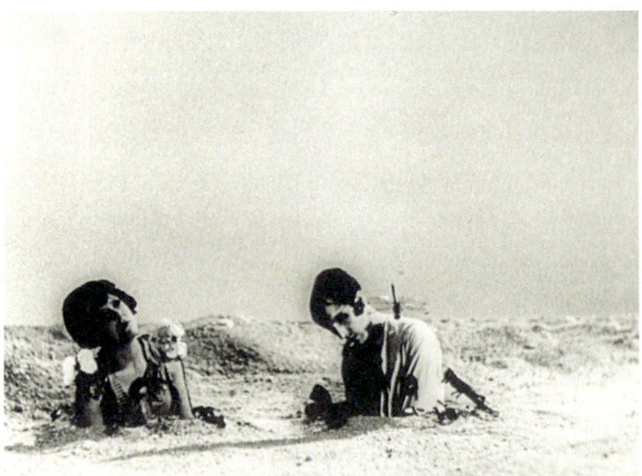

fig. 28
LUIS BUÑUEL, SALVADOR DALÍ
Un chien andalou, 1929

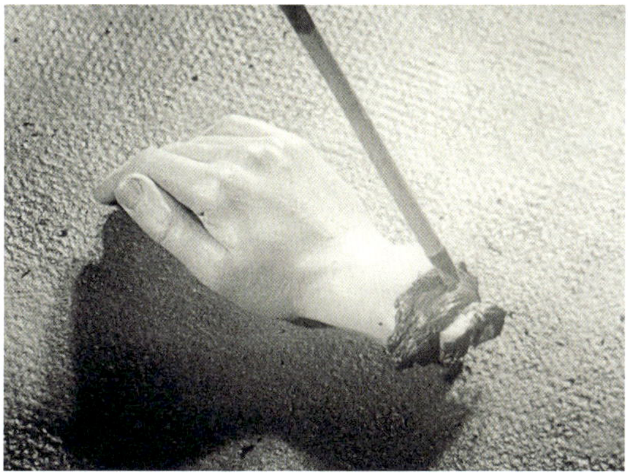

fig. 29
LUIS BUÑUEL, SALVADOR DALÍ
Un chien andalou, 1929

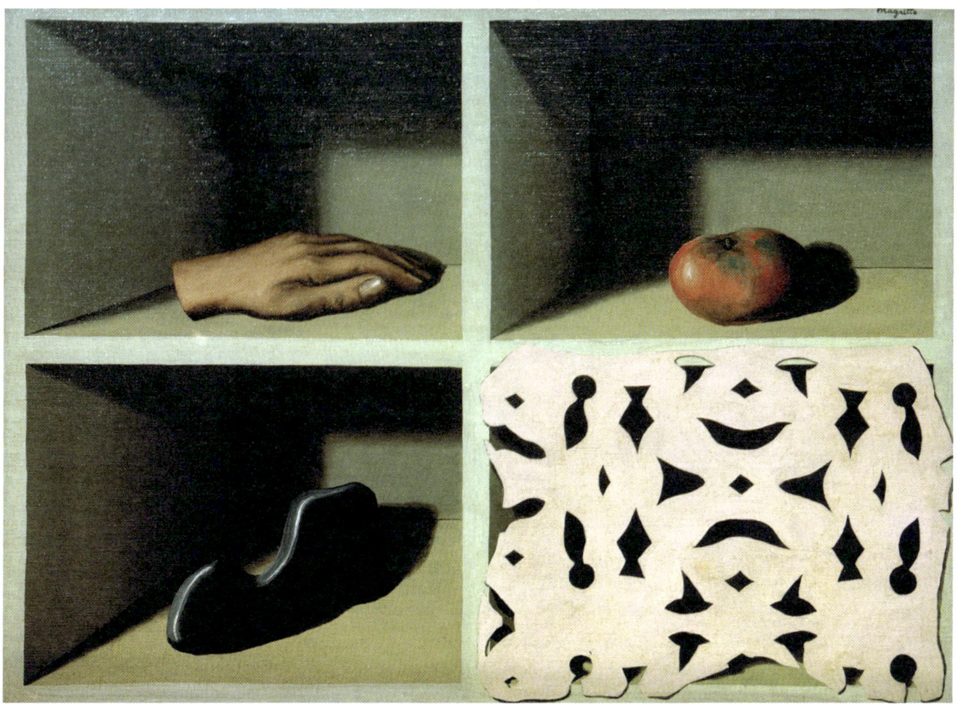

fig. 30
RENÉ MAGRITTE, *Le musée d'une nuit*
(*One Night Museum*), 1927
Private collection, London

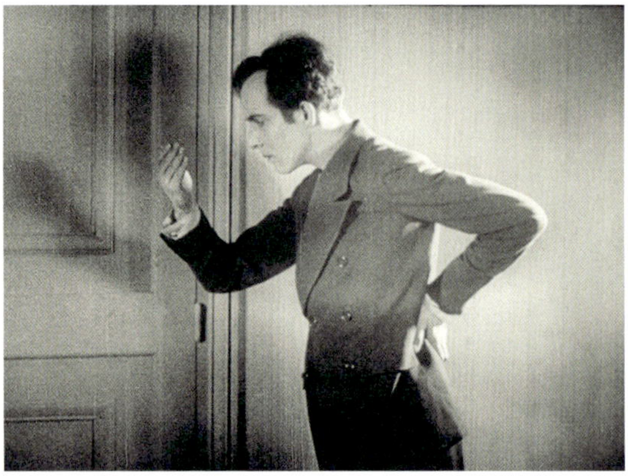

fig. 31
LUIS BUÑUEL, SALVADOR DALÍ
Un chien andalou, 1929

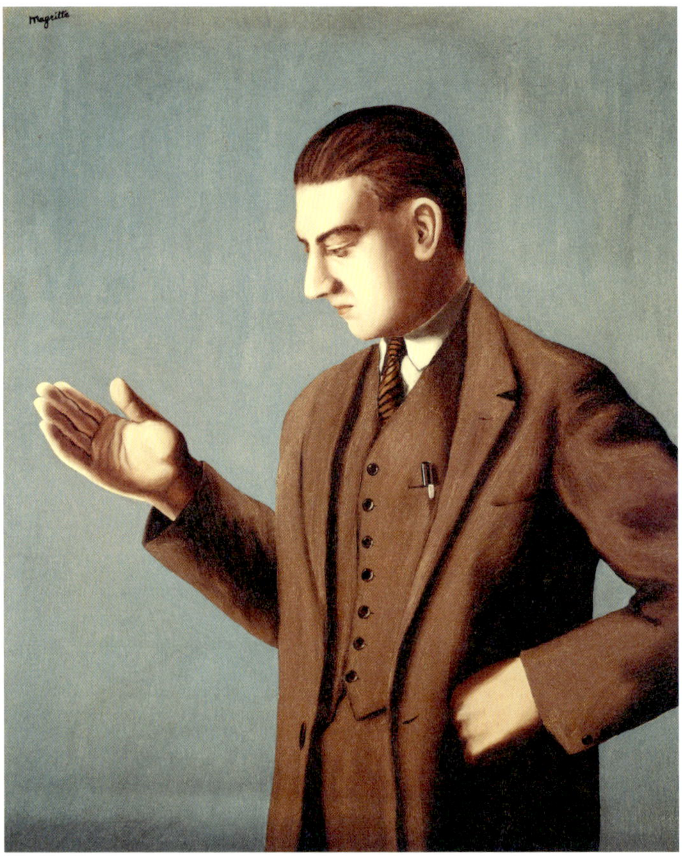

fig. 32
RENÉ MAGRITTE, *Le soupçon mystérieux*
(*The Mysterious Suspicion*), 1928
Private collection

is a soundtrack with its own connotations. There is, for example, the off-screen voice in the garden scene, in which the two lovers can be heard talking without moving their lips. We seem to be given an insight into the deepest recesses of the woman's mind when she says: "What joy! What joy in having killed our children."

Between the beginning, penned by Fabre, and the end, inspired by Sade, *L'âge d'or* is above all a Freudian film. The brochure published for the premiere and the supporting manifesto by the Surrealist group are full of expressions such as "Freudian slip," "sex drive—death wish," "sublimation," "primitive taboos," "regression," "unconscious language," and "paranoid tendencies." This can be observed from the very moment when the scorpions living under the rocks give way to a group of starving and unkempt bandits, scattered across the craggy terrain of the Cap de Creus. They are, effectively, the last survivors of a primitive horde, soon to be displaced by a posse of innovators who establish Imperial Rome on their remains, thus laying the foundations of Judeo-Christian culture.

The ceremony is interrupted by the lascivious cries of a woman (Lya Lys), rolling in the mud with a man (Gaston Modot). The two protagonists are promptly separated by several nuns and two policemen, and they then have to overcome all kinds of obstacles before they are reunited. The challenge, in cinematographic terms, was to synchronize the couple's gestures, which express a growing erotic attraction, by means of match cuts, a continuous soundtrack, and parallel editing. This tension intensifies when Modot spots a poster advertising hand cream, and Lya Lys is seen reclining on a sofa with a bandaged finger, thus adding a masturbatory connotation. Later she is seen in her room polishing her nails, and back in the living room playing with her ring—a gesture that is interspersed with the image of a waiter rubbing a bottle of liqueur. All of this increases the muted tension and culminates in the gamekeeper shooting his son and Modot slapping his host. The result is an extraordinary version of the kind of gags woven into the plot of his narrative films by Buster Keaton, whom Dalí and Buñuel so admired.

In *The Psychopathology of Everyday Life* (1901), Freud analyzed the case of a female patient who had injured the ring finger of her left hand while cutting her nails. It happened on her wedding anniversary, and the incident suggested marriage problems. The psychiatrist also noted that in her role in a drama about adultery the actress Eleonora Duse introduced a similar symptomatic action: after a violent scene with her husband, she is seen playing with her wedding ring while waiting for her lover, taking it off and putting it back on again—a clear expression of her desire to lie in her lover's arms.[4]

But Freud's influence is visible not only in this and many other details of *L'âge d'or,* but also in its entire structure and in the title. As mentioned previously, the posse of bandits appearing at the beginning have something of Darwin's primal horde described by Freud in his book *Totem and Taboo* (1913). In *The Future of an Illusion* (1927) he divides history into a series of periods culminating in a hypothetical golden age, in which work and pleasure would be reconciled. In contrast to Hesiod in *Theogony* or *Work and Days,* this Arcadian period is thus located not in the past but in the future.[5]

With regard to *Totem and Taboo,* Dalí introduced a significant variation to the primal horde's ritual patricide by adding filicide, as alluded to by Lya Lys's off-screen voice mentioned earlier ("What joy! What joy in having killed our children!") and enacted by the gamekeeper shooting his son. Dalí called this the "William Tell complex," portrayed in various pictures from this period following the falling-out with his fearsome father. In one picture, entitled *William Tell* (1930, P254, →fig. 33), the father is shown as castrator driving away his son, his penis exposed and wielding a pair of scissors. The beard makes him resemble the conductor who snatches the girl from Gaston Modot at the end of *L'âge d'or* (→fig. 34). Another painting, entitled *William Tell and Gradiva* (1932, P277), shows the bearded patriarchal figure, once again hypersexualized, attacking a young woman. Her name is derived from the protagonist in the eponymous novel by Wilhelm Jensen, published in 1902 and analyzed by Freud in 1907, and alludes to Gala.

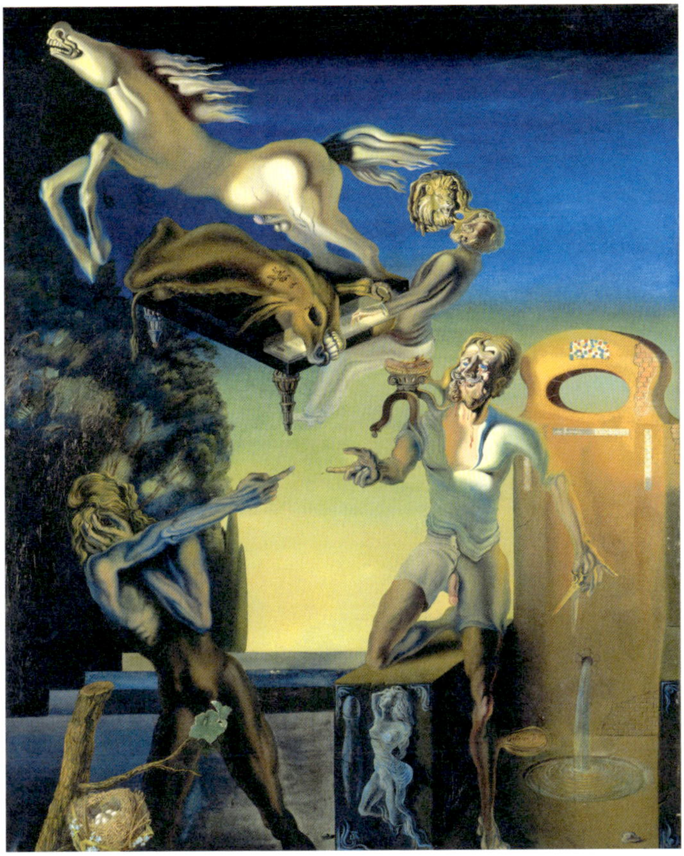

fig. 33
SALVADOR DALÍ, *Guillaume Tell* (*William Tell*), 1930
Centre Pompidou—Musée national d'art moderne—Centre de création industrielle, Paris
cat. no. P 254

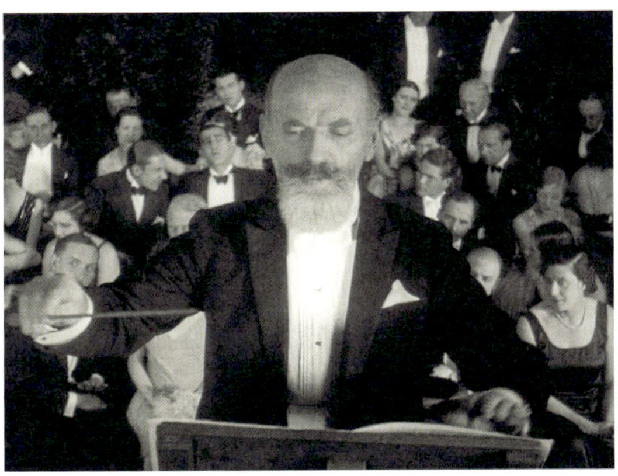

fig. 34
LUIS BUÑUEL, SALVADOR DALÍ
L'âge d'or, 1930

It is not therefore surprising that this "complex" appears repeatedly after 1930 in some of Dali's film projects, which he was already developing independently of Buñuel at the time. The most interesting of these films is the project he called "a film against the family," which draws on both psychoanalysis (Freud and Otto Rank) and historical materialism (Marx and Engels). It has occasionally been associated with *Babaouo* or the ballet *William Tell*, but surviving manuscripts suggest that it refers to a separate project. In its dominant radicalism it regards marriage as "legal prostitution," triggering neuroses and a conflict between the pleasure principle and reality. It is based on Freud's theory of infantile "polymorphous perversity" that Dalí adopted and applied to his own situation. One of the key scenes is the "butterfly hunt," also expressed in a drawing, which is evidently a hidden reference to incest between a boy and his sister.[6]

This sensitive subject was not the only one the artist was planning to explore. Other projects were aimed at a wider public. In 1933 he sketched a Surrealist amusement park in which the impulse-driven use of space is exaggerated. Also in the same year, he wrote some notes under the intriguing title Psíquica recreativa (recreational psychology).[7]

In terms of cinematographic approach, in several of his other projects Dalí reprised the cosmetics adverts sequence from *L'âge d'or* that follows the forced separation of the two lovers. Modot attempts to summon up the image of Lya Lys with the help of advertising posters for hand cream or stockings, for example, that he encounters, until he is eventually able to break through the illusion of advertising and sees the girl standing before him in the flesh. In this way, Dalí offers an astute analysis of advertising mechanisms, which aim to short-circuit and hijack desire and replace it with a socially defined and controlled narrative, a displacement activity that, once channeled into consumerism—and directed to the cash register—is intended to supplant and gratify the libido.

Interestingly, in 1944, Dalí used almost the exact same images as in *L'âge d'or* for an advert for Bryans Hosiery in *Vogue* magazine (→figs. 35 and 36). Already in 1941, in an updated version of *The Clouds*, in which he substituted the sophists lampooned by Aristophanes with Freudians and Surrealists, the artist had forsaken the avant-garde cause. By comparing psychoanalysis with sophistry, Dalí fired a broadside of considerable significance, given that he had previously declared Sigmund Freud to be the great milestone that separated ancient Greece from the twentieth century.

But we can go back even further, namely to 1939, the year Freud died. In that year, Dalí designed his *Dream of Venus* pavilion for the World's Fair in New York (→fig. 39) in a context that combined psychoanalysis with Henry Ford's assembly line. It was no coincidence that the event was planned by Freud's American nephew Edward Bernays, one of the most important popularizers of the Viennese psychiatrist, who published his uncle's work in the United States and, based on his theories, invented modern advertising. The event in New York was sponsored by major North American corporations and was like a dress rehearsal for the type of standardized mass production that laid the foundations for what was later to become known as the "consumer society," delayed by nearly two decades by the outbreak of World War II. With his pavilion, Dalí sought to create a seamless link between the ancient and modern Venus myths—while at the same time designing window displays for the Bonwit Teller department stores. From this venture into the world of fashion new opportunities arose. But it was also a different Dalí now, one who henceforth paid greater attention to Hollywood than to the Paris circles that had celebrated his cinematographic collaborations with Buñuel.

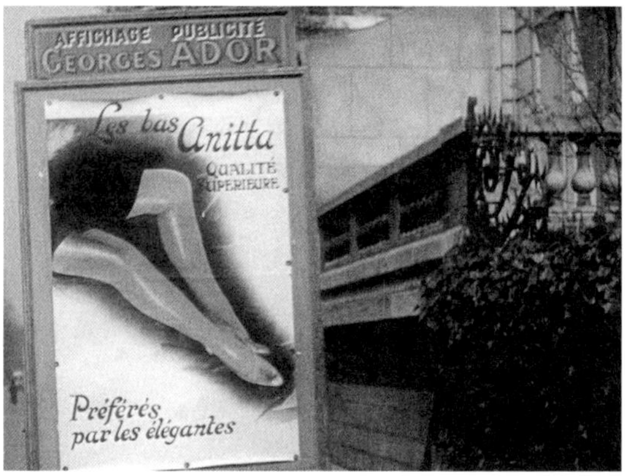

fig. 35
LUIS BUÑUEL, SALVADOR DALÍ
L'âge d'or, 1930

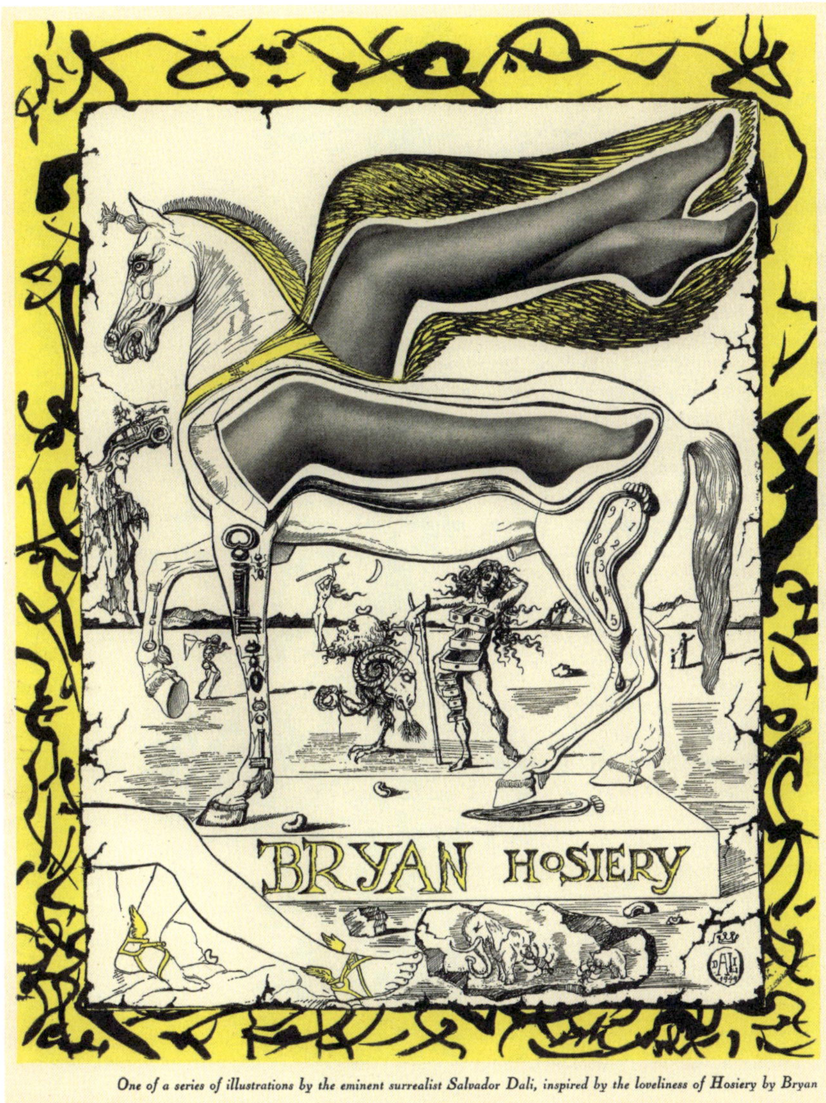

fig. 36
SALVADOR DALÍ, advertisement for Bryans Hosiery
Vogue, October 15, 1944

1 Magritte was quite perturbed, as Buñuel wrote to Dalí in a letter from Paris on June 24, 1929, describing Magritte's response to the premiere of *Un chien andalou*: "There were things that Magritte liked a lot and others that he didn't like and that even upset him. The film obviously unravels his picture somewhat," quoted from Jo Evans and Breixo Viejo (eds.), *Luis Buñuel: Correspondencia escogida* (Madrid, 2018), p. 87.

2 Dalí referred to this picture in his article "Le surréalisme spectral de l'éternel feminin préraphaélite," in *Minotaure*, no. 8, 1936, pp. 46–49.

3 Bryan Magee, *Aspects of Wagner* (Oxford, 1988), p. 36.

4 *Zur Psychopathologie des Alltagslebens*, translated into English in 1914 by A. A. Brill. It was the first book by Freud to be translated into Spanish as *Psicopatología de la vida cotidiana*, published by Biblioteca Nueva de Madrid in 1922 with a foreword by José Ortega y Gasset, marking the start of the translation of the psychiatrist's complete works into Spanish and thus initiating the exposure of Dalí and Buñuel to his theories.

5 See Paul Hammond, *L'âge d'or* (London, 1997), p. 15; Juan José Ipar, "La utopía freudiana," in *Alcmeon: Revista Argentina de Clínica Neuropsiquiátrica*, vol. 6, no. 4, March 1998, http://www.alcmeon.com.ar/6/24/a24_05.htm (accessed on June 21, 2019).

6 For details of these film projects, see my introduction and comments on Salvador Dalí, *Obra completa*, vol. III, *Poesía, prosa, teatro y cine* (Barcelona, 2004).

7 The comments on *Psíquica recreativa* were published in *Dalí: Todas las sugestiones poéticas y todas las posibilidades plásticas*, exh. cat., Museo Nacional Centro de Arte Reina Sofía, Madrid (Madrid, 2013), pp. 330–31. In 1957, André Breton described the artist in his book *L'art magique* as a "boring, anecdotal painter of religious images from the Hiroshima era," who had transformed himself "not only into an amateur physicist but also into a common thimble rigger who is tolerated by the police."

SALVADOR DALÍ'S DREAM OF VENUS: *ANALYZING THE DREAM*

Ingrid Schaffner

Billed as the "the first surrealist pavilion in exposition history," the *Dream of Venus* was Salvador Dalí's contribution to the 1939 New York World's Fair. On May 30th, just days before the much-anticipated opening, a telegram broke the news: SALVADOR Dalí *DREAM OF VENUS*...POSTPONED ...DUE TO COMPLEXITY OF SUBCONSCIOUS..." The actual situation was far more chaotic. Dalí had been commissioned mere months prior, and the exigencies of time, money, and the artist's hyper-exacting vision had reached a crisis point. When the *Dream of Venus* finally did open its door to the public, the artist and his wife Gala had already sailed to Paris, leaving open to interpretation an environmental work of art chock-full of Surrealist imagery, Freudian references, Dalínian iconography, and everyday associations—at a time when every day drew the world closer to war.

The theme of the 1939 New York World's Fair was "The World of Tomorrow," and that world was made emblematic by the streamlined Trylon and Perisphere structures that towered over the many national pavilions and edifying exhibits that comprised the fair's main plan (→fig. 37). This is not where one would have found the *Dream of Venus,* however, which existed in a parallel universe, a midway carnival zone known as the Amusement Area. Its landmark feature was the colossal Parachute Jump, towering over such attractions as "Frank Buck's Jungleland," Morris Gest's "Little Miracle Town," Admiral Byrd's "Penguin Island," and *Billy Rose's Aquacade.*

How Salvador Dalí's *Dream of Venus* came to be located amidst carnival rides, girlie shows, and other empyreans of American fun, signifies the aspirations and moment of the 1939 World's Fair. The Great Depression was at a nadir point when the fair was launched as nothing less than a juggernaut to break through economic and cultural paralysis. Paramount to its success was a democratic appeal to audiences who were widely and specifically invoked, from the general public to readers of *Vogue* magazine. It was the latter group, no doubt, that the fair's commissioners had in mind when they accepted a proposal for an Amusement Zone concession that billed itself as the "'funny house' of tomorrow."

The original plan for a Surrealist House, shaped like an eye and structured along the lines of a walk through Sigmund Freud's research and discoveries in the realm of the subconscious, was submitted by the art dealer Julien Levy and the architect Ian Woodner. The plan evolved dramatically as the project took on backers, funders, and promoters—including the theatrical agent William Morris, the art collector Edward James, and a rubber manufacturer (William Gardiner's industry proved invaluable to realizing the props and giving some wiggle to the *Dream*); their investment called for a "name" artist to headline the pavilion. Salvador Dalí's name already loomed large in the public imagination, having appeared on the cover of *Time* magazine at the time of the Museum of Modern Art's sensational exhibition *Fantastic Art, Dada, Surrealism* in 1936 (→fig. 38). Plus, he was represented by Levy's gallery in New York. On April 10, 1939, Dalí World's Fair (DWF) was incorporated.

Dalí's *Dream of Venus* opened on June 15th and operated

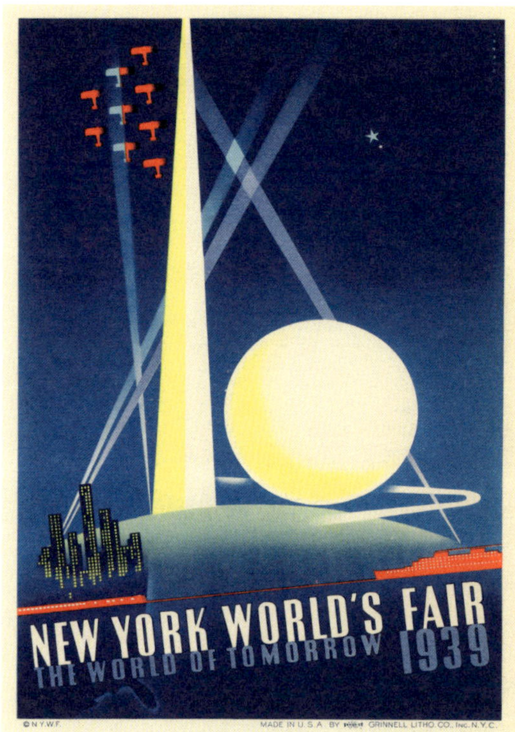

fig. 37
Poster for the New York World's Fair
The World of Tomorrow, 1939
Smithsonian Libraries, Washington, D.C.

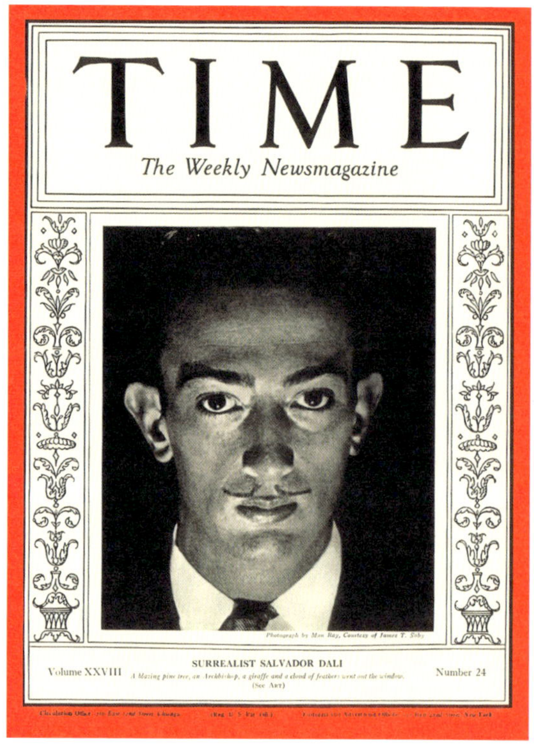

fig. 38
Salvador Dalí on the cover of *Time* magazine
December 14, 1936, photo: Man Ray

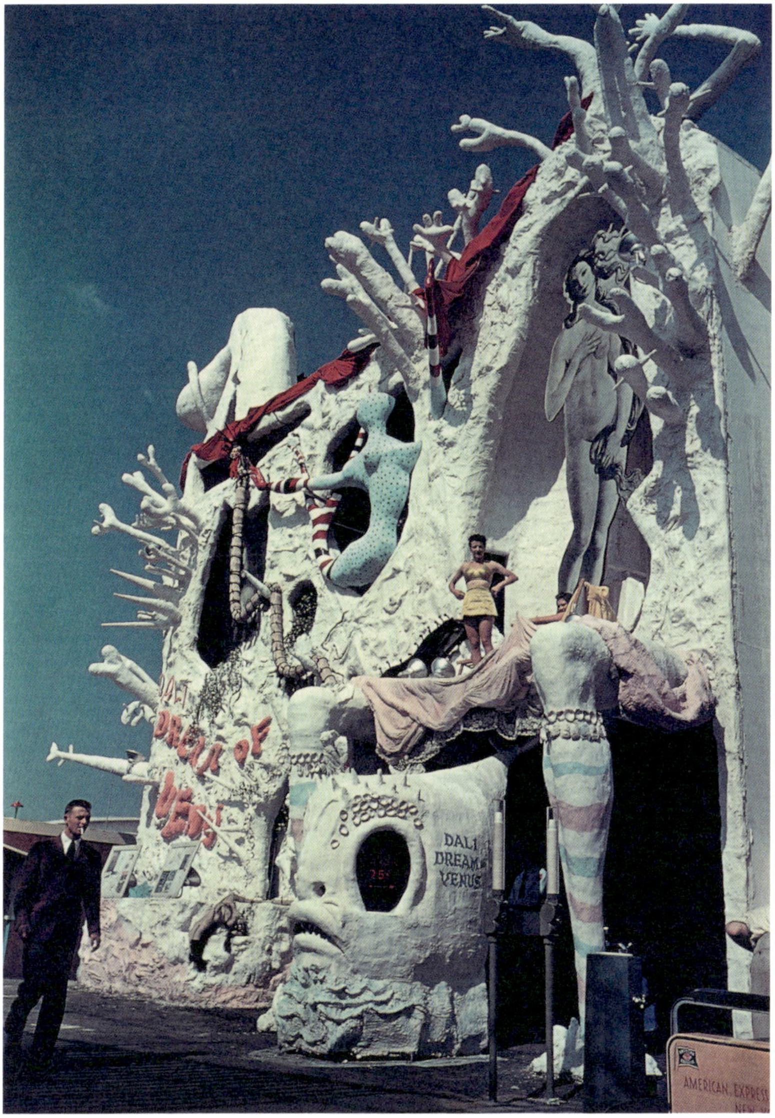

fig. 39
SALVADOR DALÍ, *Dream of Venus*
View of the pavilion, photo: Eric Schaal

through both of the fair's 1939 and 1940 seasons. It consisted of a sculpturally encrusted, free-standing building with a ticket booth at the entrance to a sequence of interior chambers, each one containing a strange diorama that was activated by a live cast of hard-working, scantily-clad performers (→fig. 39). The first chamber, and main attraction, was an underwater living room tableau with mermaids diving through the tank to tickle the keys of the "rubber piano woman," milk a fake cow, and perform other Surrealist acts. Further down the corridor, there was Venus herself, exposed topless under a luxurious red satin coverlet on a bed that was 36 feet long. Parading past, the public could hear Venus's (pre-recorded) dream, intoning images of sex, death, and fear of the void—the stock fascinations of Freudian psychology. Finally, there was the *Rainy Taxi* for Christopher Columbus—what more needs to be said to establish its Surrealist credentials?

When the fair closed, the *Dream of Venus* was destroyed. Long a footnote of Surrealist art history, the *Dream* was rediscovered through a marvelous cache of photographs taken by Eric Schaal (1905–1994), who documented Dalí's attraction from top to bottom, inside and out, on assignment for *Life* magazine. These photographs form the basis for the following analysis of the Surrealist funhouse at the 1939 New York World's Fair.

Before he became disillusioned with his *Dream of Venus*, Dalí seemed convinced that, once his intentions were properly expressed, his vision would be embraced by an appreciative American public who was sure to demand that he be given the opportunities, and means, to dream his dreams on the scale they deserved. Even more than his films *Un chien andalou* (1929) and *L'âge d'or* (1930)—Surrealist cult classics made in collaboration with Luis Buñuel—Dalí's *Dream of Venus* was a bid for future commissions in the world of mass culture. His success might be measured by the two propositions that came to Dalí from Hollywood during the 1940s: one from Walt Disney (to make a never-completed animated film called *Destino*) and one from Alfred Hitchcock (to produce the dream sequence for his cinematic psychoanalytic primer *Spellbound*).[1] Yet, here in the Amusement Zone—amid the Surrealism of the fair, public fascination with Dalí, and events of the day—the *Dream of Venus* invites the analysis that sets it apart.

Dalí's work was devoted to expressing the three basic conditions of human consciousness, based on the principles of psychoanalysis: sex, death, and fear of the cosmos. As Dalí decried in his "Declaration of the Independence of the Imagination": "Man is entitled to the enigma and the simulacrums that are found in the great vital constants: the sexual instinct, the consciousness of death, the physical melancholy caused by 'time-space.'"[2] As the architectural embodiment of those themes, Dalí's *Dream of Venus* is a craggy, skeletal, febrile mass of indeterminate structures. Both formed and formless, it threatens to collapse on itself (and anyone inside of it) if not for the branches poking abundantly askew out of its façade. These turn out to be arms and crutches, propping up the building against the crush of the void. One brittle crutch supports a pendulous blob atop the pediment. The incipient snap latent in this image represented for Dalí a sensation of falling, which he associated with both sleep (slipping into an unconscious dream state) and birth (being dropped into conscious reality).

Dalí's delirious architecture is perfectly up to Surrealist, as well as carnival, code. According to the Surrealists, there were two master builders. The first was fantastic folk builder Ferdinand "The Postman" Cheval: a Drôme letter carrier who devoted thirty-three years (1879–1912) to cementing volcanic rocks and sculpting figures and plant forms into an uninhabitable domicile that he called his "Dream Palace" in the south of France. The other was the architect Antonio Gaudí, whose undulating, tile-encrusted benches and grottos at Parc Güell (1900–1914) are some of the jewels of Barcelona—a city writhing with Art Nouveau that he studded with gems. A fellow Catalan, Gaudí was well known to Dalí, who visited the park as a child. Dalí was living in Barcelona in 1926, the year Gaudí was killed by a streetcar. Dalí's own anti-Modern brand of Modernism echoes the architect's tenacious commitment to medieval systems (both in building and society) and to the radically handcrafted.

In his own writing on architecture, Dalí praises Art Nouveau for carrying the Gothic to its illogical conclusions: form followed the function of pure desires, "desires, moreover, that are the most shady, discredited, and shameful."[3] He applauds columns "tilted, unable to support themselves on their own, like the weary necks of heavy hydrocephalic heads, [emerging] for the first time in the world of the hardened undulations of *sculpted water* with a photographic instantaneity that has been unknown until now." Given Dalí's use of double images in his own work, he loved that shape-shifting aspect of Art Nouveau, which made, for example, Hector Guimard's street lamps outside Paris subway stations appear to metamorphose into wriggling vines. He saw in this imagery of architecture consuming itself the terrifying and thrilling essence of Surrealist beauty.

Dalí trumped André Breton's call for a new "convulsive" aesthetic (which was to be the edifying subject of the human kaleidoscope inside Julien Levy's Surrealist fun house) with his own charge: "Beauty will be edible or will cease to be." Upon first beholding it in 1934, Dalí extolled the beauty of Manhattan: "It rose before me, verdigris, pink, and creamy-white. It looked like an immense Gothic Roquefort cheese. I love Roquefort." Confected as his tribute to the most gloriously medieval of modern cities, Dalí's *Dream of Venus* really was a piece of cake, ready to consume itself.

Of course, cannibalism is one of the primal fears we expect to encounter inside a carnival House of Horrors, through a nightmare tableau of, say, some gourmet monster about to tuck away a severed leg. Indeed, the constants of Dalí's art are also the basic psychological fare of the midway, where there is bound to be a concession that resembles the *Dream of Venus,* except that its Gothic façade is charcoal-colored, not pink and white. And the interior plan is tricked up to scare the bejesus out of you. Instead of good old-fashioned fright, the responses Dalí has in mind for his World's Fair confection are more ambiguous and complex—like guilt, fear of castration, a wish to go back to the womb. It is an amusement for the "world of tomorrow," where women figure eternal.

Dalí's pavilion is named after the Roman goddess of love, who rose from the sea and who stands over the doorway (→fig. 39).[4] As Dalí's elected pin-up girl, Venus comes with a conceptual caveat bound to affect the heartiest of men: her father inseminated the sea after being castrated by his son, who threw dad's genitals into the waves that then bore Venus. Another mythic babe to inspire pause is Mélusine, who appears to be bursting through the façade of the pavilion, breasts first. She extends one black wing, a neck so long it drapes, and, way at the crest of the building, her head. According to medieval lore, Mélusine was the perfect wife in every way but one: during her Saturday bath, she transformed into a winged serpent and terrorized the neighborhood. Exposed by her human husband, Mélusine is just the kind of monstrously duplicitous and beautiful woman the Surrealists admired.

In drawing on mythology, Dalí was not being as arcane as one might imagine. Myth provided the archetypes for psychoanalysis and the muses within Surrealism. But it also constituted part of the common visual language within the "World of Tomorrow," where there were mythic sculptures of Atlas, Pegasus, and Terpsichore (the muse of dance) as well as of radio waves becoming muses hurtling themselves to Earth. The mural on the Communications Building showed "the progress of the art of speech from the age of myth to the age when myths were household fixtures."[5] In other words, the 1939 present.

Dalí contrived to bring personal myth to the façade through a hybrid figure based on two famous works by his favorite painter, Leonardo da Vinci. On the shoulders of Da Vinci's finger-pointing St. John the Baptist, Dalí collaged the smiling face of the Mona Lisa. Compared to the moustache Marcel Duchamp penciled above her lips in 1919, Dalí's gesture seems less irreverent than strange; like good transvestitism, as opposed to bad drag, it almost passes unnoticed. For those intimately acquainted with Dalí, however, it would have been hard not to observe the resemblance between the sphinx-like Mona Lisa and Gala,

Dalí's wife who first attracted him with her boyish physique.

For those with more conventional tastes, there were the Sirens, "chipper gals" posted on the balcony above the entry, to lure visitors not to a Homeric death but into spending the price of admission. William Morris had suggested upping the charge, but Dalí refuted: "You will charge a quarter. I paint [...] for the masses, for the common man, for the people. If you charge the people forty cents they won't come."[6] Did anyone ask: "When is a ticket booth not a ticket booth?" Dalí had a view on that one, too: when it is shaped like a knobby fish head and is straddled between a pair of women's legs, spread wide for sex or birth, around a gaping maw of an entrance way.

Before entering, stop and notice the fish head, which has, besides its erotic placement, a menacing aspect due to a mouth full of tiny teeth (→fig. 40). Indeed, this head is imbued with a sense of horror that might come from a childhood experience of Dalí's. In his autobiography, he recalls being terrorized one day, when, while playing on the rocks at the family's seaside home in Cadaqués, he caught a little fish in his hands and saw that its face looked exactly like a grasshopper's. He cast the fish away and buried the memory, he says, until his father later prompted him to recall the incident with perfect clarity.[7] A reader of Sigmund Freud might understand this as a screen memory. Dalí alludes to a youthful suspicion that his aunt and his father were having an affair; perhaps the encounter with the soft-bellied fish (called a "slobberer") cum insect (Dalí liked to stretch out and stroke the soft pink wings hidden inside of grasshoppers' carapaces) masked an upsetting encounter with adult sexuality.

Dalí was fervently interested in Freud's theories, and he, more literally than any other Surrealist, constructed an iconography with Freudian analysis in mind. While it is possible to move past the fish/grasshopper-headed ticket booth and through Dalí's *Dream of Venus*, psychoanalyzing each detail, that was not the key to seeing it as an attraction in the Amusement Zone, where anyone could see it looked like a penis. Contemporary visitors had a general knowledge of both psychology and Surrealism (from

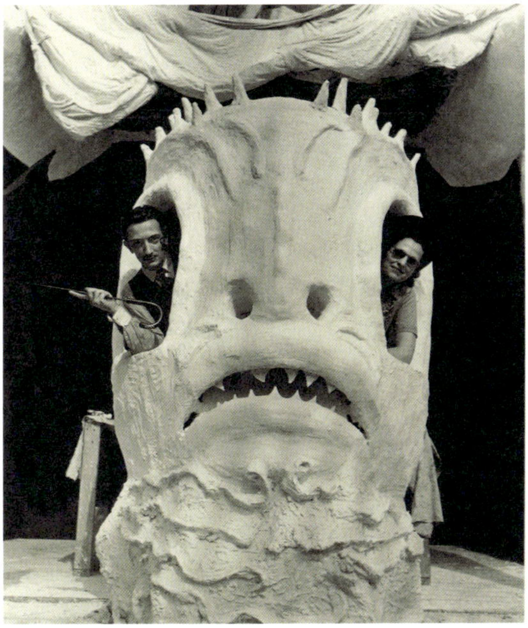

fig. 40
Salvador Dalí and Gala in the ticket booth
at the entrance to *Dream of Venus,* 1939
Photo: Eric Schaal

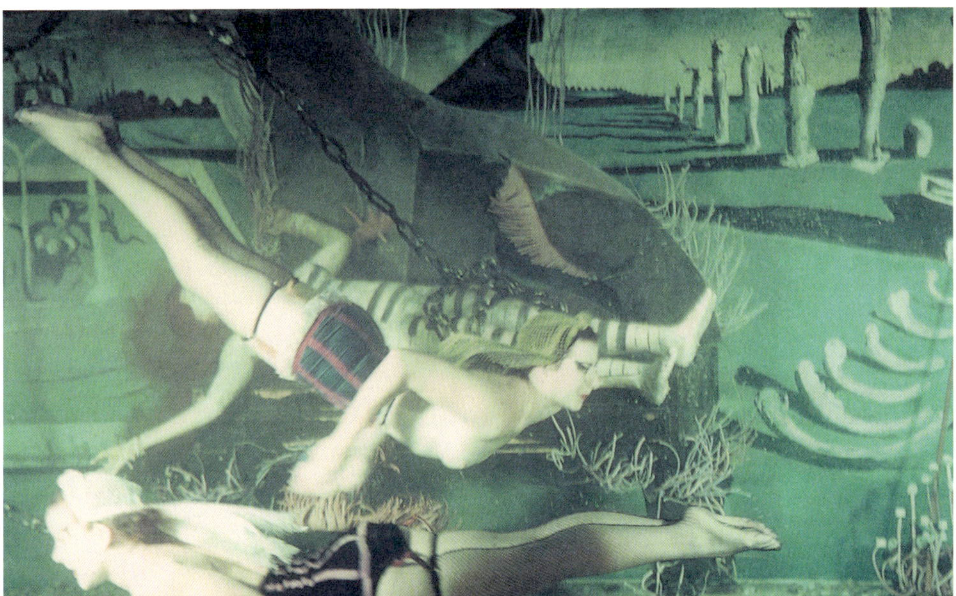

fig. 41
SALVADOR DALÍ, *Dream of Venus,*
"Venus's Pre-natal Chateau Beneath the Water"
Photo: Eric Schaal

vague to vogue) informing their perceptions—perceptions that were themselves the subject of these modern forms of representation. But what made Dalí's art so effective was its ability to trigger a sense of the surreal and psychological in terms of everyday life. His icons derived as much from personal memory, culture, and theory, as they were activated by collective memory, mass culture, and current events. Dalí seems to imply that negotiating the multivalent meaning of images—his "paranoiac-critical method"—was the real entertainment in store for thrill seekers at the World's Fair. His *Dream of Venus* simply made the roller-coaster dips and rises of eroticism and anxiety, which were a part of modern experience everywhere, into a walk-through concession.

Inside the pavilion, the first exhibit is the wet tank, or "Venus's Pre-natal Chateau Beneath the Water" (→fig. 41). It is a Dalínian living room animated by swimming female performers in costumes that leave their breasts exposed through heart-shaped cutouts or fishnet bras. Some go totally topless over lace-up bottoms that resemble Gilded Age girdles. These evoke the "World of Yesterday," which fair-goers would have visited upon leaving the Perisphere. This recreation of 1851 New York, with its cobbled streets, guttering gaslight, Victorian façades, and actors in period dress, dramatically contrasted with the "World of Tomorrow." The early telephone seen in old New York differs from those at the *Dream*, where bouquets of receivers bob like clumps of seaweed in the "Pre-natal Chateau."

The telephone receiver that combined the ear and mouth parts into one hand piece was new to the 1930s. The shape of the telephone was, according to American industrial designer Raymond Loewy's 1934 "Evolution Chart," on a parallel course with the fashioning of the female body, both becoming more streamlined as the century progressed.[8] Dalí also envisioned a sexy relationship between the two when he created his *Lobster Telephone* of 1936 (lobsters being snappy substitutes for female genitalia, →p. 148). When asked about the big black receivers in his 1939 still life paintings, Dalí said, "The telephone represents the blackened bones of my father passing between the male and female figures in Millet's *Angelus* (→fig. 27)."[9] (For Dalí, this nineteenth-century painting of pious peasants epitomized bourgeois culture at its most kitsch.) The interviewer speculates that it is more likely that his imagery of phones as black menaces, often shedding tears, reflects his aversion to the device. Dalí the technophobe waxes neurotically on the device, which is "habitually so frightfully warm and disagreeably sticky to the touch." He writes of "telephone frappé," "aphrodisiac telephone," "lobster-telephone," "Edgar Allen Poe telephones with a dead rat concealed in them," "telephones on the leash which would walk about, screwed to the back of a living turtle... telephones... telephones... telephones..."[10]

Another modern gadget in the underwater tank of the *Dream of Venus* pavilion is a typewriter. When not on the phones, the "Liquid Ladies" tap on its keys, or on those of the "rubberoid" piano woman (→fig. 41). There is also a "frustrated cow" to milk. Whatever the psychology behind this mummified pet of the pre-natal ward, her expression is not so much abject as sweetly reminiscent of Elsie, the bovine Venus of the fair. She made her debut in 1939 at the Borden Pavilion, where a "Rotolactor" demonstrated modern milking the hygienic way. (Elsie was such a celebrity, when she returned for the 1940 season, her stall was done up like a lady's boudoir.) Dalí's cow wrapped in hospital bandages was also, perhaps despite herself, a harbinger of victims of the war, which was already raging in Europe and Africa, but which still seemed unfathomable in America. An April fashion item explained that the French colonial situation had inspired a new style of turban.[11] Made from the same gauze used in bandages, it was the turban as trepan—a millinery political statement in Paris. In the *New Yorker*, it read as the "talk of the town."

In January 1939, after two-and-a-half years of struggling against the sickeningly brutal forces of Franco allied with Hitler, Spanish Loyalists had been driven out of Barcelona; in April, just days before the World's Fair opened in New York, Dalí's country was declared a Fascist state. None of this was in evidence in the *Dream of Venus* pavilion. Instead there was a touch of Andrea Palladio. Dalí painted for the

“Pre-natal Chateau” a backdrop based on an imaginary gardenscape in classical Italy. Its raking perspective of columns and figures resembles the trompe l’oeil proscenium of Palladio’s *Teatro Olympico* in Vicenza, which Dalí had already commemorated in a recent painting, *Palladio’s Corridor of Dramatic Disguises* (P 460).

One of the most important architects and theorists of the sixteenth century seems an unlikely touchstone for Dalí, whose work is the antithesis of the Vitruvian principles of harmony and proportion that Palladio avowed. And yet, Dalí’s response to the outbreak of civil war in his home country was to bury himself in the distant past and to create, through his art, a lush compound for private revolution. When the political events of 1936 (the year that Dalí’s close friend, the Catalan poet Federico García Lorca, is executed by Fascists) prevented him and Gala from summering in Port Lligat, Spain, they went instead to Italy, where Dalí absorbed the art of the Renaissance. Its immediate impact is registered in his 1936 painting *Soft Construction with Boiled Beans—Premonitions of Civil War,* which would be known as his Guernica, after the 1937 work by fellow Spaniard Pablo Picasso. The twisted violence of Dalí’s *Premonitions,* painted with a classical sense of precision and amplifying undercurrents of the Renaissance, suggests that Dalí is to the Renaissance as Surrealism is to Modernism: grotesque to baroque.

In general, Dalí’s *Dream of Venus* is both theatrical and architectural in a way that anticipates his future trajectory away from Surrealism. It also looks forward to the museum he would build for himself in his hometown of Figueres, Spain. Inaugurated in 1974, the Teatro-Museo Dalí is built on the ruins of a Neoclassical auditorium that was destroyed during Spain’s civil war. The Dalínian reconstruction features a geodesic dome, inspired by Buckminster Fuller’s biosphere for the 1967 Montreal Exposition, and chambers appointed by Dalí with objects, furniture, and his art. One room realizes his 1934 plan to transform Mae West’s face into a Surrealist apartment. At Figueres, her blonde locks curtain the doorframe, her nose is the fireplace flanked by a pair of pictures that are her eyes, and her lips are the couch. From a certain vantage, the room comes together into the visage of one of Hollywood's toughest Venuses.

As a Surrealist, Dalí was a soldier in a war to liberate the psyche from conventional behavior. Besides Freud, Marx was the other great Modernist in the Surrealist pantheon. By producing encounters with the uncanny, Surrealists intended to wreck catastrophe upon the foundations of society itself. Built upon such revolutionary principles—in a place where the populace convened during a period of seismic disruptions—the integrity of the *Dream of Venus* seems fundamentally weakened by its architect's own self-absorption. His preoccupation with being personally provocative eventually transforms Dalí into a self-cannibalizing monster of his own art and identity.

According to written accounts and some of Dalí's sketches, the doorways inside the *Dream of Venus* were meant to be zippered. No such treacherous teeth are visible in any of the publicity photographs. Nor are the cyclists who were allegedly pedaling furiously on the spot inside the next, dry chamber. Recycled from Dalí's failed 1937 film project with the Marx Brothers, the cyclists were supposedly stationed overhead a young woman playing Venus, helping her to fall asleep on an extra-long bed called "The Ardent Couch"[12] (→fig. 42). She is attended by two women, one covered in vines posted inside the headboard, another smothered and blinded by flowers and trapped behind a semitransparent mirror. Identified as the "Lunatic Narcissus," this woman was obviously maddened by a situation that enabled viewers to enjoy not only looking at her, but also seeing their own voyeuristic delight.

Covered in red satin, Venus's bed is long and laid with succulent and intoxicating snacks, including, evidently, Venus herself, who is spread half naked and dreaming. It is nighttime, judging from the shady blackness of the big umbrellas that are hanging from the ceiling in great profusion. As images in a dream world umbrellas imply many things. Psychoanalytically speaking, the closed ones suggest violent phalluses, the open ones protective wombs. They are nightmare bats, erotic octopi. In Surrealism, umbrellas are immediately associated with the Symbolist poet Lautréamont, who penned the two lines that the Surrealists adopted as anthems, "Beautiful as the chance encounter of a sewing machine and an umbrella on an operating table." And, "Poetry must be made by all, not one." Dalí brandishes an umbrella in some of the publicity shots for the *Dream of Venus*. And at the beginning of the *Declaration of the Independence of the Imagination*, Dalí invokes Lautréamont's call to poetic arms in anticipation of "the era of the wireless imagination," where people will make poetry unfettered by restraints (or rubber mermaid tails). Inside the *Dream of Venus*, Dalí's free-floating telephone receivers seem connected to the notion of wireless imagination, especially when the phones are hanging from the tips of Lautréamont's umbrellas, which also, incidentally, resemble lightening rods—for conducting bolts of creativity.

A proto-Surrealist poet was not the first person brought to mind by an umbrella, which in 1939 immediately conjured the Prime Minister of England, Lord Neville Chamberlain. The umbrella had been his trademark ever since the Munich Agreement in September 1938, when he capitulated to Hitler's threat of war by agreeing to turn Britain's back on the fate of Czechoslovakia. A Brit as inseparable from his brolly as the not-yet re-Allied Forces were reluctant to relinquish their neutrality, Chamberlain espoused "peace in our time." A vain and incriminating prop, his umbrella was everywhere. Dalí himself included it, along with a telephone receiver, in *The Enigma of Hitler*, one of the bleak still lifes that he painted during the Munich crisis, when the entire world hung on the line, listening for news. In April 1939, the *New Yorker* reported that, thanks to Chamberlain, umbrellas were currently the fastest-moving images at the Bettmann Archive.[13] (The article also thanked Hitler for sending the Berliner Dr. Otto Bettmann, along with his picture collection, into exile to America.) "You can't break it, it's a genuine Chamberlain," W. C. Fields mumbles in the 1940 film *My Little Chickadee*, after stumbling over his umbrella and while eyeing it like a twisted pool cue.

Sparking a broad range of associations, the umbrella motif travels like an overhead current throughout the rest of the pavilion. The next two rooms jump-cut from performance- to picture-based tableaux. Viewed through plate glass, these strongly resemble Dalí's department store, which was described as "an assortment of junk ranging from whiskey glasses to red hands pushing through the walls. The Greeks had a word for it and it wasn't sanity."[14] Framed inside the *Dream of Venus* is "The Beach of Gala-Salvador," a diorama composed of Dalínian images and objects. The painted backdrop was a landscape based on the desert plains around Figueres. The setting for Dalí's favorite childhood nightmares, such as encountering animal carcasses on his walk to school, this terrain represents the vast, bleak unknown, which, once contemplated, is sure to provoke physical melancholy. Dalí's signature pocket watches, hanging limply in the landscape's foreground, explain the absence, one wag noted, of stage-door suitors for the lovely "Liquid Ladies."[15]

Also prominent was "The Aphrodisiac Vampire," a mannequin covered in whiskey glasses: a sort of American cocktail-hour variation on Dalí's *Aphrodisiac Dinner Jacket* (1936). In an issue of *Cahiers d'Art,* Dalí described the original coat, covered with glasses brimming with absinthe "in which worm larvae were hatching," in terms of the legend of Saint Sebastian (→fig. 43). It could also be more simply understood, like Dalí's *Lobster Telephone* or Meret Oppenheim's fur-lined teacup, *Breakfast in Fur* (1936), as a Surrealist object par excellence—concrete evidence that the erogenous zone of dream reality was well within the reach of everyday experience and artifacts. The head of Dalí's mannequin was a leopard, which may, like the face of a lion in his *Accommodations of Desire,* represent sexual appetite. (Dalí fondly remembered waking up for the first time in New York to the sound of big cats roaring in the Central Park Zoo.) It is fierce in any case: irritated by the arrow-like straws bristling from the glasses, thirsty for more drink, full of sadomasochistic glee.

On the floor of Dalí's picture window is a vignette that Julien Levy framed nicely as "Love [...] observed by a man who is protected by a diving suit and iron diving helmet from breathing the art which has killed Venus."[16] In her

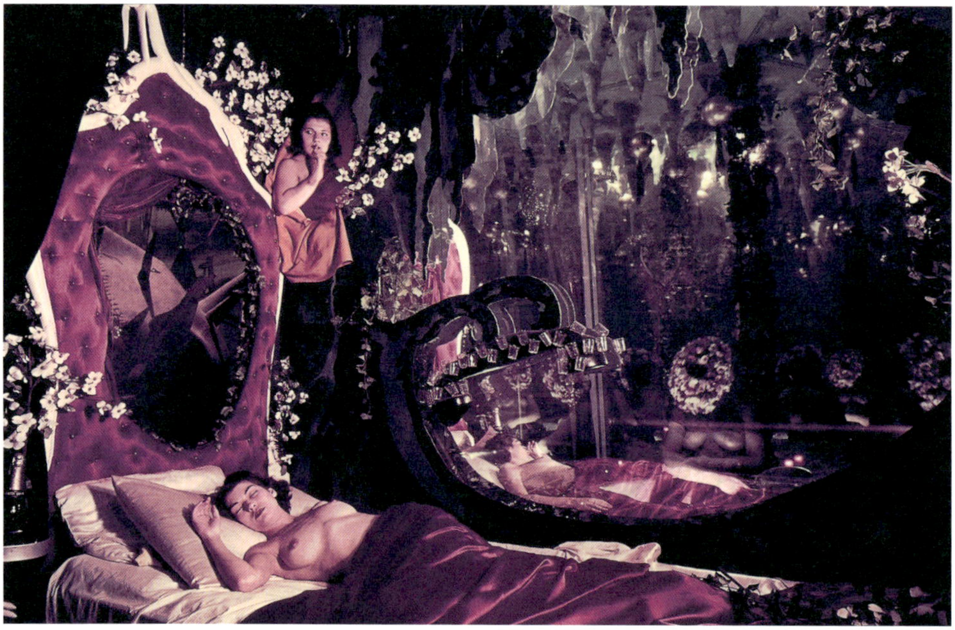

fig. 42
SALVADOR DALÍ
Dream of Venus, "Glowing Couch"
Photo: Eric Schaal

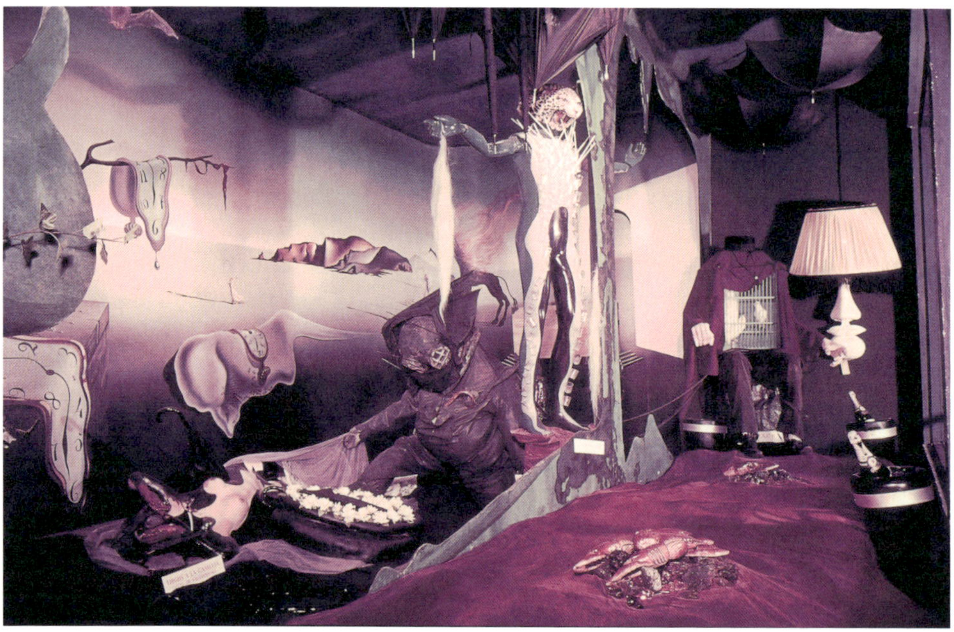

fig. 43
SALVADOR DALÍ
Dream of Venus, "Aphrodisiac Vampire"
Photo: Eric Schaal

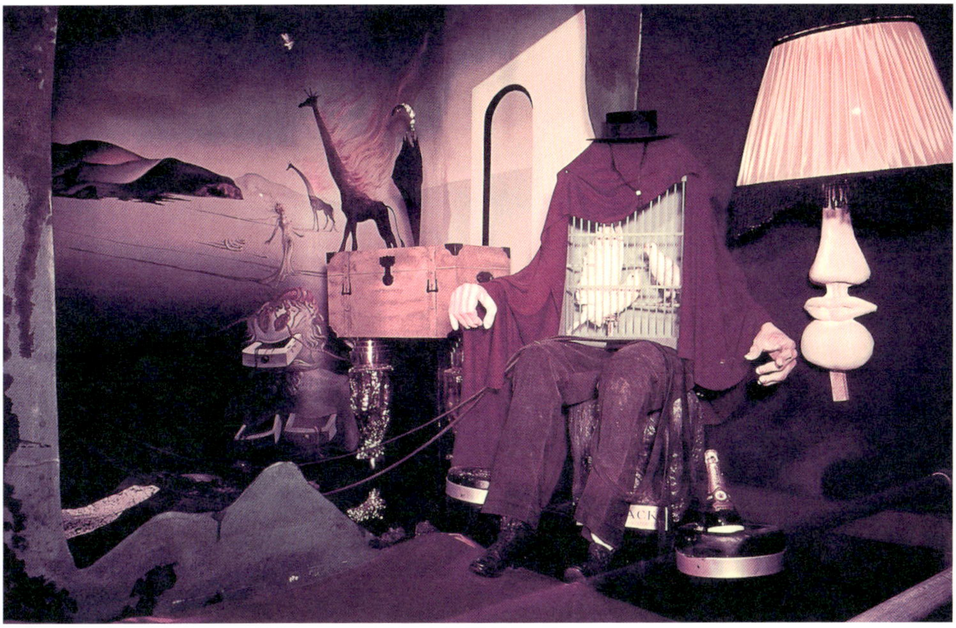

fig. 44
SALVADOR DALÍ
Dream of Venus
Photo: Eric Schaal

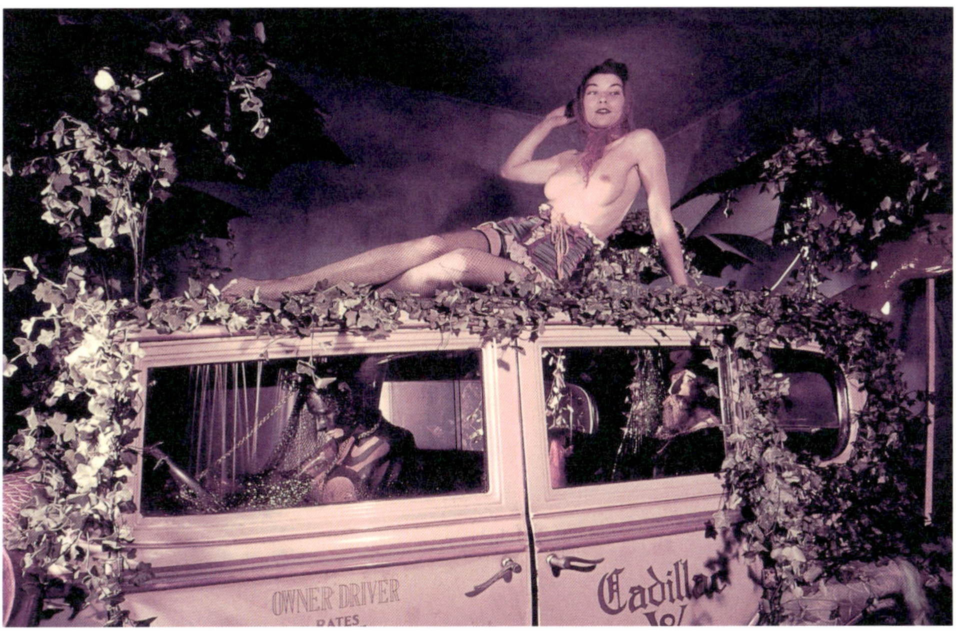

fig. 45
SALVADOR DALÍ
Dream of Venus, "Rainy Taxi"
Photo: Eric Schaal

black mask and skintight costume, Love bears more than a passing resemblance to a comic book character at the start of comic's golden age.[17] Dalí personally identified with the diving figure. In a much-publicized 1936 event, he gave a lecture in London, wearing a diving costume (→fig. 51) and attended by a pair of wolfhounds held by one leash. In the middle of his speaking about "authentic paranoiac fantasies," one came true: something went amiss with his oxygen tank. Dalí nearly suffocated—Gala had stepped out with the key—before a handyman with a wrench released him from his helmet. Dalí claimed that he was wearing the costume to demonstrate that he was diving deep into the human mind.[18] Submarines are much on the minds of 1939 visitors, who are reading in the newspapers about underwater warfare brewing. In late May, the American Navy suffered a loss of men when the *Squalus* sank during a routine dive off the coast of New Hampshire. Breathing above sea level was also an issue: people who had lived through World War I were beginning to think about gas masks again.

Surrealism's stock nightmares may have sat well in general with the populace's disquieted state of mind. Surrounding Dalí's tableaux is a cluster of icons by other Surrealists, realized in three dimensions. This portion of the exhibit appears to be a vestige of Julien Levy's original proposal for a Surrealist fun house. Given how late Dalí came on board the World's Fair project, it seems likely that he simply agreed to assimilate this part of the plan, which includes a number of objects lifted directly from the 1938 *International Surrealist Exhibition* in Paris. The most imposing piece is the figure of a man whose torso is an empty bird cage (→fig. 44). With his head shrouded in a red cape and holding a whip in his hand, he is a specter of the Marquis de Sade, a Spanish toreador, and death. He is also a little silly in his armchair, seated beside an anthropomorphized lamp with a dainty fringe-trimmed shade. Another touchy-feely furnishing is a gramophone whose horn transforms into a hand above a breast-like platter. This is a replica of *Jamais*, a 1937 object by Oscar Dominguez. The figure standing near the door is the spitting image of a collage made collaboratively among a group of Surrealists in 1927. Made of a trunk, umbrella, pots and pans, and chocolate piano legs, it brings to life "The Exquisite Corpse," which was a favorite game among the Surrealists. Working on the same piece of paper, each player contributes part of a drawing, usually of a figure, without knowing what the others are doing. The results are, as anyone can see, weirdly amusing.

The birdcage man is made after a 1937 painting by René Magritte, *The Therapeutist.* Like Dalí's art, Magritte's appeared accessible through its illustrational style of representing Surrealist precepts; he won for his work, too, a popular as well as a fine arts audience. The exchange between Dalí and Magritte went back to 1929, when they first met in Paris. In the meantime, Dalí helped himself to images by Magritte, who, in turn, showed a penchant for Dalí's flaccid forms. Dalí's appropriations, however, are fascinatingly direct: the precursors to the flaming giraffes that dot the horizon inside the *Dream of Venus* are progeny of the flaming tubas that Dalí plucked straight from Magritte. Conspicuously stolen, Dalí's liftings seem less like a botched theft job, but imply a sense of Surrealism as collective imagination. What one artist realizes becomes part of everyone's reality. And if something is compelling enough, it is worth representing in a new context, like a shop window or an amusement zone.

The faucet is running again inside the last chamber of the *Dream of Venus,* where Dalí's *Rainy Taxi* is on display (→fig. 45). Its inversion of indoors and out makes the overall inversion that Dalí was attempting to express inside his upside-down dream reality so spectacular that even a hick could get it. ("Hicks" were a target audience in Levy's Surrealist fun house prospectus, which promised "attractions for all visitors, men, women, children, 'hicks,' and intellectuals; and it will have Sex Appeal.") In recreating this Paris piece (→fig. 54), Dalí was disappointed not to be able to re-present the live snails that were passengers, dining on chicory, inside the French version, because for him snails were linked indelibly with Freud (→fig. 14). The artist recalls eating snails on a "gastronomic excursion" in the south of France, when a newspaper picture of Freud, who was leaving Vienna going into exile from the Nazis, caught his eye.[19] The meal gained significance when just moments before their meeting in 1938, Dalí stood on the pavement outside Freud's London home, riveted by the sight of a snail on a bicycle seat. (One never knows what tidbits can be extracted from the nautilus chambers of the analyzed mind.)

In lieu of the father of psychoanalysis, Dalí inserts another founding figure with a beard—this one more relevant to a New York taxi cab at the World's Fair. It is unclear whether Dalí realized his plan to give Christopher Columbus a big sign reading, "I Return." But there he sits: the Italian-born, ocean-going explorer who claimed America as part of the New World dominated by Spain. Dalí, who seems under the impression that Columbus got a transfusion of blood as well as riches from his patrons, claimed his national brotherhood with the man in the back seat. Upon his first voyage to America, when the New York skyline came into view, "immediately the pride of the Catalonian blood of Christopher Columbus which flows in my veins cried to me, 'Present!' and I in turn saluted the cosmic grandeur and the virgin originality of the American flag."[20] In Dalí's declaration of departure from the *Dream,* he again summoned Christopher Columbus, this time in person, escaping the nightmare of the "American Venus" and carrying a sign, "Am I back already?"[21] Why, he asks, does Columbus sit in his taxi pointing toward Europe? "Why is he accompanied by the invisible ghosts of the Duke and Duchess of Windsor? Why is a somnambulistic Spanish girl attached to the steering wheel of his deluxe Cadillac with golden chains?" Watching Dalí's ship disappear on the horizon, having so furiously absolved himself of anything further to do with the *Dream of Venus* or the World's Fair, there is but one response: is it any wonder?

Left to their own devices, the American public came up with their own take. In a radio interview with a performer playing Venus, she quips, "Well, personally—I call it 'Queen Isabella Driving Christopher Columbus to Distraction.'"[22]

The original version of this text was first published in: Ingrid Schaffner, *Salvador Dalí's Dream of Venus: The Surrealist Funhouse from the 1939 World's Fair*, Princeton Architectural Press, New York, 2002, pp. 110–36. It is presented here with a new introduction by the author and with permission from Princeton Architectural Press.

1 In conversation with Harry Morgan, he shared the story his father told him that Gregory Peck may have worked as a barker outside the *Dream of Venus*. According to the actor, he did earn $25 a week as a barker at the 1939 World's Fair, but outside the Meteor Speedway. (Gerard Molyneaux, *Gregory Peck: A Bio–Bibliography* [Westport, Connecticut, 1995], p. 5.) It is nice to think he may have moonlighted outside the Surrealist pavilion, because, in 1945, Peck would co-star with Ingrid Bergman in *Spellbound*, Hitchcock's thriller that featured a sequence by Dalí.

2 Salvador Dalí, "Declaration of Independence of the Imagination and the Rights of Man to His Own Madness," *The Collected Writings of Salvador Dalí*, ed. Haim Finkelstein (Cambridge, 1998), p. 333.

3 Salvador Dalí, "Concerning the Terrifying and Edible Beauty of Art Nouveau Architecture," *The Collected Writings of Salvador Dalí*, p. 195. See also Fèlix Fanés, ed., *Dalí: Architecture* (Barcelona, 1996).

4 At some point during the 1939 fair the Botticelli Venus was removed from the façade and stuck onto one of the sides of the building. A contemporary cheesecake Venus replaced it over the entryway.

5 Edmund Gilligan, "The Report of a Subway Explorer of His Trip to a Magic City," *The Sun*, April 29, 1939, p. 49.

6 Margaret Case Harriman, "A Dream Walking," *New Yorker*, July 1, 1939, p. 27.

7 In Robert S. Lubar's catalogue entry on Dalí's painting *Myself at the Age of Ten When I Was a Grasshopper Child (Castration Complex)* (1933, → p. 135), he recounts Dalí's version of the grasshopper/fish episode and offers further psychoanalytic insights. Robert S. Lubar, *Dalí: The Salvador Dalí Museum Collection* (Boston, 2000), p. 85. It is interesting to note that the artist Joseph Cornell, who also showed with Julien Levy, originally purchased this painting from the gallery, but got rid of it after an unpleasant incident (recounted by Julien Levy in his *Memoirs*) with Dalí in 1936. Cornell later based one of his daguerreotype collage constructions on a photographic image of one of the women in a lobster headdress from Dalí's *Dream of Venus*.

8 Raymond Loewy, *Evolution Chart of the Desk Telephone* and *Evolution Chart of Female Dress*, 1934, reproduced in Richard Guy Wilson, ed. *The Machine Age in America 1918–1941* (New York, 1986), p. 44.

9 Dalí quoted in Harriman, "Dream Walking" (see note 6), p. 27.

10 Salvador Dalí, *The Secret Life of Salvador Dalí* (1942; reprint, St. Petersburg, Florida, 1986), p. 271.

11 "Talk of the Town," *New Yorker*; April 22, 1939, p. 11.

12 See Dalí's 1937 drawings for the Marx Brothers film project, *Surrealist Gondola above Burning Bicycles*, and, in anticipation of the food-studded "Ardent Couch" inside the *Dream of Venus, Surrealist Dinner on a Bed.* Both are reproduced in Robert Descharnes and Gilles Néret, *Salvador Dalí, 1904–1989, The Paintings Part I, 1904–1946* (Cologne, 2001), p. 296.
13 "Talk of the Town," *New Yorker*, April 22, 1939, p. 14.
14 The article describes Dalí's 1939 window for Bonwit Teller. "Surrealism Shows," *New York City Retailing*, December 28, 1939.
15 "Surrealist Babes," *New Yorker*, July 22, 1939, p. 13.
16 Julien Levy, *Memoir of an Art Gallery* (New York, 1977), p. 218.
17 Batman, for example, made his debut in a May 1939 issue of *Detective Comics*.
18 The infant Dalí lived on a street named for Narcissus Montirol, the manufacturer of the first submarine and a fellow Spaniard—a point of pride for the adult Dalí, who refers to Montirol in his writings.
19 Dalí, *Secret Life* (see note 10), p. 23.
20 Dalí, Secret Life (see note 10), p. 331.
21 Dalí, "Declaration" (see note 2), p. 334.
22 "NBC Special Events Booking: Talent from the World of Tomorrow" (September 19, 1939). For sharing a copy of this script and reminiscence of his grandmother, mermaid Mary Spence Francis, I am extremely grateful to Guy Richards Smit. Smit's watercolor drawings based on his grandmother's "Venus" experience were part of the 2001 exhibition *Crossing the Line* at the Queens Museum of Art. The artist also staged the radio play for Stephen Vitiello's contribution to the exhibition, a CD compilation of sound pieces related to the show.

THE TWO OR THREE LIVES OF EDWARD JAMES (EXCURSES)

Juan Manuel Bonet

Edward James (1907–1984) was one of the last of the great English eccentrics, a personality whose biography actually seems to consist of two or three lives and resembles a novel (→fig. 46). Famous mainly for his ties with Dalí, Magritte, and other Surrealists, James himself was not strictly speaking a Surrealist, but more of a dandy in the manner of George "Beau" Brummell, an aesthete and the last exponent of the curious social set of British individualists that included personalities like Max Beerbohm and the ubiquitous heiress and patron of the arts Nancy Cunard, or versatile talents such as Lord Gerald Berners and Rex Whistler, whom we will encounter later on in this story.

At the tender age of five, James already became fabulously rich, following the death of his father, a wealthy Anglo-American. Rumors abound as to whether he was his biological father, some even suggesting that he was the illegitimate son of Edward VII, although another version of events casts his mother as the king's child.

Educated at Eton and Oxford, the young aesthete—who, in 1922, at the age of just fifteen, received an award for drawing from Roger Fry—studied in the company of a long list of famous names: Harold and William Acton; John Betjeman; Randolph Churchill, son of Winston Churchill; Brian Howard; Diana Mitford, the future wife of Oswald Mosley (who later joined the fascist party); Diana's brother, Tom; Harold Nicolson; Edith Sitwell; Evelyn Waugh; and Peter Watson, who later became Lucian Freud's friend and model and went on to publish *Horizon*, the magazine edited by Cyril Connolly. Many in his social circle were interested in artistic styles largely disdained until that time, such as the Baroque (Dalí later borrowing many elements from this artistic era), as well as "the stupid nineteenth century," as Léon Daudet put it. This interest in the nineteenth century was shared by many twentieth-century artists, including the Surrealists in James's circle, such as the "gothic" Leonora Carrington, Giorgio de Chirico (whose father was a railway engineer, a particularly typical nineteenth-century profession), Max Ernst (with his penchant for using magazines from that era as springboards for his collages), Joseph Cornell (who had fallen for the voices [albeit never recorded] of the most acclaimed Romantic singers), and, of course, Dalí himself, who wrote his analysis on the edible beauty of the *modern style* during the 1930s. As for James, his own interest in the Baroque consolidated during those few months in 1930 he spent as a trainee diplomat at the British Embassy in Rome, the first of many visits to Italy during the decade that had just begun.

Returning to Giorgio de Chirico, James later said that his passion for the artist was ignited after seeing some of his pictures in the window of a Paris gallery, an anecdote that recalls a similar encounter but starring André Breton as the bewitched spectator.

James's first vocation was poetry, which he would later combine with writing novels. His unique literary work, ranging from Neo-Romanticism to Surrealism, comprises some fifteen titles, the first being his *Poems*, printed in 1926 in the Shakespeare town of Stratford-upon-Avon. Other notable titles, some published by The James Press and a few appearing under the pseudonym Edward Selsey, include: *Carmina Amico* (1932), printed in Verona as one of the exquisite editions produced by Giovanni Mardersteig's Officina Bodoni; *The Venetian Glass Omnibus* (1932), published by Oxford University Press and illustrated by Oliver Messel; *The Next Volume: Poems* (1932) with Neo-Rococo vignettes by Rex Whistler; *La belle au bois dormant and Other Poems* (1933), illustrated by the perceptive Edward Bawden; *Reading Into the Picture* (1934), designed by Jörg von Reppert-Bismarck (he and his wife Jack von Reppert-Bismarck, née Elisabeth Meyer, were close to Cecil Beaton, Lord Berners, Messel, Rex Whistler, and other personalities already mentioned in this text); and *The Bones of My Hand* (1938), also published by Oxford University Press, with a frontispiece by Pavel Tchelitchew, whom James greatly admired, and an ode that was set to music by Henri Sauguet, an exquisitely edited volume, of which I am lucky to own the copy the author had dedicated to Michel de Brunhoff, then editor-in-chief of the French edition of *Vogue*. Several of these books, graced with eloquent dedications, are now held in the library formerly belonging to Dalí.

A decisive event in Edward James's life was his marriage, in 1931, to the Austrian-Jewish dancer Tilly Losch, who was immortalized in wonderful portrait photographs by Emil O. Hoppé and Cecil Beaton, as well as in an oil painting by Tchelitchew. Edward James's admiration for Tilly Losch was first sparked in 1928 after seeing her performance in a Noël Coward revue. The ultra-modern bathroom he had designed for her by Paul Nash for their house at 35 Wimpole Street seems to have been Edward James's first interior design commission and the only occasion he opted for a functionalist aesthetic. His own Pompeian-style bathroom was designed for him by Geoffrey Houghton Brown, a minor painter remembered primarily for his 1928 murals at the Blue Train restaurant in London. The restaurant's name alludes to the famous French express service to the Mediterranean, which four years previously had been the title of a ballet by Darius Milhaud, with a set designed by Henri Laurens, costumes by Coco Chanel, and a curtain by Picasso. In overall charge of the Blue Train restaurant's interior design, a project on which Rex Whistler also collaborated, was the Italian Marquese Piero Malacrida de

Saint-August, who subscribed to the style wryly described by Osbert Lancaster in 1938 as "Curzon Street Baroque." But let us return to 35 Wimpole Street, where another part of the interior décor, leading up the stairs to Tilly Losch's bathroom, was a carpet designed by Norris Wakefield. This carpet incorporated as its main motif the dancer's footprint (→fig. 47), which, following the couple's separation, James had replaced with a new design featuring the paw prints of his favorite dog.

In 1931, James had been one of the instigators of the chamber music society La Sérénade (where he encountered the Marquesa de Casa Fuerte, the Vicomtesse de Noailles, and the Princess de Polignac, as well as Georges Auric, Roger Désormière, Igor Markevitch, Darius Milhaud, Nicolas Nabokov, Francis Poulenc, Sergei Prokofiev, Maurice Ravel, Vittorio Rieti, and Henri Sauguet). Two years later, his love for Tilly Losch—and his constant fear of losing her, which eventually became reality: the couple divorced in 1934—prompted him to embark on a risky and exorbitantly expensive adventure as a musical impresario.

Fascinated by George Balanchine and Boris Kochno, he became the main funder of their company Les Ballets 1933, which, in June of that year, performed a series of ballets, first in Paris at the Théâtre des Champs-Elysées (famous in the history of modern ballet as the stage where Igor Stravinsky's *Le sacre du printemps* premiered in 1913) and later at the Savoy in London. I am unable to go into detail here about the individual ballets in this series. Charles Koechlin, Darius Milhaud, Nicolas Nabokov, Henri Sauguet, and Kurt Weill were the composers involved, some with their own compositions, others with arrangements of classical works. Bertolt Brecht and James himself were the librettists. The performers included Tilly Losch and the singer Lotte Lenya; set designers were Christian Bérard, André Derain, Caspar Neher, José María Sert, Pavel Tchelitchew, and, as one of the few architects, Emilio Terry. Chief conductor of the Orchestre Symphonique de Paris was Maurice de Abravanel, a student of Kurt Weill. The list of names is certainly spectacular. As far as Dalí is concerned, the following are named in *The Secret Life of Salvador Dalí*:

Bérard (the Catalan even referred to the "Dalí–Bérard axis"[1] in his memoirs), Eugene Berman (his paintings being described as "romantic with classicism"[2]), Lord Berners (a brilliant character, straight from a novel: composer, painter, writer, decorator, friend of Acton, Fortunato Depero, Picasso, Stravinsky, and Gertrude Stein, an inspiration for Beaton and Bill Brandt; today Gavin Bryars and Michael Nyman cite him as an influence; some regard him as an English Erik Satie, although I personally do not consider their music to be that similar), Sert, Tchelitchew, and Emilio Terry (a member of Dalí's Zodiac group of patrons; in 1934 Dalí produced a sensational portrait of him, which has recently been acquired by the Foundation), and Peter Watson, who, according to Dalí, had a penchant for Pre-Raphaelitesque Picassos. Needless to say, all of these were names whom Breton viewed with disdain, partly because many of them were in the circle of his bête noire Jean Cocteau, whose drawings also featured in Edward James's collection.

It was around this time that James first met Dalí. The stage was set in the winter of 1932/33 when James stayed at the Villa Noailles in Hyères, one of the most famous buildings designed by Robert Mallet-Stevens. James was fascinated by Dalí's portrait of Marie-Laure de Noailles, already mentioned in relation to La Sérénade, and with whom he had a brief and passionate affair in Hyères. Soon after that, Dalí and James met at a concert in the garden of the Princess de Polignac in Paris. James was accompanied by Bettina Bergery, née Shaw-Jones, to whom he deliberately dropped a comment within earshot of Dalí, about Hitler and his "gingerbread chest," a phrase originally coined by Dalí that he knew about from Marie-Laure de Noailles. Dalí was touched: "How do you know that? What you say is true. Who are you?"

Bettina Bergery, whose life inspired Yves Pourcher to write a novel in the form of a quest (*Trois coupes de champagne*, 2009), is described in *The Secret Life of Salvador Dalí* as "the soul and the biology" of Elsa Schiaparelli's establishment on the Place Vendôme and "one of the women of Paris most highly endowed with fantasy."[3] James frequented this store and presented clothes designed by the couturier to one of his great friends, whom he unsuccessfully tried to marry: the American actor Ruth Ford, sister of the poet Charles Henri Ford and model for paintings by Tchelitchew and photographs by Cecil Beaton, Man Ray, and Carl Van Vechten.

Whereas for James this chance meeting with Dalí marked the beginning of a pivotal friendship in his life and his first step toward Surrealism, for the painter it was the start of his connection to Britain. This ran in parallel with his ties to Neo-Romantic painters in Paris, especially Bérard, Eugene Berman, and Tchelitchew, as well as to fashionable figures such as Étienne de Beaumont (who inspired the Comte d'Orgel in Raymond Radiguet's novel), Carlos de Beistegui, Marie-Louise Bousquet, Eugenia Errázuriz, de Faucigny-Lucinge, Daisy Fellowes, Natalia Paley, and Misia Sert—not forgetting de Noailles herself. But back to the British connection: it was undoubtedly with James (and, to a lesser extent, Lord Berners) in mind that the Catalan wrote in his memoirs the notable sentence, "London brought to Paris a gleam of Pre-Raphaelism which I was the only one to understand and to savor."[4] James, meanwhile, is described as the "hummingbird poet, [who] ordered aphrodisiac lobster-telephones, bought the best Dalís, and was naturally the richest."[5] The name "hummingbird poet" was not Dalí's invention, as the painter himself explains in *Les morts et moi* (edition of the manuscript published by Carles Fontserè in 1991, first appeared in French in *La Parisienne* in 1954), but was coined by Federico García Lorca, whom Dalí had introduced to James in Catalonia in 1935.

The friendship between Dalí and James really took off properly in Italy in the year 1935. Breton's aversion to Italy is well known, and partly arose from his view that the Romans were to blame for the destruction of Gaul. He never set foot on Italian soil as a result. Dalí, on the other hand, encouraged by Gala, felt a growing desire during the 1930s—the decade that brought the rift between him and the founder of Surrealism—to visit Italy (→fig. 48). This was not a quest for the Italy of Giorgio de Chirico, Alberto Savinio,

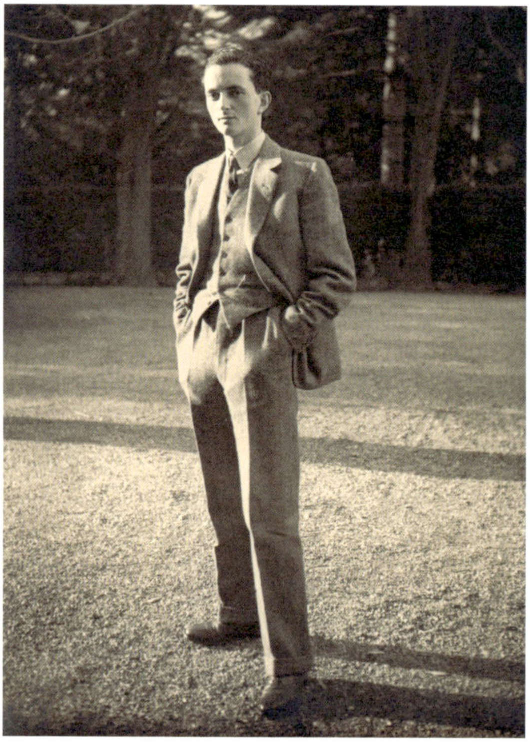

fig. 46
Edward James in West Dean Gardens, c. 1930

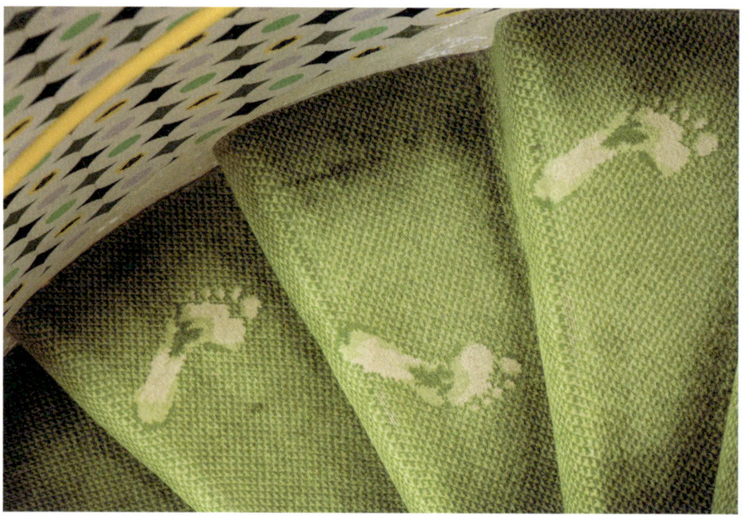

fig. 47
Carpet with Tilly Losch's footprints
in West Dean House, reconstruction from the 1950s
Design: Norris Wakefield

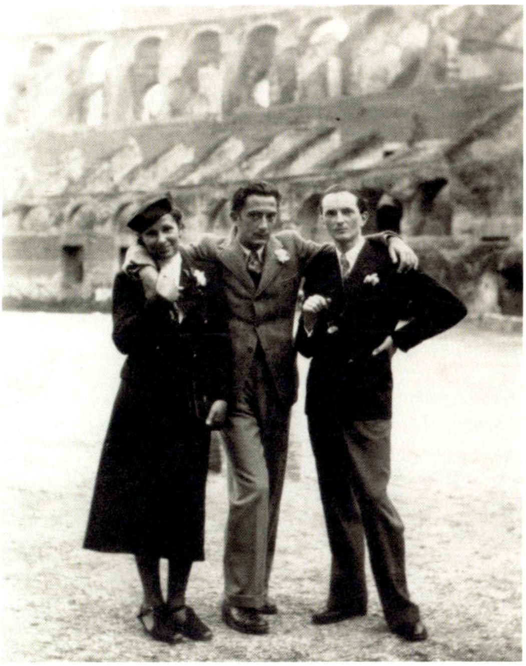

fig. 48
Gala, Salvador Dalí and Edward James
in Rome, 1935

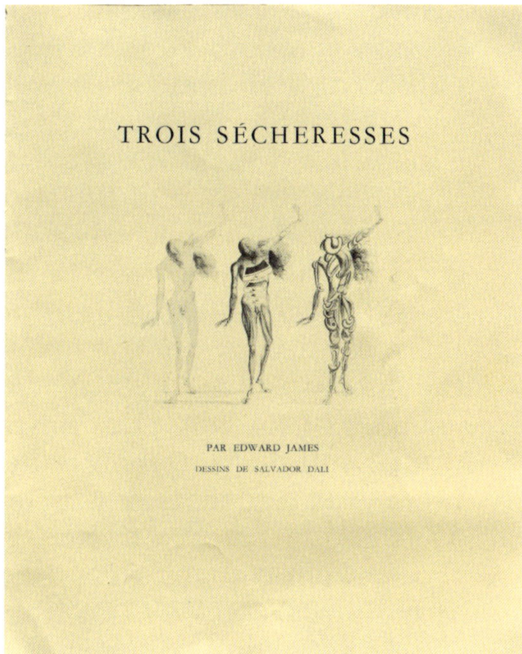

fig. 49
SALVADOR DALÍ, Illustration for
Edward James's poem "Trois sécheresses," 1936
Minotaure, no. 8, 1936

or Giorgio Morandi, as envisaged during his days as a subscriber to *Valori Plastici*, a magazine that taught him, too, like everyone else, to appreciate the art of the Italian primitives. Instead, his aim now was to discover the Italy of Palladio (incidentally, James was a friend of the Brazilian Bertie Landsberg, owner of Villa Foscari, "La Malcontenta") and Bramante, the Italy of Perugino, Raphael, and Leonardo da Vinci. As it happened, the trip eventually took place at a time when Dalí was in a deep depression, following the death of Prince Alexis Mdivani at the wheel of his Rolls-Royce after a summer party at Mas Juny, a residence of the prince's sister Roussie and José María Sert in Palamós. As a literary companion, the travelers took with them the Pléiade edition of Stendhal's Italian journeys. Although they also traveled to Florence and Rome, the main destination of their expedition, which was almost joined by García Lorca, was the Villa Cimbrone in Ravello on the Amalfi Coast. For most of the decade, James was renting this villa from his compatriots and friends Lord and Lady Grimthorpe. When the Dalís returned again in 1937, they spent part of the year there. It was here, too, that Wagner composed his *Parsifal*, the inspiration for *Tristan le fou*, as the Wagnerian ballet in memory of Ludwig II of Bavaria was then called. Dalí wrote it for Léonide Massine's Ballets Russes, but it eventually premiered under its new title *Bacchanale* at the Metropolitan Opera in New York in 1939. In fact, Dalí had at some point toyed with the idea of involving García Lorca in the project.

As sponsor of the last two issues of *Minotaure*, James's poems "Trois sécheresses," written in French and illustrated by none other than Dalí himself (later set to music by Poulenc; →fig. 49) featured in no. 8, while the ninth included an article by James about Holbein and Cranach at the Kunsthistorisches Museum in Vienna. He failed, however, in his attempt to give Albert Skiras's magazine a British twist, since the editorial board rejected his proposed contributions by John Betjeman, Lord Berners, and the Catholic and Chestertonian Hilaire Belloc.

Edward James's "Dalí years" were from 1934 to 1940. In a letter cited by John Lowe, which James wrote to Edith

Sitwell in 1935, he said he considered Dalí—whom he visited several times in Portlligat—one of the three most important painters of his day, on a par with Picasso and Tchelitchew, whom he so admired, although, in this latter case, James was obviously confusing his wish with reality. From 1936 onward, James acquired the following works by Dalí—for a while even purchasing the artist's entire output—all of which are listed in the catalogue raisonné and, notably, all of which are also still possible to locate today: *Phantom Cart* (1933, P 321); *Mediumnistic-Paranoiac Image* (c. 1934, P 427); *Suburbs of the "Paranoiac-Critical Town" (Afternoon on the Outskirts of European History)* (1935, P 434); *Paranoiac Face* (c. 1935, P 404); *Paranoiac-Critical Solitude* (1935, P 408); *Sun-Table* (1935, P 425); *White Calm* (1935, P 429); *The Fossil Automobile of Cape Creus* (1936, P 409); *Diurnal Melancholy: The Chemist of Figueres In Search of Absolutely Nothing* (1936, P 416); *City of Drawers: The Anthropomorphic Cabinet* (1936, P 444, →fig. 5); *A Couple with Their Heads Full of Clouds* (1936, P 443); *"Geodesical" Portrait of Gala* (1936, P 438); *Autumnal Cannibalism* (c. 1936, P 447); *Feminine Head Which Has the Form of a Battle* (1936, P 436); *The Great Paranoic* (1936, P 435); *Anthropomorphism, Extra Flat* (1936, P 430); *Girl Skipping in a Landscape* (1936, P 419); *Average Pagan Landscape* (1937, P 449); *Enchanted Beach* (c. 1937, P 452); *Swans Reflecting Elephants* (1937, P 454, →p. 139), which includes an image of James; *Metamorphosis of Narcissus* (1937, P 455, →fig. 17); *Sleep* (c. 1937, P 456); *Anbattet: The Spit* (c. 1937, P 622); *Imperial Violets* (1938, P 474); *Spain* (1938, P 468); *Palladio's Corridor of Thalia* (c. 1938, P 461); *Melancholic Eccentricity, Mountain Lake* (1938, P 473); *Impression of Africa* (c. 1938, P 462); *Landscape with Telephones on a Dish* (1939, P 478); *Original Sin* (1941, P 501); and *Project for "Labyrinth"* (1941, P 584). In addition to the painting mentioned above, James is also depicted in the *Invention of the Monsters* (c. 1937, P 457, →fig. 50).

In the end, however, their friendship deteriorated into endless squabbling, with the result that, when James met the Dalís in California in 1942, he described this friendship, which had been so mutually important, as "amitié en aspic" (friendship in aspic). And in 1947 he made it very clear that what Dalí was exhibiting at the Bignou Gallery in New York was no longer of any interest to him. Later he remarked acerbically that, in his eyes, the one who had always condemned opportunism had now turned into an opportunist himself, into someone who solemnly declared himself to be a Catholic, and, ultimately, into a traitor, a Quisling (Minister President of Norway and a Nazi collaborator) of the art world. He imagined that one could warn an artist who was losing his way by cautioning him to watch out that he did not turn into a Dalí.

But back in 1936, the friendship between Dalí and James was still strong and buoyed by the *International Surrealist Exhibition* at London's New Burlington Galleries. At the opening on June 11, Dalí gave a talk wearing a diving suit (→fig. 51), which, incidentally, had been hired by Lord Berners. The suppliers of this item of equipment had asked him for details about how deep the wearer was intending to venture, to which Lord Berners replied that the dive would be into the depths of the human subconscious. The manuscript of the lecture was translated by Edward James, who also loaned the above-mentioned *Paranoiac Face* as well as a work by Picasso to the exhibition. James was also closely involved in a further presentation shown in parallel: Dalí's solo exhibition at the Reid and Lefevre Gallery. Dawn Ades and other art historians have pertinently pointed out that James was not on the same wavelength as the official English Surrealism of Roland Penrose, David Gascoyne, or the Belgian artist E.L.T. Mesens, although he did own a work by the latter.

While James and Tilly Losch had been living primarily at West Dean in Sussex, with its magnificent nineteenth-century gardens, after their split, James's focus shifted to Monkton, a hunting lodge on the estate that his father had commissioned from the great Edwin Lutyens. Here, the collector had free rein to design the interiors in the style of the eighteenth and nineteenth centuries or of Surrealism (→fig. 52). In this endeavor he enjoyed technical support from Kit Nicholson and his assistant Hugh Casson, as well as the aforementioned Norris Wakefield. As has been

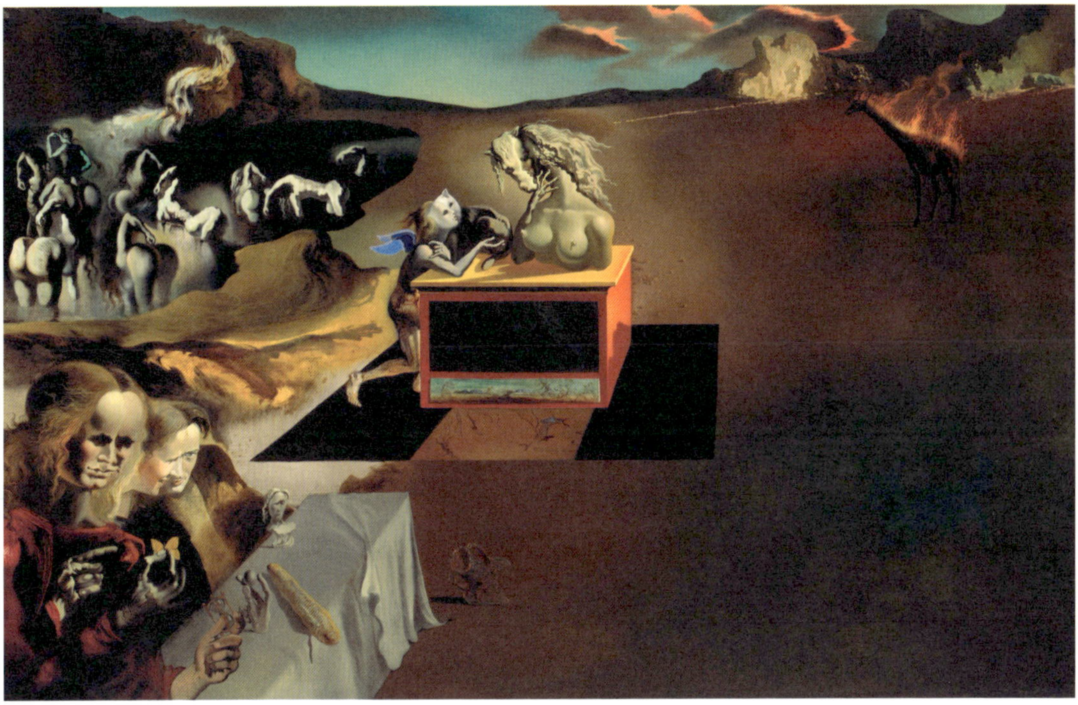

fig. 50
SALVADOR DALÍ, *Invention of the Monsters*
c. 1937, The Art Institute of Chicago
Cat. no. P 457

pointed out by architectural historians, after the interventions of James and his collaborators—including Dalí—nothing remained of Edwin Lutyens's elegant simplicity. Some of James's ideas for the interior design were discussed with Nicholson and Casson at a meeting also attended by Dalí. The artist made various suggestions, some of which were embraced with great enthusiasm, while others never got past the drawing board, generally for reasons of practicality—such as, for example, a wall that heaved like the belly of a panting dog.

The now famous collaborations between Dalí and James in objects and furniture include the *Lobster Telephone* (→p. 148), one of the most iconic Surrealist objects of the time. Apparently, the idea came from James after seeing a friend eat a lobster on his bed and then toss the shell at a telephone: a Lautréamontesque encounter. The pink or red velvet sofas inspired by Mae West's lips were also one of James's ideas (→fig. 53), based on Dalí's gouache *Mae West's Face which May be Used as a Surrealist Apartment* of 1934/35 (at the Art Institute of Chicago). The two versions by Jean-Michel Frank for Elsa Schiaparelli deserve special mention; Dalí and James also devised caterpillar-shaped patches to repair any wear and tear in the fabric. And, finally, there are the comparatively less well known chair with hands and a pair of lamps created from stacked champagne glasses. The *Rainy Taxi* (→fig. 54), Dalí's contribution to the major Surrealism exhibition staged at the Galerie Beaux-Arts in Paris in 1938, was the result of his collaboration with James and an incident while waiting for a rental car in Verona.

Immediately after this exhibition opened, the Dalís spent two months in Lord Berners's Roman palace near the Forum Romanum, where Dalí painted *Impression of Africa,* an explicit homage to Raymond Roussel, his memory of the writer having recently been rekindled during a stay in Sicily, where, five years earlier, Roussel had taken his own life at the Grand Hotel et des Palmes in Palermo. It was at around this time that James gave Dalí a stuffed polar bear he had purchased from a Parisian taxidermist and which still stands guard in its full magnificence in a corner of Dalí's house in Portlligat.

In 1937, René Magritte made a significant contribution to the décor of the house on Wimpole Street, where he took up residence for over a month. The relationship between James and Magritte was courteous, but never as close and complicit as James's friendship with Dalí. James introduced Magritte to Henry Moore and Roberto Matta, who was passing through at the time. Interior design scholars have pointed out the similarity between James's *Tent Room* (scene of Norman Parkinson's 1939 photograph, depicting James in the company of Igor Markevitch in front of Picasso's Neoclassical work *Femme assise au chapeau* of 1922, now at Kunsthaus Zürich) and Tchelitchew's stage sets for *L'errante* (The Wanderer), a performance by Les Ballets 1933 to Koechlin's orchestration of Schubert's music. The same scholars have also singled out a carpet designed by Rex Whistler. Magritte painted three works for the ballroom at Wimpole Street: *The Red Model* and *Youth Illustrated*, both now in the Rotterdam Museum Boijmans Van Beuningen (a museum well known for its Dalís originally from James's collection), and *On the Threshold of Liberty*, today at the Art Institute of Chicago. Especially famous is the mirror depiction *Not to Be Reproduced*, also now in the Rotterdam gallery, which is based on a photograph taken by Magritte himself, capturing a rear view of James in front of *On the Threshold of Liberty*. On the mantelpiece in *Not to Be Reproduced*, we can see a Calmann-Lévy edition of Edgar Allan Poe's *The Narrative of Arthur Gordon Pym* in its French translation by Baudelaire.

James was also the model for *The Pleasure Principle* (→figs. 55 and 57), a painting inspired by a photograph taken that same year by Man Ray (→fig. 56). For the staircase, Magritte painted *Time Transfixed* a year later in 1938, which has also found its way to the Art Institute of Chicago. Another of Parkinson's 1939 photographs—a dramatically illuminated, breathtaking snapshot—shows James with his eyes closed in front of Magritte's famous sculpture *The Future of Statues*: a cast of Napoleon's death mask onto which Magritte had painted a cloudy sky. There are five versions of this object, the one at Tate Modern originating from James's collection. Wimpole Street certainly encapsulates the

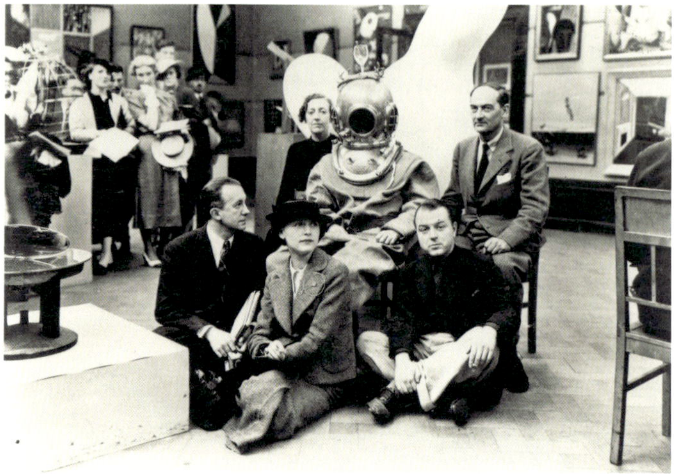

fig. 51
Salvador Dalí in a diver's suit at the
International Surrealist Exhibition in London, 1936
(with Paul Éluard, Nusch Éluard, Diana Brinton Lee,
ELT Mesens, Rupert Lee), Tate, London

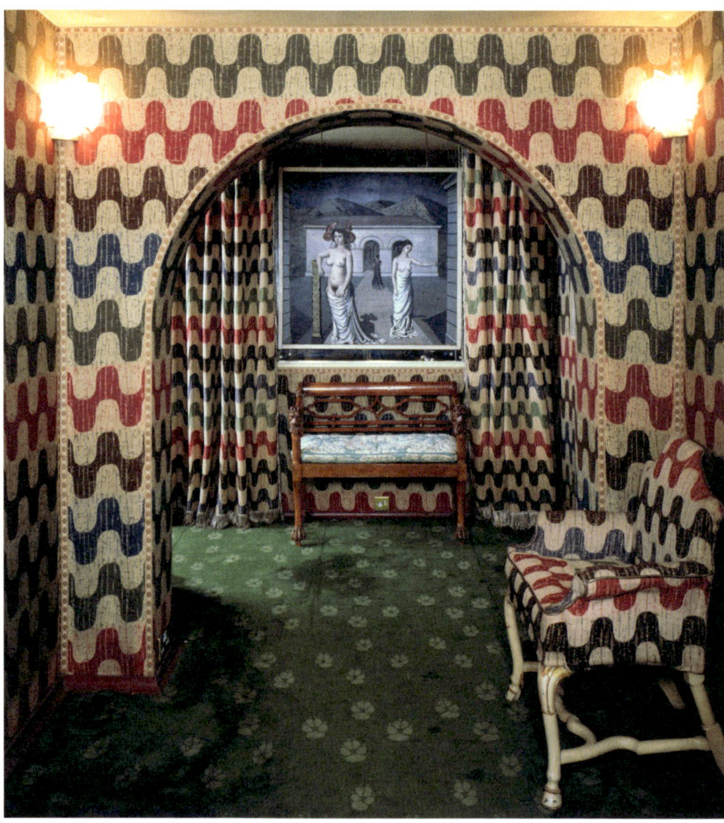

fig. 52
Hall of Monkton House

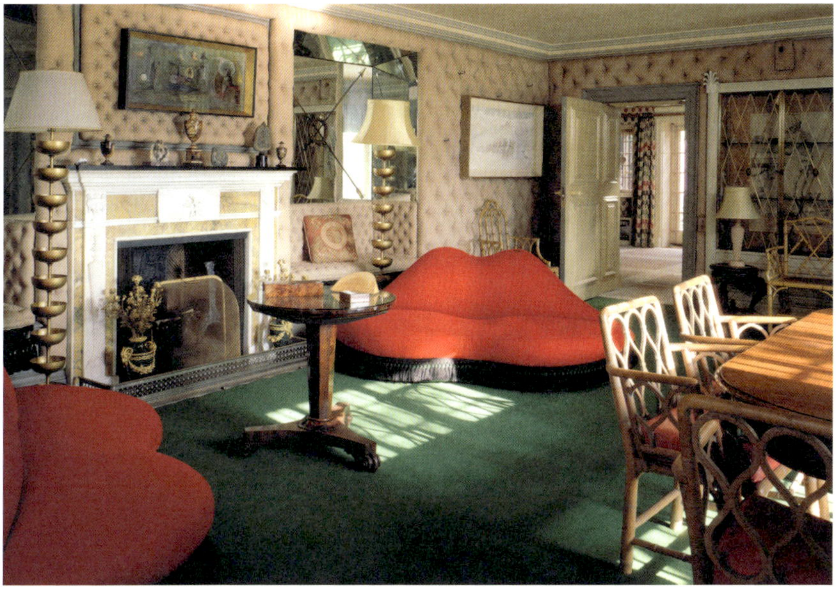

fig. 53
Dalí's *Mae West Lip Sofas* and lamps designed by him made of champagne glasses in Monkton House

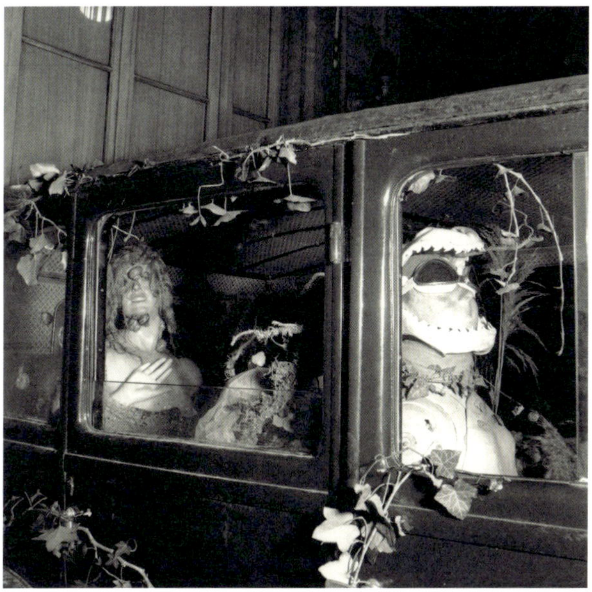

fig. 54
SALVADOR DALÍ, *Taxi pluvieux* (*Rainy Taxi*)
Photo taken at the *Exposition internationale du surréalisme*, Paris, Galerie Beaux-Arts, January/February 1938, photo: Denise Bellon

eclectic tastes of its owner: an Edwardian setting, the classic English eccentric Rex Whistler among its decorators, Cubist and Surrealist images (Magritte's paintings being displayed next to a work by his compatriot Paul Delvaux), Neo-Romantic pictures. We also know that James wanted to commission Dalí to create a grotto for the house, inspired by rocks from Cap de Creus, a project he eventually abandoned.

I have already mentioned Man Ray and Norman Parkinson, but James—who across all of his two or three lives always enjoyed masquerade and posing—was also portrayed by Cecil Beaton, Sasha, and Madame Yevonde.

The setting of the Spanish Civil War has given rise to an urban myth—its credibility admittedly discounted by Román Gubern and Paul Hammond, great experts on the subject—namely Buñuel's account that Edward James proposed funding a bomber for the Republican army in return for a traveling exhibition in Czechoslovakia comprising masterpieces from the Prado.

Despite the fact that the collaboration between Dalí and James came to a bittersweet end in 1939/40 with *The Dream of Venus* (→figs. 40–45)—Dalí's New York project, which was based on his interpretation of Botticelli, Leonardo da Vinci, and other Italian old masters, and was so expertly photographed by Eric Schaal, but ultimately ended in a pre-Pop-style fiasco—for the purposes of this text, it seems more important to look at Dalí's meeting with Freud, which took place on July 19, 1938, at Freud's residence in Primrose Hill in the company of James and Stefan Zweig, the latter brokering the meeting and assuming the role of interpreter.

The great Austrian novelist, who, like his compatriot, the father of psychoanalysis, was living in exile in London at the time, had read James's novel *The Gardener Who Saw God*, published the previous year with a dust jacket designed by Tchelitchew. Along with the Austrian, the novel also mentions Breton, Dalí, Marx, and Sade: a Who's Who of Surrealist figureheads. In his enthusiasm, it occurred to him that the author of the book could potentially be the right person to compose Freud's biography. He therefore decided to introduce them to each other. James took Dalí with him on the visit. Dalí had been an avid reader of Freud's work ever since his student days in Madrid. Since 1922, he had always devoured every new publication by Freud as soon as it appeared in its Spanish translation by Luis López-Ballesteros y de Torres, published by Biblioteca Nueva. Three times, he recounts in his memoirs, he had traveled to Vienna, where he invariably sought out the Czernin Collection for its Vermeer, but had *never* managed to meet Freud, who on each occasion was away in the countryside for health reasons.

Before the London visit, Dalí and James decided to take a key painting by the Catalan artist from James's collection to show to their host: the already-mentioned *Metamorphosis of Narcissus* (→fig. 17). It is a painting that clearly takes us to Freud's and Zweig's native country, as James pointed out that the brightness in the air was that of the Austrian Alps, where, on a walking trip in April, the two had seen early daffodils flowering in the snow. As far as the visit itself is concerned, Dalí (who failed to awaken Freud's interest in his "paranoiac-critical method") concentrated on drawing a portrait of the father of psychoanalysis. Documenting the visit we have Dali's account in his memoirs and his two drawings, one now at the Freud Museum in London, Zweig's writings in his own memoirs, and a letter from Freud to Zweig, written the following day, in which he writes: "For until then I was inclined to look upon the Surrealists—who have apparently chosen me as their patron saint—as absolute (let us say 95 per cent, like alcohol), cranks. That young Spaniard, however, with his candid and fanatical eyes, and his undeniable technical mastery, has made me reconsider my opinion." During the visit itself, Dalí had overheard Freud say to Zweig: "I have never seen a more complete example of a Spaniard. What a fanatic!" It is moreover common knowledge that innumerable portraits of Freud and allusions to him and his writings appear throughout Dalí's oeuvre.

James's second life, which seems even more like a novel than his first, is not our subject here and I will summarize it only briefly. It began in 1939 in New York, where he

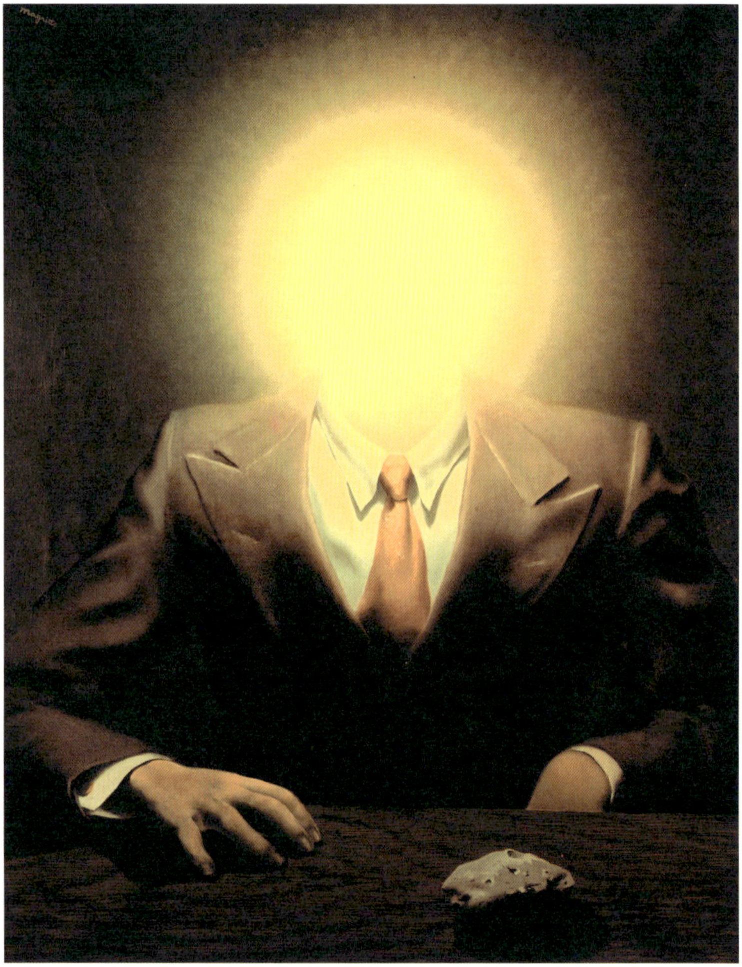

fig. 55
RENÉ MAGRITTE, *Le principe du plaisir*
(*The Pleasure Principle*), 1937
Private collection, formerly owned by Edward James

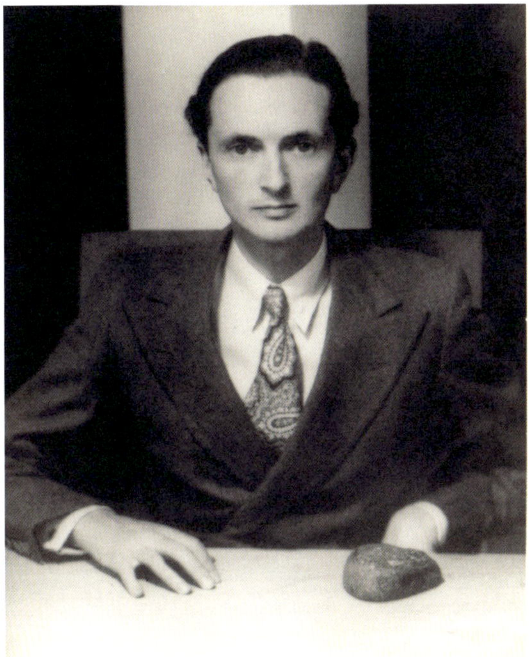

fig. 56
MAN RAY, Portrait of Edward James
(model for René Magritte's *The Pleasure Principle*), 1937
West Dean College of Arts and Conservation

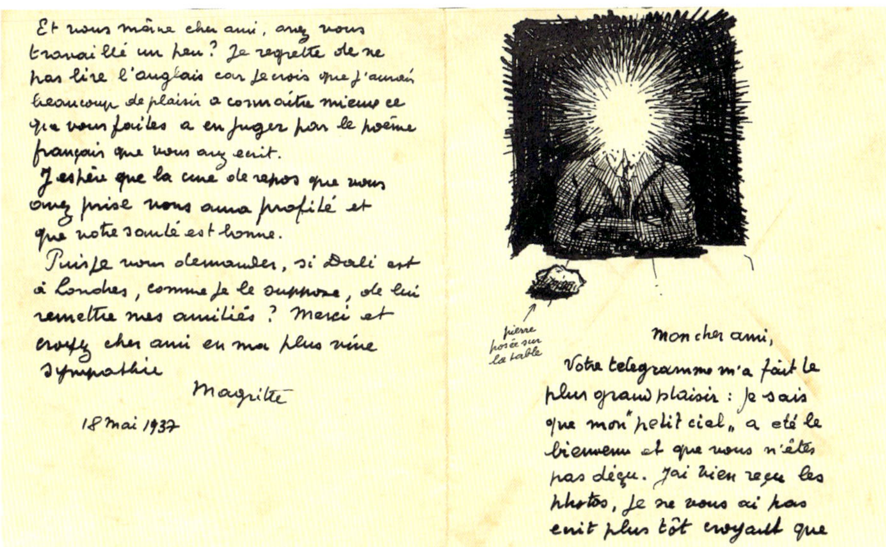

pierre
posée sur
la table

Mon cher ami,

Votre telegramme m'a fait le plus grand plaisir : je sais que mon "petit ciel" a été le bienvenu et que vous n'êtes pas déçu. J'ai bien reçu les photos, je ne vous ai pas écrit plus tôt croyant que

Et vous même cher ami, avez vous travaillé un peu? Je regrette de ne pas lire l'anglais car je crois que j'aurais beaucoup de plaisir à connaître mieux ce que vous faites à en juger par le poème français que vous avez écrit.
J'espère que la cure de repos que vous avez prise vous aura profité et que votre santé est bonne.
Puis-je vous demander, si Dali est à Londres, comme je le suppose, de lui remettre mes amitiés? Merci et croyez cher ami en ma plus vive sympathie

Magritte

18 mai 1937

fig. 57
RENÉ MAGRITTE, Letter to Edward James
with a sketch for *The Pleasure Principle*, May 18, 1937
West Dean College of Arts and Conservation

associated, among others, with Esteban Francés, George Grosz, Julien Levy, George Platt Lynes, Isamu Noguchi, and James Thrall Soby, and continued in 1940 in Taos, New Mexico, in the social circle of D.H. Lawrence. That same year, James moved to California, where he was in contact with Gerald Heard, Aldous Huxley, and Christopher Isherwood and was involved in saving the Watts Towers by the eccentric artist Simon Rodia. He then moved to Cuernavaca in Mexico, where he was reunited with his fellow student Geoffrey Gilmore and, through Huxley, got to know Erich Fromm. Still in Mexico, which became his adopted home country, he eventually settled in the town of Xilitla near San Luis Potosí. Arriving there in 1945, he created his last Surrealist architectural folly, Las Pozas (→fig. 58), "the Englishman's garden," as it is known to the locals, surrounded by an abundant tropical paradise filled with orchids and a selection of local fauna, which regularly accompanied James on his travels: parrots, toucans (→fig. 59), crocodiles, caimans, iguanas, armadillos, boas, cobras, and so on, as well as his widely known dogs. This is documented in numerous photographs, in which he looks like an embodiment of Robinson Crusoe, and is also referenced by Elena Poniatowska, who alluded to his "prohibitive and prohibited private zoo." It also features in a late work by Sauguet (a friendship that had lasted from James's European days), a musical setting of the *Ode to a Dying Crocodile*. Las Pozas, with its fantastical architectural structures, recalls Bomarzo (visited by Dalí in 1948, before he found another example of magical architecture, in 1965, with the Sicilian Villa Palagonia or "Villa of Monsters" in Bagheria near Palermo), but also the Palais idéal du facteur Cheval or Gaudí's Park Güell, and, with its reminiscences of Max Ernst or Henry Moore, is now a place of pilgrimage for friends of the surreal. "El Castillo," the flamboyant house designed by Plutarco Gastélum, also matches the follies of Las Pozas, and here we again encounter the decorative use of footprints, this time belonging to James himself.

At the time, James was friendly with four of Surrealism's great women artists, all, like himself, from far-off lands: three painters, comprising his compatriots Leonora

Carrington and Bridget Bate Tichenor and the Catalan Remedios Varo, as well as the Hungarian photographer Kati Horna, who sometimes housed James's traveling zoo in her chalet at Calle Tabasco, where I visited her in 1989. James commissioning Leonora Carrington to create two murals in Xilitla was his last venture into the patronage of painting. Among his visitors from abroad, Bona and André Pieyre de Mandiargues deserve a mention. James had met the latter during the interwar years in Paris through Leonor Fini, whose work he owned as well. Also worth mentioning is the fantastical magazine *S.NOB* from the year 1962, created by Salvador Elizondo and Juan García Ponce, with contributions from Leonora Carrington and Kati Horna. The latter portrayed James several times at the Francis Hotel in Mexico City, and one of the portraits was published in the magazine's seventh issue, dedicated to the theme of narcotics. James, who occasionally financed the magazine, contributed the autobiographical text "Cuando cumplí cincuenta años" ("My Fiftieth Birthday"), illustrated with said photograph, a reproduction of Mantegna's *Dead Christ*, two drawings by Leonora Carrington, and one by José Horna (the photographer's Spanish husband who was a cabinetmaker and sculptor; a photograph by Kati Horna shows him working on a model for James's palace). The text itself talks about his experience of taking hallucinogenic mushrooms, given to James by the painter Bridget Bate Tichenor.

Among James's male friends, Pedro Friedeberg stands out, an idiosyncratic Surrealist painter, sculptor, and designer of absurd furniture, which inevitably attracted James's attention. In his memoirs, *De vacaciones por la vida* (A Lifelong Vacation, 2011), the Mexican artist describes his collaboration with James in Las Pozas, manifested in a relief showing hands. A photograph from 1968 by Kati Horna shows Friedeberg, in typical James fashion, playing the violin dressed as a zebra. Also of interest in connection with James's Mexican presence is the following quote from a 1958 essay by Octavio Paz, published in *Puertas al campo* (1966) and preceded by a few sentences about Leonora Carrington: "Also among the meteorites that landed in Mexico during

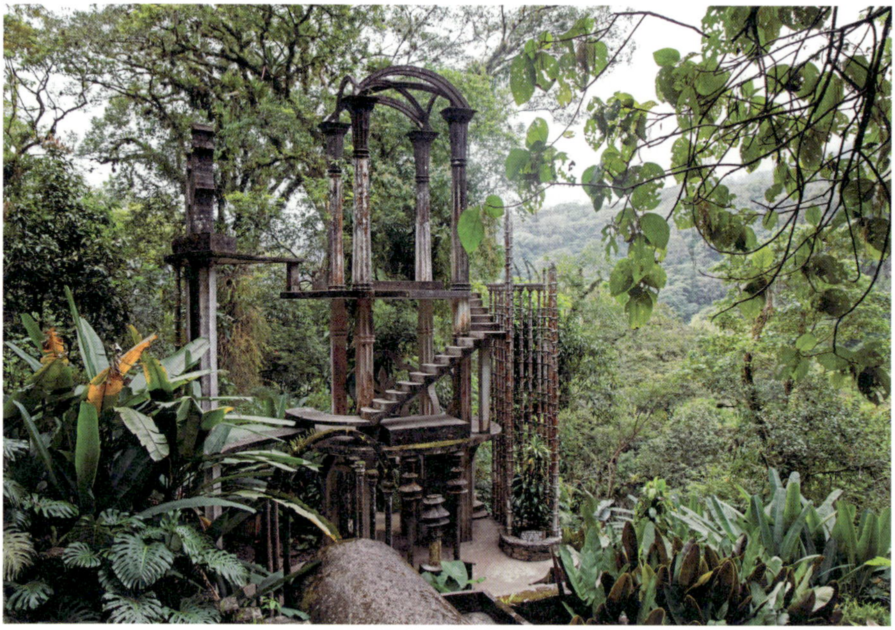

fig. 58
Edward James's Surrealist sculpture and landscape garden Las Pozas in Xilitla, Mexico

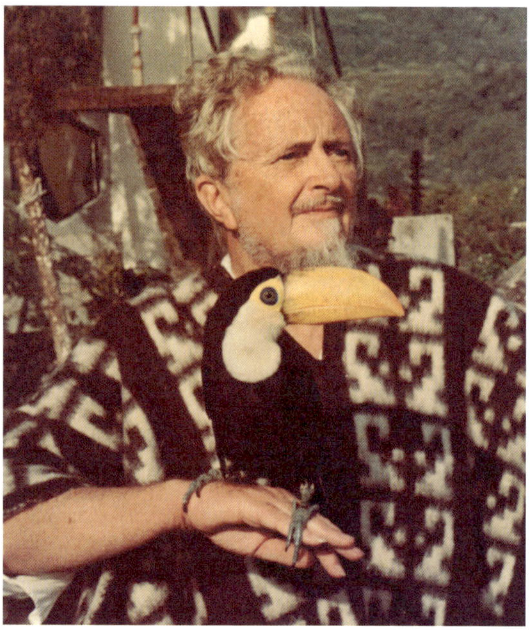

fig. 59
Edward James with a toucan in Las Pozas, 1970s

World War II is the English Surrealist Edward James. Comparable to Gaudí or the anonymous architects and sculptors from the gardens of Bomarzo, he transformed his tropical estate into a park of chimeras. Architecture and sculpture carved in stone by madness."

As time went on, James's life evolved into an existence between two continents. Which is why, in the title of this essay—now gradually drawing to a close—I even alluded to a third life of this English eccentric. In 1964, he turned West Dean into a foundation, while keeping Monkton for himself. In the 1970s he had a house built in the Algarve in Portugal. Later, he built one in Perinaldo, near San Remo in Italy, where he died in 1984. He also often frequented the Irish retreat of his friend Desmond Guinness. In 1983 he travelled around India. In addition to looking after his gesamtkunstwerk in Mexico, he continued to move his collection of paintings between his various residences scattered across two continents. He curated exhibitions, such as the Dalí retrospective in 1970, first shown at the Boijmans Van Beuningen Museum in Rotterdam and then at the Kunsthalle in Baden-Baden; he organized an anamorphosis exhibition with the Dutch photographer Michael Schuyt, who introduced him to Niki de Saint Phalle, another woman who fascinated James. At a public auction he sold some of the treasures he had amassed; and he reinvented his life, for example, by publishing his childhood memories under a title borrowed from Dalí, *Swans Reflecting Elephants* (1982), having dictated them to the photographer and singer George Melly, whereby, so it would appear, one or two anecdotes were added...

In his biography *Edward James: A Surrealist Life* (1991), his former collaborator John Lowe describes how, in 1982, James tried to visit the now widowed Dalí in Figueres, an endeavor that was thwarted, apparently as a result of mistaken identity, as was explained to him afterwards in a letter he deemed unconvincing. A few years earlier, writes Lowe, the two had met for the last time in Paris, then still with Gala present. According to James, he had the impression that, while Dalí was pleased to see him, Gala was not. This probably refers to their meeting at Hôtel Le Meurice, also mentioned by Amanda Lear in her collected memories of Dalí, citing some rather disparaging comments made by the Catalan artist about how old James had become, his white beard, and his Mexican dream: "How unfortunate! [...] such an educated man. And then he ends up in Mexico, the most dreadful country that exists!"

In memoriam Pierre Le-Tan

1 Salvador Dalí, *The Secret Life of Savaldor Dalí*, translated by Haakon M. Chevalier (New York, 1993), p. 378.
2 Ibid., p. 378.
3 Ibid., p. 340.
4 Ibid., p. 340.
5 Ibid., p. 340.

JULIO ROMERO DE TORRES – SALVADOR DALÍ: A UNIQUE VISUAL RELATIONSHIP

Jaime Brihuega Sierra

> "To return to the analysis of the dream of the plaster inundation, here are some preliminary data for determining the intentional role of certain elements of the preceding waking period—a symbolic role of the first order. First of all, the two prepared canvases which I have at the foot of my bed and which I look at with self-satisfaction before going to sleep: these two canvases had previously been two studies executed in the class in what was called 'drapery,' which was under the auspices of the painter [...] Julio Romero de Torres."[1]

Why discuss Julio Romero de Torres in a publication about the genesis of Salvador Dalí's work?[2] It may seem absurd, and yet, although the two artists differ significantly in both essence and appearance, one cannot draw an unbreachable line between certain paintings by Julio Romero de Torres and some of Salvador Dalí's 1920s works. *Portrait of Luis Buñuel* (1924, P 141, →fig. 26), *Portrait of My Sister* (1925, P 166, →p. 27), and *Girl's Back* (1926, P 179) come to mind.

These paintings are early examples of the young Dalí's foray into Modernism and affirm his connection to the new European "verisms." They therefore have little in common with the portentous, mysterious oeuvre cultivated by the Córdoba-born Romero de Torres during the same period, the consequence of repeated adaptations of his primitive Symbolism. It is clear, however, that the metaphysical thread—which permeates several paintings by both artists—the pathologically melancholic uncertainty in the faces of their protagonists, and the hyper-realism of the tangible objects around them (be they alive, lifeless, or an element of the composition that alludes to necrophilia) now enable us to leap from one world of artistic conception to the other without getting too dizzy; or, one might say, in perfectly controlled schizophrenia.

Of the numerous examples that allow us to create a link between Dalí and Romero de Torres, I would like to draw attention to one in particular. I have often asked myself what the curious hand gesture—beseeching or as if raised in the Elevation of the Host—of the kneeling blind man in Julio Romero de Torres's *La Saeta* (1918, →fig. 60) is trying to tell me.[3] For these hands appear to represent something beyond exaggerated religious supplication. I have long suspected as much, since there is usually more to Romero's figures than mere hand gestures, designed to shift or direct the pattern of culturally coded symbols, or to give form to a hermetic metalanguage of lost ciphers. Their gestures seem to go beyond all of that and to give form to invisible shapes, thus generating anamorphisms, "double images," riddles, pictorial metaphors, and even dizzying spectral images... Mechanisms also frequently employed by Dalí.

Hands... fingers... There are few themes that are more typical of Dalí's work. The figures in Julio Romero's paintings endeavor to make exaggerated gestures with their hands. They cramp, flex, separate, and contort the complex apparatus of bones, muscles, and sinew beneath the taut skin with particular intensity and suggestively perplexing expressivity.[4] In principle, this is an iconographic key that, above all, references the wide repertoire of gestures found in Italian and international Mannerism. Yet we

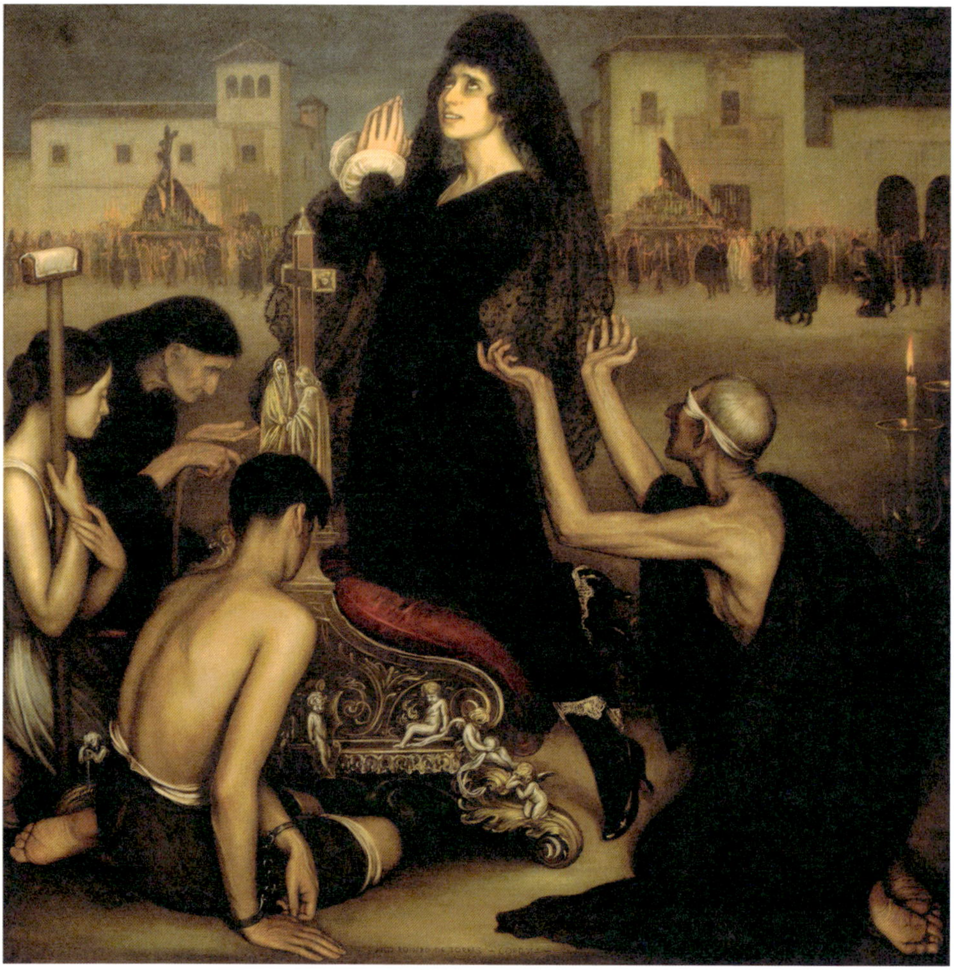

fig. 60
JULIO ROMERO DE TORRES, *La Saeta*, 1918
Palacio de Viana, Fundación Cajasur,
Córdoba

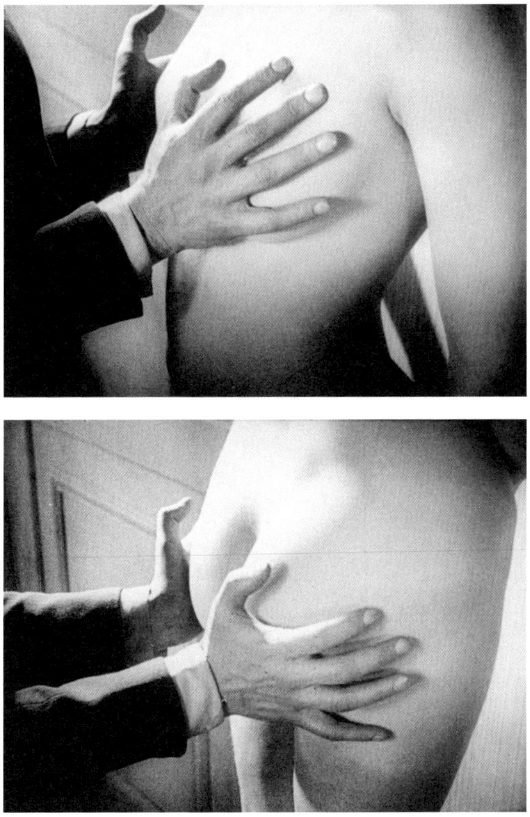

fig. 61
LUIS BUÑUEL, SALVADOR DALÍ
Un chien andalou, 1929

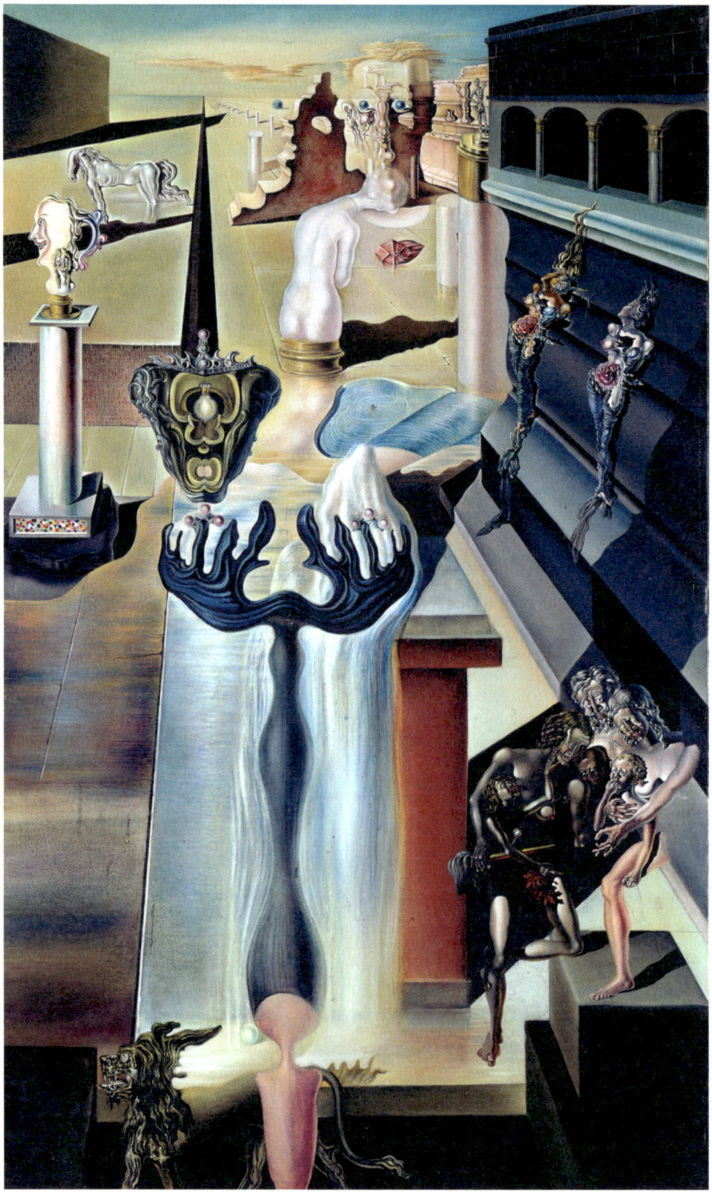

fig. 62
SALVADOR DALÍ, *L'homme invisible*
(*The Invisible Man*), 1929–32
Museo Nacional Centro de Arte Reina Sofía,
Madrid, cat. no. P 237

can sense immediately that these painterly statements are abundant with tautological significance. For, in general, there are always two fingers on the hands of Romero's figures (almost all female) that touch, open, or bend independently of each other, until they eventually form a double image that suggests the legs of a female body in miniature, her sex concealed in between.

However, Romero de Torres's sexual references, especially the phallus or vagina—themes also highly characteristic of Dalí—take on very different dimensions. All the typical symbols and metaphors of psychoanalysis are clearly evident in his painting: male ones, like the pocketknife, the waterspout of a well or fountain, the rocket, gun, or fireworks missile—which lead us once again to Dalí[5]—and female ones, such as lilies, fruits revealing their insides through a slit, high-heeled shoes, jugs and carafes, guitars with exaggerated curves and hollows, braziers, and other vessels. Comparing the iconic position of the blind man's hands in *La Saeta* with these examples (and I could name many others), one can easily reach similar conclusions. Through a gesture of touch, an imaginary projection in the air, these hands could also be seen as caressing two round, symmetrical shapes. Two breasts, perhaps? Buttocks? Is this not, after all, what underlies several key sequences in *Un chien andalou* (→fig. 61)?

Examining the painting's complex narrative more closely, we may be looking at a figurative evocation, synaesthetically triggered within the figure of the blind man by the Saeta, a song performed by a female voice. And, indeed, one that gradually dissolves into a formless acoustic-olfactory blend of religiosity and eroticism. If we then look at Dalí's picture *The Invisible Man* (1929–32, P 237, →fig. 62, sketch →p. 99)—a work brimming over with double images, pictorial shifts, anamorphoses, "pictorial amalgamations," and "the paranoid surveillance of the gaze"—turned upside down, we can suddenly see a pair of hands, bearing a surprising resemblance to the hands of the blind man in Romero's painting. My intention is not to use a positivist hypothesis to suggest that, in 1929, Dalí was directly inspired by this picture painted in 1918 by his professor at the Academy in

San Fernando; rather, I wish to draw attention to the fact that Julio Romero de Torres's paintings were deeply embedded in the collective consciousness of the era, and that it is certainly quite plausible, especially bearing in mind that the ambivalent interpretations of the works of the Cordoban artist would have held a strong attraction for the young Dalí.

In fact, following the description of a convoluted, paranoid dream, Dalí makes explicit reference to the three-dimensional exercises he took part in at the academy during a lesson with Romero de Torres.[6] Reinforcing this in its ironic coincidence is the significant role of the crutch in the narrative design of *La Saeta*; a crutch, which not much later would take center stage in Dalí's painting as an allegory for his fear of sexual impotence.

If we compare the two paintings, we get the impression that in *The Invisible Man*, the Catalan artist has reproduced the hands of the blind man from *La Saeta*, only from the opposite direction, looking out from inside the painting. More specifically, from inside the body of the woman, who is singing, gripped by an ecstatic trance—a psychological state which Dalí, in turn, was obsessed with, as can be surmised from his collage *The Phenomenon of Ecstasy* (→p. 113).[7] Moreover, the hands painted by Romero suggest two imaginary breasts, placed precisely where they could be caressed by the blind man's hands. In the case of Dalí, the association of this shape with female breasts (and also with eyes) can be better appreciated in a drawing (1936/37), which in a way is linked to *The Invisible Man*, as well as in the breasts of the female figure in *The Memory of the Woman-Child* (1929, P 236) and other representations of breasts and buttocks from the same period.

Given the expressive mythology developed by Dalí around Jean-François Millet's *Angelus* (1857/59; →fig. 27),[8] this suggestion is not as spurious as it may sound, but, much rather, is a line of thought complementary to those offered by contemporary critics regarding these aspects. It is an important one, however. Undeniably, such mechanisms for the articulation of puzzles, double images, pictorial metaphors, and hallucinations were already in ample supply in the pictures of Romero de Torres, whom Dalí became acquainted with at the Real Academia de Bellas Artes de San Fernando.

There are also a number of overt references to necrophilia, a common thread between Romero and Dalí, essentially arising from the iconography of the severed head—an absolutely crucial element in Dalí's iconography, and one that is expressed in Romero's work through themes such as Magdalena, the hagiography of the female martyr, Salome, and Judith. The two latter themes are, in turn, closely connected to the conceptual world of fin-de-siècle Symbolism (Gustave Moreau, Aubrey Beardsley, Gustav Klimt, Émile Fabry, Lovis Corinth, Franz von Stuck...).

More difficult to overlook is the image of the greyhound Pacheco,[9] who is strolling back and forth between the paintings of Julio Romero de Torres and the poetry collection *Poema del cante jondo* (*Poem of the Deep Song*), believed to have been written by Lorca in 1921, who then developed its themes between 1924 and 1927 with *Romancero gitano* (*Gypsy Ballads*). And, of course, Dalí always emerges like a shadow from the depths of this spider's web of connections. A shadow that reveals its shape like an Indonesian puppet once we compare the silhouette of the greyhound Pacheco by Romero with the sketches and works connected to *Invisible Sleeping Woman Horse Lion* (1930, P 246).

Much more concrete is the comparison with the greyhound gnawing on raw meat at the bottom right of *Metamorphosis of Narcissus* (1937, P 455, →fig. 17). And it was this very painting that Dalí presented to Sigmund Freud at their meeting in 1938.

1 Salvador Dalí, *The Secret Life of Salvador Dalí*, translated by Haakon M. Chevalier (New York, 1993) p. 168.

2 I have explicitly explored this topic in a major exhibition about Javier Pérez Segura. See Jaime Brihuega, "Materialidad obsesiva del símbolo: La pintura de Julio Romero de Torres a partir de 1915," in *Julio Romero de Torres: Símbolo, materia y obsesión*, ibid., exh. cat., Fundación Provincial de Artes Plásticas "Rafael Botí," Córdoba (Madrid, 2003), pp. 43–70.

3 "Saeta" is a religious song performed in Andalusia during the Holy Week processions.

4 In an essay in the aforementioned catalogue, Juan Antonio Ramírez explores this aspect in a monograph, connecting Romero to an intense pictorial codification of the expression of passion, undeniably an update of a classical theme in Western painting; Juan Antonio Ramírez, "Nota (apasionada) sobre gestos y pasiones," in *Julio Romero de Torres: Símbolo, materia y obsesión*, eds. Jaime Brihuega and Javier Pérez Segura, exh. cat., Fundación Provincial de Artes Plásticas "Rafael Botí," Córdoba (Madrid, 2003), pp. 157–62.

5 Once again, the link between Romero and Dalí shows in explicit connections. *Un chien andalou* (which also implicitly references Lorca) begins with a shocking photogram featuring a razor. When mapping the relationship between "passion" and "dynamite," a line can be drawn between Romero's commercials for the Unión de Explosivos Río Tinto and Dalí's *Board of Demented Associations* (1930/31, P 1185), made using an advert for fireworks.

6 This reference to Romero is found in Dalí, *The Secret Life*, (see note 1), p. 168. In Ramírez 2003 (see note 4), a whole range of potential connections between Romero and Dalí are also proposed.

7 Published in issue 3/4 of the magazine *Minotaure*, Paris 1933.

8 See "El Mito Trágico del 'Angelus' de Millet," in *Salvador Dalí: Ensayos 2*, ed. Montse Aguer, (Barcelona, 2005), vol. V, pp. 403–548.

9 The black greyhound Pacheco belonged to Julio Romero de Torres; he is depicted in a number of Torres's paintings.

APPENDIX

SALVADOR DALÍ I DOMÈNECH
Figueres, May 11, 1904 – January 23, 1989, Figueres

Jaime Brihuega Sierra

1904
Born on May 11 in Figueres, Girona, as the son of the notary Salvador Dalí Cusí (→ p. 29) and his wife, Felipa Domènech Ferrés.

1908
Birth of his only sister, Ana María (→ p. 27).

1910
His father enrolls him at the Hispano-French Colegio de la Inmaculada Concepción in Figueres, where he learns French, henceforth his language of habitual use.

1916
Socializes with the Pichot family, whose collection of paintings by Ramón Pichot introduces him to Impressionism. Starts secondary education at the Colegio de los Hermanos Maristas and the Instituto de Figueres. Receives tuition from Juan Núñez at the municipal drawing school in Figueres.

1919
Takes part in a group exhibition in the salon of the Societat de Concerts at the municipal theater of Figueres, later the Dalí Theatre-Museum. Founds, with others, the magazine *Studium*, in which he publishes his first articles. Begins a personal diary titled "Les meves impressions i records íntims" (My impressions and personal memoirs), which he continues throughout the following year (published in Spanish under the title *Un diario: 1919–1920. Mis impresiones y recuerdos íntimos*).

1920
His father sends him to study at the school of painting, sculpture, and engraving at the San Fernando Royal Academy of Fine Arts in Madrid.

1921
In February his mother dies. The following year his father marries her sister Catalina Domènech Ferrés.

1922
Takes part in the *Students' Original Art Works Competition Exhibition* of the Catalan Students' Association at the Galeries Dalmau in Barcelona. In Madrid he attends the Real Academia de Bellas Artes de San Fernando and lives at the Residencia de Estudiantes (British-style student halls of residence, → p. 37). There he befriends a group of young students, including Luis Buñuel, Federico García Lorca, Pedro Garfias, Eugenio Montes, Pepín Bello, and others who later become prominent intellectuals and artists (→ p. 45).

1923
Expelled from the San Fernando Royal Academy after being accused of leading a protest against the rejection of painter Daniel Vázquez Díaz as Chair of Painting. Returns to Figueres, where he resumes lessons with Juan Núñez who teaches him engraving techniques.

1924
In the autumn he returns to the Academy, where he is forced to repeat a year.

1925
Takes part in the *First Exhibition of the Society of Iberian Artists* in Madrid and presents his first solo exhibition at the Galeries Dalmau in Barcelona. At this stage his work reflects the influences of the various Modernist trends. In 1925 and 1926 he does not return to the Academy in San Fernando. Federico García Lorca spends his holidays with Dalí in Cadaqués.

1926
Dalí discovers the writings of Sigmund Freud, which have been published in Spanish translation by Biblioteca Nueva since 1922 (→ p. 50). He and Lorca become interested in the histological drawings of Santiago Ramón y Cajal (→ pp. 55–72). He is also increasingly receptive to the influence of the Surrealists and produces his first drawings marked by these influences. Takes part in various exhibitions in Madrid and Barcelona. Travels to Paris for the first time, together with his aunt and sister, where he meets Picasso and visits the Louvre. Expelled permanently from the Academy in Madrid. Returns to Figueres where he devotes himself to painting.

1927
Holds his second solo exhibition at the Galeries Dalmau in Barcelona. Takes part in the *Saló de Tardor*, the second autumn exhibition of the Sala Parés gallery in Barcelona. The early influences of Surrealism are already in clear evidence in the exhibited works. Undertakes his military service at Sant Ferran Castle in Figueres. Starts contributing to the avant-garde magazine *L'amic de les arts*.

1928

Publishes, together with Lluís Montanyà and Sebastià Gasch, the Catalan anti-art manifesto *Manifest groc*, a scathing attack against conventional art. Takes part in the third *Saló de Tardor* at the Sala Parés and the *Twenty-seventh International Exhibition of Paintings* in Pittsburgh, USA.

1929

Travels to Paris again and, through Joan Miró, makes contact with the group of Surrealists led by André Breton. The film *Un chien andalou* (→ p. 86), a collaboration with Luis Buñuel, is produced and premieres at the Studio des Ursulines in Paris. Spends the summer in Cadaqués, where he is visited by the gallery owner Camille Goemans and his wife, René Magritte and his wife, Luis Buñuel, as well as Paul Éluard and Gala, along with their daughter Cécile. From that moment on, Gala never leaves his side (→ p. 93). He has his first solo exhibition at Galerie Goemans in Paris. Breaks with his family. Affirms his Surrealist pictorial language with works such as *Face of the Great Masturbator* (P 235, → fig. 12) and *The Lugubrious Game* (P 232, → p. 91).

1930

L'âge d'or (→ p. 88), his second film with Buñuel, premieres at Studio 28 in Paris. His illustrated book *La femme visible* (*The Visible Woman*) is published by Éditions surréalistes and includes essays that had previously appeared in various magazines, one of them "L'âne pourri" (The Rotting Donkey), which laid the foundation for his "paranoiac-critical method."

1931

Holds his first solo exhibition at Galerie Pierre Colle in Paris, where he presents the work *The Persistence of Memory* (1931, P 265). Takes part in the first Surrealist exhibition in the United States, which is held at the Wadsworth Atheneum in Hartford. His book *L'amour et la mémoire* (Love and Memory) is published.

1932

Takes part in the exhibition *Surrealism: Paintings, Drawings and Photographs* at the Julien Levy Gallery in New York. In Paris, his second solo exhibition at Galerie Pierre Colle is held. Publishes his book *Babaouo*, in which he outlines his views about cinema. At the end of this year, Dalí announces to the Vicomte de Noailles the founding of the "Zodiac Group," a group of friends who agree to sponsor him by commissioning and regularly purchasing his works.

1933

Publishes the essay "Interprétation paranoïaque-critique de l'image obsédante 'L'Angélus' de Millet" (Paranoiac-critical interpretation of the obsessive image of Millet's *Angelus*, → p. 115) in the first issue of the magazine *Minotaure*. Takes part in the joint exhibition of Surrealists at Galerie Pierre Colle, where he also presents his third solo exhibition. First solo exhibition at the Julien Levy Gallery in New York.

1934

Civil marriage to Gala (née Helena Ivanovna Diakonova). Exhibits at the Salon des Indépendants' *Exposition du Cinquantenaire* at the Grand Palais in Paris, despite the other Surrealists' decision to boycott the exhibition. This almost results in his expulsion from the group led by André Breton. Holds his first solo exhibition at the Zwemmer Gallery in London. First trip to the United States, accompanied by Gala, on board the *Champlain*. Two solo exhibitions in the US, one at the Julien Levy Gallery and the other at the Avery Memorial of the Wadsworth Atheneum in Hartford, Connecticut.

1935

Dalí and Gala return to Europe on the *Normandie*. In March, Salvador Dalí goes to Figueres, where he reconciles with his family. Éditions surréalistes publishes *La conquête de l'irrationnel* (*Conquest of the Irrational*, → p. 145).

1936

Takes part in the *Exposition surréaliste d'objets* at Galerie Charles Ratton in Paris in May and the *International Surrealist Exhibition* at London's New Burlington Galleries in June (→ fig. 51). On December 14, *Time* magazine dedicates its cover to him, with a photograph taken by Man Ray (→ fig. 38). Takes part in the exhibition *Fantastic Art, Dada, Surrealism* at MoMA in New York. His third solo exhibition at the Julien Levy Gallery in New York is held.

1937

Meets the Marx Brothers in Hollywood in February. Starts working together with Harpo on the screenplay for the film *Giraffes on Horseback Salad* (known in its final version by the title *The Surrealist Woman*); however, the film is never produced. Dalí and Gala return to Europe. From April they spend some time in Austria. In Vienna, Dalí attempts unsuccessfully to visit Freud and is fascinated by Vermeer's *The Art of Painting*. At the Galerie Renou et Colle in Paris he presents his portrait of Harpo Marx and the drawings the two had produced for their film. His poem "Métamorphose de Narcisse" (Metamorphosis of Narcissus) is published simultaneously by Éditions surréalistes and in English by Julien Levy.

1938

On January 17, the *Exposition internationale du surréalisme*, organized by André Breton and Paul Éluard, opens at the Galerie Beaux-Arts in Paris. Exhibited at the entrance to the gallery is Salvador Dalí's *Rainy Taxi* (→ fig. 54). On July 19, Dalí, with the help of Stefan Zweig and accompanied by Edward James, succeeds in meeting Freud, who is living in exile in London. He shows him the painting *Metamorphosis of Narcissus* (1937, P 455, → fig. 17) and draws several portraits of him.

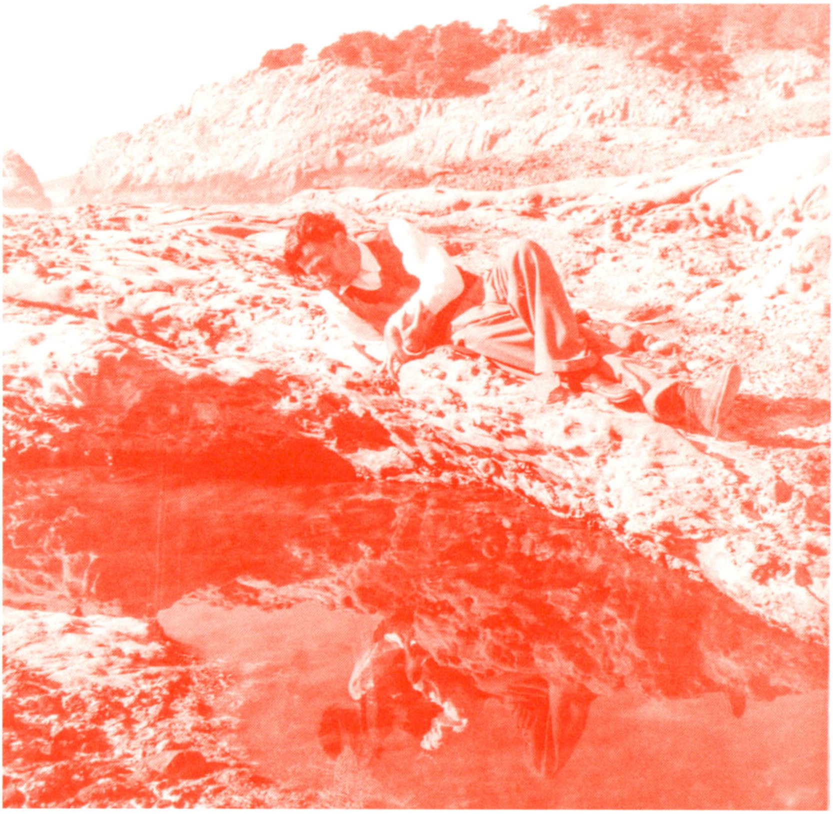

fig. 63
Salvador Dalí at Punta dels Tres Frares in Cala Galladera, Cap de Creus, 1930s

SALVADOR DALÍ ON SIGMUND FREUD: TEXT FRAGMENTS

Compiled by Jaime Brihuega Sierra

The texts in which Dalí mentions Sigmund Freud are taken from the official complete Spanish edition of Dalí's writings, unless otherwise stated: Salvador Dalí, *Obra completa*, 7 vols. (with studies by Montse Aguer, Agustín Sánchez Vidal, Juan José Lahuerta, Juan Manuel Bonet, and Francisco Calvo Serraller; Barcelona, 2003). Page and volume references as per each citation.

The Surrealist revolution has upheld the names of the Comte de Lautréamont, of Trotsky, of Freud, of the Marquis de Sade, of Heraclitus, of Uccello, etc.
— Vol. IV, p. 198, originally from Salvador Dalí, "Posición moral del surrealismo," *Hélix*, no. 10, Villafranca del Penedés, 1930. Translation from Salvador Dalí, "The Moral Position of Surrealism," in *The Collected Writings of Salvador Dalí* (Cambridge / New York, 1998), p. 222.

Through Freud we have become acquainted with the purity of literal interpretation, that is, the non-interpretation of platitudes and common expressions.
— Vol. IV, p. 209, originally from Salvador Dalí, *La femme visible* (Paris, 1930).

My three voyages to Vienna were exactly like three drops of water which lacked the reflections to make them glitter. On each of these voyages I did exactly the same things: in the morning I went to see the Vermeer in the Czernin Collection, and in the afternoon I did *not* go to visit Freud because I invariably learned that he was out of town for reasons of health.
— SALVADOR DALÍ, *The Secret Life of Salvador Dalí* (London, 1949), p. 23.

Several years after my last ineffectual attempt to meet Freud [...] in France. We started the dinner with snails [...] All of a sudden I saw a photograph of Professor Freud on the front page of a newspaper [...] I had just that instant discovered the morphological secret of Freud! Freud's cranium is a snail! His brain is in the form of a spiral. [...] This discovery strongly influenced the portrait drawing which I later made from life, a year before his death.
— SALVADOR DALÍ, *The Secret Life of Salvador Dalí* (London, 1949), p. 23.

I was to meet Freud at last, in London. I was accompanied by the writer Stefan Zweig and by the poet Edward James. While I was crossing the old professor's yard I saw a bicycle leaning against the wall, and on the saddle, attached by a string, was a red rubber hot-water bottle which looked full of water, and on the back of the hot-water bottle walked a snail! The presence of that assortment seemed strange and inexplicable in the yard of Freud's house.
— SALVADOR DALÍ, *The Secret Life of Salvador Dalí* (London, 1949), p. 24.

Contrary to my hopes we spoke little, but we devoured each other with our eyes. Freud knew nothing about me except my painting, which he admired, but suddenly I had the whim of trying to appear in his eyes as a kind of dandy of "universal intellectualism."
— SALVADOR DALÍ, *The Secret Life of Salvador Dalí* (London, 1949), p. 24.

Before leaving I wanted to give him a magazine containing an article I had written on paranoia [...] begging him to read it if he had time. Freud continued to stare at me without paying the slightest attention to my magazine. [...] I explained that it was not a Surrealist diversion, but was really an ambitiously scientific article. [...] Then, continuing to stare at me, Freud exclaimed, addressing Stefan Zweig, "I have never seen a more complete example of a Spaniard. What a fanatic!"
— SALVADOR DALÍ, *The Secret Life of Salvador Dalí* (London, 1949), p. 25.

We have learned, thanks to Freud, the symbolic significance charged with a well determined erotic meaning that characterizes everything relating to aviation, and especially to its origins.
— SALVADOR DALÍ, *The Secret Life of Salvador Dalí* (London, 1949), pp. 30.

The remarkable stroke of genius, however, was not this discovery itself, but its interpretation. [...] At this period I had just begun to read Sigmund Freud's *Interpretation of Dreams*. This book presented itself to me as one of the capital discoveries in my life, and I was seized with a real vice of self-interpretation.
— SALVADOR DALÍ, *The Secret Life of Salvador Dalí* (London, 1949), p. 167.

She [Gala] was destined to be my Gradiva. *Gradiva*, the novel by W. Jensen, interpreted by Sigmund Freud (*Der Wahn und die Träume*). Gradiva is the heroine of this novel, and she effects the psychological cure of the other, the male protagonist. When I began to read this novel, even before coming upon Freud's interpretation, I exclaimed, "Gala, my wife, is essentially a Gradiva."
— SALVADOR DALÍ, *The Secret Life of Salvador Dalí* (London, 1949), p. 233.

As soon as we had got settled in Port Lligat I painted a portrait of Gala with a pair of raw chops poised on her shoulder. [...] The chops were in effect the expiatory victims of abortive sacrifice—like Abraham's ram, and William Tell's apple [...] this being the prime condition for the cannibalistic sacrifice. [...] Freud relates a desert sacrifice of totemic character, in which the entire tribe in a few hours devoured a raw camel, of which only the bones remained at sunrise
— SALVADOR DALÍ, *The Secret Life of Salvador Dalí* (London, 1949), p. 319.

The day I went to visit Sigmund Freud in his London exile, on the eve of his death, I understood [...] how many things were at last ended in Europe with the imminent end of his life. He said to me, "In classic paintings, I look for the subconscious—in a Surrealist painting, for the conscious."
— SALVADOR DALÍ, *The Secret Life of Salvador Dalí* (London, 1949), pp. 397.

Freud particularly clarified for me some thoughts I had had on religion. In fact, I should not have been able to express them at all if it had not been for this contact.
— Vol. VII, p. 77, originally from Alfred Frankenstein, "Around the Art Galleries: Artist Dalí Sits For a Portrait," *San Francisco Chronicle*, August 24, 1941, p. 11.

Before I have been much with the influence of Sigmund Freud, and my pictures show the effect of this influence. That is the first stage of my life. Now this interest is still there, but I am with much more interest in the same thing, made to be extended by the work of Einstein. They are interested in the same. It is that Freud wrote about the subconscious, the mysteries of the mind, and Einstein has found the theory of the material. [...] I spend much time

reading in both Freud and Einstein.
— Vol. VII, p. 163, originally from William M. Freeman, "No More Freud for Dalí; Now He's Painting the Einstein Theories!," *Globe Democrat*, Saint Louis, January 31, 1950, p. 19.

When I got closer to them [the Surrealists] and defended Freud, since I had the impression he was able to explain better than anyone the human soul and its conflicts, the Communist group within the Surrealists, led by Louis Aragon, accused me of being bourgeois and reactionary.
— Vol. VII, p. 178, originally from Jose Ma Massip, "Dalí, Hoy," *Destino*, Barcelona, April 1, 1950, p. 4

My fanatism, aggravated by Freud and Einstein, both of them forced out of Germany by Hitler, made it obvious that the latter interested me only as an object of my delirium and because he seemed to me of incomparable catastrophic value.
— SALVADOR DALÍ, *Diary of a Genius* (Chicago, 2007), p. 26

Once more I thank Sigmund Freud and proclaim louder than ever his great truths. I, Dalí, […] have just discovered that, without realizing it, I have painted nothing but rhinoceros horns all my life.
— SALVADOR DALÍ, *Diary of a Genius* (Chicago, 2007), p. 49.

This is the day to think of the dead and of myself. The day to think about the death of Federico Garcia Lorca, shot in Granada, about the suicide of René Crevel in Paris. […] About the death of surrealism. […] About the deaths of Princess Mdivani and of Sigmund Freud, exiled in London. About the double suicide of Stefan Zweig and his wife. […] About the deaths of Gertrude Stein and of José-Maria Sert. […] Of Robert Desnons and Antonin Artaud. Of existentialism. About the death of my father. The death of Paul Eluard.
— SALVADOR DALÍ, *Diary of a Genius* (Chicago, 2007), p. 69.

Nor should I forget a singing scene in which Nietzsche, Freud, Ludwig II of Bavaria, and Karl Marx will sing their doctrines with incomparable virtuosity […] to some music by Bizet.
— SALVADOR DALÍ, *Diary of a Genius* (Chicago, 2007), p. 90.

I have already remarked […], that his [Freud's] skull looked like a Burgundy snail. […] If you want to eat his thoughts you have to pick them out with a needle. Then they come out whole. […] Today while reminding you of Freud's death, I shall add that the Burgundy snail, outside its shell, is one of the things that look quite stunningly like a painting by El Greco.
— SALVADOR DALÍ, *Diary of a Genius* (Chicago, 2007), p. 115

Freud's brain, one of the most savory and important of our age, was *par excellence* the snail of terrestrial death.
— SALVADOR DALÍ, *Diary of a Genius* (Chicago, 2007), p. 117

It seems that without realizing it I drew Freud's terrestrial death in the pencil portrait I did of him a year before his death.
— SALVADOR DALÍ, *Diary of a Genius* (Chicago, 2007), p. 117

Zweig […] claimed that Freud had greatly appreciated "the delicacy of the features." […] Freud had never seen his own portrait. Zweig had piously lied to me. According to him, my portrait so strikingly forecast Freud's impending death that he did not dare show it to him […] and knowing him to

be already very sick with cancer.
— SALVADOR DALÍ, *Diary of a Genius* (Chicago, 2007), pp. 117–18

Without hesitation, I place Freud among the heroes. He dispossessed the Jewish people of the greatest and most influential of all its heroes—Moses.
— SALVADOR DALÍ, *Diary of a Genius* (Chicago, 2007), p. 118

At daybreak, I dreamt that I was the author of several white turds, very clean and extremely agreeable to produce. When I woke up, I said to Gala: "Today there is going to be gold!" For this dream, according to Freud, indicated in bald terms that I was related to the hen with the golden eggs and the legendary ass who, when his tail was lifted, would shit golden coins, without mentioning Danaë's divine diarrhea of semiliquid gold.
— SALVADOR DALÍ, *Diary of a Genius* (Chicago, 2007), p. 156

While waiting for the faith that is the grace of God, I have become a hero. I made a mistake—two heroes! The hero, according to Freud, is a man, who revolts against the paternal authority and the father, and finally vanquishes them. This was the case with my father, who loved me so much. […] The situation is the same with Picasso, who is my second spiritual father.
— SALVADOR DALÍ, *Diary of a Genius* (Chicago, 2007), p. 169

The two places that I do not want to stop seeing on each of my returns from New York […] are still the glorious doors of the Paris métro, viscous incarnation of all the spiritual nourishment of the New Era—Marx, Freud, Hitler, Proust, Picasso, Einstein, Max Planck, Gala, Dali […] the other place is the very insignificant Perpignan station where,

[…] Dalí's brain and soul have found the most sublime ideas.
— SALVADOR DALÍ, *Diary of a Genius* (Chicago, 2007), p. 173

I met Sigmund Freud two years before Sigmund Freud died in London. My first period is influenced by Freud completely. Now, psychoanalysis is no more interest for me because now I am interested only about nuclear physics and these extraordinary heavens in the metaphysics.
— Vol VII, p. 570, originally from "Wallace versus Dalí," interview, *Town and Country*, New York, May 31, 1957.

I would like to write an opera starring Freud, Stalin, Karl Marx, Hitler, among others. Each of them would sing their ideas. This is feasible because they have been disseminated via the radio and newspapers. And then, when Freud explains psychoanalysis in an aria, everybody will understand what it is about.
— Vol. VII, p. 613, originally from "Walt Disney y Dalí no se ponen de acuerdo" (Walt Disney and Dalí are in dispute, interview), *Fotogramas*, Barcelona, October 11, 1957.

According to Freud, the father of psychoanalysis, "a hero is a man who revolts against the authority of his father and finally overcomes it." This applies to me.
— Vol. VII, p. 672, originally from "El estudiar con los niños pobres fue muy importante en el desarrollo de mi natural tendencia a la megalomanía" (Studying with poor children was essential to the development of my natural predilection for megalomania), *Solidaridad nacional*, Barcelona, August 30, 1958.

In the first period of my life my hero was Sigmund Freud. I depicted all the anguish and neurotic visions in those days, whereas now my hero is the physicist

Werner Heisenberg, because his ideas show a closer relationship to God and cosmic unity.
— Vol. VII, pp. 721–22, originally from "Dalí the Great," interview with Selden Rodman, *Controversy*, Philadelphia, May 31, 1959, p. 32.

Since knowing Freud, I have come to the conclusion that one must sleep on things. During sleep, one recapitulates them, and the following morning they seem clear. Plato called it "the sleep of truth." And already the meaning emerges.
— Vol. VII, p. 785, originally from "García Lorca y la Costa Brava," (García Lorca and the Costa Brava, fragment), *Usted*, Girona, June 30, 1961.

The works by Millet that I discover today are composed of clear antecedents to the erotic tendencies manifested by their author, tendencies that, we shall see, seem to lie in the latent content of the *Angelus* [...] Thus [...] [he] gives us a direct example of the enigma of the penis [...] a parallelism confused with the famous *Virgin and Child* by Leonardo da Vinci, which contains the invisible vulture discovered by Freud, in *A Souvenir of the Childhood of Leonardo da Vinci.*
— Vol. V, pp. 881–82, originally from Salvador Dalí, *The Tragic Myth of Millet' Angelus* (St. Petersburg, FL, 1986) p. 43–45

Freud was of the opinion that the dreamlike aspect of my pictures was too obvious.
— Vol. VII, pp. 881–82, originally from "Picasso es un genio como yo, pero un genio demoníaco" (Picasso is a genius like I am, albeit a demonic one, interview), *Pueblo*, Madrid, November 11, 1964.

When I had the honor of meeting Sigmund Freud in London, he explained to me in a few words that superstition has an erotic and, with regard to the dark forces, effective background. Since then, I have been digging deeper into superstition.
— Vol. VII, p. 1112, originally from Alain Bosquet, *Entretiens avec Salvador Dalí* (Paris, 2000), p. 136.

Cumulative discontent leads to a process which Freud calls sublimation. All unfulfilled erotic desires are sublimated in artwork.
— Vol. VII, p. 1126, originally from Alain Bosquet, *Entretiens avec Salvador Dalí* (Paris, 2000), p. 157.

So, if I am a hero, according to Freud, it is because I have succeeded in appropriating my father's power.
— Vol. II, p. 107, originally from Louis Pauwels, *Les passions selon Dalí* (written 1966/1967) (Paris, 1968).

When I held back the crap // The hidden gold // My painting is like an iceberg // What Freud said to me // A few words about cathartic love.
— Vol. II, p. 185, originally from Louis Pauwels. *Les passions selon Dalí* (written 1966/67) (Paris, 1968).

Flicking through a book about Freud by Raymond de Becker, I came across the only drawing ever made by the father of psychoanalysis. [...] During his four-year engagement Freud wrote one thousand five hundred letters. One of them was accompanied by a sketch of his room at the Vienna General Hospital. [...] Why did he deem it necessary to draw up this plan, if not to follow an unconscious impulse in the face of a structure identical to the structure of the entrance to Perpignan station, the structure par excellence?
— Vol. II, p. 185, originally from Louis Pauwels, *Les passions selon Dalí* (written 1966/67) (Paris, 1968).

"The Firefighters" [representatives of academy arts] Meissonier and Detaille, upon whom the historical task of maintaining the genetic code of the homeland was incumbent, as embodied through the

person and the spirit of Karl Marx (*Das Kapital*, 1857), Max Planck, Friedrich Hegel, Albert Einstein, Sigmund Freud, Antonio Gaudí, Cézanne, Marcel Proust, Raymond Roussel, Mariano Fortuny, Pablo Picasso, and their contemporary Norbert Weimer.
— Vol. IV, p. 759, originally from *Hommage à Meissonier*, exh. cat., Hôtel Meurice de Paris (Paris, 1967).

(Can one be a Surrealist without realizing it?)
Especially without realizing it. Besides, that was Freud's view. One day he claimed to me that the Surrealists did not interest him. And since I was puzzled, because I knew how much they referred to him, he said to me "I prefer the pictures with no obvious trace of Surrealism. Those I do indeed examine. And in them I find real treasures of subconscious thought."
— Vol. VII, p. 1195, originally from "El delirio de Dalí" (Dalí's Delirium, interview), *La Galerie*, Paris, January 1971.

I had often thought about Freud before meeting him. I think he would have been the only man who could talk as an equal to my paranoia. He admired my painting greatly. I would have liked to dazzle him. When I met him in London, introduced by Stefan Zweig, I made great efforts to appear to him as I imagined he imagined me; a Beau Brummel of universal caliber. But I failed. He listened to me talk with great attention and finally exclaimed to Zweig: "What a fanatic! What a perfect Spanish type!" To him, I was a case, not a person. His snail's skull had not sensed my intuitions or my intimate strength. But I did make a deep impression on him, since the next day he wrote to Zweig:

"I must really thank you for the introduction that brought me yesterday's visitors. For until then, it seems, I had tended to think the Surrealists, who apparently have chosen me as their patron saint, were completely crazy (or let us say 95% so, as in the case of pure alcohol). The young Spaniard, with his candid fanatic's eyes and his undeniable technical mastery, led me to reconsider my opinion. It would indeed be most interesting to study analytically the genesis of a picture of this type. From a critical viewpoint, it could however always be said that the notion of art does not lend itself to any extension when the qualitative relationship, between unconscious material and preconscious elaboration, does not remain within determined limits. At any rate, these are serious psychological problems."

But what interested him obviously was his own theory, not my personality. He was no longer really in the running. I sketched him on a blotter. This was in 1938, a year before his death.

Two geniuses had met without making sparks [...] I am convinced that our meeting was a turning-point in Freud's artistic conception. I am persuaded that I forced the great master of the subconscious to rethink his attitude. Before me—Dalí—Freud had never met any really modern artist. Before our meeting, he thought—as he wrote—that the Surrealists were crazy; after me, he "reconsidered" his opinion. Freud had a hunch that the Surrealists, and the Expressionists along with them, took the mechanics of art for art itself. My work—my technical mastery—and my person showed him that his concept had been foolhardy. Yes, I am convinced that if we had met earlier, or several times, some of his views on art might have been modified. My paranoia-critical method would have opened new vistas to him. Freud thought that the unconscious was a psychic content which can no longer return to the consciousness once it has been driven out.
He brought about the psychology of depths—as compared to formal psychology, which in this domain is a superficial geography of the mind—he put his finger on the reality of reason, man's

invention for realizing himself in a world perpetually in confrontation and conflict. With him, we found out that the psyche is not the conscious alone, but I could have been his living and fundamental proof that paranoia, which is one of the most extraordinary forms of the irrational unconscious, can perfectly well give impetus to rational mechanisms and fertilize the real with an efficacity as great as experimental logic. Paranoia-critical delirium is one of the most fascinating formulas of human genius. Freud was probably too old to reopen his theses and make way for new experiments.
— SALVADOR DALÍ, *The Unspeakable Confessions of Salvador Dalí as told to André Parinaud* (London / Melbourne / New York, 1974), pp. 120–21.

That same summer, 1932, a madman in a fit punched a hole in Millet's *Angelus* at the Louvre, after having long hesitated, he later stated, between it and Watteau's *Embarkation for Cythera* or the *Mona Lisa*. (Freud's demonstration of the incestuous attraction of that Da Vinci work is well known.)
— SALVADOR DALÍ, *The Unspeakable Confessions of Salvador Dalí as told to André Parinaud* (London / Melbourne / New York, 1974), pp. 1156.

I was not unhappy to check out this new strength of mine by meeting Sigmund Freud. When Stefan Zweig introduced me to him in London, the fanaticism of my personality deeply impressed the father of psychoanalysis.
— SALVADOR DALÍ, *The Unspeakable Confessions of Salvador Dalí as told to André Parinaud* (London / Melbourne / New York, 1974), pp. 1185

One of Dalí's most recent discoveries has revealed that monotheism is currently hidden in the "pee" of a squid. The rhinoceros is only missing the wings of a vulture. You know, of course, that, according to Freud, the vulture is the symbol for mother […] All mothers. On the left side and on the ground is a book by Sigmund Freud titled *Monotheism* [*The Man Moses and Monotheistic Religion*] […] in which he explains that Moses was not a Jew but an Egyptian. This must have been a dramatic discovery for Freud. The book is marvelous.
— Vol. VII, p. 1347, originally from "El museo Dalí explicado por el propio Dalí" (The Dalí Museum explained by Dalí himself, interview), *La actualidad española*, Madrid, October 10, 1974.

Yes, but Freud has interesting views about sex that are all wrong. Freud places too much emphasis on male sex. Sex is not in the body of one man; the pointed, erected, minute clitoris is the man becoming the girl, the girl becoming the boy. In this manner the woman makes love inside the sex of the boy.
— Gregory Battcock, "An Interview with Salvador Dalí," *Art and Artist*, London, August 1975, p. 5

Even those who disagree with Freud consider the act of flight to be […] self-evident, the winged phallus is an internal human organ possessing the extraordinary ability to fly.
— Vol. VII, p. 1468, originally from "Dalí: 'Soy el pompier de la pintura moderna,'" (Dalí: "I am the Fire Fighter of Modern Painting"), *Paris Match*, December 9, 1977.

Yes. I believe I was the only one in the group of Surrealists who was in contact with Freud. Before he met me, he thought Surrealism was based on drugs and a ludicrous Romanticism. When I brought him my picture, he wanted to talk about it, but I

wanted him to read my theory on paranoid psychosis, which was different from Jacque Lacan's. Freud, who took me for a painter, turned back to the picture. I became annoyed, thumped my fist on the table, and said "I really want you to read my theory on paranoia." He paused for a moment and said to Stefan Zweig: "The perfect Spaniard. What a fanatic!"
— Vol. VII, p. 1509, originally from "Dalí: 'Mi ética es la estética,'" ("Dalí: 'My Ethic is Aesthetic,'" interview), *Destino*, Barcelona, October 4, 1978.

That is why a vulture appears in Leonardo da Vinci's work [...] Hence the interest of Freud and of Salvador Dalí, who recalls it in the article on these pages. The helicopter is the vulture discovered by Freud. Like the vulture, which intruded through the window and whose tail Leonardo da Vinci felt in his mouth [...] Gala! Submarine! Submarine, suspended for a moment between sky and sea, chasms of heaven and beyond. King Oedipus! Incest! Saint Anne and the Virgin in one! The mother vulture goddess of Egypt! The vulture's tail in the mouth! Living on scents and essences. Inventing everything in the dark! Theology. Malebranche! We still live off you! All or nothing. Speechless, confused, our longings for the limited eternal. Federico García Lorca, we still live in you!
— Vol. IV, p. 897, originally from "El buitre, Leonardo y el ictíneo," (The Vulture, Leonardo, and the Submarine), *El país*, Madrid, February 11, 1985.

As a typical, fanatical Spaniard—that is how Freud defined me, incidentally. If there is one thought that I'm obsessed by, it is Spanish unity. Every time I hear the national anthem, although musically mediocre, I get goosebumps.
— Vol. VII, p. 1609, originally from "Dalí. Si no divino, inmortal," (Dalí: If Not Divine, Then Immortal At Least, interview), *Época*, Madrid, April 28, 1985.

I have intense memories of my life in the womb. It was the same for Casanova. And Freud confirmed it when I met him in London. I saw—and see—fried eggs without plates, their edges phosphorizing, expanding and contracting [...] true reproductions of the forgotten paradise, the prenatal paradise.
— Vol. VII, p. 1639, originally from "No me he drogado nunca, porque yo soy la droga" (I Have Never Done Drugs. I Am Drugs, interview) in Joaquín Soler Serrano, *Personajes a fondo* (Barcelona, 1987).

Metamorphosis of Narcissus // *How to visually observe the metamorphosis of Narcissus in my picture on the opposite page: // Dali has endowed Surrealism with an instrument of primary importance, in particular the paranoiac critical method, which has immediately shown itself capable of being applied with equal success to painting, poetry, the cinema, to the construction of typical Surrealist objects, to fashions, to sculpture and even, if necessary, to all manner of exegesis. /* André Breton, *What is Surrealism? //* If one looks for some time, from a slight distance and with a certain "distant fixedness," at the hypnotically immobile figure of Narcissus, it gradually disappears until at last it is completely invisible. / The metamorphosis of the myth takes place at that precise moment, for the image of Narcissus is suddenly transformed into the image of a hand which rises out of his own reflection. At the tip of its fingers, the hand is holding an egg, a seed, the bulb from which will be born the new narcissus—the flower. Beside it can be seen the limestone sculpture of the hand—the fossil hand of the water holding the hatched, blossoming flower. / *The first poem and the first painting obtained entirely through the unrestrained application of the paranoiac-critical method. /* For the first time, a Surrealist painting and poem objectively allow the coherent interpretation of a developed irrational subject. The paranoiac-critical method is beginning to establish the indestructible pudding of the "exact details" that Stendhal demanded for the description of Saint Peter's Church in Rome, and it is doing this in the domain of the most paralyzing Surrealist poetry. / The lyricism of poetic images is philosophically important only when it has attained, in its operation, the same exactness as mathematics do in their operation. / The poet must, before anyone, prove what he says. // *First Port-Lligat Fisherman.*—What's wrong with that chap, glaring at himself all day in his looking-glass? / Second Fisherman.—If you really want to know (*lowering his voice*) he has a bulb in his head. // "A bulb in the head," in Catalan, corresponds exactly with the psychoanalytic notion of "complex." / If a man has a bulb in his head, it might break into flower at any moment, Narcissus! // Under the split in the retreating black cloud / the invisible scale of Spring / is oscillating / in the fresh April sky. / On the highest mountain, / the god of the snow, / his dazzling head bent over the dizzy space of / reflections, / starts melting with desire / in the vertical cataracts of the thaw / annihilating himself loudly among the excremental / cries of minerals, / or / between the silences of mosses / towards the distant mirror of the lake / in which, / the veils of winter having disappeared, / he had newly discovered / the lightning flash / of his faithful image. / It seems that with the loss of his divinity the whole / high plateau / pours itself out, / crashes and crumbles / among the solitude and the incurable silence of iron / oxides / while its dead weight / raises the entire swarming and apotheosis / plateau from the plain / from which already thrust towards the sky / the artesian fountain of grass / and from which rise, / erect, / tender, / and hard, / the innumerable floral spears / of the deafening armies of the germination of the / narcissi. // Already the heterosexual group in the renowned poses of preliminary / expectation, conscientiously ponders over the threatening libidinous / cataclysm, the carnivorous blooming of its latent morphological atavisms. // In the heterosexual group, / in that kind date of the year / (but not excessively beloved or mild), / there are / the Hindou / tart, oily, sugared / like an August date, / the Catalan with his grave back / well planted / in a sun-tide, / a Whitsuntide of flesh inside his brain, // the blond flesh-eating German, / the brown mists / of mathematics / in the dimples / of his cloudy knees, // there is the English woman, / the Russian, / the Swedish woman, / the American / and the tall darkling Andalusian, / hardy with glands and olive with anguish. // Far from the heterosexual group, the shadows of the advanced afternoon draw out across the countryside, and cold lays hold of the adolescent's nakedness as he lingers at the water's edge. // When the clear and divine body of Narcissus / Leans / down to the obscure mirror of the lake, / when his white torso folded forward / fixes itself, frozen, / in the silvered and hypnotic curve of his desire, / when the time passes / on the clock of the flowers of the sand of his own flesh // Narcissus loses his being in the cosmic vertigo / in the deepest depths of which / is singing / the cold and Dionysiac siren of his own image. / The body of Narcissus flows out and loses itself / in the abyss of his reflection, / like the sandglass that will not be turned again. // Narcissus, you are losing your body, / carried away and confounded by the millenary / reflection of your disappearance / your body stricken dead / falls to the topaz precipice with yellow wreckage of / love, / your white body, swallowed up, / follows the slope of the savagely mineral torrent / of the black precious stones with pungent perfumes, / your body… / down to the unglazed mouths of the night / on the edge of which / there sparkles already / all the red silverware / of dawns with veins broken in

“the wharves of / blood.” // Narcissus, / do you understand? / Symmetry, divine hypnosis of the mind’s geometry, / already fills up your head, / with that incurable sleep, vegetable, atavistic, slow / which withers up the brain / in the parchment substance / of the kernel of your nearing metamorphosis. // The seed of your head has just fallen into the water. // Man returns to the vegetable state / by fatigue-laden sleep / and the gods / by transparent hypnosis of their passions. / Narcissus, you are so immobile / one would think you were asleep. / If it were a question of Hercules rough and brown, / one would say: he sleeps like
a bole / in the posture / on an Herculean oak. / But you, Narcissus, / made of perfumed bloomings of transparent / adolescence, / you sleep like a water flower. / Now the great mystery draws near, / the great metamorphosis is about to occur. // Narcissus, in his immobility absorbed by his reflection /
With the digestive slowness of carnivorous plants, becomes invisible. // There remains of him only / the hallucinatingly white oval of his head, / his head again more tender, / his head, chrysalis of hidden biological designs, / his head held up by the tips of the water’s fingers, / at the tips of the fingers /
of the insensate hand, / of the terrible hand, / of the excrement-eating hand, / of the mortal hand / of his reflection. // When that heads slits / when that head splits / when that head bursts, / it will be the flower, / the new narcissus, / Gala—my narcissus.

(1936) Poem translated by Francis Scarpe.
— Vol. III, p. 261, English version from *The Collected Writings of Salvador Dalí*, edited and translated by Haim Finkelstein (Cambridge, 1998), pp. 324–29.

PAINTINGS

SALVADOR DALÍ
Paisaje en Madrid (*Landscape of Madrid*), 1922
Oil on paper on cardboard, 30.1 × 35.8 cm
Museo de Arte Contemporáneo, Madrid
Cat. no. P 108, → p. 39

SALVADOR DALÍ
Naturaleza muerta (*Still Life*), c. 1923
Oil on cardboard, 50 × 56 cm
Museo Nacional Centro de Arte Reina Sofía, Madrid
Cat. no. P 123, → p. 40

SALVADOR DALÍ
Pierrot con guitarra (*Pierrot with Guitar*), c. 1923
Oil and collage on cardboard, 54.5 × 52.3 cm
Museo Nacional Thyssen-Bornemisza, Madrid
Cat. no. P 137, → p. 41

SALVADOR DALÍ
Desnudo en el agua (*Nude in the Water*), c. 1924
Oil on cardboard, 50.5 × 47 cm
Museo Nacional Centro de Arte Reina Sofía, Madrid
Cat. no. P 160, → p. 24

SALVADOR DALÍ
Retrat de la meva germana
(*Portrait of My Sister*), 1925
Oil on canvas, 99 × 99 cm
Museo Nacional Centro de Arte Reina Sofía, Madrid
Cat. no. P 166, → p. 27

SALVADOR DALÍ
Composició amb tres figures. "Acadèmia neocubista" (*Composition with Three Figures. "Neo-cubist Academy"*), 1926
Oil on canvas, 190 × 200 cm
Museu de Montserrat, Barcelona,
donated by Josefina Cusí, 1999
Cat. no. P 171, → p. 43

YVES TANGUY
Quand on me fusillera (*When They Shoot Me*), 1927
Oil on canvas, 61 × 47 cm
Musée des Beaux-Arts de Brest
→ p. 74

SALVADOR DALÍ
Le jeu lugubre (*The Lugubrious Game*), 1929
Oil and collage on cardboard, 44.4 × 30.3 cm
Private collection, Switzerland
Cat. no. P 232, → p. 91

SALVADOR DALÍ
Homme poisson (*Fish Man*), 1930
Oil on canvas, 26.7 × 19.1 cm
Meadows Museum, Dallas, purchased with funds from the Meadows Foundation, Holly Bock, Doug Deason, Mrs. Eugen McDermott, Linda P. and William A. Custard, and Gwen and Richard Irwin, MM.2014.11
Cat. no. P 383, → p. 103

SALVADOR DALÍ
Untitled. Woman Sleeping in a Landscape, 1931
Oil on canvas, 27.2 × 35 cm
Peggy Guggenheim Collection, Venice
Cat. no. P 269, → p. 101

SALVADOR DALÍ
La solitude (*Solitude*), 1931
Oil on canvas, 35.2 × 27.2 cm
Wadsworth Atheneum, Hartford, CT, purchased through the gift of Henry and Walter Keney, 1932.218
Cat. no. P 274, → p. 105

SALVADOR DALÍ
Remorse. Sphinx Embedded in the Sand, 1931
Oil on canvas, 19 × 26.7 cm
Eli and Edythe Broad Art Museum, Michigan State University, Gift of John Wolfram, 61.8
Cat. no. P 268, → p. 107

SALVADOR DALÍ
Gradiva retrouve les ruines anthropomorphes (fantaisie rétrospective) (*Gradiva Rediscovers the Anthropomorphic Ruins. [Retrospective Fantasy]*), c. 1931/32
Oil on canvas, 65 × 54 cm
Museo Nacional Thyssen-Bornemisza, Madrid
Cat. no. P 281, → p. 125

SALVADOR DALÍ
Pa antropomorf (*Anthropomorphic Bread*), 1932
Oil on canvas, 24 × 16.5 cm
Town Hall of Figueres, on permanent deposit at the Fundació Gala-Salvador Dalí, Figueres
Cat. no. P 291, → p. 121

SALVADOR DALÍ
The Birth of Liquid Anguish, 1932
Oil on canvas, 55 × 38.5 cm
Hamburger Kunsthalle
Cat. no. P 313, → p. 123

SALVADOR DALÍ
Moi-même à 10 ans quand j'étais l'enfant-sauterelle (complexe de castration) (*Myself at the Age of Ten When I Was a Grasshopper Child [Castration Complex]*), c. 1933
Oil on wood, 21.9 × 16.2 cm
The Dalí Museum, Saint Petersburg (Florida)
Cat. no. P 208, → p. 135

SALVADOR DALÍ
The Alert, c. 1934
Oil on wood, 24 × 18 cm
Ulla and Heiner Pietzsch Collection, Berlin
Cat. no. P 469, → p. 137

SALVADOR DALÍ
Paranonïa, c. 1935
Oil on canvas, 38.1 × 46 cm
The Dalí Museum, Saint Petersburg (Florida)
Cat. no. P 422, → p. 131

SALVADOR DALÍ
Cisnes reflejando elefantes (*Swans Reflecting Elephants*), 1937
Oil on canvas, 51 × 77 cm
Esther Grether Family Collection
Cat. no. P 454, → p. 139

OBJECTS

Bronze of a hand holding an egg, Roman, 1st–2nd century BCE
Bronze, 8.5 × 6 × 6 cm
Freud Museum London
→ fig. 68

SANTIAGO RAMÓN Y CAJAL
Microscope with lenses, Carl Reichert, Vienna
Instituto Cajal, CSIC, Madrid

SALVADOR DALÍ, EDWARD JAMES
Lobster Telephone, 1938
Steel, plaster, rubber, resin, and paper, 18 × 31 × 12.5 cm
West Dean College of Arts and Conservation
→ p. 148

SALVADOR DALÍ, EDWARD JAMES
Cat's Cradle Hands Chair, 1938
Wood, leather, 105 × 63 × 42.5 cm
West Dean College of Arts and Conservation
→ p. 149

FILMS

LUIS BUÑUEL (director, script, producer), SALVADOR DALÍ (script)
Un chien andalou, 1929
Black-and-white silent film, 17 min
Film restored in 2020 by La Cinémathèque française and the Filmoteca Española in collaboration with Les Grands Films Classiques, thanks to the support of Creative Europe.
→ pp. 86/87

LUIS BUÑUEL (director, script), SALVADOR DALÍ (script)
L'âge d'or, 1930
Black-and-white film, 35 mm, with sound, 1 h 3 min
Centre Pompidou—Musée national d'art moderne, Paris
→ pp. 88/89

LUIS BUÑUEL
Menjant garotes (*Eating Sea Urchins*), 1930
Black-and-white silent film, 4 min
Filmoteca de Catalunya
→ p. 30

JOAN DOLÇ
Dalí. Eine Freud'sche Skizze (*Dalí: A Freudian Sketch*), 2021
Documentary, 16 min
Production: Gran Angular Indústries Culturals for the Belvedere, Vienna

DRAWINGS AND PRINTS

SIGMUND FREUD
Spinal Ganglia and Spinal Cord of Petromyzon Fish (*Ganglions spinaux et moelle épinière de la lamproie marine*), 1878
Ink on paper, 20.4 × 26.3 cm
Freud Museum London
→ p. 54

SANTIAGO RAMÓN Y CAJAL
Histological drawing: Sección del bulbo a la altura del núcleo facial de un ratón (*Cross section of the olfactory bulb of a mouse at the level of the facial nerve*), c. 1898
Ink and pencil on paper, 20 × 16.5 cm
Instituto Cajal, CSIC, Madrid
→ p. 62

SANTIAGO RAMÓN Y CAJAL
Histological drawing: Células de axón corto grandes de la circunvolución central anterior de niño de 25 días (*Long and short axons from the cells of the anterior central gyrus of a 25-day-old infant*), c. 1899
Ink and pencil on paper, 16 × 17 cm
Instituto Cajal, CSIC, Madrid
→ p. 64

SANTIAGO RAMÓN Y CAJAL
Histological drawing: Células de axón corto de la capa quinta de la corteza acústica humana (Short axons of the cells in layer 5 of the human auditory cortex), c. 1900
Ink and pencil on paper, 17.6 × 7.1 cm
Instituto Cajal, CSIC, Madrid
→ p. 66

SANTIAGO RAMÓN Y CAJAL
Histological drawing: Corte frontal de comisura posterior de gato (Frontal section through the posterior commissure of a cat), c. 1903
Ink and pencil on paper, 15.2 × 13 cm
Instituto Cajal, CSIC, Madrid
→ p. 70

SANTIAGO RAMÓN Y CAJAL
Histological drawing: Esquema de las vías motrices superiores e inferiores del cerebelo (Diagram of the upper and lower motor pathways of the cerebellum), c. 1904
Ink and pencil on paper, 18.3 × 14.7 cm
Instituto Cajal, CSIC, Madrid
→ p. 68

SANTIAGO RAMÓN Y CAJAL
Histological drawing: Células de axón corto de la corteza esfeoidal olfativa (Short axons of the olfactory cells in the zone of the sphenoid bone), c. 1904
Ink and pencil on paper, 16 × 22.7 cm
Instituto Cajal, CSIC, Madrid
→ p. 55

SANTIAGO RAMÓN Y CAJAL
Histological drawing: Células neuróglias de la sustancia blanca del cerebro (Neuroglial cells of white matter in the brain), c. 1913
Ink and pencil on paper, 20 × 12.7 cm
Instituto Cajal, CSIC, Madrid
→ p. 57

SANTIAGO RAMÓN Y CAJAL
Histological drawing: Aparato reticular de Golgi en las neuronas motrices (Golgi apparatus of motor neurons), c. 1914
Ink and pencil on paper, 12.7 × 16.1 cm
Instituto Cajal, CSIC, Madrid
→ p. 72

SANTIAGO RAMÓN Y CAJAL
Histological drawing: Corte horizontal del centro cerebroide de sepia (Horizontal section through the midbrain of a cuttlefish), c. 1917
Ink and pencil on paper, 13.1 × 19.2 cm
Instituto Cajal, CSIC, Madrid
→ p. 60

SALVADOR DALÍ
Tertúlia en un cafè, 1926
Pencil and ink on paper, 20.2 × 26.8 cm
Museu de Montserrat, Barcelona
→ p. 44

SALVADOR DALÍ
Pep Ventura, 1926
Ink on paper, 27 × 19 cm
Museu de Mataró
→ p. 71

SALVADOR DALÍ
Trovador ecuestre 2 (Equestrian Troubadour 2, from the series: *Putrefactos)*, 1927
Ink on paper, 20.8 × 16.5 cm
Museo Nacional Centro de Arte Reina Sofía, Madrid
→ p. 49

SALVADOR DALÍ
Sketch for *Pescadores al sol (Fishermen in the Sun)*, 1928
Pencil on paper, 20 × 18 cm
Collection Pere Vehi
→ p. 73

FEDERICO GARCÍA LORCA
Sin título (Untitled), 1928/30
Ink on paper, 19.8 × 11.8 cm
Gregorio Prieto Foundation
→ p. 67

FEDERICO GARCIÁ LORCA
Dos figuras sobre una tumba (Two Figures over a Tomb), c. 1929/31
Ink on paper, 24.9 × 20.2 cm
Fundación Federico García Lorca
Centro Federico García Lorca, Granada
→ p. 65

SALVADOR DALÍ
La femme visible, La chasse aux papillons (The Visible Woman, Chasing Butterflies), 1930
Ink on paper on cardboard, 27.8 × 22 cm
Courtesy Galerie Natalie Seroussi, Paris
→ p. 97

SALVADOR DALÍ
Frontispiece for *Second manifeste du surréalisme*, 1930
Stencil print on paper, 28 × 22.5 cm
Museo Nacional Centro de Arte Reina Sofía, Madrid
→ p. 85

SALVADOR DALÍ
Artine, 1930
Heliogravure and etching on Japan paper, 24 × 18.5 cm
Museo Nacional Centro de Arte Reina Sofía, Madrid
→ p. 100

SALVADOR DALÍ
Sketch for *El hombre invisible* (*The Invisible Man*), c. 1930
Graphite, colored pencil, and ink on laid paper, 27.7 × 20.7 cm
Museo Nacional Centro de Arte Reina Sofía, Madrid
→ p. 99

SALVADOR DALÍ
Solitude mental (*Mental Solitude*), 1932
Ink on paper, 22.4 × 30.8 cm
Colecciones Fundación Mapfre, Madrid
→ p. 127

SALVADOR DALÍ
Sketch for *Soft Construction with Boiled Beans. Premonition of Civil War 1*, 1934
Pencil on paper, 22.7 × 17.7 cm
Asociación Colección Arte Contemporáneo—Museo Patio Herreriano, Valladolid
→ p. 129

FEDERICO GARCIÁ LORCA
Parque con linea envolvente (*Park Enveloped by a Line*), 1935/36
Ink on paper, 22.6 × 16.5 cm
Fundación Federico García Lorca
Centro Federico García Lorca, Granada
→ p. 69

SALVADOR DALÍ
Portrait Sketches of Edward James, 1936
Pencil and ink on paper, 21 × 15.7 cm
West Dean College of Arts and Conservation
→ p. 147

EDWARD CARRICK
Sketches for the *Mae West Lips Sofa*, 1937
West Dean College of Arts and Conservation

SALVADOR DALÍ
Sketch for *The Metamorphosis of Narcissus*, c. 1937
Pencil on paper, 20.3 × 15.6 cm
Fundació Gala-Salvador Dalí, Figueres
→ fig. 67

SALVADOR DALÍ
Portrait of Sigmund Freud, 1937
Ink and gouache on paper, 35.1 × 25.5 cm
Fundació Gala-Salvador Dalí, Figueres
→ p. 158

SALVADOR DALÍ
Portrait of Sigmund Freud, 1938
Ink on paper, 34.5 × 28 cm
Freud Museum London
→ p. 167

BOOKS

SIGMUND FREUD
"Über Spinalganglien und Rückenmark des Petromyzon," 1878
From: *Sitzungsberichte der kaiserlichen Akademie der Wissenschaften (mathematisch-naturwissenschaftliche Classe)*, 3rd dept., vol. 78, pp. 81–167, plate II
Sigmund Freud Privatstiftung, Vienna
→ p. 53

SIGMUND FREUD
"Über Spinalganglien und Rückenmark des Petromyzon," 1878
From: *Sitzungsberichte der kaiserlichen Akademie der Wissenschaften (mathematisch-naturwissenschaftliche Classe)*, 3rd dept., vol. 78, pp. 81–167, plate I
Sigmund Freud Privatstiftung, Vienna
→ p. 52

EDUARD PLIETZCH
Vermeer van Delft (Salvador Dalí's copy), Leipzig 1911
Fundació Gala-Salvador Dalí, Figueres

SIGMUND FREUD
La interpretación de los sueños I: Flectere si nequeo superos, acheronta movebo, Madrid 1923
Belvedere, Vienna
→ p. 50

SIGMUND FREUD
El chiste y su relación con lo inconsciente: El delirio y los sueños en la "Gradiva" de W. Jensen, translated by Luis López-Ballesteros y de Torres, Madrid 1923
Belvedere, Vienna
→ p. 50

SIGMUND FREUD
Introducción a la psicoanálisis: I. Los actos fallidos y los sueños, translated by Luis López-Ballesteros y de Torres, Madrid 1923
Belvedere, Vienna
→ p. 50

SIGMUND FREUD
Introducción a la psicoanálisis: II. Teoría general de las neurosis, translated by Luis López-Ballesteros y de Torres, Madrid 1923
Belvedere, Vienna
→ p. 51

SIGMUND FREUD
Tótem y tabú: Un recuerdo infantil de Leonardo da Vinci, translated by Luis-López Ballesteros y de Torres, Madrid 1923
Belvedere, Vienna
→ p. 51

WENCESLAO FERNÁNDEZ FLÓREZ
Visiones de neurastenia, Madrid 1924
Belvedere, Vienna
→ p. 51

SIGMUND FREUD
La histeria: Charcot: Un caso de curación hipnótica, translated by Luis López-Ballesteros y de Torres, Madrid 1925
Belvedere, Vienna
→ p. 51

BENJAMIN PÉRET
Dormir, dormir dans les pierres, 1927
with illustrations by Yves Tanguy
Galería de Osma, Madrid
→ pp. 76/77

SIGMUND FREUD
Un souvenir d'enfance de Léonard de Vinci (Salvador Dalí's copy), Paris 1927
Fundació Gala-Salvador Dalí, Figueres

C. G. JUNG
L'inconscient dans la vie psychique normale et anormale (Salvador Dalí's copy), Paris 1928
Fundació Gala-Salvador Dalí, Figueres

SIGMUND FREUD
Una teoría sexual y otros ensayos, translated by Luis López-Ballesteros y de Torres, Madrid 1929
Belvedere, Vienna
→ p. 51

SIGMUND FREUD
La interpretacion de los sueños II: Psicología de los procesos oníricos, Madrid 1934
Belvedere, Vienna
→ p. 51

SALVADOR DALÍ
La conquête de l'irrationnel, Paris 1935
Fundació Gala-Salvador Dalí, Figueres
→ p. 145

SALVADOR DALÍ
La conquête de l'irrationnel with a dedication and a drawing by Salvador Dalí, Paris 1935
West Dean College of Arts and Conservation
→ p. 146

SALVADOR DALÍ
Metamorphosis of Narcissus, New York 1937
Fundació Gala-Salvador Dalí, Figueres
→ p. 155

EDWARD JAMES
The Bones of My Hand, London 1938
Fundació Gala-Salvador Dalí, Figueres

SALVADOR DALÍ
The Secret Life of Salvador Dalí, translated by Haakon M. Chevalier, London 1942
Fundació Gala-Salvador Dalí, Figueres
→ p. 21

SALVADOR DALÍ
Cover for Raymond de Becker, *La vie tragique de Sigmund Freud*, Paris 1967
Fundació Gala-Salvador Dalí, Figueres

MAGAZINES

SALVADOR DALÍ
San Sebastiá, 1927
From: *L'Amic de les Arts*, no. 16, July 1927 (reprint)
Belvedere, Vienna

SALVADOR DALÍ
Homenaje a Góngora (*Homage to Góngora*), 1927
From: *Litoral*, nos. 5/7, October 1927 (reprint)
Private collection
→ p. 63

La révolution surréaliste, no. 12, December 15, 1929
Belvedere, Vienna

SALVADOR DALÍ
"Rêverie," from: *Le surréalisme au service de la révolution*, no. 4, 1931
University Library, Vienna

Sigmund Freud to André Breton, December 26, 1932, from: *Le surréalisme au service de la révolution*, no. 5, 1933
University Library, Vienna

JACQUES LACAN
"Le problème du style et la conception psychatrique des formes paranoiaques de l'expérience"
From: *Minotaure*, no. 1, 1933
University Library of University of Applied Arts Vienna

SALVADOR DALÍ
"Interprétation paranoïaque-critique de l'image obsédante 'L'Angelús' de Millet," 1933
From: *Minotaure*, no. 1, 1933
Colección MJM, Madrid
→ p. 115

SALVADOR DALÍ
"Le phénomène de l'extase," 1933
From: *Minotaure*, nos. 3–4, 1933
Colección MJM, Madrid
→ p. 113

EDWARD JAMES
"Trois sécheresses," with illustrations
by Salvador Dalí
from: *Minotaure*, no. 8, 1936 (reprint 1968)
University Library of University of Applied Arts
Vienna
→ fig. 49

SALVADOR DALÍ
Magazine cover of *Minotaure*, no. 8, 1936
Colección MJM, Madrid
→ p. 116

Trajectoire du rève no. 7, Cahiers G.L.M, Les textes & illustrations composant ce cahier consacré au rêve ont été assemblés par André Breton (Paris, 1938).
University Library of University of Applied Arts
Vienna
→ p. 119

PHOTOGRAPHS

SALVADOR DALÍ
Photograph of the painting *La mel és més dolça que la sang* (*Honey Is Sweeter than Blood*), 1927
Oil on unknown support, measurements unknown, whereabouts unknown, cat. no. P 194,
Fundación Federico García Lorca
Centro Federico García Lorca, Granada
→ p. 83

MAN RAY
Portrait of Edward James, 1937
Black-and-white photograph
West Dean College of Arts and Conservation
→ fig. 56

ARCHIVAL MATERIALS

Santiago Ramón y Cajal's diploma conferring honorary membership of the Vienna Society of Psychiatry and Neurology
Instituto Cajal, CSIC, Madrid

FEDERICO GARCIÁ LORCA
Oda al pintor Salvador Dalí (*Ode to the Painter Salvador Dalí*), 1926
Autograph
Fundación Federico García Lorca
Centro Federico García Lorca, Granada
→ p. 46

Postcard from Salvador Dalí to Edward James with a portrait of Gala Dalí and a drawing of a horse and rider on the reverse, 1935
West Dean College of Arts and Conservation
→ pp. 150/151

Postcard from Cadaqués sent from Salvador Dalí to Edward James, May 29, 1936
West Dean College of Arts and Conservation

Contract between Salvador Dalí and Edward James for the *"Geodesical" Portrait of Gala* (1936), July 31, 1936
West Dean College of Arts and Conservation

Letter from René Magritte to Edward James with a sketch for *The Pleasure Principle*, May 18, 1937
West Dean College of Arts and Conservation
→ fig. 57

Letter from Salvador Dalí to Edward James with a sketch for *Metamorphosis of Narcissus*, June 15, 1937
West Dean College of Arts and Conservation
→ fig. 66

Telegram from Edward James to Salvador Dalí at Südbahnhotel in Semmering, August 31, 1937
West Dean College of Arts and Conservation
→ fig. 2

EDWARD JAMES
Letter to Christopher Sykes describing the meeting of Dalí and Freud, 1938
West Dean College of Arts and Conservation
→ pp. 165/166

STEPHANIE AUER studied art history and Romance studies at the universities of Innsbruck and Granada. She completed her master's thesis in 2006, spending several months in Madrid conducting research into Federico García Lorca as a visual artist. She was project researcher at the Oskar Kokoschka Center, University of Applied Arts Vienna. Since 2007, she has been assistant curator for the collections of nineteenth and twentieth century art at the Belvedere, contributing to numerous catalogues and helping to research and curate various exhibitions, including *Klimt and Antiquity* (2017), *Beyond Klimt: New Horizons in Central Europe* (2018), *Kiki Smith—Procession* (2019), and *The Age of Dürer: Austria at the Gate of the Renaissance* (2021). Her research focuses on Austrian and international classical Modernism, specifically in Vienna c. 1900.

JUAN MANUEL BONET is a writer and art critic. He was director of the Institut Valencià d'Art Modern (IVAM), the Museo Nacional Centro de Arte Reina Sofía, Madrid, and the Instituto Cervantes in Paris. Bonet is the author of several volumes of poetry, the *Diccionario de las vanguardias en España, 1907–1936*, and numerous artist monographs. He has curated exhibitions on Spanish Ultraism, Ramón Gómez de la Serna and Morton Feldman, Polish Constructivism, and Spanish and Latin American Surrealism, as well as retrospectives on Pablo Picasso, Juan Gris, Giorgio Morandi, Henri Michaux, Josef Sudek, Ramón Gaya, Esteban Vicente, José Guerrero, Alex Katz, Bernard Plossu, and others.

JAIME BRIHUEGA SIERRA is professor emeritus of art history at the Universidad Complutense de Madrid and teaches at numerous universities in Spain and overseas. As a lecturer and speaker at international conferences he specializes in the historical avant-garde and the iconology of mass communication, and has published more than two hundred titles on these subjects. From 1985 to 1988, he was director of the Instituto de Conservación y Restauración de Obras de Arte in Spain and deputy director of the Instituto de Conservación y Restauración de Bienes Culturales, which are both under the auspices of the Spanish Ministry of Culture and Sport. From 1988 to 1991, he was Director General of Fine Arts and Archives at the Spanish Ministry of Culture and Sport. He has been involved in more than one hundred contemporary art exhibitions in Europe and America, and curated over forty of these.

ULRIKE KADI is a specialized doctor in psychiatry and psychotherapeutic medicine and an independent psychoanalyst (WAP/IPA). She is currently associate professor at the Department of Psychoanalysis and Psychotherapy at the Medical University of Vienna and an external lecturer of philosophy at the University of Vienna. Kadi was project leader for the FWF project "Topographien des Körpers: phänomenologische, genealogische und psychoanalytische Forschungen" at the Department of Psychoanalysis and Psychotherapy at the Medical University of Vienna (2014–19). She has also been involved in the WWTF project "Transferences: Psychoanalysis—Art—Society" of the Viennese psychoanalytic research group stuzzicadenti (2009–11) at the Institute of Philosophy, University of Vienna.

ROBERT LUBAR MESSERI teaches art history at the Institute of Fine Arts at New York University. As an expert in twentieth-century French and Spanish painting, he has authored numerous publications on artists such as Dalí, Picasso, and Miró. He is a Trustee of the Fundació Joan Miró in Barcelona and Curator at Large at the Museu de Arte Contemporânea de Serralves in Porto.

STELLA ROLLIG has been CEO and artistic director of the Belvedere since January 2017. She studied German and art history at the University of Vienna and later worked as an arts journalist (for ORF, *Der Standard*, and others). From 1994 to 1996, Rollig was the Austrian Federal Curator for the Fine Arts; during this time she also founded the discussion platform "Depot, Kunst und Diskussion" at MuseumsQuartier Wien. From 2004 to 2016, she was artistic director of the LENTOS art museum in Linz and from 2011 also director of NORDICO Stadtmuseum Linz. In addition to her curatorial roles, Rollig has taught at numerous institutions.

AGUSTÍN SÁNCHEZ VIDAL is professor emeritus of art history (cinema and other audiovisual media) at the Universidad de Zaragoza. He was visiting professor at several universities in America and Europe, including Princeton and Paris-Nanterre. His more than sixty publications include *Buñuel, Lorca, Dalí: el enigma sin fin*, for which he received the 1988 Premio Espejo de España prize for literature. He has published three monographs on Salvador Dalí and the third volume of Ediciones Destino's *Salvador Dalí: Obra completa* (2004). Vidal has contributed to the 1993 monograph on *L'âge d'or*, published by the Centre Pompidou and the catalogue *Dalí & Film* for the exhibition of the same name at the Tate Modern, London, and the Museum of Modern Art, New York, in 2007/08.

INGRID SCHAFFNER is an American curator, art critic, and author, specializing in contemporary art. She is currently curator of the Chinati Foundation in Marfa, Texas. Previously she worked for the 57th Carnegie International (Ci18) at the Carnegie Museum of Art, Pittsburgh. Renowned for her comprehensive knowledge of art history and her outstanding collaborations with artists such as Richard Artschwager, Barry Le Va, Karen Kilimnik, Maira Kalman, and Anne Tyng, Schaffner often combines themes such as archiving and collecting, photography, feminism, and alternative Modernism, in particular Surrealism, in her work. From 2000 to 2015, Schaffner was chief curator for the exhibition program of the Institute of Contemporary Art (ICA) at the University of Pennsylvania.

PICTURE CREDITS

ABANCA Art Collection, A Coruña: p. 133
akg-images: pp. 15 (top), 161 (top); figs. 3, 30
akg-images / Album: p. 84
akg-images / Denise Bellon: fig. 54
Allen Phillips / Wadsworth Atheneum: p. 105
ANNO / Austrian National Library: fig. 1
Archivo Fotográfico. Asociación Colección Arte Contemporáneo – Museo Patio Herreriano, Valladolid: p. 129
Arterra Picture Library / Alamy Stock fig. 58
Biblioteca Digital Memoria de Madrid: p. 61
bpk / Bayerische Staatsgemäldesammlungen: fig. 13
bpk / Hamburger Kunsthalle / Elke Walford: p. 123
bpk / Kunstsammlung Nordrhein-Westfalen, Düsseldorf / Walter Klein: fig. 5
bpk / The Art Institute of Chicago / Art Resource, NY: fig. 50
Bridgeman Images: fig. 32
Carl Van Vechten / Bridgeman Images: p. 15 (bottom)
Centre Pompidou, MNAM-CCI, Dist. RMN-Grand Palais / Bertrand Prévost: fig. 10
Centre Pompidou, MNAM-CCI, Dist. RMN-Grand Palais / Guy Carrard: pp. 25, 95;
Centre Pompidou, MNAM-CCI, Dist. RMN-Grand Palais / Jean-Claude Planchet: fig. 33
Centro Federico García Lorca: pp. 46, 47, 59, 65, 69, 83
Colecciones Fundación Mapfre: p. 127
Collection Pere Vehi: p. 73
Courtesy Galerie Natalie Seroussi: p. 97
Digital image, The Museum of Modern Art, New York / Scala, Florence: fig. 20
Ediciones Litoral: p 63
Eli and Edythe Broad Art Museum, Michigan State University: p. 107
Elizabeth Whiting & Associates / Alamy Stock Foto: figs. 52, 53
Eric Schaal; scan from: Ingrid Schaffner, *Salvador Dalí's Dream of Venus: The Surrealist Funhouse from the 1939 World's Fair* (New York, 2002): figs. 39, 40, 41, 42, 43, 44, 45
Freud Museum London: pp. 54, 152, 157, 159, 160, 161 (bottom), 167; fig. 68
Freud Museum, London / Bridgeman Images: fig. 15
Fundació Gala-Salvador Dalí, Figueres: pp. 21, 23, 26, 31, 92, 93, 94, 121, 145, 155, 158; figs. 7, 8, 14, 48, 63, 67
Galería de Osma, Madrid: pp. 76, 77
Gordon Roberton Photography Archive / Bridgeman Images: fig. 55
Gregorio Prieto Foundation: p. 67
http://content.time.com/: fig. 38
https://archive.vogue.com/: fig. 36
Instituto Cajal, CSIC: pp. 55, 57, 58, 60, 62, 64, 66, 68, 70, 72
Jochen Littkemann, Berlin: p. 137
Man Ray Trust: p. 117
Michael Bodycomb: p. 103
Musée d'Orsay, Dist. RMN-Grand Palais / Patrice Schmidt: fig. 27
Musée des Beaux-Arts de Brest métropole: p. 74
Museo de Arte Contemporáneo, Madrid: p. 39
Museo Nacional Thyssen-Bornemisza, Madrid: pp. 41, 125
Museu de Mataró: p. 71
Museu de Montserrat, Montserrat (Barcelona): pp. 43, 44
Museu Nacional d'Art de Catalunya, Barcelona, 2022: p. 29
Palacio de Viana, Fundación CajaSur, Córdoba: fig. 60
Peggy Guggenheim Collection, Venice: p. 101;
Photographic archives Museo Nacional Centro de Arte Reina Sofía, Madrid: pp. 24, 27, 40, 49, 85, 99, 100; figs. 6, 11, 12, 26, 62
PVDE / Bridgeman Images and Toy Museum of Catalonia / Figueres: p. 22
Residencia de Estudiantes, Madrid: p. 37, 45
RMN-Grand Palais (Musée du Louvre) / René-Gabriel Ojeda: fig. 18
RMN-Grand Palais (Musée national Picasso – Paris) / Mathieu Rabeau: fig. 4
Robert Bayer, Bildpunkt AG, CH-4142 Münchenstein: p. 139
Scan: Belvedere Research Center, Vienna: pp. 50, 51
Sigmund Freud Privatstiftung, Vienna: pp. 52, 53
Smithsonian Institution / Bridgeman Images: fig. 37
Sotheby's London: p. 163
Source gallica.bnf.fr / Bibliothèque nationale de France: pp. 113, 115, 116, 119
SZ Photo / picturedesk.com: p. 153
Tate, London: figs. 17, 51, 64
The Dalí Museum, Saint Petersburg (Florida): pp. 131, 135; figs. 9, 19

NOTE

The English work titles in this volume are based on the *Catalogues Raisonnés of Works by Salvador Dalí*, https://www.salvador-dali.org/en/artwork/catalogue-raisonne. The catalogue raisonné numbers (cat. no.) are also derived from this source.

COVER

Salvador Dalí, detail of a letter from Salvador Dalí to Edward James with a sketch for *Metamorphosis of Narcissus*, June 15, 1937, West Dean College of Arts and Conservation

COLOPHON

This catalogue is published on the occasion of the exhibition *Dalí – Freud: An Obsession* Belvedere, Vienna, January 28 – May 29, 2022

Artistic Director / CEO
STELLA ROLLIG
CFO
WOLFGANG BERGMANN

Curator
JAIME BRIHUEGA SIERRA
Assistant Curator
STEPHANIE AUER
Project Coordinator
EVA LORENZO (PONTE: Organisation für kulturelles Management)

Exhibition Management and Loans
STEPHAN PUMBERGER
Exhibition Production
TATJANA GAWRON-DEUTSCH
Exhibition Architecture
MARGULA ARCHITECTS
Chief Curator
HARALD KREJCI
Education
SUSANNE WÖGERBAUER
Communications and Marketing
KATHARINA STEINBRECHER
Visitor Services
MARGARETE STECHL
Research Center
CHRISTIAN HUEMER
Conservation Department
STEFANIE JAHN

Belvedere
Prinz Eugen-Strasse 27
1030 Vienna
Austria
www.belvedere.at

Editors
STELLA ROLLIG
JAIME BRIHUEGA SIERRA
Authors
STEPHANIE AUER
JUAN MANUEL BONET
JAIME BRIHUEGA SIERRA
ULRIKE KADI
ROBERT LUBAR MESSERI
STELLA ROLLIG
AGUSTÍN SÁNCHEZ VIDAL
INGRID SCHAFFNER
Catalogue Concept
STEPHANIE AUER
JAIME BRIHUEGA SIERRA
EVA LAHNSTEINER
EVA LORENZO
WILLI SCHMID
Graphic Design
WILLI SCHMID
Editorial Team
STEPHANIE AUER
EVA LAHNSTEINER
EVA LORENZO
Copy-Editing (English)
BETTI MOSER
Translation (German → English)
REBECCA LAW (Bonet, captions and quotes)
NICK SOMERS (Auer, Kadi, Rollig, Vidal)
JESSICA WEST (Brihuega Sierra, biographies, Dalí quotes)
Publication Management
EVA LAHNSTEINER
Picture Editing
PIXELSTORM
Printed and bound by
GERIN DRUCK, Wolkersdorf
Stock
Surbalin moiré 2060 (cover)
Munken Lynx 150 g (endpapers)
Munken Lynx 120 g
Typefaces
Larish Neue
Custom font
(www.radimpesko.com)

Published by
Verlag der Buchhandlung
Walther und Franz König
Ehrenstrasse 4
50672 Cologne
Germany

Bibliographic information published by the Deutsche Nationalbibliothek
The Deutsche Nationalbibliothek lists this publication in the Deutsche Nationalbibliografie; detailed bibliographic data are available on the internet at http://dnb.d-nb.de.

Distribution
— Europe
Buchhandlung Walther König
Ehrenstrasse 4
50672 Cologne
Germany
T: +49 (0) 221 205 9653
verlag@buchhandlung-walther-koenig.de
— UK & Ireland
Cornerhouse Publications Ltd. – home
2 Tony Wilson Place
Manchester M15 4FN, UK
T: +44 (0) 161 212 3466
publications@cornerhouse.org
— Outside Europe
D.A.P. / Distributed Art Publishers, Inc.
75 Broad Street, Suite 630
New York, NY 10004, USA
T: +1 (0) 212 627 1999
orders@dapinc.com

ISBN 978-3-7533-0133-4 (retail edition, english)
ISBN 978-3-903327-30-6 (museum edition, english)

belvedere

In cooperation with

PONTE
ORGANISATION FÜR KULTURELLES MANAGEMENT GMBH

EPILOGUE

AMBIGUOUS IMAGES WITHOUT ECHO

Ulrike Kadi

A relationship between art and psychoanalysis was recognized by the Surrealists early on. While still a student in Madrid, Salvador Dalí "devoured" the works of Sigmund Freud.[1] He later hoped to find an ally in psychoanalysis for his own project of liberating unconscious forces and fantasies. Among the psychoanalysts, Jacques Lacan in particular was inspired by this idea. He published a text in the Surrealist magazine *Minotaure* on everyday paranoid forms of experience, thereby expressing his opposition, like Dalí, to all forms of naïve realism.[2]

Dalí traveled to Vienna several times in the hope of meeting Sigmund Freud in person, albeit in vain. Freud was preparing at the time to escape the terrible reality of the fanatical racist Nazi ideology. As he was on the verge of his departure from Vienna, he was unable to receive visitors. As for Dalí, he filled the time visiting art galleries, browsing in antiques shops, and consoling himself with Sacher torte. To deal with the sad reality of yet another failed attempt to visit Freud, he conducted long imaginary conversations with the psychoanalyst, which he conjured up while sitting alone in his hotel room.[3]

A psychoanalytic treatment is not unlike a work of art. Using words, syllables, sounds, phrases and sentences, metaphors, and other rhetorical figures of speech as its materials, something new is created. This something is fleeting and delicate—the words fade away in space. Often even the memory of what has been heard falls away, sometimes within the hour of it being said. The fragility of psychoanalytical therapy calls for a strict setting: free association at fixed times and a fixed place in the presence of a person trained in psychoanalysis. With this in mind, hearing the unconscious in a painting such as Dalí's *Metamorphosis of Narcissus* (1937, P 455, → fig. 64) presents certain problems: How can a picture be heard?[4] And who is the subject of the analysis when it is a work of art that is being analyzed? The painter with reference to his biography and his psychological constitution, the picture and its components, or the viewers of the artwork and their experience of individual works?

To this day, psychoanalysts have offered more than enough answers to such questions, for example in their considerations about Leonardo da Vinci's character, whom Freud made the subject of an analysis using one of the artist's childhood memories;[5] conjectures about Paul Klee's skin disease, seen as a personal processing through art of collective guilt;[6] theories about Diego Velázquez's painting *Las Meninas,* which Lacan used to develop and present psychoanalytical hypotheses on seeing and the eye;[7] speculation regarding Francis Bacon's pictorial use of violence as an illustration of claustrophobia;[8] or museum education considerations regarding the unconscious background to viewers' scopophilic drives.[9]

Dalí, meanwhile, turned this on its head and aimed to use his art for psychoanalysis. He was convinced that his theory of paranoiac-critical activity was the key to accessing the unconscious through art, analogous to psychoanalysis. His declared ambition was to "materialize the images of concrete irrationality with the most imperialist fury of precision"[10] and in this way to go beyond manifestations susceptible to psychoanalysis. His combative approach, with its echoes of an almost war-like conquest of the irrational, is clearly evident here.

In his use of double images, which reveal different things depending on the way they are focused on—Ludwig Wittgenstein's rabbit–duck illusion is a classic example—Dalí appears at first to be giving priority to the viewers and their perception. In doing so, he is able to draw on the tenets of perceptual psychology, since every perception is also permeated by irrational aspects and imagination-led expectations: viewers see what they want or desire to see, or even what they imagine they are seeing. In *Metamorphosis of Narcissus*, a double image is disassembled into its component parts. Dalí shows several versions of Narcissus. He paints him, in line with the myth, as a figure bending over the water admiring his own reflection (→fig. 64a). He then transforms him into the sculpture of an oversized human hand, which—matching the form of Narcissus's head—is holding an egg between its thumb and middle finger, with a daffodil sprouting from it in place of Narcissus's hair (→fig. 64b).

Even the title of the painting plays on the theme of the ambiguous image. The original title is *Metamorphose de Narcisse*. The French word "narcisse" can refer to both the mythological character or the flower. Unconscious motivations are known to hide within words with double meanings, and some psychoanalysts are therefore very alert to such equivocations. We could further conjecture that the title alludes to Dalí's desire to see himself as being on a par with a psychoanalyst or even as a psychoanalyst himself. Yet, he was acting not only as a quasi-analyst but also as an artist, endeavoring in his works to actively amplify the irrational component. He thus encouraged daydreaming to evoke third and fourth images.[11] The results of such forced productivity can also be seen in *Metamorphosis of Narcissus*. Apart from the reflections in the water, a further Narcissus sculpture is visible on the horizon, peeping out from behind a mountain, and the youth posing on the pedestal in the middle of the chessboard also brings narcissistic qualities to the fore (→fig. 64c).

Coercive persuasion is obviously not part of the inventory of psychoanalytical techniques. Links between the (pre-)conscious fantasies that manifest themselves in this way and the unconscious are barely perceptible. Dalí took *The Metamorphosis of Narcissus* with him when he finally met Freud in London on July 19, 1938. But the echo on Freud's side remained weak. In a letter he later wrote to Stefan Zweig, who had brokered the meeting, Freud expressed his interest in analyzing how the picture had come about, but he also emphasized that a high degree of preconscious revision of the unconscious material placed limits on the psychoanalytical method.[12] In other words, art remains art and cannot compete with psychoanalysis, even if it adopts fragments of psychoanalytical theory.

Like the painting itself, the accompanying poem *Narcissus,* written with pedagogical intentions,[13] is an expression of extensive secondary revision. Insofar as the genesis of the painting reflects the artist's personal character traits, it would perhaps be possible to delve into Dalí's private unconscious—if he was still alive today to freely associate in a psychoanalytical setting—to obtain new information about his brother, who died three years before Dalí was born, about his perception of himself as a genius, and his sense of mission, his relationship to objects, his fantasies, and much more besides. In the absence of this possibility, the access is more hermeneutic than psychoanalytical. Dalí has laid down a few markers for this in his poem, but also in the painting itself.

The multiple depictions of Narcissus can be read as something that was central to Freud's interpretation of narcissism: Although narcissism is considered a stage in the development of the ego, some aspects of it will remain for life.[14] And must do so. The development of libido in the corporeal individual[15] is also of constitutive significance when the early auto-eroticism opens up to embrace object-love. Freud, in fact, described the libidinal components of auto-eroticism and object-love as being fluid.[16]

The reflection that causes Narcissus's death by drowning in the myth is reinterpreted by Dalí as a more fluid process of transformation. He describes the petrified hand as being "insensate," "mortal," even "terrible" and "excrement-eating."[17] This recalls early fantasies about his own body being fragmented.[18] Through the stone hand crawling with ants[19]—an image that is of autobiographical significance for Dalí—he makes it clear that this is his own hand. The stone hand becomes the artist's hand. This draws attention to the creative aspect of narcissism. Transcending the myth, the object held in the artist's hand marks a floral new beginning—although some also wish to interpret the egg as a symbol of power (→fig. 64b).[20] In the poem, Dalí connects the flower, which in itself is genderless, with Gala, his muse and life companion.[21] Is this genderless Gala a queer fantasy *avant la lettre*?

One of the formative factors in subjective development is the question of gender. Lacan emphasizes that the growing child looking at itself naked in front of a mirror will inevitably ask the (today almost improper-sounding) question: am I a boy or a girl?[22] Dalí paints the Narcissus figures practically without external sexual characteristics, even if the narrow hips and broad shoulders of the figure above the chessboard would suggest a male imprint. The eight bathers are to be seen, in line with the myth, as haplessly in love with the small statue of Narcissus on the right (→fig. 64d). Their gender is not always clear. In his poem, Dalí describes the eight naked or half-naked figures as a heterosexual group with a Hindu, a Catalan, a predatory German, and an English, Russian, Swedish, American, and Andalusian woman.[23] Their graceful—by no means unhappy-looking—pose would suggest that the group is a further ambiguous image, a multiple reflection of the small self-contained statue.

The nymph Echo, whose function in the myth is to personify Narcissus's unattainability, is absent from Dalí's picture. It can only be conjectured whether he wished, by emphasizing the heterosexuality of the bathers in his poem, above all to present an antithesis to the solitariness of the self-reflecting Narcissus. The relationship with Gala, alluded to between the artist's hand and the daffodil sprouting from the egg, is placed in the composition above the group—as if to hint at an alternative and superior form of relationship. The implications of this interpretation are, however, limited by the fact that the relationship seems rather abstract, as if constructed on a chessboard. There is no question of likening it to a heterosexual relationship. In fact, it is easier to see Gala as the artist's alter ego, his transsexual transformation into the other sex.

The pile of ashes on the right-hand edge of the picture, and the dog in front of it eating meat and bones, symbolize remnants (→fig. 64e). According to the myth, Narcissus dissolves completely into his own reflection. His body can no longer be found. Yet Dalí's version makes it clear that a body can never disappear completely, in whichever gender it may continue to live.

1 Dawn Ades, "Dalí, Freud and the Metamorphosis of Narcissus," in *Freud, Dalí and the Metamorphosis of Narcissus*, exh. cat., Freud Museum London (London, 2018), pp. 13–31, here p. 17.
2 Jacques Lacan, "Le problème du style et la conception psychiatrique des formes paranoïaques de l'expérience," in *Minotaure*, no. 1, 1933, pp. 68–69.
3 Salvador Dalí, *The Secret Life of Salvador Dalí*, translated by Haakon M. Chevalier (New York, 1993).
4 See Ulrike Kadi, *Bilderwahn: Arbeit am Imaginären* (Vienna, 1999).
5 Sigmund Freud, "Leonardo da Vinci and a Memory of his Childhood" (1910), in *The Standard Edition of the Complete Psychological Works of Sigmund Freud*, translated by James Strachey (London, 1953), vol. XI, pp. 63–138.
6 Ralf Bohn, *Inszenierung als Widerstand: Bildkörper und Körperbild bei Paul Klee* (Bielefeld, 2009).
7 Jacques Lacan, "'L'objet de la psychanalyse,' Séminaire XIII (1965–1966)," for different versions cf. http://gaogoa.free.fr/SeminaireS.htm (accessed on October 24, 2021).
8 Katherine Stroczan, "In Gewalt verliebt: die Anatomiestunde Francis Bacons," in *Psyche*, vol. 54, no. 1, 2000, pp. 1–27.
9 August Ruhs, *Lacan* (Vienna, 2010).
10 Salvador Dalí, *Conquest of the Irrational* (New York, 1935), p. 12.
11 Peter Gorsen, *Salvador Dalí, der "kritische Paranoiker"* (Frankfurt am Main, 1983).
12 Sigmund Freud, *The Letters of Sigmund Freud*, selected and edited by Ernst L. Freud, translated by Tania and James Stern, letter 302, (New York, 1975).
13 Salvador Dali, "Metamorphosis of Narcissus" (1937), in *Freud, Dalí and the Metamorphosis of Narcissus*, exh. cat., Freud Museum London (London, 2018), p. 6.
14 Sigmund Freud, *Totem and Taboo: Some Points of Agreement between the Mental Lives of Savages and Neurotics* (1913), in *Standard Works*, vol. XIII, pp. 1–162; ibid., "On Narcissism: An Introduction" (1914), *Standard Works*, vol. XIV, pp. 73–104.
15 Ibid., "Psychoanalytical Notes on an Autobiographical Account of a Case of Paranoia (Dementia paranoides)" (1911), *Standard Works*, vol. XI, pp. 9–84.
16 Ibid., "A Difficulty in the Path of Psychoanalysis" (1917), *Standard Works*, vol. XVII, pp. 135–44.
17 Dalí, 2018 (see note 13).
18 Jacques Lacan, "Le stade du miroir comme formateur de la fonction du Je telle qu'elle nous est révélée dans l'experience psychanalytique" in ibid., *Écrits* (Paris, 1966), pp. 93–100.
19 Dalí, 1984 (see note 3).
20 Ades, 2018 (see note 1).
21 Dalí, 2018 (see note 13).
22 Jacques Lacan, "De nos antécédents," in ibid., *Écrits* (Paris, 1966), pp. 65–72.
23 Dalí, 2018 (see note 13).

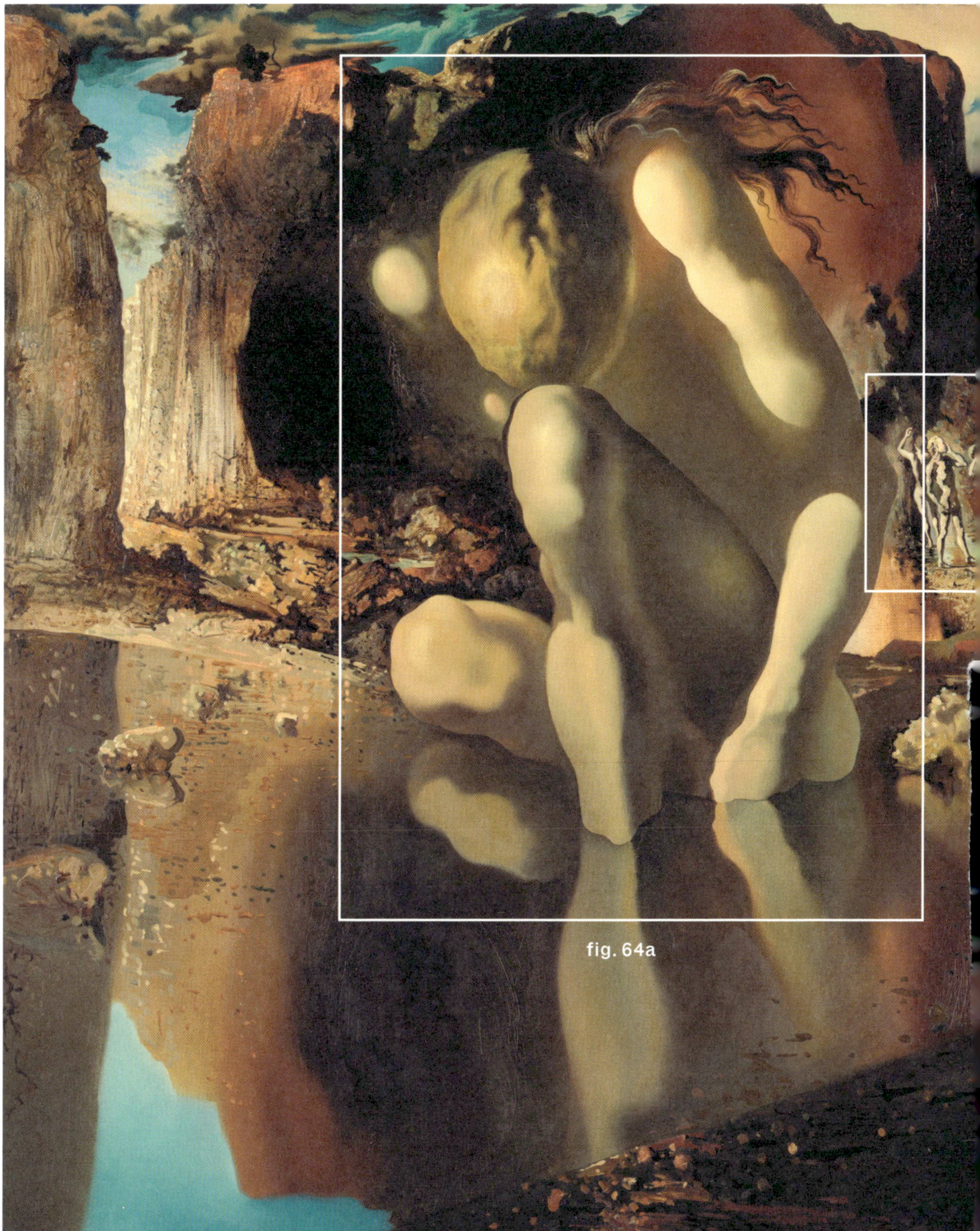

fig
SALVADOR DALÍ, *Mé*
(*Metamorphosis c*
Tate Modern, Lor

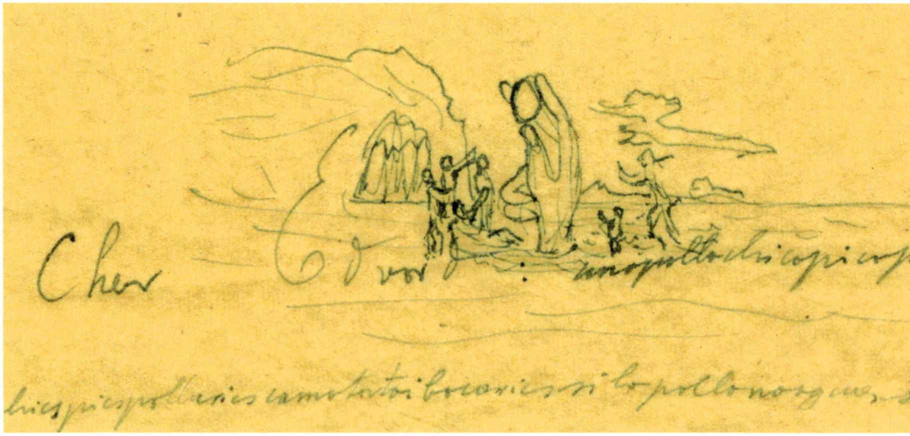

fig. 66
SALVADOR DALÍ, detail of a letter to Edward James with a sketch for *Metamorphosis of Narcissus*, June 15, 1937, West Dean College of Arts and Conservation

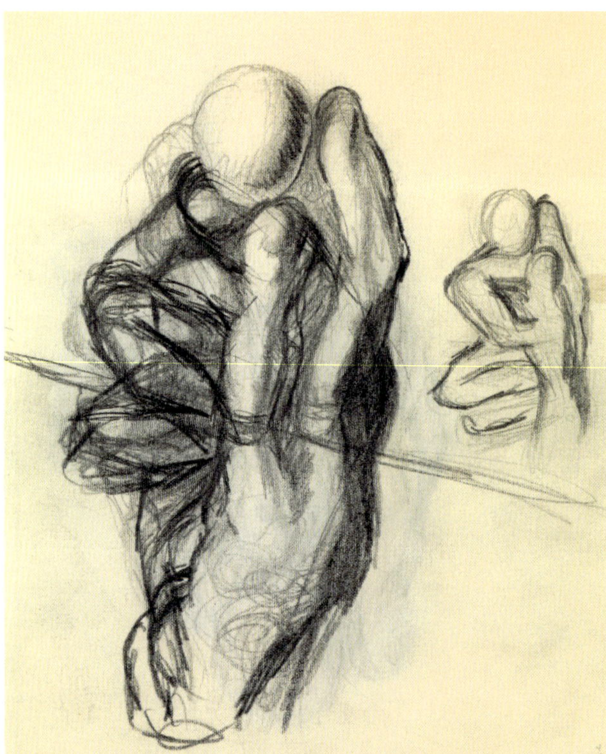

fig. 67
SALVADOR DALÍ, Study for *Metamorphosis of Narcissus*, c. 1937
Fundació Gala-Salvador Dalí, Figueres

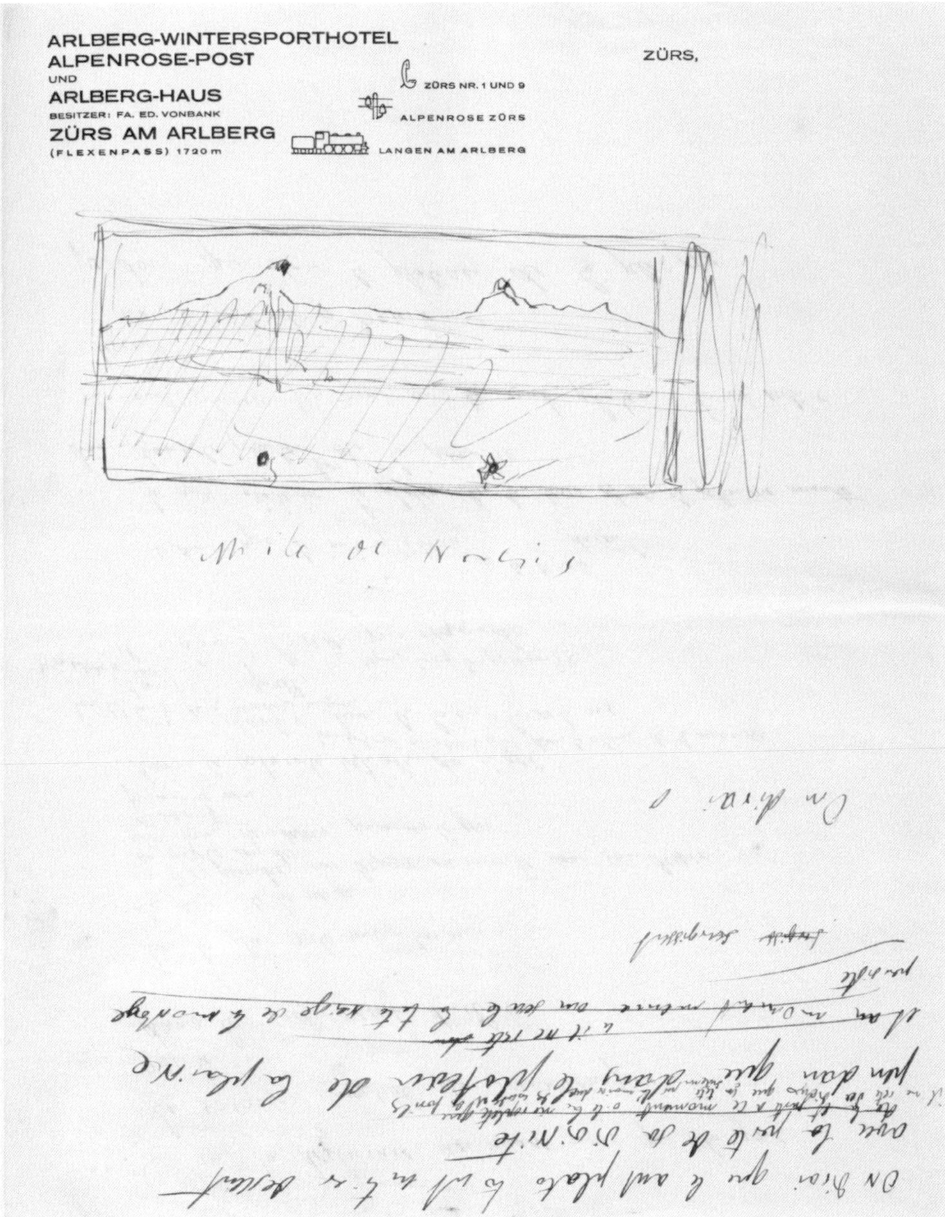

ARLBERG-WINTERSPORTHOTEL
ALPENROSE-POST
UND
ARLBERG-HAUS
BESITZER: FA. ED. VONBANK
ZÜRS AM ARLBERG
(FLEXENPASS) 1720 m

ZÜRS NR. 1 UND 9
ALPENROSE ZÜRS
LANGEN AM ARLBERG

ZÜRS,

fig. 65
SALVADOR DALÍ, letter to Edward James, sent from Zürs, with a sketch for *Metamorphosis of Narcissus*, West Dean College of Arts and Conservation

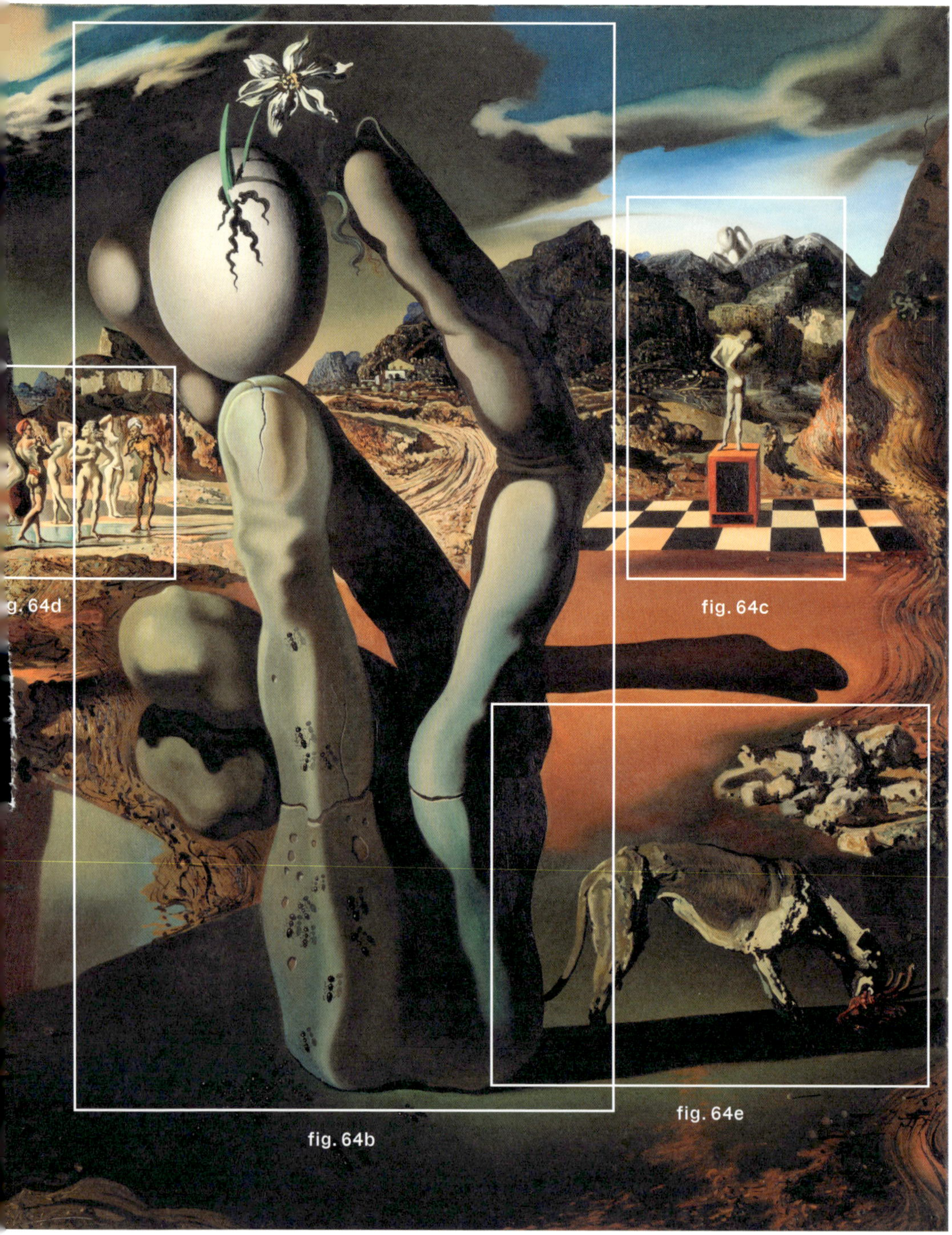

ɜ4
ımorphose de Narcisse
Narcissus), 1937
on, cat. no. P 455